Communications
in Computer and Information Science   418

Limin Sun Huadong Ma Feng Hong (Eds.)

Advances in Wireless Sensor Networks

7th China Conference, CWSN 2013
Qingdao, China, October 17-19, 2013
Revised Selected Papers

 Springer

Volume Editors

Limin Sun
Chinese Academy of Sciences, Beijing, China
E-mail: sunlimin@iie.ac.cn

Huadong Ma
Beijing University of Posts and Telecommunications, China
E-mail: mhd@bupt.edu.cn

Feng Hong
Ocean University of China, Qingdao, China
E-mail: hongfeng@ouc.edu.cn

ISSN 1865-0929   e-ISSN 1865-0937
ISBN 978-3-642-54521-4   e-ISBN 978-3-642-54522-1
DOI 10.1007/978-3-642-54522-1
Springer Heidelberg New York Dordrecht London

Library of Congress Control Number: 2014932219

Typesetting: Camera-ready by author, data conversion by Scientific Publishing Services, Chennai, India

Printed on acid-free paper

Springer is part of Springer Science+Business Media (www.springer.com)

Preface

This volume of *Communications in Computer and Information Science* contains the proceedings of the 7th China Conference of Wireless Sensor Networks (CWSN 2013), which was held in Qingdao, China, during October 17-19, 2013. CWSN represents the highest research level of sensor networks in China. CWSN 2013 served as a forum for researchers, developers, and users to compare their experiences of sensor network research and applications, and to discuss the key challenges and research directions facing the sensor network community.

CWSN 2013, with its focus on sensor network design and implementation, aimed to promote the exchange of the theories and applications surrounding sensor networks. In addition, the conference provides the opportunity to consider research on CPS and the Internet of Things. Six prominent experts were invited to attend and present keynote speeches. Moreover, several industries demonstrated their state-of-the-art products and technologies on sensor networks and Internet of Things. In all, 324 papers were submitted to CWSN 2013 among which 191 were completed in English. Of these, 35 high-quality papers, focusing, amongst other things, on node systems, infrastructures, communication protocols, data management, etc., were recommended by the Program Committee to be presented at the conference and included in this volume of CCIS.

On behalf of the Organizing Committee, we would like to thank Springer for publishing the proceedings of CWSN 2013. We would also like to express our gratitude to the reviewers for providing extra help in the review process, and to the authors for contributing their research results to the conference.

We look forward to seeing all of you next year at CWSN 2014. With your support and participation, CWSN will continue its success for a long time.

October 2013

Limin Sun
Huadong Ma
Feng Hong

Organization

The 7th China Conference of Wireless Sensor Networks (CWSN2013) was held in QingDao, China, and was organized by Ocean University of China.

General Chair

Dexing Wu   President of Ocean University of China
Jianzhong Li   Director of Sensor Network Special Committee

Honorary Chair

Hao Dai   Academician of Chinese Academy
     of Engineering

Co-chair

Limin Sun   Institute of Information Engineering Chinese
     Academy of Sciences
Huadong Ma   Beijing University of Posts and
     Telecommunications

Organizing Chair

Zhongwen Guo   Ocean University of China

Organizing Vice-Chair

Junyu Dong   Ocean University of China
Bing Zheng   Ocean University of China

Local Chair

Feng Hong   Ocean University of China

Organizing Committee

Liyan Jiang   Ocean University of China
Yuan Feng   Ocean University of China
Yongguo Jiang   Ocean University of China

Haipeng Qv	Ocean University of China
Zuojuan Liang	Ocean University of China
Yanxiu Sheng	Ocean University of China
Hua Li	Ocean University of China
Chao Liu	Ocean University of China

Table of Contents

Vehicle Speed Estimation Based on Sensor Networks and Signal Correlation Measurement

Wei Zhang, Guozhen Tan, and Nan Ding

School of Computer Science and Technology,
Dalian University of Technology, 116023, Dalian, P.R. China
wesley.cheung@163.com, {gztan,dingnan}@dlut.edu.cn

Abstract. This paper proposed a novel method for accurate vehicle speed estimation based on magnetic sensors. The estimation system consists of triple sensors and signals are collected synchronously when vehicles travel over it. Taking into consideration the difference of sensor sensitivity and self-disturbance of Earths magnetic field, a signal correlation model is introduced to improve the measurement precision of vehicle traveling time. Spectrum analysis and correlation model are used to accurately estimate the phase difference of sensor signals. In addition, an efficient clock synchronization algorithm based on active compensation is designed to reduce the time estimation error and enhance the vehicle speed estimation accuracy. Simulation and on-road experiment show that the method introduced in this paper has better performance and robustness than other approaches.

Keywords: intelligent transportation systems, wireless sensor networks, binary proximity sensors, vehicle speed estimation, signal correlation model, clock synchronization, active compensation.

1 Introduction

The intelligent transportation systems (ITS) is highly depends on the quality and quantity of road traffic data, and how to obtain exact and reliable traffic data with higher spatial-temporal resolution becomes more and more important [1]. Vehicle speed is one of the key parameters which can be used in traffic light control, safety assurance, over speed monitoring, and travel time estimation, etc [2]. In existing traffic control systems such as SCOOT, SCATS and REHODES, vehicle speed is a significant parameter to timing optimization algorithm [3]. In Jamitons model introduced by M.R. Flynn et al [4], vehicle speed is used as one of the important parameters to revel the cause of traffic congestion formation.

Nowadays, broadly used traffic surveillance technologies include loop sensor, digital video, microwave radar, infrared sensor, acoustic detector, float vehicle equipped with GPS, satellite image, UAV, and even mobile phone, etc [5,6]. But generally, current existing methods have many disadvantages such as high maintenance cost, low accuracy, poor real-time performance, can not work under all weather conditions, or can not deploy in large scale, etc. Modern traffic control

L. Sun, H. Ma, and F. Hong (Eds.): CWSN 2013, CCIS 418, pp. 1–12, 2014.

systems challenge traditional traffic surveillance technologies with both exactness and scale [7].

Wireless sensor networks (WSNs) have shown many attractive features in a lot of physical world sensing applications that motivate their rapid and wide diffusion in urban traffic surveillance and signal control [8,9]. Researchers in IBM predicts that sensors will appear on every mobile phone and every vehicle within 5 years. In PATH program joint research launched by UC Berkeley in collaboration with Caltrans (*California Department of Transportation*), P. Varaiya *et al* creatively applied wireless sensor networks in traffic surveillance to replace traditional technologies [8], and proposed adaptive threshold based algorithms for vehicle surveillance. The overall recognition rate of vehicle detection is beyond 98.2%, but because some inconsiderate respects or quite unexpected reasons, classification and speed estimation is not so efficient with lower precision below 60%. The main problems include: (1). The thresholds on individual sensor node are independent from each other, with no reference value, and that may led to spray drift and accumulated errors under different environment conditions; (2). The deviations from signal amplitude and phase changes caused by vehicle trajectory offset is inconsiderate; and (3). The short-time and exact clock synchronization of sensor nodes is out of consideration, which is very important to such a time-dependent detection system to estimate speed in a transient interval.

Under the background mentioned above, an accurate and novel vehicle speed estimation algorithm based on binary sensor networks and signal correlation analysis, named SEACM (*Speed Estimation Algorithm based on Correlation Measurement*), is proposed in this paper. The detection system consists of an access point (AP) and many detection points, and every detection point includes two detection sensor nodes and one surveillance node. This algorithm tries to improve speed estimation precision based on exact measurement of the time difference between signals achieved from detection sensor nodes. Models introduced in this paper are used to decrease magnetic field self-disturbance caused by environmental factors, to eliminate the measurement error resulted from sensor sensitivity difference, and to decrease clock synchronization deviations in short time. Result of simulation and on-road experiment show that the algorithm proposed in this paper enhanced the precision of vehicle speed estimation with better performance.

2   Related Work and Problem Statement

The typical scenario of vehicle detection and classification based on magnetic sensor networks carried in Berkeley PATH project is illustrated in Fig. 1 [8,9]. Magnetic sensors are deployed at detection point on segments near intersection and exchange data with AP via multi-hop communication.

A three-axis magnetometer on magnetic sensors can detect the changes of magnetic field in three directions, denoted by X, Y and Z. The magnetic field change will generate instant current in loop, which can be measured in disturbance signal, as shown in Fig. 2. The raw signal of sensor readings is s(t),

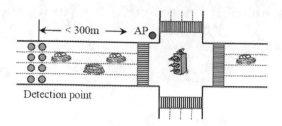

Fig. 1. Scenario of magnetic sensor based vehicle speed estimation

the digital data sent by sensor node is a(k) with sampling frequency f, which will be send to AP and processed by a state machine of the adaptive threshold detection algorithm (ATDA) to perform vehicle detection after band-pass filtering. The adaptive threshold in timeslot k is h(k), which will be updated by a forgetting factor α. The detection flag d(k)=1 is generated when continuous N signal samples exceed the threshold, and d(k)=0 is generated when M signal samples below the threshold continuously. Here the parameters α, N and M are all empirical values achieved from field experiment data.

In the speed estimation algorithm, double sensor nodes are used to measure instant speed based on an adaptive threshold. Assume the sensor nodes numbered A and B, and the separate distance between two nodes is D, and vehicle travel from A to B. Assume the time when d(k)=1 and d(k)=0 are denoted by t_{up} and t_{down} respectively. The vehicle speed can be calculated when detect d(k) changes from 1 to 0, via equation (1) as below.

$$v = \frac{1}{2} * \left(\frac{D}{t_{B,up} - t_{A,up}} + \frac{D}{t_{B,down} - t_{A,down}} \right) \tag{1}$$

However, the overall precision of vehicle speed estimation in this algorithm is below 60 %. Firstly, the result of on-road experiment of UC Berkeley shows that the collected signals of sensor node fluctuates greatly during different sunshine and relative humidity conditions [9], which will cause self-distortion of magnetic disturbance signals. That means speed estimation may vary largely when environment conditions change in short time. Secondly, threshold changes independently and different accumulated errors on sensor nodes may led to uncontrolled drift of vehicle speed estimation. Thirdly, if the vehicle trajectory is not parallel along the sensor nodes, the offset will cause hysteresis and deformation of measured signals. In addition, the minor fluctuation caused by clock synchronization will produce remarkable deviation drift in speed estimation, because both the separate distance and time interval are very short in actual application, and the effective signal length always sustains only 1 to 2 seconds. How to eliminate influence of self-distortion, environmental difference and trajectory offset, to estimate vehicle speed with higher precision, are the main issues studied in this paper.

3 Speed Estimation Based on Correlation Model

3.1 Correlation Model

In essence, ATDA only take into consideration N+M discrete signal simples to perform rough judgment according to a threshold, which is accurate enough to detect vehicle presentence, but lack of fault-tolerance performance and adaptive adjustment to environment changes. This paper proposed an algorithm based on signal correlation model [10] with the tentative idea to provide accurate and noise-tolerance approach for vehicle speed estimation. Given two signals x(t) and y(t) generated from the same source by two receivers deployed in different locations, to study their similarity, need to transform signal y(t) to y(t-τ) by time-shift τ, and calculate the correlation of y(t) and (t-τ). Here τ is delay. In vehicle speed estimation scenario, assuming sensor signals caused by traveling vehicle as stochastic variables, the correlation coefficient can indicate the strength and direction of the linearity between two signals, which can be defined in a general form as below:

$$R_{xy}(\tau) = \int_{-\infty}^{+\infty} x(t)y(t-\tau)\,dt \qquad (2)$$

To exam the change of $R_{xy}(\tau)$, if $|R_{xy}(\tau)|$ reach the maximum at time τ_0, that means the signal y(t) is most similar with x(t) with time-shift of τ_0, and here τ_0 is the time difference. In this paper, the proposed speed measurement algorithm based on correlation model uses two identical sensor nodes to monitor signals caused by the same travelling vehicle. Assume the sensor readings are shown in Fig. 3, the separate distance between sensor nodes is D, the signals generated by sensor A and B are x(t) and (t) respectively, and detection time window is T, thus the correlation function can be rewrote in a given limited time interval as equation (3).

$$R_{xy}(\tau) = \lim_{T \to +\infty} \frac{1}{T} \int_0^T x(t)y(t-\tau)\,dt \qquad (3)$$

Usually the data collected by sensor is sampled from raw signals, which is discrete in time domain. The discrete form of equation (3) is given in equation (4). Where δ is sampling interval, N is the total number of samples, m denotes time-shift scale in delay and

$$R_{xy}(m\delta) = \frac{1}{N} \sum_{n=0}^{N-1} x(n\delta)y(n\delta + m\delta) \qquad (4)$$

With the traffic measurement dataset achieved from field experiment based on magnetic sensors [11], the correlation function is analyzed and the result of two selected signals is shown in Fig. 2. From the statistical deviation of travelling time estimation from adaptive threshold based method and correlation analysis as shown in the scatter diagram of Fig. 3, where the unit of both coordinate axes is time in second. Correlation function based method is better in time resolution.

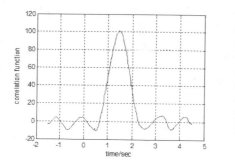
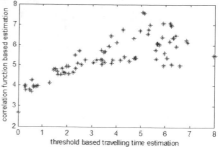

Fig. 2. Correlation function of two signals   **Fig. 3.** Deviation in time estimation

Given $m = m_0$ when $R(m\delta)$ reaches the maximum value $R(m_0\delta)$, then vehicle speed can be estimated via $D/m_0\delta$. In actual application, proper values of D and δ are meaningful to decrease computation complexity of the whole algorithm, which can be achieved from field experiment.

3.2 Offset Error Analysis and Complementation Model

If vehicle travelling trajectory is not parallel along the sensor nodes, the offset will cause hysteresis and deformation of measured signals, which will produce estimation error. In fact this phenomenon is uncontrolled and unavoidable. In error analysis model as shown in Fig. 4, A and B are sensor nodes, the ideal travelling trajectory is parallel along the sensor nodes, and the offset trajectory is declining at a slight angle θ.

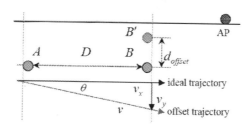

Fig. 4. Vehicle trajectory offset and error model

Under such condition, to simulate this condition, we can model that sensor B is located in B' with a offset d_{offset} in vertical direction, and sensor node move from B' to B with a speed related to vehicle speed when vehicle travel from A to B. During measurement, because of the density of magnetic field, the frequency of signal measured by sensor node far from vehicle become sparse, and frequency shift phenomenon similar to Doppler Effect will generate. Assuming the vehicle speed is v as the estimation variable, which can be projected to

v_x and v_y in horizontal and vertical direction respectively, thus below equation holds according to trigonometric formulas.

$$v_y = v \frac{d_{offset}}{\sqrt{D^2 + d_{offset}^2}} \tag{5}$$

Thus the vehicle trajectory offset problem can be transformed to one sensor node move on the vertical direction. Based on Doppler frequency shift equation, we introduce an empirical formula to express the relation of vehicle speed and frequency shift, as shown in equation (6), with which the speed deviation caused by offset can be compensated. Here f is the measured frequency of sensor node A, and f' is the measured frequency of node B. The parameter β is a relaxation factor and $|\beta| < 1$, v_y is vertical speed projected by vehicle speed v, v_m is critical speed, both β and v_m are empirical parameters. The vehicle magnetic signal is a non-periodic function of time, and currently there many frequency estimation methods can estimate the frequency characteristics based on signal samples. In this paper Hilbert-Huang transformation is used to estimate the instant frequency [12].

$$f' = (1 - \beta)f \frac{v_m \pm v_y}{v_m \mp v_y} \tag{6}$$

4   Sensor Networks Deployment and Signal Processing

4.1   Network Topology and Vehicle Detection

A binary proximity sensor network [13,14] topology model as shown in Fig. 5 (a) is proposed under the application scenario of vehicle speed estimation based on sensor networks and correlation model. The detection system deployed near an intersection consists of an AP and multiple detection points, which includes two detection sensor nodes A and B, and a surveillance node G for clock synchronization, are all deployed on the paralleling line with lane. Denote the distance between sensor node and vehicle travelling trajectory is D_{offset}, effective radius of sensor node is R, sensor separate distance is D. The buffer distance L is reserved for clock synchronization. The length of D and L will be studied based on data achieved from on-road experiment. When vehicle is detected by surveillance node G, the detection sensor nodes will be notified and clock synchronization is performed between detection sensor nodes A and B before vehicle reach the effective range of node A. To ensure the clock of sensor node A and B is synchronized accurately before vehicle speed is estimating, we use an efficient clock synchronization algorithm which will be discuss in later chapter.

Sensor node will perform ATDA to detect data, synchronize local clock and transmit data to AP, and AP exchange data with sensor node via single-hop or multi-hop depending on distance. The AP has more computation resource and power, which collects data from all sensor nodes, calculate correlation function to estimate vehicle speed, and manages the network topology. The raw signals will be filtered and smoothed to eliminate noise, and then send to ATDA state machine to detect vehicle. In actual application scenario, vehicles may travel from the sensor node continuously. In this paper we modified the state machine of ATDA to improve the performance. As shown in Fig. 5 (b), a detection window W is introduced to avoid vehicle detection missing under high density traffic flow, and an intermediate Count10 with corresponding threshold Φ is appended to process state transfer immediately after vehicle detection.

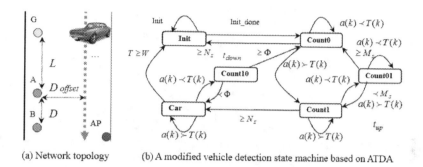

(a) Network topology   (b) A modified vehicle detection state machine based on ATDA

Fig. 5. Sensor deployment and modified state machine

For some special scenarios such as still vehicle in stopped traffic, the measured magnetic signals will be constant values, thus the time difference calculated by correlation model is zero. In this condition the model proposed in this paper can identify it and give output that the vehicle speed is zero.

4.2 Signal Pre-processing and Noise Elimination

Because the sensor is high sensitive, the raw data collected by sensor node is error-prone to be effected by environmental changes and random noise, which will decrease performance. In this paper band-pass filter is used to remove random noise, and then signal is smoothed with median filtering. Assuming the detection window is W, total number of samples is N, filter window is m, here m is an odd number. Raw data is a(k), and the output data smoothed by median filtering is $a'(k)$, thus below equation hold.

$$a'(k) = Median(a(k-v), ..., a(k), a(k+1), ..., (a(k+v)), v = (m-1)/2 \quad (7)$$

The processing of time-domain features extraction and median filtering is illustrated in Fig. 9 and Fig. 10 respectively. Signal is intercepted by window W based on threshold judgment. The running average is obtained from N samples.

4.3 Clock Synchronization Based on Active Compensation

In this paper we want to estimate vehicle speed as accurate as possible, consequently the clock synchronization needs more consideration. Currently there

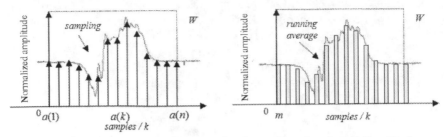

(a). Time-domain features extraction   **(b).**Signal smoothness based on median filtering

Fig. 6. Feature extraction and median filtering

exist many clock synchronization algorithms [15]. For the simple application scenario and network topology proposed in this paper, as shown in Fig. 5 (a), we design an efficient clock synchronization algorithm based on TPSN (Timing-sync Protocol for Sensor Networks) [16]. The basic steps include: to sample local clock value periodically, and then calculate the deviation between local clock and the reference clock, and finally fix local clock with the difference.

TPSN is a clock synchronization algorithm based on sender-receiver communication. As we know, the most power consumption is radio, and the power of sensor nodes will affect the overall lifespan of the detection system, thus we need to consider power-efficient approach. In the model proposed in this paper, the network topology is very simple, so we can modify the work mode of TPSN to receiver-only that synchronize clock based on the local clock of the node with less power to decrease communication cost and save power [17].

Assuming the case that node B has less power, node A will communicate with node B and adjust its local clock to keep synchronous with node B while node B just need to exchange synchronization packets with node A without clock adjustment. In this process, node A will complete the receiver-only synchronization, and different to TPSN, node A·will calculate a clock deviation compensation which is predicted based on clock deviation obtained from frontal packets and maximum likelihood estimation model. The active compensation is helpful to speed deviation convergence. In this paper, the value of clock deviation compensation is denoted in equation (8), here $T_{k,i}$, $k \in [1, 4]$ is time packet sending or receiving, and $t_i{}^A$, $i \in [1, n]$ is local clock value in the i-th iteration.

$$\theta_{offset}^{AB} = \frac{1}{2i}(\sum_{k=1}^{i}(T_{2,i}{}^B - T_{1,i}{}^A) - \sum_{k=1}^{i}(T_{4,i}{}^A - T_{3,i}{}^B) \pm \sum_{k=1}^{i}\xi_k) \qquad (8)$$

5   Speed Estimation Algorithm

The diagram of the overall processing of vehicle speed estimation algorithm is illustrated in Fig. 7. In idle time, all nodes are sleeping to save power. The surveillance node G will shutdown radio when it in sleeping state and keep sensor active. When detect M times d(k)=1 in ATDA state machine, that means vehicle is detected by node G, it will awake detection nodes A and B to perform clock synchronization and switch to work mode when local clock is nearly full synchronous. In actual scenario, sensor node is error-prone in wireless communication condition, and unstable wireless channel maybe cause unexpected noise, such as high frequency pulse or signal loss. In work mode, the sampled raw signal is sent to band-pass filter to remove environmental noise, and smoothed by mean filter to eliminate random noise, then signals will be sent to ATDA to detect vehicle. Meanwhile correlation factor R of the signals received by two detection sensor nodes is calculated via FFT, and time difference is obtained when R reaches the maximum value. At the same time, the time difference is modified by offset and phase compensation obtained from frequency shift estimation and empirical equation (6). Finally the vehicle speed can be estimated via nodes separate distance and time difference.

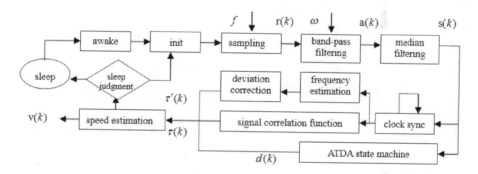

Fig. 7. Diagram of speed estimation algorithm

6   Experiment and Performance Analysis

In the simulation and on-road experiment, the hardware and software platform we used are Mica2 series sensor toolkits and the TinyOS respectively, that is designed and developed by UC Berkeley. The sensor nodes consist of three data processing boards equipped with Honeywell HMC1002 2-axis magnetic sensors, a gateway MB510 as AP which is connected to computer by USB.

The experimental parameters are setting as below: sampling frequency of sensor node is f=128Hz, threshold with empirical values that N=11 and M=12, forgot factor α=0.15, detection window W=60, the offset from sensor node to middle of lane D_{offset}=1.8m, sensor separate D is 1m, buffer distance for clock synchronization L is 2m. For performance comparison, we use a high speed camera to record vehicle traveling video, and measure vehicle speed based on image processing and the reference lines on the ground. The on-road experiment scenario is shown in Fig. 8 (a). The signals under conditions of different vehicle trajectory offset are collected, and the data samples are shown in Fig. 8 (b)

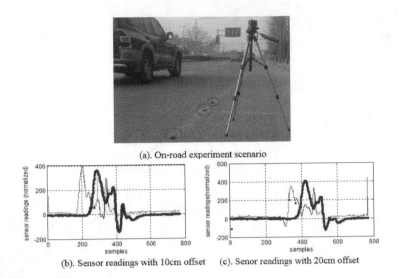

(a). On-road experiment scenario

(b). Sensor readings with 10cm offset   (c). Senor readings with 20cm offset

Fig. 8. On-road experiment scenario and signals under different vehicle trajectory offset

and Fig. 8 (c). From the figures, it obvious that the environmental factors and vehicle trajectory offset may greatly affect the shape and time-domain attribute of sensor signals.

For speed estimation performance analysis, we calculate the speed of the same vehicle based on video image, correlation model (SEACM) and direct ATDA algorithm respectively. The performance result is illustrated in Fig. 9. ATDA can only estimate vehicle speed when both up/down thresholds are detected, and SEACM can estimate vehicle speed from the first threshold exceeding is detected. The variation of error in clock synchronization used in SEACM is shown in Fig. 10. Owing to active compensation and receiver-only strategy, the clock deviation of two detection sensor nodes is fast convergent and local clock becomes exact synchronous in short time. The performance is better than traditional TPSN algorithm in both convergence time and stable precision.

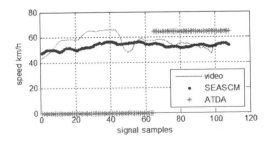

Fig. 9. Speed estimation performance

The experiment result shows that the measurement of sensor nodes fluctuates greatly under different environmental conditions, especially in ATDA the vehicle trajectory offset and loss of clock synchronization will cause self-distortion which may led to remarkable deviation in vehicle travelling time estimation. The SEACM algorithm proposed in this paper decreases the error of vehicle travelling time estimation based on signals correlation function analysis, and the speed estimation precision is improved.

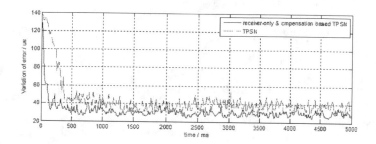

Fig. 10. Variation of error in clock synchronization

7   Conclusions and Next Steps

This paper proposed an efficient algorithm for accurate vehicle speed estimation based on wireless sensor networks and signal correlation measurement. Focus on the physical characteristics that magnetic field disturbance signal is error-prone to be affected by environment conditions and vehicle trajectory offset, this paper introduced models such as correlation function, frequency estimation and time-shit compensation, median filtering, active compensation based clock synchronization in short time, etc, to improve vehicle speed estimation precision and enhance robustness. The result of simulation and on-road experiment show good performance.

On another hand, there are some empirical parameters in models that make this algorithm just adaptive to common scenario, and the performance in extreme or special conditions such as high traffic density need more considerations. In addition, to implement this algorithm on sensor nodes, the complexity needs more optimization because the resource is restricted on embedded systems on sensor node. These problems will be studied in next steps.

References

1. Orosz, G., Wilson, R.E., Stepan, G.: Traffic jams: dynamics and control. Phi. Trans. of the Royal Soc. A 368, 4455–4479 (2010)
2. Klein, L.A., Milton, K.M.: Traffic detector handbook, 3rd edn. FHWA, Joint Program Office for Intelligent Transportation Systems, Department of Transportation, U.S.A. (2006)

3. Mirchandani, P., Wang, F.Y.: RHODES to intelligent transportation systems. IEEE Int. Sys. 20, 10–15 (2005)
4. Flynn, M.R., Kasimov, A.R., Nave, J.C., Rosales, R.R., Seibold, B.: Self-sustained nonlinear waves in traffic flow. Physical Review E 79, 61–74 (2008)
5. Mimbela, L.E.Y., Klein, L.E.Y. : A summary of vehicle detection and surveillance technologies used in intelligent transportation systems. FHWA, Joint Program Office for Intelligent Transportation Systems, Department of Transportation, U.S.A. (2007)
6. Toral, S.L., Torres, M.R.M., Barrero, F.J., Arahal, M.R.: Current paradigms in intelligent transportation systems. IET Int. Trans. Sys. 4, 201–211 (2010)
7. Lint, J.W.C., Valkenberg, A.J., Binsbergen, A.J., Bigazzi, A.: Advanced traffic monitoring for sustainable traffic management - experiences and results of five years of collaborative research in the Netherlands. IET Int. Trans. Sys. 4, 387–400 (2010)
8. Amine, H., Robert, K., Pravin, V.: Wireless magnetic sensors for traffic surveillance. Trans. Res. Part C 16, 294–306 (2008)
9. Cheung, S.Y., Varaiya, P.: Traffic surveillance by wireless sensor networks: final report. Department of Electrical Engineering and Computer Science, University of California, Berkeley (2007)
10. Han, X.Y.: Study on measurement method of running velocity. Master dissertation, Xi'an University of Technology (2004)
11. Cheung, S.Y., Varaiya, P.: Traffic measurement data-set, http://paleale.eecs.berkeley.edu/~varaiya/sensors.html
12. Huang, N.E., Zheng, S., Long, S.R.: The empirical mode decomposition and the Hilbert spectrum for nonlinear non-stationary time series analysis. Proc. of the Royal Soc. of London Series A 454, 903–995 (1998)
13. Shrivastava, N., Mudumbai, R., Suri, S.: Target tracking with binary proximity sensor networks. ACM Transactions on Sensor Networks 5, 1–33 (2009)
14. Singh, J., Kumar, R., Madhow, U., Suri, S., Cagley, R.: Multiple-target tracking with binary proximity sensors. ACM Trans. on Sen. Net. 8, 1–26 (2011)
15. Sivrikaya, F., Yener, B.: Time synchronization in sensor networks: a survey. IEEE Network 18, 45–50 (2004)
16. Ganeriwal, S., Kumar, R., Srivastava, M.B.: Timing-sync protocol for sensor networks. In: Proc. of the 1st Int. Conf. on Embedded Networked Sensor Systems, pp. 138–149 (2003)
17. Guo, W.J., Wang, Y.L., Wei, N., Guo, Q., Zhou, S.W.: A time synchronization protocol for wireless sensor network based on Kalman filter. J. of Shandong University (Natural Science) 45, 32–36 (2010)

Human Tracking with Pyroelectric Sensors Based on Clutter Environment Modeling

Jingyuan Zhang, Fangmin Li, and Ji Xiong

Key Laboratory of Fiber Optic Sensing Technology and Information Processing
Ministry of Education, School of Information Engineering,
Wuhan University of Technology, Wuhan 430070, China
lifangmin@whut.edu.cn
http://i.whut.edu.cn/

Abstract. With the segmentation and coding of the field of views (FOVs) by using Fresnel lens arrays, we can realize the human body target positioning tracking. The observation noise will be uneven distributed when using the angular measurement error model, furthermore, the model can't work in the event of missing inspection. Based on these two defects, in this paper we design a clutter environment tracking model by changing angle measurement into clutter coordinates to make the observation noise homogenization. We calculate all the associated probability of the clutter and use the probability as weight values to update the target state in the location phase. The simulation results show that the error of our model is smaller than angular measurement error model, and our model can also be used in the high missing rate of inspection.

Keywords: human tracking, pyroelectric sensor, clutter.

1 Introduction

Human body motion tracking includes getting body displacement and body motions. It is widely used in various environment detection system, security systems, intelligent auxiliary system, etc. Human body tracking usually needs to collect the stable and reliable physical characteristics [1], such as fingerprint, iris, voice spectrum, facial features or behavior features. Traditional detection and tracking system generally use the video device to detect the image of access area [2,3], this kind of system is mainly used to track individual facial features, greatly restricted by factors such as lighting condition, shooting angle, or clothing. And the system which is based on video image usually has high computational overhead and data throughput, and advanced infrared video system [4] are very expensive.

Compared with the traditional video tracking system, wireless pyroelectric sensor network has many advantages [5]. Pyroelectric infrared sensor has higher capacity to detect infrared radiation. It has many characteristics, such as small size, low power consumption, low cost, high sensitivity. Combined with low prices Fresnel lens array, it can obtain higher (FOV) angle domain, and select input wavelength, and only through human radiation wavelength. That is very important to distinguish between human and the human body target. This basis, the

L. Sun, H. Ma, and F. Hong (Eds.): CWSN 2013, CCIS 418, pp. 13–22, 2014.

researchers have to try and develop the human detection and tracking system based on pyroelectric sensor, in order to realize target tracking and recognition to human body [6,7].

Qi Hao et al. presents some human tracking algorithm [7,8,9] in the study of pyroelectric sensors to the human body tracking system. It takes full advantage of the characteristics of regional pyroelectric sensor and encode the detection area regional segmentation. When human body movement in different regions, the sensor will produce different coding and obtain initial positioning of the body. And then through the corresponding filter, get the final aim. Because in the process of system simulation, the system takes the angle error model and the positioning accuracy of the simulation is very good, but the actual positioning error is larger.

This paper points out that the positioning accuracy of angle error model is uneven and in missing cases it's unable to track . And then it puts forward the thought of clutter environment modeling, which turns the observation of pyroelectric infrared sensor node value into a set of clutter by angle and use the probability as weight values to update the target state and forecasts. At last, it gives a coarse positioning mechanism which can be work in a real environment when missing happens. The simulation results show that the positioning error is smaller than the angle error model in reference [10] error, and it can track normally when missing rate increased.

2   A Pyroelectric Infrared Sensor Detection Model

The simulation environment of this paper uses dual-column pyroelectric sensor nodes, whose visual field modulation is horizontal side angle sensing mode [9]. The physical maps of the node and single-node detection area are shown in Figure 1.

In Figure 1, each node consists of eight sensors, a double-column distribution, and each sensor visual field adjusts its angle through the Fresnel lens [9], thus producing 14 different detection zones.

The position of a fan-shaped region can be achieved through the method mentioned above, but the specific coordinates from the region 1 to the region 14 is unknown because it needs multiple pyroelectric nodes collaborate together to get the exact location of the target. The principle of the design is shown in Figure 2.

As can be seen from Figure 2, the four pyroelectric sensor nodes can constitute a detection unit, and the detection area of neighboring sensor nodes are partially overlapping, which are numbered 1, 2, 3, 4. The target in the intersection area can be detected by two sensors simultaneously. Based on the detected position of the node itself and its label of the observation area, we can get the angle of the central intersection area. By using the angle as observed values, the state value of the target can be got through Kalman Filtering, which is the positioning process of angle measurements error modal. The specific formula derivation can be found in the literature [10].

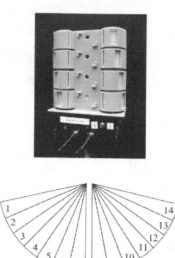

Fig. 1. Two-column radiation sensor node and its detection area

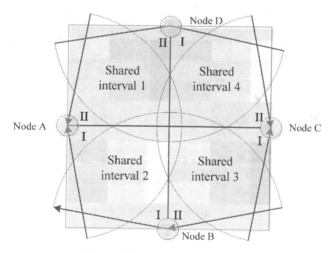

Fig. 2. Node detection area [10]

3   Clutter Environment Modeling

The introduction part has pointed out that angular measurement error model used in the pyroelectric sensors system has good precision in simulation but large error in actual measurement. All above, there are two main reasons contribute to this.

On the one hand, in actual measurement, angular error increases with decreasing the distance from the human body to the pyroelectric sensors. This phenomenon is especially obvious when the distance is relatively close. As Figure 3 shows the angular error increases from θ_1 to θ_2 while the distance decreases from L_1 to L_2. That reduces the location precision.

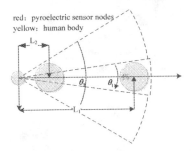

Fig. 3. Uneven angular error schematic of pyroelectric sensors

On the other hand, in actual measurement, missing occurs frequently due to the hardware threshold detection features. When comes to this situation, angular measurement error model will discarding the incomplete observation information. It will cause a loss of effective observation information and make the detection rate greatly reduced, as shown in figure 4.

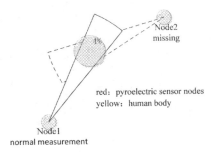

Fig. 4. Missing schematic of pyroelectric sensors

Based on these two defects, this paper put forward the idea of clutter environment modeling which turns observed value from the angle to the coordinates of the clutters to make the observation noise homogenized. The model consists of (1) to (4) as follows.

State transfer equation:

$$X_k = A^* X_{k-1} + G^* w_k \tag{1}$$

Observation equation:

$$z_k = H X_k + v_k \tag{2}$$

$$R_k^{(i,j)} = \begin{cases} 1, \text{ if } \left|(\arctan \frac{y_k - y_s^{(i)}}{x_k - x_s^{(i)}} - \theta_s^{(i)} + m\pi) - \text{angle}^{(i,j)}\right| < \frac{FOV^{(i,j)}}{2} \\ 0, \text{ otherwise} \end{cases} \tag{3}$$

$$Z_k^{1:n} = \left\{\text{clutter}^{(i,j)} | R^{i,j} = 1\right\} \tag{4}$$

(1) shows that the state transition equation using the uniform motion model. X_k represent the moving state of human body which consist of X position, X-velocity component, Y position, Y-velocity component. w_k and v_k are process noise and measurement noise which are independent zero mean additive noise sequence with covariance of Q_k and S_k.

Here,

$$A = \begin{bmatrix} 1 & 1 & 0 & 0 \\ 0 & 1 & 0 & 0 \\ 0 & 0 & 1 & 1 \\ 0 & 0 & 0 & 1 \end{bmatrix}, \quad G = \begin{bmatrix} \lambda & 0 \\ 1 & 0 \\ 0 & \lambda \\ 0 & 1 \end{bmatrix} \tag{5}$$

A and G make (1) be uniform motion model, $0 < \lambda < 1$.
Observation equation is clutter measurement model. Here,

$$H = \begin{bmatrix} 1 & 0 & 0 & 0 \\ 0 & 0 & 1 & 0 \end{bmatrix}, \quad z_k = \begin{bmatrix} x_k \\ y_k \end{bmatrix} \tag{6}$$

In (3), $R_k^{(i,j)} = 1$ means that the real observation z_k appears in j^{th} observation area of sensor i, angle$^{(i,j)}$ is the center angle of jth observation area of sensor i. $FOV^{(i,j)}$ is the size of the jth observation area of sensor i. $m\pi$ is used to ensure the values in parentheses in the range of $(-180°, 180°]$.

Therefore, the measured values used in state estimation is a set of clutters called clutter$^{(i,j)}$ which represent the clutters in j^{th} observation area of sensor i. Assume that sometime human body is detected by three pyroelectric nodes, then the relationship of true value, observed value and observed clutters is shown in Figure 5.

The clutters are spread evenly in the detection area with granularity of λ. During the initialization phase the fusion center builds a clutter distribution table as (7) shows.

$$\text{clutter}^{(i,j)} \{i = 1, \ldots, 4, j = 1, \ldots, 14\} \tag{7}$$

In subsequent time we just need to search the table to get the observation clutters. By modeling clutter environment angular measurement error can be converted to coordinate error. On the one hand, the measurement error is even; on the other hand, only one set of clutters is need to be observed data for tracking filter which is significant while dealing with missing.

4   Tracking Filter Technology in Clutter

Suppose $Z_{k+1}^{1:n}$ is the observed clutter set at k_1, for these n observed clutters can define n interconnected events, that is:

$$\theta_i(k+1) = \left\{\text{the } i^{\text{th}} \text{ clutter is the true observation value}\right\}, i = 1, 2, 3, \ldots, n \tag{8}$$

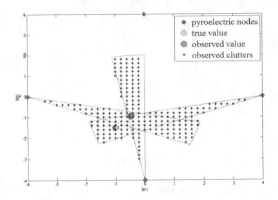

Fig. 5. Clutter environment model target detection schematic

The corresponding interconnection probability to the above infinite events are:

$$\beta_i(k+1) = \frac{e_i}{\sum\limits_{j=1}^{n} e_j}, \quad i = 1, 2, \ldots, n \tag{9}$$

In the formula (8)

$$e_j = \exp\left\{ -\frac{1}{2} V_j'(k+1) S^{-1}(k+1) V_j(k+1) \right\} \tag{10}$$

Among (9),

$$V_j(k+1) = Z_{k+1}^j - H\hat{H}(k+1|k) \tag{11}$$

$V_j(k+1)$ is the corresponding innovation of the jth effective measurement. Using the interconnection probability-weighted sum in Equation [9], the equivalent echo of the target can be obtained and the status of the target can be updated as follows:

$$\hat{X}(k+1|k+1) = \sum_{i=1}^{n} \beta_i(k+1)\hat{X}_i(k+1|k+1)$$
$$= \hat{X}(k+1|k) + K(k+1)V(k+1) \tag{12}$$

In formula (11), $V(k+1)$ is combination innovation, $\hat{X}(k+1|k)$ is the one-step prediction of the target state, $K(k+1)$ is Kalman filter gain, namely

$$V(k+1) = \sum_{i=1}^{n} \beta_i(k+1)V_i(k+1) \tag{13}$$

$$K(k+1) = P(k+1|k)H'(k+1)S^{-1}(k+1) \tag{14}$$

$$S(k+1) = H(k+1)P(k+1|k)H'(k+1) + R(k+1) \tag{15}$$

$P(k+1|k)$ is one-step prediction of the covariance of the state. $S(k+1)$ is the innovation covariance.

State covariance update equation:

$$P(k+1|k+1) = P(k+1|k) + K(k+1)\left[\sum_{i=1}^{n}\beta_i(k+1)V_i(k+1)V_i^{'}(k+1)\right.$$
$$\left. -V_i(k+1)V_i^{'}(k+1)\right]K^{'}(k+1) \tag{16}$$

Thus, the equation (8), (11), (12), (13), (15) constitute basic equation of Kalman filter state estimation in the clutter environment modeled.

5   Simulation Example

This paper takes an $8 \times 8m$ room for the simulation scene where four pyroelectric infrared sensor nodes are arranged. The detection radius is $6m$, while the target actual path is assumed as a circular trajectory. On this circular curve, a uniform circular motion at the linear speed of $1m/s$ takes place, and by cycling sampling with $0.2s$ as a period, 500 sampling points are obtained as the real trajectory of the simulation. A 0.2 of variance of white Gaussian noise based on the real trajectory is taken to simulate the observed trajectory in actual environment. By adoption of Kalman filter algorithm with angle error model as mentioned in Reference [10] for track-up, the results obtained are shown in Figure 6. The mean errors on Axis X and Y are $0.4399m$ and $0.5195m$ respectively; and the tracking results by application of filtering algorithm with clutter environment modeling in this paper are shown in Figure 7, wherein, the mean errors on Axis X and Y are $0.3352m$ and $0.3560m$ respectively. Figure 8 shows the average error distribution histograms of the two models.

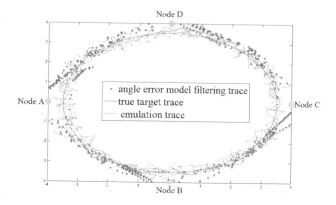

Fig. 6. Tracking trajectory of angle error

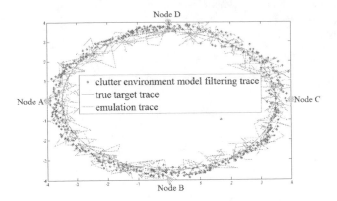

Fig. 7. Tracking trajectory of clutter environment

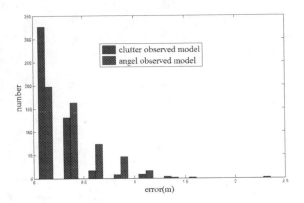

Fig. 8. Histogram for distribution of tracking errors of different models

In case that residual occurs to detection of pyroelectric sensor nodes, with direct discarding of incomplete information, then errors would be increased. If clutter positioning mechanism as pointed out in this paper is adopted, then tracking errors arisen from missed detection would be reduced to a certain extent. In this paper, switch variables are adopted to simulate missed detection under actual conditions, in which case, the sensor observation information falls short; while the observation information is complete. Figure 9 demonstrates the tracking errors in case of clutter positioning mechanism and direct discarding of incomplete observation results, wherein, when the undetected rate is 0.1, then it would be indicated that there would be 10 missed detection occurrences for each 100 sampling times. From Figure 9, we can see that when the undetected rate is 1, i.e. the observed information sampled in each period is incomplete, then by adoption of clutter confirmation mechanism, the positioning errors on Axis X and Y are deemed as $0.6813m$ and $0.6302m$ respectively, thus the tracking and positioning of targets are still available. In case direct discarding mechanism is adopted in other models and the undetected rate is greater than 0.6, then it can be basically regarded as failed.

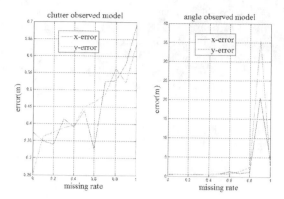

Fig. 9. Relationship between missing rate and tracking error using different models

6 Conclusion

This paper puts forward the idea of using the modeling of the clutter environment, turning the observed value from the angle into clutter coordinates, to solve the problem of uneven tracking accuracy caused by using angle error model in regional detection such as pyroelectric sensor nodes. In the tracking phase, we presents a clutter tracking filter algorithm, which looks the observational information of pyroelectric sensor nodes to a group of clutter. In the integration phase, we adopts the voting integration based on the collection of observations clutter. Simulation results show that this model has a good tracking accuracy during single human target tracking. And in the real situation, when the undetected situations occur, it can be accurately tracked. The future work is to make the emulate model algorithm implemented in a real environment, and finally establish a perfect pyroelectric sensor network tracking system.

Acknowledgments. This work was supported by the National Natural Science Foundation of China under Grant No. 61170090.

References

1. Bourgeois, N.V., Hoatzins, D., Plantaniotis, K.N.: Gait recognition. IEEE Signal Process. Mag. 22(6), 78–90 (2005)
2. Hong, L., Ze, Y., Hongbin, Z., Yuexian, Z., Lin, Z.: Robust human tracking based on multi-cue integration and mean-shift. Pattern Recognition Letters 30(9), 827–837 (2009)
3. Jialue, F., Wei, X., Ying, W., Yihong, G.: Human tracking based neural networks. IEEE Transactions on Neural Networks 21(10), 1610–1623 (2010)
4. Cheng, S.Y., Park, S., Trivedi, M.: Multi-spectral and multi-perspective video arrays for driver body tracking and activity analysis. Computer Vision and Image Understanding 106(2-3), 245–257 (2007)

5. Morinaka, K., Hashimoto, K., Tanaka, S., et al.: Human information sensor. Sensor and Actuators 66, 1–8 (1988)
6. Hao, Q., Hu, F., Xiao, Y.: Multiple human tracking and identification with wireless distributed pyroelectric sensor systems. IEEE Syst. J. 3(4), 428–439 (2009)
7. Zhou, X., Hao, Q., Hu, F.: 1-bit walker recognition with distributed binary pyroelectric sensors. In: 2010 IEEE Intl. Conf. on Multisensor Fusion and Integration for Intelligent Systems, University of Uath, Slat Lake City, UT, USA, pp. 168–173 (2010)
8. Hao, Q., Fang, J.S., Brady, D.J., Guenther, B.D.: Real-time walker recognition using pyroelectric sensors. Submitted to IEEE Sensors Journal
9. Hao, Q., Brady, J.D., Guenther, D.B., Burchett, J.B., Shankar, M., Feller, S.: Human tracking with wireless distributed pyroelectric sensors. IEEE Sensors Journal 6(6), 1683–1694 (2006)
10. Hao, Q.: Multiple Human Tracking and Identification with Wireless Distributed Pyroelectric Sensor. Ph.d thesis, Duke University (2006)

An Adaptive Virtual Area Partition Clustering Routing Protocol Using Ant Colony Optimization for Wireless Sensor Networks[*]

Dexin Ma[1,2], Jian Ma[1], and Pengmin Xu[3,**]

[1] State Key Lab of Networking & Switching Technology,
Beijing University of Posts and Telecommunications, Beijing 100876, China
[2] Communication College, Qingdao Agricultural University, Qingdao 266109, China
[3] Network Management Center, Qingdao Agricultural University,
Qingdao 266109, China

Abstract. Clustering is an energy efficient techniques that extends the network's lifespan, and routing is an efficient techniques that reduces the communication delay and balances the network traffic loads. In this paper, we propose and analyze an Adaptive Virtual Area Partition Clustering Routing protocol using Ant Colony Optimization (AVAPCR-ACO), a protocol that clusters the network field adaptively, then uses ant colony optimization to build a routing path among cluster heads. The simulation results show that AVAPCR-ACO can improve system lifetime obviously.

Keywords: wireless sensor networks, ant colony optimization, adaptive virtual area partition.

1 Introduction

Wireless sensor networks (WSNs) are application-specified networks, and have a great number of applications such as military surveillance, natural disaster rescue etc. This has been enabled by the availability of sensors that are smaller, cheaper, and intelligent. These sensors are equipped with antennas with which they can communicate each others to form a network. So when we design a WSN, we must take the factors such as the object, application environment, hardware, cost and other system constraints into consideration [1].

A wireless sensor network consists of hundreds to thousands of small multi-functioning devices with limit energy supply. Once they are deployed, the sensor nodes are often unreachable to users, the replacement or recharge of batteries are impossible, so energy efficient is the vital factor for WSNs. Clustering is

[*] Research supported by Shandong Province Independent Innovation Achievements of Major Projects under grant No.2011ZHZX1A0406, National Natural Science Foundation of China (NSFC) under grant No.61271041, FP7 Integrated Project iCore (Internet Connected Objects for Reconfigurable Eco-systems) under grant No.287708.
[**] Corresponding author.

one of the energy efficient techniques that extending the sensor network's lifetime [2], we cluster the network using virtual area partition scheme adaptively; and routing is one of the efficient techniques that reduces the communication delay and balances the network traffic loads, we takes advantage of ant colony optimization to build a routing path among the cluster heads.

Ant Colony Optimization (ACO) has been inspired by the behavior of real ant colonies, in particular, by their foraging behavior [3], [4]. It has the advantage of robust, excellent distributed calculated mechanism, easy to combine with other methods [5], etc.

In this paper, we design an Adaptive Virtual Area Partition Clustering Routing protocol using Ant Colony Optimization (AVAPCR-ACO), which uses virtual area partition scheme to cluster the network, and takes advantage of Ant Colony Optimization to build a routing path among the cluster heads. The protocol clusters the network adaptively, then builds a routing path among the cluster heads to reduce the communication delay, balance the network traffic loads. The protocol accords the idea of energy efficient to obtain good performance in terms of energy consumption and system lifetime. Our simulation results show that AVAPCR-ACO can improve system lifetime and minimize energy dissipating obviously.

2   Related Work

Low-Energy Adaptive Clustering Hierarchy (LEACH) is proposed in [6] that randomly rotating the role of a cluster head in the network among all the nodes, it is an adaptive clustering scheme. VAP-E [7] is based on virtual area partition for heterogeneous wireless sensor networks, but it is not partitions the network adaptively.

Ant Colony Optimization based routing algorithms have been used for improving the system performance. By finding the maximum number of connected covers, it [8] proposes an ACO-based scheme to prolong the lifespan of heterogeneous WSNs. The authors [9] have investigated a routing protocol and used ant colony optimization (ACO) algorithm to this protocol for homogeneous WSNs. A routing protocol [10] considers remainder of node along the path and the path energy cost concurrently, and tries finding the tradeoff between them.

Our design clusters the network adaptively and takes advantage of ACO, considers the network states information deliberately, and selects the best path to the BS to further improve energy efficiency and balance the energy dissipation.

3   AVAPCR-ACO Algorithm

We proposed an adaptive energy-efficient clustering routing algorithm, aiming to enhance the existing clustering algorithms' performance. In this section, we design AVAPRC-ACO, partitions the network into clusters, then use ant colony optimization to build routing path among the cluster heads. The flow chart of AVAPCR-ACO is as shown in Fig. 1.

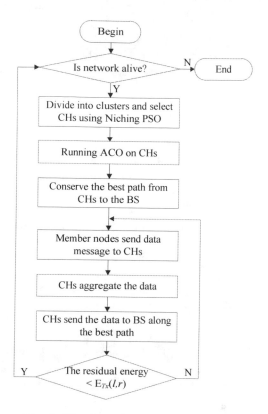

Fig. 1. The flow chart of AVAPRC-ACO

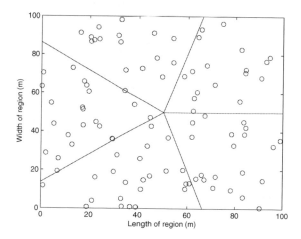

Fig. 2. Virtual area partition clustering with K=5

3.1 Adaptively Virtual Area Partition Clustering

The optimal number of clusters is determined by $K = \frac{\sqrt{N}}{\sqrt{2\pi}}\sqrt{\frac{\varepsilon_{fs}}{\varepsilon_{mp}}}\frac{M}{d_{toBS}^2}$ [6], then we perform virtual area partition clustering, the network is partitioned into clustering adaptively according the network states. As shown in Fig. 2, a 100m × 100m region with 100 nodes distributed randomly, we use virtual area partition clustering that divided the network by K=5.

3.2 Ant Colony Optimization

Ant Colony Optimization (ACO) [3], [4], [5] is a population-based approach which has been applied to NP-hard combinatorial optimization problems successfully [8], [9]. ACO has been inspired by the behavior of real ant colonies, especially by their foraging behavior. Based on the trails of a chemical substance which called pheromone that real ants use for communication, each ant communicates indirectly among a colony of ants. The pheromone trails are a kind of distributed numeric information which is modified by the ants to reflect their experience accumulated while solving a particular problem. The ACO meta-heuristic has been presented to provide a unifying framework for most applications of ant algorithms [4], [5] to combinatorial optimization problems.

ACO algorithms make use of ants to construct candidate solutions iteratively of a combinatorial optimization problem. Guiding by problem-dependent heuristic information and pheromone trails, the solution is constructed. The candidate solutions constructed by individual ant starts with an empty solution, then adds solution components iteratively until we get an integrated candidate solution. The ants give feedback on the solutions by depositing pheromone on it after complete the solution construction. Solution components which are used by many ants will receive a higher amount of pheromone, and will be used by ants in the future iterations more likely. We should avoid the pheromone accumulate infinitely before the pheromone trails get enhanced, so all pheromone trails are decreased by a factor.

We define the transition probability from cluster head i to j for the kth ant as:

$$p_{ij}^k(t) = \begin{cases} \frac{[\tau_{ij}(t)]^\alpha \cdot [\eta_{ij}]^\beta}{\sum\limits_{k \in allowed_k} [\tau_{ik}(t)]^\alpha \cdot [\eta_{ik}]^\beta}, & j \in allowed_k \\ 0, & \text{otherwise} \end{cases} \tag{1}$$

Where α is the pheromone heuristic factor, it reflect the residual pheromones importance of degree, β is the expectation heuristic factor, it reflect the expectation's importance of degree. η_{ij} is the expectation degree that transit from i to j. $allowed_k = \{C - tabu_k\}$ is the cluster head that ant k can select (i.e. the cluster head that ant k didnt visit). $\eta_{ij}(t) = 1/d_{ij} = \left[(x_i - x_j)^2 + (y_i - y_j)^2\right]^{1/2}$, that means the smaller d_{ij}, the bigger $\eta_{ij}(t)$ for ant k.

In order to avoiding the residual pheromone overwhelm the heuristic information, we use the following formula to update the residual pheromone.

$$\tau_{ij}(t+1) = (1 - \rho) \cdot \tau_{ij}(t) + \Delta\tau_{ij} \tag{2}$$

$$\Delta\tau_{ij}(t) = \sum_{k=1}^{m} \Delta\tau_{ij}^{k}(t) \tag{3}$$

Where ρ is the coefficient such that $(1 - \rho)$ represents the evaporation of trail. $\Delta\tau_{ij}$ is the quantity per unit of length of trail substance laid on edge (i, j) by kth ant.

3.3   Optimal Routing Path

In order to reduce the communication delay and balance the network traffic loads, we adopt the multi-hop communications between cluster heads. In this paper, we run ACO among the cluster heads to achieve this goal. Fig. 3 shows

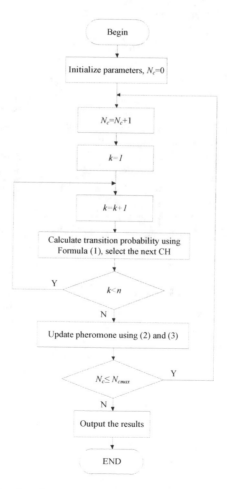

Fig. 3. The flowchart of AVAPCR-ACO for routing selection

the flowchart of AVAPCR-ACO algorithm for optimal routing selection. The detailed steps are as follows:

1. Initialize parameters. Set the maximum number of cycles $N_{c\,\text{max}}$, the number of cycles $N_c = 0$, $\tau_{ij}(t) = const$, and $\Delta\tau_{ij}(t) = 0$.
2. Place m ants on n cluster heads randomly.
3. $N_c \leftarrow N_c + 1$.
4. Set the index of Tabu tables $k=1$.
5. $k = k + 1$.
6. Calculate the transition probability using Formula (1) for ants to select cluster head j, $j \in \{C - tabu_k\}$.
7. Select the maximum transition probability, move ant to this cluster head, and add this cluster head to the tabu table.
8. If ant does not visit all the cluster head, that is $k < n$, go to step 5; otherwise go to step 9.
9. Update the pheromone using Formula (2) and (3).
10. Output the results if the maximum number of cycles is reached; otherwise clear the tabu and go to step 3.

We select the optimal routing using ACO among CHs, this is effective and efficient for it optimized the inter-clustering routing mechanism, thus reduce the energy consumption and balance the network traffic loads.

4   Simulation

We appraised the performance of the proposed protocol, let's suppose there are 100 nodes randomly distributed in a $100m \times 100m$ network field with the BS located at $(x = 50, y = 175)$. We compares the performance of our protocol with

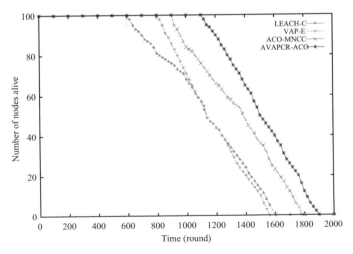

Fig. 4. Number of nodes alive over time

the clustering protocols for wireless sensor networks, LEACH-C [6], VAP-E [7], ACO-MNCC [8]. The simulation parameters of the radio model are as used in [6], [7], [8].

The number of nodes alive over time is shown in Fig. 4, we can define it the system lifetime. Obviously our proposed protocol can prolong the network lifetime compared to LEACH-C, VAP-E and ACO-MNCC. This is because our protocol produces better network partitioning as we partitions the network adaptively, and uses ACO to select the optimal routing path among the CHS. While in LEACH-C, VAP-E and ACO-MNCC some nodes have to transmit long distances in order to reach a cluster head due to poor network clustering or the cluster head consume more energy for data gathering and transmitting, so some nodes dissipate a large amount of energy.

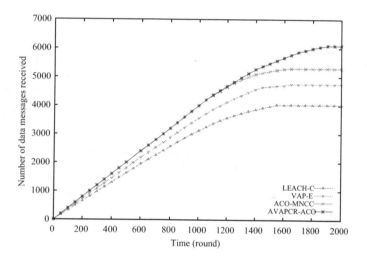

Fig. 5. Total data messages received at the BS over time

Fig. 5 illustrates the total data messages received at the base station, it clearly indicates the effectiveness of the proposed protocol in delivering more data messages than LEACH-C, VAP-E and ACO-MNCC. The reason is that the proposed protocol can take advantage of virtual area partition to form clusters and use ACO to form an optimal routing path, thus balance the energy consumption and send more data messages to the base station. On the contrary, LEACH-C do not take the energy of a node when selecting the cluster head into account, and may select the cluster head with minimal energy that have not enough energy to remain alive during that round, though VAP-E considers the distance to the BS and the energy of a node, its still randomly select the cluster head, ACO-MNCC only emphasis use ACO to find the maximum number of disjoint connected covers. While our protocol partition the network adaptively and build the optimal routing using ACO.

5   Conclusion

In this literature we have presented an Adaptive Virtual Area Partition Clustering Routing protocol using Ant Colony Optimization (AVAPCR-ACO). We partition the network effectively and adaptively and using ACO to build an optimal routing path among the cluster heads. Results from the simulations indicate that the proposed protocol using virtual are partition and ACO algorithm gives a higher network lifespan, delivers more data to the base station compared to LEACH-C, VAP-E and ACO-MNCC. Our future work includes the implicit parallelism of the ACO framework can be utilized for for reducing the computational time and tackling large-scale WSNs.

References

1. Yick, J., Mukherjee, B., Ghosal, D.: Wireless sensor network survey. Computer Networks 52(12), 2292–2330 (2008)
2. Abbasi, A., Younis, M.: A survey on clustering algorithms for wireless sensor networks. Computer Communications 30(14-15), 2826–2841 (2007)
3. Bonabeau, E., Dorigo, M., Theraulaz, G.: Inspiration for optimization from social insect behavior. Nature 406(6), 39–42 (2000)
4. Jackson, D.E., Holcombe, M., Ratnieks, F.F.W.: Trail geometry gives polarity to ant foraging networks. Nature 432(7019), 907–909 (2004)
5. Dorigo, M., Maniezzo, V., Colorni, A.: Ant System: Optimization by a Colony of Cooperating Agents. IEEE Trans. Systems, Man, and Cybernetics-Part B 26(1), 29–41 (1996)
6. Heinzelman, W.B., Chandrakasan, A.P., Balakrishnan, H.: An Application-Specific Protocol Architecture for Wireless Microsensor Networks. IEEE Trans. Wireless Commun. 1(4), 660–770 (2002)
7. Wang, R., Liu, G., Zheng, C.: A Clustering Algorithm based on Virtual Area Partition for Heterogeneous Wireless Sensor Networks. In: 2007 IEEE International Conference on Mechatronics & Automation, pp. 372–376. IEEE Press, Harbin (2007)
8. Lin, Y., Zhang, J., Chung, H.S., Ip, W.H., Li, Y., Shi, Y.: An Ant Colony Optimization Approach for Maximizing the Lifetime of Heterogeneous Wireless Sensor Networks. IEEE Trans. Systems, Man, and Cybernetics-Part C 42(3), 408–420 (2012)
9. Okdem, S., Karaboga, D.: Routing in wireless sensor networks using ant colony optimization. In: 1st NASA/ESA Conf. Adapt. Hardware Syst., pp. 401–404 (2006)
10. Zhong, Y.P., Huang, P.W., Wang, B.: Maximum lifetime routing based on ant colony algorithm for wireless sensor networks. In: Proc. IET Conf. Wireless, Mobile, Sensor Networks, pp. 789–792 (2007)

Virtual Backbone Construction Algorithms Based on Protocol Interference Model

Guomin Yan, Jiguo Yu*, Congcong Chen, and Lili Jia

School of Computer Science,
Qufu Normal University, Rizhao, 276826, Shandong, P.R. China
{guominyanrz,congcchen}@126.com,
jiguoyu@sina.com, lljiasd@163.com

Abstract. Interference is one of the main challenges in designing energy efficient protocols for wireless sensor networks. Decreasing interference can reduce energy consumptions of nodes and prolong the lifetime of the network. Combining graph matching and the protocol interference model, in this paper, we propose a Matching Based Interference-Aware Dominating Set Construction Algorithm (MBIDSC), in which we consider a connected dominating set as a virtual backbone. The upper bounds of message complexity of the algorithm is $O(nr\Delta)$ and the time complexity is $O(r\Delta)$. Where n is the total number of nodes, Δ is the maximum degree of the network, r is the round of the algorithm, and d is the diameter of the network. We show the correctness of the algorithms and complexity of time and message by theoretical analysis. To the best of our knowledge, the proposed algorithm is the first results for the protocol interference model based on graph matching.

Keywords: wireless sensor network, dominating set, virtual backbone, graph matching, interference.

1   Introduction

A wireless sensor network (WSN) consists of lots of mobile sensor nodes equipped with many radio communication devices, such as RF transceivers. Sensor nodes perform sensing, processing and communication tasks. In recent years, wireless sensor networks have been widely applied in various fields and deployed for many kinds of applications. Since WSNs can be quickly distributed in some geographical areas where humans fail to arrive, they play an important role in many fields, such as habitat monitoring, health care, military surveillance, target tracking, disaster relief and so on. Since sensor nodes are powered by batteries which reserve limited energy and can not be recharged, every node only communicates with nodes within its transmission range. Nodes fail to directly communicate with each other, if the Euclidean distance between them is larger than their transmission range. Therefore, their communication is dependent on other nodes (usually called relay nodes) within their transmission range, if there

---

* Corresponding author.

L. Sun, H. Ma, and F. Hong (Eds.): CWSN 2013, CCIS 418, pp. 31–40, 2014.
© Springer-Verlag Berlin Heidelberg 2014

are such relay nodes. In a word, communication among nodes in WSNs may be single hop or multiple hops.

WSNs usually are assumed to be homogeneous and work for certain time, since energy conservation is one of the essential issues in every research field of WSNs. In normal case, topology control in WSNs can perform the task to prolong the lifetime of the networks. Given a connected network graph, topology control is considered to compute a subgraph with specific required properties, such as connectivity, sparsity, low interference and so on. Dominating sets based on clustering are always used in topology controls. The great flexibility is the best advantage of a WSN, and the worst disadvantage of such networks is their lack of infrastructure. The disadvantage results in many difficulties in their applications. For example, broadcast is liable to cause greatly excessive transmission redundancy. Such problem is the well known broadcast storm problem [1]. Apart from broadcast, there exist many other operations such as routing, data gathering, or query which can also result in excessive redundant messages. According to these problems, virtual backbones arise since they tremendously reduce redundant messages and improve performance of the network. In many existing works, connecting dominating sets are usually constructed to play the role of virtual backbones, since they preserve many good geometrical properties [2]. Although many CDS construction algorithms have been developed, most of them do not take interference into consideration.

In this paper, we pay our attention to the construction of dominating sets and virtual backbones with low interference, where virtual backbones are computed by constructing connected dominating sets. Given a graph $G = (V, E)$, V denotes the set of nodes in the wireless network, E is the set of edges among nodes (communication links between nodes in the network). A subset $D \subseteq V$ is a dominating set of G, if every node $v \in V$ is either in D or has a neighbor in D. D is a connected dominating set if the subgraph induced by D is connected. Finding a dominating set and finding a connected dominating set both have been proved to be NP-complete problems [3], even if the given graph is a unit disk graph (UDG) [4]. A unit disk graph has a wide application in WSNs, which consists of a set of unit disks centered at each node in the graph. There exists an edge between u and v if and only if the Euclidean distance between u and v is at most 1. Since the amount of the energy consumption caused by transmitting a message increases at least quadratically with increases of distances, it makes sense to replace a long link by a sequence of short links, that is, replace single-hop communication by multiple-hop communication. Under this condition, it not only reduces the transmission power level of nodes, but also reduces the number of collision, thus energy consumptions of nodes can be reduced. In this paper, bases on the protocol interference model, we propose edge interference capability, that is, the number of nodes that can interfere the endpoints of one edge when the endpoints communicate along the edge. We propose two algorithms, one is to construct a dominating set with minimized edge interference capability, and the other is to construct a connected dominating set as a virtual backbone with minimized edge interference capability.

2   Related Works

In this section, we introduce some existing algorithms for dominating sets and connected dominating sets.

In [5], Alzoubi et al. proposed a algorithm for constructing a connected dominating set by selecting an arbitrary maximal independent set (MIS) as the dominating set, and then connecting it. In [6], Wan et al. proposed a distributed algorithm for constructing a connected dominating set included two phases, with a approximation ratio 8. In the first phase, the algorithm constructs a span tree, then adds more nodes to connect the independent set in the second phase. In [7], Yu et al. proposed two heuristic algorithms for constructing connected dominating sets with minimum size and bounded diameter in wireless networks. The first phase of both algorithms is to construct an MIS for the graph, and the second is to select connectors with heuristic information to connect the nodes in the MIS. All the algorithms above assume that the given graph is a unit disk graph, and more details about UDGs are in [8].

The minimum dominating set (MDS) problem is to find a dominating set with minimum size in given graph, and the minimum connected dominating set (MCDS) problem is to look for a connected dominating set with minimum size in given graph. Both problems have been proved to be NP-complete [2]. Cheng et al. designed a $PTAS$ with $(1 + 1/s)$-approximation factor for MCDS in a unit disk graph [9], with time complexity $n^{O((s \log s)^2)}$. In [10], Wang et al. proposed a nodes neighborhood based algorithm to construct a minimum connected dominating set in a WSN, where the complexities of time and message are $O(\log n)$ and $O(n)$, respectively. According to the changes of the topology caused by power constraint, the authors also designed a repair algorithm to reconstruct the MCDS. In [11], Dubhashi et al. designed a $O(\log \Delta)$-approximation for constructing a MCDS, where Δ is the maximum degree of the given graph. The algorithm has low stretch property that any two adjacent nodes in the network have their dominators at a distance of at most $O(\log n)$.

If the given graph is weighted, finding a dominating set with minimum total weight is called minimum weighted dominating set (MWDS) problem. Minimum weighted connected dominating set problem is to construct a connected dominating set with minimum total weight. In [12], Ambühl et al. gave a 72-approximation algorithm for a MWDS, and they proposed the first constant-factor algorithm for a MWDS with approximation ration 89. In [13], Huang et al. improved the approximation ratio of a MWCDS from 89 to $(10 + \epsilon)$ with a 4-approximation ratio of the connecting part. In [14], Zou et al. proposed a $(4 + \epsilon)$-approximation algorithm for a MWDS based on a dynamic programming algorithm for a min-weight chromatic disk cover. Meanwhile, by connecting a minimum connected dominating set, a $(5 + \epsilon)$-approximation algorithm for a MWCDS was presented. For latest results on dominating sets, one can refer to [15,16].

Interference is one of the most important challenges to solve when we design protocols for wireless networks. Most of the work in the literature assumes localized or hop-based interference models in which the effect of interference is neglected beyond a certain range from the transmitter. In [17], Scheideler et al. first presented a distributed dominating set protocol for wireless networks with $O(1)$ approximation bound based on the physical interference model introduced in [16], which accounts for interference generated by all nodes in the network. The protocol is fully distributed and extensively uses physical carrier sensing to reduce message overhead and do not need any kind of prior information about the system. The physical interference model considering all interference in the network is more practical, in which a message is correctly received if and only if the SINR value at the receiver is larger than a certain threshold. Another interference model commonly used in the design of protocols for WSNs is the protocol interference model in [18]. In this model, a transmission from node v to node u is considered to be successful if and only if there exists no other transmitter within a constant range centered at node u. In this paper, we consider the number of nodes in a certain area as edge interference capability, where the area is centered at the endpoints of an edge respectively, and the radius of which is the Euclidean distance between the endpoints. More details about it will be introduced in Section 3. Most of the existing literatures for dominating sets and virtual backbones do not take the interference into consideration, or simply consider that low degree can result in low interference. Most of the existing protocols aiming at constructing a dominating set with low interference make sure that there is less interference when the network works effectively. Apart from this, considering interference issue from another different point of view, Huang et al. proposed a algorithm to reduce interference when construct a connected dominating set which is considered as the virtual backbone in [19]. The algorithm is a fully distributed, interference-aware virtual backbone construction algorithm. Meanwhile, authors applied it on the leader election problem and present a fully distributed, interference-aware leader election algorithm with the complexity of time $O(n \log n)$.

The rest of this paper is organized as follows. In Section 3, we describe the network model, and give the definition of edge interference capability. The proposed algorithms for a dominating set and a virtual backbone are presented in Section 4. The detailed analysis about the correctness of the algorithms and time and message complexity are shown in Section 5. Conclusions and future works are described in Section 6.

3   Model and Definition

3.1   Network Model

We make some reasonable assumptions as follows.

(1) Each node has a unique node identity id.
(2) Each node can adjust its transmission power to any value between zero and its maximum power level.

(3) All the nodes have the same maximum power level.

(4) The nodes are stationary.

(5) The edge interference capability is the same for both endpoints incident with one edge.

Based on these assumptions, the network can be modeled as a weighted undirected unit disk graph $G_w = (V, E_w)$, V is the set of vertices (nodes of the network), E_w is the set of weighted edges. The edge $e(u, v)$ exists if and only if node u and node v can successfully receive messages from each other. The values of edge interference capability are presented by the weight of the edge. More details about it will be given in the following section.

3.2   Edge Interference Capability

In the protocol interference model, node u successfully receive a message from node v, if and only if every other node w, which is simultaneously transmitting over the same channel, satisfies,

$$d(u, w) \geq (1 + \Delta)d(u, v) \tag{1}$$

where $\Delta > 0$, $d(u, v)$ is the Euclidean distance between nodes u and v.

We propose the edge interference capability, a new parameter based on the protocol interference model, which is the total number of nodes interfering the endpoints of one edge when they communicate with each other. A larger edge interference capability results in less probability of successful transmission. Let $N(u)$ denote the neighbor set of node u, $N(u) = \{v \in V \mid e(u, v) \in E_w\}$. If $e = (u, v)$, we define the edge interference capability as follows.

$$IL(e) = \mid \{w \in V \mid d(u, w) \leq d(u, v)\} \cup \{w \in V \mid d(v, w) \leq d(u, v)\} \mid \tag{2}$$

$IL(e, u)$ denotes the number of nodes generating interference when node u transmits along the edge. $IL(e, v)$ denotes the number of nodes generating interference when node v transmits along the edge, and $IL(e, u) = IL(e, v) = IL(e)$. Moreover, $AIL(u)$ is defined as the average interference level (AIL) of u.

$$AIL(u) = \frac{\sum_{e \in E_w} IL(e, u)}{deg(u)} \tag{3}$$

where $e(u, v)$, $v \in N(u)$, $deg(u)$ is the degree of node u, and $deg(u) = \mid N(u) \mid$. We consider the average interference level of nodes as one of the main factors when selecting dominating nodes. The proposed algorithms construct a dominating set and a virtual backbone with low interference. Therefore, energy consumptions of nodes can be reduced greatly and the lifetime of the wireless network can be extended.

3.3   Graph Matching

A matching $M \subseteq E$ in a graph G is a set of non-loop edges with no shared endpoints. That is, if $t, u \in M$ and $t, v \in M$ then $u = v$. If the graph is weighted, then the problem is called weighted matching [20]. More details about graph matching can be referred to [20,21]. In this paper, we consider weighted matching in which the weights of edges denote the interference capability $IL(e)$. If $Min(IL(e, u)) = IL(e)$ when $e = (u, v)$, then node v is the candidate of u. The candidate with minimum id is the best candidate of node u. If the nodes are the best candidates for each other, then the nodes are matched. Meanwhile, $Min(IL(e, u)) = Min(IL(e, v)) = IL(e(u, v))$. The number of nodes interfering two endpoints (u and v) of one edge will be minimum, if they transmit along the edge $e = (u, v)$. Then we select the node with smaller average interference level as dominator, thus it makes sure that there is minimum interference during transmission between dominators and dominatees.

4   Matching Based Interference-Aware Dominating Set Construction Algorithm (MBIDSC)

In this section, the proposed algorithm for dominating set with low interference are described in detail. In a given network graph $G_w = (V, E_w)$, each node knows the edge interference capability of the edge incident to it. Initially, each node in the network is an *empty node*, which is neither a dominator nor a dominatee.

4.1   MBIDSC Details

The following algorithm simultaneously runs at every node in the network.

Step 1. Each node u sends a $Request\_Msg$ to its best candidate v, if u is the best candidate of v, then they are matched, v replies u with a $Request\_Ack\_Msg$, or v replies with a $Reject\_Msg$.

Step 2. If one of the matched two nodes (u and v) has already been a dominator, then the other becomes its dominatee, or if $AIL(u) < AIL(v)$, then u is selected to be a dominator and v becomes its dominatee. If $AIL(u) > AIL(v)$, then v is a dominator and u is its dominatee. Otherwise, the node u (or v) with smaller id becomes a dominator and v (or u) is its dominatee. Once the dominatee determines its role, it broadcasts a $Dominatee\_Msg$.

Step 3. Every dominator u broadcasts a $Dominator\_Msg$ after determining its role. If node w receiving the $Dominator\_Msg$ from u has already been the dominatee of u, then it replies with a $Dominator\_Ack\_Msg$. If w has already been a dominator or a dominatee of another dominator, it replies with a $Reject\_Msg$. If w is the candidate of u or u is the best candidate of w, then w replies with a $Dominator\_Ack\_Msg$ and becomes a dominatee of u. Once w determines its role as a dominatee, it broadcasts a $Dominatee\_Msg$.

Step 4. If there is an *empty node* w which has at least one *empty node* or one dominator in its neighborhood, then it computes its best candidate and goes to Step 1 of the next round. If the neighbors of w are all dominatees, then it becomes a dominator and broadcasts a $Dominator\_Msg$. If every selected dominator has at least one *empty node* in its neighborhood, it selects its best candidate from such empty neighbors and goes to Step 1 of the next round.

Until there is no *empty node* in the network, all the selected dominators form a dominating set. During above process of the algorithm, every node receiving a *Dominatee_Msg* replies with a *Dominatee_Ack_Msg*, such that nodes transmit successfully. When nodes perform the MBIDSC algorithm in rounds, they only require local information of their one-hop neighbors. Once there is no *empty node* in the whole network, that is, the selected dominating set can dominate all nodes in the network, the MBIDSC algorithm terminates. We consider that a dominator and its dominatees form a *dominating clique*. If there is only one dominator in a *dominating clique*, then the dominator is called a *single dominator*.

5   Theoretical Analysis

5.1   Proof of Correctness

Lemma 1. *In MBIDSC, if a node sends a Request_Msg to its best candidate, then it receives a Reject_Msg or Request_Ack_Msg from the candidate.*

Proof. We consider the following three cases.

Case 1. If the best candidate is an *empty node*, and its best candidate is the source node, it replies with a *Request_Ack_Msg*.

Case 2. If the best candidate is an *empty node*, but its best candidate is not the source node, then it replies with a *Reject_Msg*.

Case 3. If the candidate of the source node is already a dominator or a dominatee, the it replies with a *Reject_Msg*.

Therefore, the lemma gets proved.

Lemma 2. *In MBIDSC, if a node sends a Dominator_Msg to its candidate, then it receives a Reject_Msg or Dominator_Ack_Msg from the candidate.*

Proof. The proof is the same as Lemma1. After the destination node receives a *Dominator_Msg*, there are three cases as follows.

Case 1. If the destination is already the dominatee of the source node, then it replies with a *Dominator_Ack*.

Case 2. If the destination is already a dominator or a dominatee of another dominator, then it replies with a *Reject_Msg*.

Case 3. If the destination node is an *empty node* and it is the best candidate of the source node, or the source node is the best candidate of the destination node, then it replies with a *Dominator_Ack_Msg*.

Theorem 1. *After performing the MBIDSC, each node in the network is either a dominator, or a dominatee.*

Proof. By contradiction. Assume that there is an *empty node* in the network after performing the MBIDSC. According to step 4 of the algorithm, at the end of every round of the algorithm, if there are still empty nodes, they continue to perform the algorithm by two cases.

Case 1. If all the neighbors of the empty node are already the dominatees of some dominator, then it becomes a dominator and broadcasts a *Dominator_Msg*.

Case 2. If there is at least a dominator or an empty node in its neighborhood, then it selects its best candidate and continues the algorithm.

The empty node determines its role finally which contradicts with our assumption.

According to Lemma 1, Lemma 2, every session is guaranteed to be answered successfully. Therefore, the proposed algorithm are free from deadlock and starvation which can make sure that the algorithms perform successfully.

5.2   Complexity Analysis

Theorem 2. *The upper bound of the message complexity of MBIDSC with r rounds is $O(nr\Delta)$, where Δ is the maximum degree of the network, n is the number of nodes. The lower bound for message complexity of MBIDSC is $\Omega(n\Delta)$.*

Proof. Assume that there is a node with maximum degree locally transmit and exchange information with their neighbors. The amount of information of every round is the sum of a constant times of Δ and a constant which is easily known from the algorithm. If every node in the network has a maximum degree, the algorithm requires $O(nr\Delta)$ messages when the algorithm completes after r rounds. If $r = 1$, that is, the algorithm terminates successfully after one round, then it only demands $\Omega(n\Delta)$ messages.

Theorem 3. *The time complexity for MBIDSC with r rounds is $O(\Delta r)$, where Δ is the maximum degree of nodes.*

Proof. Since the MBIDSC algorithm is distributed, the running time of one round is $O(\Delta)$ based on the description of the algorithm and the proof of Theorem 6.3. Therefore, the time complexity for MBIDSC with r rounds is $O(r\Delta)$.

6   Conclusions

Interference is one of the most important challenges to deal with when we design protocols for WSNs. Since the energy consumption caused by interference is greatly high, minimizing interference of dominating sets can reduce energy consumptions of nodes and optimize the network. Thus the lifetime of the network can be extended. In this paper, we are the first to combine graph matching technique and the protocol interference model in designing dominating sets. The proposed algorithm MBIDSC, only require local information of nodes during the construction of a dominating set and a virtual backbone. In section 5, we show that the correctness of the algorithm and complexity of time and message by theoretical analysis. The topology obtained by the algorithm effectively reduce the energy consumptions of nodes with lower interference levels, and thus prolong the lifetime of the network.

In the future, we will study a algorithm for constructing a virtual backbone with low interference. Therefore, the amount of transmission messages are be greatly reduced. Meanwhile, the number of collision also decrease, which guarantees to save the energy of nodes and thus to prolong the lifetime of the whole network.

It is known that there are special nodes called *single dominator* which maybe increase the size of dominators, but they can reduce the amount of interference. It can prolong the effective lifetime of dominating set and virtual backbone. In the future, we will study a trade-off between the number of *single dominator* and the amount of interference generated in the network. We will contributes to construct a better topology with minimum interference which is beneficial for improving the performance of WSNs.

Although a protocol based on the physical interference model has better behavior in a practical scenario, the physical interference model tremendously increases the complexity of the design of protocols. In the future, we will improve our algorithms based on the physical interference model, then we obtain topology controls with better performance in a practical scenario.

Acknowledgments. This work was partially supported by the NSF of China for contract (61373027, 11101243), NSF of Shandong Province for contract (ZR2012FM023, ZR2012FQ011), STPU of Shandong Province for contract (J10LG09, J12LN06), PFMYS of Shandong Province for contract (BS2009DX024, BS2010DX013).

References

1. Ni, S.Y., Tseng, Y.C., Chen, Y.S., Sheu, J.P.: The broadcast storm problem in a mobile ad hoc network. In: Proc. 5th ACM/IEEE International Conf. Mobile Computing Networking (MobiCom), pp. 151–162 (1999)
2. Cheng, X., Ding, M., Du, D.H., Jia, X.: Virtual backbone construc-tion in multihop ad hoc wireless networks: research articles. Wireless Communications and Mobile Computing 6(2), 183–190 (2006)
3. Garey, M.R., Johnson, D.S.: Computers and Intractability: A Guide to the Theory of NP-Completeness. W. H. Freeman, San Francisco (1979)
4. Clark, B.N., Colbourn, C.J., Johnson, D.S.: Unit disk graphs. Discrete Mathematics 86(1-3), 165–177 (1990)
5. Alzoubi, K.M., Wan, P.J., Frieder, O.: Message-Optimal Connected Dominating Sets in Mobile Ad Hoc Networks. In: ACM Mobihoc, pp. 157–164 (2002)
6. Wan, P.J., Alzoubi, K.M., Frieder, O.: Distributed Construction of Connected Dominating Set in Wireless Networks. In: Proceedings of IEEE Conference on Computer Communications (INFOCOM), pp. 141–149 (2002)
7. Yu, J., Wang, N., Wang, G.: Heuristic Algorithms for Constructing Connected Dominating Sets with Minimum Size and Bounded Diameter in Wireless Networks. In: Pandurangan, G., Anil Kumar, V.S., Ming, G., Liu, Y., Li, Y. (eds.) WASA 2010. LNCS, vol. 6221, pp. 11–20. Springer, Heidelberg (2010)
8. Schmid, S., Wattenhofer, R.: Algorithmic models for sensor networks. In: Proc. of the 14th International Workshop on Parallel and Distributed Real-Time Systems, p. 11 (2006)

9. Cheng, X., Huang, X., Li, D., Wu, W., Du, D.: A polynomial-time approximation scheme for the minimum-connected dominating set in ad hoc wireless networks. Networks 42(4), 202–208 (2003)
10. Wang, N., Yu, J., Qi, Y.: Nodes Neighborhood Relation-based Construction Algorithm for Minimum Connected Domination Set. Computer Engineering 36(13), 105–107 (2010)
11. Dubhashi, D., Mei, A., Panconesi, A., Radhakrishnan, J., Srinivasan, A.: Fast distributed algorithms for (weakly) connected dominating sets and linear-size skeletons. J. Computer System Sciences 71(4), 467–479 (2005)
12. Ambühl, C., Erlebach, T., Mihalák, M., Nunkesser, M.: Constant-factor approximation for minimum-weight (connected) dominating sets in unit disk graphs. In: Díaz, J., Jansen, K., Rolim, J.D.P., Zwick, U. (eds.) APPROX and RANDOM 2006. LNCS, vol. 4110, pp. 3–14. Springer, Heidelberg (2006)
13. Huang, Y., Gao, X., Zhang, Z., Wu, W.: A better constant-factor approximation for weighted dominating set in unit disk graph. Journal of Combinatorial Optimization 18(2), 179–194 (2008)
14. Zou, F., Wang, Y., Xu, X., Li, X., Du, H., Wan, P., Wu, W.: New approximations for minimum-weighted dominating sets and minimum-weighted connected dominating sets on unit disk graphs. Theoretical Computer Science 412(3), 198–208 (2009)
15. Du, H., Ye, Q., Wu, W., Lee, W., Li, D., Du, D., Howard, S.: Constant approximation for virtual backbone construction with Guaranteed Routing Cost in wireless sensor networks. In: Proc. of INFOCOM, pp. 1737–1744 (2011)
16. Yu, J.G., Wang, N., Wang, G.: Constructing minimum extended weakly-connected dominating sets for clustering in ad hoc networks. Journal of Parallel Distributed Computing 72(1), 35–47 (2012)
17. Scheideler, C., Richa, A., Santi, P.: An $O(\log n)$ Dominating Set Protocol for Wireless Ad-Hoc Networks under the Physical Interference Model. In: Proceedings of the 9th ACM International Symposium on Mobile Ad Hoc Networking and Computing, pp. 91–100 (2008)
18. Gupta, P., Kumar, P.R.: The Capacity of Wireless Networks. IEEE Transactions on Information Theory 42(2), 388–404 (2000)
19. Huang, S.C.H., Sun, M.T., Liang, Q.L., Wan, P., Jia, X.: Interference-Aware, Fully-Distributed Virtual Backbone Construction and its Application in Multi-Hop Wireless Networks. IEEE Transactions on communications 58(12), 3550–3560 (2010)
20. West, D.: Introduction to Graph Theory, 2nd edn., pp. 107–109. Prentice Hall (2001)
21. Bunke, H.: Graph Matching: Theoretical Foundations. Algorithms, and Applications. In: Proc. VI 2003, pp. 82–88 (2000)

An Algorithm for Constructing Strongly Connected Dominating and Absorbing Sets in Wireless Networks with Unidirectional Links

Shengli Wan, Jiguo Yu*, Nannan Wang, Cui Wang, and Fang Liu

School of Computer Science,
Qufu Normal University, Rizhao, 276826, Shandong, P.R. China
jiguoyu@sina.com

Abstract. It is effective to construct a strongly connected dominating and absorbing set (SCDAS) instead of a virtual backbone network in a wireless network with unidirectional links. However, there exist few studies on the strongly connected dominating and absorbing sets in wireless networks. In this paper, we propose an addition-based localized heuristic algorithm for constructing a SCDAS in a wireless network. The algorithm can obtain a small SCDAS with a constant approximation ratio through three executive phases. Theoretical analysis demonstrates the correctness of our algorithm.

Keywords: wireless network, unidirectional link, disk graph (DG), strongly connected dominating and absorbing set (SCDAS).

1 Introduction

In Wireless Networks (WNs), nodes communicate directly with each other through the shared media, sometimes with the help of intermediate nodes. To make sure that sensed data can be transmitted to the sink node in such network, control information need to be flooded by all nodes. But, such solution results in serious redundancy, contention, and collision at the same time [1]. Thus, it is natural that to built a Virtual Backbone Network (VBN), which decreases the routing overhead and energy consumption. In virtual backbone networks, routing information is exchanged between backbone nodes other than among all nodes. Such routing fashion is simpler, and it adapts to the rapid changes in network topology. And forwarding the data only between nodes in the built virtual backbone network can reduces energy consumption.

Connected dominating sets were introduced into the built of a virtual backbone network in wireless network for the first time [2]. Given an undirected graph $G = (V, E)$, where V and E represents the vertices and edges respectively. $D \subseteq V$ is a dominating set (DS) of G if either v belongs to D or shares an edge with another node $u \in D$ for any node $v \in V$. $S \subseteq V$ is a connected dominating set of G if S is a dominating set and the subgraph induced by S is connected.

---

* Corresponding author.

L. Sun, H. Ma, and F. Hong (Eds.): CWSN 2013, CCIS 418, pp. 41–50, 2014.

$I \subseteq V$ is a independent set (IS) of G if no two nodes in I are adjacent. An independent set of G is a maximal independent set (MIS) if no more node can be added to form a larger independent set. Obviously, a MIS is a dominating set. A connected dominating set facilitates routing and adapts to the rapid changes of the network topology. Constructing a minimum connected dominating set in unit disk graph is a notable problem. In a unit disk graph, the range of each node is identical, and there exists an edge between any pair of nodes if and only if the Euclidean distance between them not more than 1. That is to say, they can communicate with each others. In [3], it is proved that minimum connected dominating set problem in unit disk graph is NP-hard.

However, the communication ranges of all nodes are not the same in physical networks. In such situation, a wireless network can be modeled as a directed graph $G = (V, E)$, where all elements in V located in a plane, and that for each node $v_i \in V$, $r_i \in [r_{\min}, r_{\max}]$, here r_i is the communication radius of v_i. A directed edge $(v_i, v_j) \in E$, if and only if $d(v_i, v_j) \leq r_i$. Such graph is a disk graph (DG). (v_i, v_j) is a unidirectional edge if $(v_i, v_j) \in E$ and $(v_j, v_i) \notin E$. If both $(v_i, v_j) \in E$ and $(v_j, v_i) \in E$, that is to say $d(v_i, v_j) \leq \min\{r_i, r_j\}$, then (v_i, v_j) is a bidirectional edge. Given a directed graph $G = (V, E)$, $S \subseteq V$ is a dominating set of G if $v \in S$ or there exists $u \in S$ that $(u, v) \in E$. S is a strongly connected dominating set of G if there has at least one directed path from u to v for any pair of nodes $u, v \in S$. C is a strongly connected dominating set of G if $G[C]$ is strongly connected and C is a dominating set of G. The strongly connected dominating set problem is also NP-hard for connected dominating set problem is NP-hard in unit disk graph(UDG) and the unit disk graph(UDG) is one special case of disk graph(DG). Not only node u should be dominated by one node in C, which is a strongly connected dominating set, but also there exists one absorbing neighbor of u being an element of C. This is the problem of strongly connected dominating and absorbing set (SCDAS) we try to solve in this paper. In a directed graph, a strongly connected dominating set is built for routing instead of a virtual backbone. Such structure maintains the advantage of connected dominating set in an undirected graph. It has been proved that the problem of finding a strongly connected dominating set is also NP-hard [3].

The problem of constructing a minimum connected dominating set in a undirected graph is proved to be NP-hard [3], but great effort has been devoted to find a approximation of the minimum connected dominating set (MCDS). These works take a common assumption that the whole topology is known by all nodes in the network. However, such assumption is not match with the physical network. Encouragingly, many schemes have been proposed to generate a small connected dominating set with information of local topology. Such protocols can be catalogued into two types. The first one is based on pruning strategy, at the beginning of pruning, all nodes try to exclaim to be a dominator, then algorithm delete some nodes to build a connected dominating set. The marking process proposed by Wu and Li is the best well-known scheme based on pruning [4]. Another one is based on adding strategy. Algorithms begin with an unconnected subset of nodes. Then more nodes will be added to form a connected dominating set. According to the differences between unconnected subsets, the corresponding protocols can be catalogued into Maximal Independent Set-based protocols [5] and Tree-based protocols [6] [7]. It is shown that the scale of connected dominating set generated by adding strategy is less than that of pruning strategy [6]. The overhead of Tree-based protocols is less than others. The set of all nodes constituting the virtual backbone for broadcast is a connected dominating and absorbing set (CDAS). We can form a connected dominating and absorbing set in a directed graph just adopting one of the above two methods. Wu adopted an extended marking process and two pruning rules to build a connected dominating and absorbing set in directed graph [8]. In this paper, we apply the adding strategy to form a small connected dominating and absorbing set. The proposed scheme is divided into three phases. First, locally build a dominating set with information of adjacent nodes. Second, extend the dominating set into a dominating and absorbing set. Last, add some nodes to connect all nodes in the dominating and absorbing set. At the last period, we design two different ways to form a connected dominating and absorbing set (CDAS).

The rest of this paper is organized as follows: in section 2, we overview current works about both the connected dominating set problem in an undirected graph and the connected dominating and absorbing set problem in a directed graph. Preliminary work is provided in section 3. In section 4, the proposed algorithm is detailed and the performance is analyzed. The simulation and corresponding analysis is presented in section 5. The last section is a conclusion of this paper.

2   Related Work

The connected dominating set problem has acquired great attention, and a large mount of works has been proposed to solve it in undirected graphs. On the basis of whether relying on global information, the algorithms of building a connected dominating set can be classified into the following types: centralized algorithms and decentralized ones. The resulting connected dominating set built by centralized algorithms shows better performance than that of decentralized algorithms. The decentralized algorithms can be further divided into two sub types: distributed algorithms and localized ones. The process of distributed algorithms is decentralized. In localized algorithms, the decision process is distributed with constant rounds communication. The network models applied are directed graph model and undirected graph model. The undirected graph model can be subdivided into general undirected graph model, unit disk graph model and disk graph model. When transforms another network model into a general undirected graph G, the factor of the algorithm performance usually relates with Δ. Here Δ is the maximum cardinality of G. At the same time, the factor of the algorithm performance is a constant for the special geometry structure of the unit disk graph when modeled as a unit disk graph.

Recently, many schemes have been proposed to solve the connected dominating set problem in undirected graph. Wu and Li developed a simple and efficient localized algorithm to form a connected dominating set rapidly, which is called marking process [4]. In the process, each host will be marked as dominating node if there are at least two unconnected neighbors. The resulting dominating set will be reduced by applying two dominating node pruning rules: rule 1and rule 2. Dai and Wu, taking a further step, designed a general dominating node pruning role: rule k, following which the nodes covered by other k dominators is not marked again, thus the size of the connected dominating set is reduced further[9]. The computational complexity is $O(\sigma^2)$ and message complexity is $O(\sigma)$, where σ is the maximum node degree. Wu and Dai et al proposed a common framework to iterative localized solve the connected dominating set problem in ad-hoc networks [10]. Such framework iteratively applied the localized dominator selection method, combining with coping with the dynamic network topology. A spinning tree-based algorithm has been proposed by Wan et al to solve the weakly connected dominating set problem (WCDS) [11]. A maximal independent set (MIS) was selected to form a dominating set, where each node connected with the spinning tree through a temp node. For the size of an independent set is at most four times than that of the minimum connected dominating set, the approximation factor of such algorithm is 8. Han et al. proposed an area-based localized algorithm to calculate a weakly connected dominating set (WCDS) [12]. The process consists of three parts: area partition, WCDS construction for each area and adjustment along the area borders. The outstanding advantages of such algorithm are both the computational complexity and the message complexity are linear and the approximation factor is 110. Chen et al. proposed two centralized algorithms based on a new conception piece to form a weakly connected dominating set and a distributed algorithm [13]. Qayyam et al discussed the mechanism of multipoint relays (MPRs) to efficiently do the flooding of broadcast messages in the mobile wireless networks [14]. The technique of multipoint relays provides an adequate solution to reduce flooding of broadcast messages in the network, while attaining the same goal of transferring the message to every node in the network with a high probability.

Several schemes on the building of connected dominating and absorbing sets in directed graphs have been proposed. In [8], Wu applied a extended marking process and two pruning rules to form a connected dominating and absorbing set in wireless network for broadcast and routing. A proximate algorithm has been designated to build a minimum strongly connected dominating and absorbing set under unit disk graph model [15]. But both the maximum approximation factor and the minimum approximation factor are confined. To enhance the fault-tolerant ability of wireless ad-hoc networks, Tiwari et al proposed a general algorithm to form a k-strongly connected and m-dominating and absorbing set [16]. In [17],Thai et al introduced building a strongly connected dominating set in a disk graph model, and then the authors provide two constant approximation algorithms to build strongly connected dominating sets. In [18], the authors proposed two approximate algorithms to construct strongly connected dominating sets, both of which have constant approximation factors. To the best of our knowledge, little effort has been devoted to build a strongly connected dominating and absorbing set in a directed graph.

3   Preliminaries

Here, we address the problem of building a virtual backbone in a network with different transmission ranges. A network with different transmission ranges can be modeled as a directed graph $G = (V, E)$, where all elements in V located in a plane and for each node $v_i \in V$, $r_i \in [r_{\min}, r_{\max}]$, here r_i is the communication radius of v_i. A directed edge $(v_i, v_j) \in E$, if and only if $d(v_i, v_j) \leq r_i$. Such graph is a disk graph (DG). (v_i, v_j) is a unidirectional edge if $(v_i, v_j) \in E$ and $(v_j, v_i) \notin E$. If both $(v_i, v_j) \in E$ and $(v_j, v_i) \in E$, that is to say $d(v_i, v_j) \leq \min\{r_i, r_j\}$, then (v_i, v_j) is a bidirectional edge. An undirected edge between u and v means both the unidirectional edge from u to v and the unidirectional edge from v to u belong to the edge set. Thus, in this paper, we also take the two-way link into consideration other than the directed links only.

Before we describe the proposed algorithm formally, we introduce the definitions that will be used in the following parts.

Definition 1. *Given a graph $G = (V, E)$, the absorbing neighbor of $u \in V$ is defined as $N^-(u) = \{v \in V | (u \to v) \in E\}$, where $(u \to v)$ is a dominating edge of u. And the dominating neighbor is defined as $N^+(u) = \{v \in V | (v \to u) \in E\}$, where $(v \to u)$ is an absorbing edge of u. $|N^-(u)|$ is the dominating node degree of u, denoted by $d_d(u)$. $|N^+(u)|$ is the absorbing node degree of u, denoted by $d_a(u)$.*

Definition 2. *$S \subseteq V$ is a dominating set of G, if $S \cup N^-(S) = V$, where $N^-(S) = \cup_{u \in S} N^-(u)$.*

Definition 3. *$S \subseteq V$ is an independent dominating set of G, if $S \cup N^-(S) = V$ and $S \cap N^-(S) = \emptyset$.*

Definition 4. *G is strongly connected, if there is a directed path from every node to every other node. Similarly, $S \subseteq V$ is strongly connected, if the induced graph of S $G[S]$ is strongly connected.*

Definition 5. *$S \subseteq V$ is a dominating and absorbing set of G, if S is a dominating set of G and $N^+(v) \cap S \neq \emptyset$ holds for each $v \notin S$(That is to say, there is a absorbing neighbor in S for each node not in S).*

Definition 6. *$S \subseteq V$ is a strongly connected dominating set of G, if S is a dominating set of G and $G[S]$ is strongly connected. S is a strongly connected dominating and absorbing set of G, if S is a strongly connected dominating set and $N^+(v) \cap S \neq \emptyset$ holds for each $v \notin S$*

For brevity, we take the grade of node as a dominating and absorbing node selection basis in the following localized algorithm. The definition of the grade of node is an order pair $(d(u), id(u))$, where $(d(u)$ is the degree of node u and $id(u)$ is the identification of u. $(d(u), id(u)$ is greater than $(d(v), id(v)$, if $d(u) > d(v)$ or $id(u) < id(v)$ while $d(u) = d(v)$. Here $d(u) > d(v)$ holds if $d_d(u) > d_d(v)$ or $d_a(u) > d_a(v)$ while $d_d(u) = d_d(v)$.

4 Algorithm Description

In this section, an algorithm of building a strongly connected dominating and absorbing set in a wireless network with different transmission ranges is detailed and the corresponding theoretical analysis of the performance also is presented. The proposed algorithm consists of three phases. In the first phase, a dominating set of the directed graph corresponding to the network will be constructed with information of small-scale neighbors. Then, extend such dominating set into a dominating and absorbing set. In the last phase, connects all nodes in the dominating and absorbing set to form a strongly connected dominating and absorbing set. And in the last phase, two schemes have been designated to build the strongly connected dominating and absorbing set. One of them is based on connected components; another is based on Steiner Tree. Now we formally introduce the proposed algorithm.

Phase 1. Construction of a dominating set

1. Find the node with the maximum dominating node degree in its single-hop neighbors, mark it black and broadcast it color message.

2. All nodes received the message from a black node mark themselves to be gray.

3. Such process continues until there is no white node in the network.

Phase 2. Construction of a dominating and absorbing set

1. Search all gray nodes to find whether there is an absorbing neighbor colored black.

2. If no such black neighbor, then the absorbing neighbor with of current gray node will be colored black(the Ext_SCDS algorithm proposed in [19] can be used in this step).

3. Such process continues until each gray node in the graph has at least an absorbing neighbor colored black.

4. All black nodes form a dominating and absorbing set of the directed graph.

Phase 3. Connecting the dominating and absorbing set to form a strongly connected dominating and absorbing set

1. Examine that whether the dominating and absorbing set is strongly connected or not.

2. If not strongly connected, one of the following methods can be used to connect the dominating and absorbing set

(1) Find the gray node connecting the maximum black nodes and color the resulting node blue, which is a breakpoint. Repeat steps 1 and 2 until the dominating and absorbing set is strongly connected.

(2) Build a directed Steiner tree to connect the dominating and absorbing set strongly. Mark node u with the maximum degree in the dominating and absorbing set as the leader of the Steiner tree. Then examine whether there exists a directed path, consisting of black nodes only, between each node(except u) in the dominating and absorbing set according to the descending order sequence of its degree one by one and the leader. If such path does not exist, a path containing the least gray nodes and the dominating node degree of the contained gray nodes

being relative big enough is selected. All gray nodes on the path turn their color to be blue.

3. All nodes colored black or blue form a small-scale strongly connected dominating and absorbing set of the directed graph.

Here we show the execution process of the proposed algorithm with a concise network, shown in Figs 1.

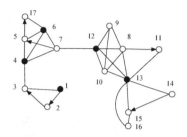

Fig. 1(a) {1,4,6,12,13} is a dominating set of G

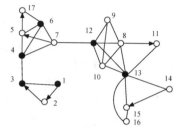

Fig. 1(b) {1,3,4,6,12,13} is a dominating and absorbing set of G

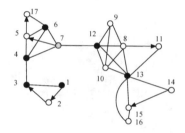

Fig. 1(c) {1,3,4,6,7,12,13} is a connected dominating and absorbing set of G

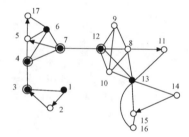

Fig. 1(d) {3,4,7,12} is a hierarchical connected dominating and absorbing set of G

Fig. 1. The size of area is 30*40 and the transmission range is [10, 15]

The specific implementation process of our algorithm is as follows.

Nodes 1, 4, 6, 12 and 13 will be colored black and black messages will be broadcast to all neighbors for all of them have the maximum dominating degree in the graph, shown as Fig 1(a). After received the black message, nodes 2, 3, 5, 7, 8, 9, 10, 11, 14, 15, 16 and 17 become gray nodes. Now the black nodes form a dominating set of the graph. Examine whether a black neighbor exist or not for each gray node. Node 2 has no such neighbor, thus color node 3 black for it is the absorbing neighbor of node 2. Until now, the black nodes form a dominating and absorbent set of the graph, shown as Fig 1(b). Node 7 will be colored blue to connect the dominating and absorbing set strongly, Thus, a strongly connected dominating and absorbing set has been constructed. The execution finished, shown as Fig 1(c). What's more, we can apply such localized algorithm iteratively to build a hierarchical dominating and absorbing set of the whole graph, shown as fig. 1(d).

The following is the analysis of both the correctness and the performance of the proposed algorithm. Here S is the solution generated by the above localized heuristic algorithm.

Theorem 1. *S contains all intermediate node on the shortest path between any pair nodes in V.*

Proof. By contradiction. Select two node u and v in graph G randomly. For it is a strongly connected graph, there exists one shortest path from v to u. Assume that there is a node v_i that is not contained in S on the path: $(v, \cdots, v_{i-1}, v_i, v_{i+1}, \cdots, u)$. Due to v_i is not contained, there is a direct connection between v_{i-1} and v_{i+1}. Thus, path $(v, \cdots, v_{i-1}, v_{i+1}, \cdots, u)$ is shorter than $(v, \cdots, v_{i-1}, v_i, v_{i+1}, \cdots, u)$, which contradicts with the above assumption.

Theorem 2. *the induced graph of S, $G[S]$ is a strongly connected graph.*

Proof. Select two node v and u in graph G randomly. Assume that $(v, v_1, \cdots, v_k, u)$ is the shortest path from v to u. Then, $(v, v_1, \cdots, v_k, u)$ also is a path in $G[S]$ according to theorem 1. Thus, the theorem holds.

Theorem 3. *S is a dominating and absorbing set of G*

Proof. In the first phase of the proposed, all nodes with the maximum degree in single hop neighbors is colored black, thus the resulting set of black nodes dominates all nodes in the whole network. Such strategy promises the size of the resulting dominators is smallest. In the second phase, by examining whether there is a black absorbing neighbor for each gray node, the absorbing property is guarantee. Thus the solution is a dominating and absorbing set of the graph.

Corollary 1. *there is a dominating neighbor and a absorbing neighbor in S for each node in S*

Lemma 1. *In a disk graph $G = (V, E)$. The size of any dominating set D is confined by the following constraint: $|D| \leq 2.4(k + \frac{1}{2})^2 \bullet opt + 3.7(k + \frac{1}{2})^2$, where $k = \frac{r_{\max}}{r_{\min}}$ and opt is the optimal solution to build a strongly connected dominating set.*

This lemma has been proved in [18]. The strongly connected dominating and absorbing set is a special case of a strongly connected dominating set. Thus, the following theorem holds at the same time.

Lemma 2. *In a disk graph $G = (V, E)$. The size of any dominating set D is confined by the following constraint: $|D| \leq 2.4(k + \frac{1}{2})^2 \bullet opt + 3.7(k + \frac{1}{2})^2$, where $k = \frac{r_{\max}}{r_{\min}}$ and opt is the optimal solution to build a strongly connected dominating and absorbing set.*

Corollary 2. *In a disk graph $G = (V, E)$. The size of any absorbing set D is confined by the following constraint: $|D| \leq 2.4(k + \frac{1}{2})^2 \bullet opt + 3.7(k + \frac{1}{2})^2$, where $k = \frac{r_{\max}}{r_{\min}}$ and opt is the optimal solution to build a strongly connected dominating and absorbing set.*

Theorem 4. *the size of the resulting strongly connected dominating and absorbing set generated by the proposed scheme is confined by the following constraint:*
$|S| \leq 7.2(k + \frac{1}{2})^2 \bullet opt + 11.1(k + \frac{1}{2})^2 - 1$,
where $k = \frac{r_{max}}{r_{min}}$ and opt is the optimal solution to build a strongly connected dominating and absorbing set.

Proof. Assume that S is the strongly connected dominating and absorbing set, D is the dominating set generated after the execution of the first phase of the proposed algorithm, A is the absorbing set and C is the connecting nodes set. Then we have $|S| = |D| + |A| + |C| \leq 2|D| + |C|$. If we want to get a strongly dominating and absorbing set, the number of the connecting nodes should be confined by the following constraint: $|C| \leq |D| - 1$. And based on the above, we have $|S| \leq 3|D| - 1$. While according to theorem 6, we have $|D| \leq 2.4(k + \frac{1}{2})^2 \bullet opt + 3.7(k + \frac{1}{2})^2$. Thus, $|S| \leq 7.2(k + \frac{1}{2})^2 \bullet opt + 11.1(k + \frac{1}{2})^2 - 1$.

5   Conclusion

In this paper, we proposed a node added-based localized heuristic method to solve the strongly connected dominating and absorbing set problem in wireless network. Both theoretical analysis and simulation results demonstrate that our scheme is efficient and the performance is acceptable. This paper is very important for it contribution on the building of a virtual backbone in wireless sensor network with different transmission ranges. In the future, we will try to develop other localized algorithms to build a better virtual backbone in a directed graph.

Acknowledgments. This work was partially supported by the NSF of China for contract (61373027, 11101243), NSF of Shandong Province for contract (ZR2012FM023, ZR2012FQ011), STPU of Shandong Province for contract (J10LG09, J12LN06), PFMYS of Shandong Province for contract (BS2009DX024, BS2010DX013).

References

1. Tseng, Y.C., Ni, S.Y., Chen, Y.S., Sheu, J.P.: The broadcast storm problem in a mobile ad hoc network. Wireless Networks 8(2-3), 153–167 (2002)
2. Das, B., Bharghavan, V.: Routing in ad-hoc networks using minimum connected dominating sets. In: Proceedings of ICC 1997, pp. 376–380 (1997)
3. Gary, M.R., Johnson, D.S.: Computers and Intractability: A Guide to the Theory of NP-completeness (1979)
4. Wu, J., Li, H.: On calculating connected dominating set for efficient routing in ad hoc wireless networks. In: Proceedings of the 3rd International Workshop on Discrete Algorithms and Methods for Mobile Computing and Communications, pp. 7–14 (1999)
5. Wan, P.J., Alzoubi, K.M., Frieder, O.: Distributed construction of connected dominating set in wireless ad hoc networks. In: Proceedings of INFOCOM 2002, pp. 1597–1604 (2002)

6. Sakai, K., Shen, F., Kim, K.M., Sun, M.T., Okada, H.: Multi-initiator connected dominating set construction for mobile ad hoc networks. In: Proceedings of ICC 2008, pp. 2431–2436 (2008)
7. Zhou, D., Sun, M.T., Lai, T.H.: A timer-based protocol for connected dominating set construction in ieee 802.11 multihop mobile ad hoc networks. In: Proceedings of Symposium on Applications and the Internet 2005, pp. 2–8 (2005)
8. Wu, J.: Extended dominating-set-based routing in ad hoc wireless networks with unidirectional links. IEEE Transactions on Parallel and Distributed Systems 13(9), 866–881 (2002)
9. Dai, F., Wu, J.: An extended localized algorithm for connected dominating set formation in ad hoc wireless networks. IEEE Transactions on Parallel and Distributed Systems 15(10), 908–920 (2004)
10. Wu, J., Dai, F., Yang, S.: Iterative local solutions for connected dominating set in ad hoc wireless networks. IEEE Transactions on Computers 57(5), 702–715 (2008)
11. Guha, S., Khuller, S.: Approximation algorithms for connected dominating sets. Algorithmica 20(4), 374–387 (1998)
12. Han, B., Jia, W.: Clustering wireless ad hoc networks with weakly connected dominating set. Journal of Parallel and Distributed Computing 67(6), 727–737 (2007)
13. Chen, Y.P., Liestman, A.L.: Approximating minimum size weakly-connected dominating sets for clustering mobile ad hoc networks. In: Proceedings of the 3rd ACM international Symposium on Mobile Ad Hoc Networking and Computing, pp. 165–172 (2002)
14. Qayyum, A., Viennot, L., Laouiti, A.: Multipoint relaying for flooding broadcast messages in mobile wireless networks. In: Proceedings of HICSS 2002, pp. 3866–3875 (2002)
15. Park, M.A., Willson, J., Wang, C., Wu, W., Farago, A.: A dominating and absorbent set in a wireless ad-hoc network with different transmission ranges. In: Proceedings of the 8th ACM International Symposium on Mobile Ad Hoc Networking and Computing, pp. 22–31 (2007)
16. Tiwari, R., Mishra, T., Li, Y., Thai, M.T.: K-Strongly connected m-dominating and absorbing set in wireless ad hoc networks with unidirectional links. In: Proceedings of WASA 2007, pp. 103–112 (2007)
17. Thai, M.T., Wang, F., Liu, D., Zhu, S., Du, D.Z.: Connected dominating sets in wireless networks with different transmission ranges. IEEE Transactions on Mobile Computing 6(7), 721–730 (2007)
18. Du, D.-Z., Thai, M.T., Li, Y., Liu, D., Zhu, S.: Strongly connected dominating sets in wireless sensor networks with unidirectional links. In: Zhou, X., Li, J., Shen, H.T., Kitsuregawa, M., Zhang, Y. (eds.) APWeb 2006. LNCS, vol. 3841, pp. 13–24. Springer, Heidelberg (2006)
19. Thai, M.T., Tiwari, R., Du, D.Z.: On construction of virtual backbone in wireless ad hoc networks with unidirectional links. IEEE Transactions on Mobile Computing 7(9), 1098–1109 (2008)

Activity Recognition via Distributed Random Projection and Joint Sparse Representation in Body Sensor Networks

Ling Xiao*, Renfa Li, Juan Luo, and Mengqin Duan

Laboratory of Embedded Systems and Networks,
Hunan University, Changsha 410082, China
{xiaoling,juanluo}@hnu.edu.cn, lirenfa@vip.sina.cn

Abstract. Designing power-aware signal processing algorithms for activity recognition is challenging as special care needs to be taken to maintain acceptable classification accuracy while minimizing the energy consumption. This paper utilizes the theory of distributed random projection and joint sparse representation to develop a simultaneous dimension reduction and classification approach for multi-sensor activity recognition in BSNs. Both temporal and spatial correlations of sensing data among the multiple sensors are exploited for the purpose of compression and classification. Activity recognition with multiple sensors is formulated as a multi-task joint sparse representation model to combine the strength of multiple sensors for improving the classification accuracy. This method is validated on the WARD dataset using inertial sensors placed on various locations on a human body. Experimental result shows that the proposed DRP-JSR approach achieves better classification performance that is competitive with traditional classifier.

Keywords: Activity Recognition, Joint Sparse Representation, Random Projection, Body Sensor Network.

1 Introduction

Wireless body sensor networks (BSN) with multiple inertial sensors are widely used in various studies on human body movement[1]. A lot of pattern recognition and machine learning algorithms were developed to model and recognize human activities. As for the recognition techniques, a large number of classification methods have been investigated [2]. Some studies incorporated the idea of simple heuristic classifier, whereas others employed more generic and automatic methods from the machine learning literature including the decision trees , nearest neighbor (NN), Bayesian networks, support vector machines (SVM), Artificial neural networks (ANN) and Hidden Markov Model (HMM). A particular interest of multi-sensor fusion is classification, where the ultimate question is how

---

* This work was partially supported by Program for New Century Excellent Talents in University(NCET-12-0164), Natural Science Foundation of Hunan(13JJ1014).

L. Sun, H. Ma, and F. Hong (Eds.): CWSN 2013, CCIS 418, pp. 51–60, 2014.

to take advantage of having related information from different sensors recording the same physical event to achieve improved classification performance. In activity recognition of multi-sensor, a final decision can be made using either a data fusion or a decision fusion scheme. In the data fusion, features from all sensor nodes are fed into a central classifier. The classifier then combines the features to form a higher dimensional feature space and classifiers movements using the obtained features [3]. In the decision fusion, however, each sensor node makes a local classification and transmits the result to a central classifier where a final decision is made according to the received labels [4]. However, most existing techniques are designed for single observation based classification, which are clearly not optimal due to the failure of exploiting the correlations among the multiple observations of the same physical object.

However, the battery limitations of the BSN severely limit the maximum deployment time for continuously monitoring human body. This problem is often solved by shifting some processing to the local sensor nodes to reduce a very heavy communication cost. Designing power-aware signal processing algorithms for activity recognition is challenging as special care needs to be taken to maintain acceptable classification accuracy while minimizing the energy consumption. This paper focuses on developing a computationally simple and energy-efficiency algorithm for action recognition. Compressive sensing (CS) [5] is new method for recovering of sparse or compressible signals from a small set of non-adaptive, linear measurements. It has been shown that random projections (RP) are a near-optimal measurement scheme. Distributed compressive sensing (DCS) [6] is an extension of the CS acquisition framework to correlated signal ensembles. Using DCS as the data acquisition approach in BSNs can significantly reduce the energy consumed in the process of sampling and transmission through the network, and also lower the wireless bandwidth requirements for communication.

Sparsity has been the key factor of compressive sensing and has been playing an important role in many fields. Sparse signal representations from over-complete dictionaries have far-reaching significance in signal processing. Recently, a sparse representation classification (SRC) method for face images is developed in [7], this work has shown that the sparse coefficients are also discriminative. The term Joint Sparsity was first coined in [6]. Yuan et al. [8] investigated the problem of multi-task joint sparse representation and classification and its applications to visual recognition. Zhang et al. [9] proposed a joint sparse representation for multi-view face recognition.

The goals and contributions of this paper are as follows: 1) to combine distributed random projection with joint sparse representation for power-aware classification; 2) to extend the sparsity-based classification approach to handle the multi-sensor classification problem with joint-structured-sparsity priors; 3) to propose the DRP-JSR classification algorithm and to find a sparse Bayesian learning algorithm for solving this problem.

The rest of the paper is organized as follows: In Section 2, we define the problem of activity recognition and review the sparse representation classification method. In Section 3, we present the proposed distributed random projection and joint sparse representation classification for multi-sensor. In Section 4, we evaluate the efficacy of the proposed method under various compression ratios. Finally, we make some discussions and conclude this paper in Section 5.

2   Problem Descriptions

2.1   Problem Definition

Beginning with the problem formulation, let there be a set of J wearable sensors, each with consisting of a 3-axis accelerometer (x,y,z) and a 2-axis gyroscope (θ, φ), attached to the human body. Then, let

$$a^j(t) = (x^j(t), y^j(t), z^j(t), \theta^j(t), \varphi^j(t),) \in \mathbb{R}^5 \qquad (1)$$

denotes the 5 measurements provided by node j at time t, and

$$v^j = [a^j(1), a^j(2), \cdots, a^j(h)]^{\mathrm{T}} \in \mathbb{R}^{5h} \qquad (2)$$

corresponds to an action segment of length h by node j.

Consider a multi-task (multi-sensor) C-class classification problem. Suppose we have a training set of n samples in which each sample was collected by J different sensors. For each sensor $j = 1, \cdots, J$, we denote $V^j = [V_1^j, V_2^j, \cdots, V_C^j]$ as a $N \times n$ training feature matrix in which $V_i^j = [V_{i,1}^j, V_{i,2}^j, \cdots, V_{i,n_i}^j] \in \mathbb{R}^{N \times n_i}$ with respect to C classes. Here, each sub-dictionary represents a set of training data from the jth sensor labeled with ith class. Accordingly, , which we usually call an atom in the dictionary is the kth training sample for jth sensor and ith class. In addition, we have a training label vector $L \in \mathbb{R}^n$ associated with v. Notice that n_i is the number of training sample for class ith and N is the feature dimension of each sample ($N = 5h$), therefore, the total samples is $n = \sum_{i=1}^{C} n_i$. Given a test sample v_{test} collected by J sensors $\{v_{test}^1, v_{test}^2, \cdots, v_{test}^J\}$, we want to decide which class the sample v_{test} belongs to. This can be formally represented as

$$\hat{i} = argminE(V, L, v_{test}) \qquad (3)$$

Where $E(V, L, v_{test})$ is a cost function defining the classification problem.

2.2   Sparse Representation-Based Classification

We first review the single task (single sensor) sparse representation based classification method. A SRC method for single image based face recognition has been proposed in [7]. This method casts the task of face recognition as one of classifying between linear regression models via sparse representation. The sparsest linear combination of a test face image is sought using all the training images, and the dominant sparse coefficients reveal its identity.

A single new test sample v_{test}^j (i.e., $J=1$) can be represented in terms of the atoms form a structured dictionary V^j as follows:

$$v_{test}^j = V^j \alpha^j + \varepsilon \tag{4}$$

where $\alpha^j = [0, \cdots 0, \alpha_{k,1}, \alpha_{k,2}, \cdots, \alpha_{k,n_i}, 0, \cdots 0]^{\mathrm{T}} \in \mathbb{R}^n$, α^j is a sparse representation vector whose entries are zero except those associated with the same class as v_{test}^j.

The theory of sparse representation and compressive sensing reveals that the solutions exist to uniquely recover sparse solution α^j via l_1-minimization:

$$\hat{i} = argmin \|\alpha\|_1 \; subject \; to \left\| v_{test}^j - V^j \alpha^j \right\|_2 \le \varepsilon \tag{5}$$

After recovering the sparse representation vector α^j, the class label for $v_{k,test}$ is assigned to the class with the smallest residual

$$\hat{i} = SRC(v_{test}^j) = argmin \left\| v_{test}^j - V^j \delta_i^j(\hat{\alpha}) \right\|_2 \tag{6}$$

Where $\delta_i^j(\hat{\alpha})$ is defined as a vector indicator function, keeping the coefficients corresponding to the ith class while setting all others to be zero.

In this paper, we extend SRC to handle the multi-sensor classification problem with joint-structured-sparsity priors. It is important to note that Human body motions usually exhibit a high degree of coherence and correlation in patterns. By temporal correlation, body signs sensed by a single node typically change smoothly and slowly. By spatial correlation, body signs measured on different nodes are typically correlated because body components are connected and they normally move with certain rhymes. On the other hand, sensors of the same node may also exhibit strong spatial correlations, especially among the three axes of a triaxial accelerometer. We call such spatial correlations intra-node spatial correlations and those among sensors of different nodes inter-node spatial correlations. By exploiting the structural information across the multiple sparse representation vectors for the multiple sensors, we can reduce the number of measurements required for proper model estimation and improve the accuracy of classification.

Three different models are investigated in this paper. 1) Separate sparse representation and their sparse patterns may be quite different. 2) All the representation vectors have equal values. 3) Sparse coefficient vectors share similar patterns, but with different coefficient values.

3   DRP-JSR Classification

3.1   Distributed Random Projection

Random projections of the signal measurements are performed at each source node, only taking into account the temporal correlation of the sensor readings.

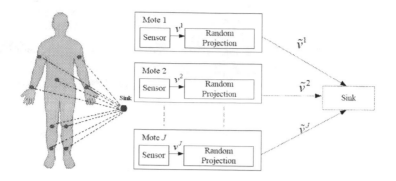

Fig. 1. Framework of distributed random projection

We denote by Φ_j the measurement matrix for sensor j; Φ_j is $M \times N$ and, in general, the entries of Φ_j are different for each j. After random projection matrix Φ_j is chosen on each node j, there are:

$$\tilde{v}^j = \Phi_j v^j \tag{7}$$

Where $\tilde{v}^j$ is a vector after RP.

Gaussian and Bernoulli random matrix have been proven to follow RIP with a very high probability [10].

After RP, typically the feature dimension M is much smaller than N. Furthermore, by exploiting the relationships between these J sets of sensor measurements, the number of transmissions to the sink can be further reduced, with a consequent reduction of the energy consumed by the sensor nodes.

3.2 Classification by Joint Sparse Representation

Every sensor sends random projection vector $\tilde{v}^j$ to the base station.

The spatial correlation is then exploited at the sink by means of suitable decoders through a joint sparsity model able to characterize different types of signals. For each sensor, there is equation:

$$\tilde{v}^j_{test} = \Phi_j V^j \beta^j + \varepsilon_j \tag{8}$$

To handle multi-sensor classification, the simplest idea would be to perform SRC method for each sensor separately and the recovered spare representation vectors may be quite different, as shown by a graphical illustration in figure.3 (a). The final decision is based on the lowest total reconstruction error accumulated from all the sensors, which is called by SRC-S.

It is clear that the SRC-S approaches do not exploit the relationship between different sensors except at the post-processing step where decision is made via fusion. Rather than doing post-processing during the decision fusion, it is more

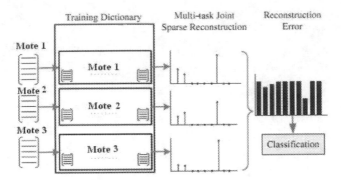

Fig. 2. Scheme illustration of activity recognition with multi-sensor joint sparse representation

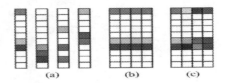

Fig. 3. Pictorial illustration of different sparsity models for coefficient matrix

robust to recover the sparse representation vectors for the J sensors simultaneously. This can be done by exploiting the correlations among measurements of multiple sensors during the sparse representation process, and then make a single decision based on the J sparse representation vectors jointly. In the following, we exploit the correlations among the multiple measurements of multi-sensor by imposing different joint-structured-sparsity constraints on their sparse coefficient vector.

The most direct method to enforce joint structures on the multiple sparse representation vectors would be making the assumption that all the measurements would have the same sparse representation vector with respect to a dictionary, as shown by a graphical illustration in figure.3 (a), which is called SRC-A. The base station collects J sensors random projection vector and constitutes as $\tilde{v}$:

$$\tilde{v} = [\tilde{v}^1, \cdots, \tilde{v}^J]^{\mathrm{T}} = \Phi v \tag{9}$$

Where $\Phi \in \mathbb{R}^{MJ \times NJ}$ is a block-diagonal matrix which constitutes by J nodes random projection matrices.

Correspondingly, we form a large concatenated dictionary as

$$V = [V^{1^{\mathrm{T}}}, \cdots, V^{J^{\mathrm{T}}}]^{\mathrm{T}} \tag{10}$$

where each V^j can be constructed by the training samples from the corresponding jth sensor. The sparse representation can be formulated by equation (9), we enforce all the sparse representation vector is the same, i.e., $B = \beta^1 = \beta^1 = \cdots = \beta^J \in \mathbb{R}^N$.

$$\tilde{v}_{test} = \Phi V \beta + \varepsilon \tag{11}$$

Although the SRC-A can reduce the degrees of freedom greatly, the constraint that all the measurements would have the same sparse representation vector is a restrictive, which is often violated in typical sparsity-based classification problems.

Therefore, we make a relax assumption by assuming that the sparse representation vector for multi-sensor share the location of nonzero coefficients, but the values of the coefficients may be different for different sensors, as shown in figure 3.(c). The joint sparse representation can be represented by equation (12), which is named DRP-JSR.

$$\tilde{v}_{test}^1 = \Phi_1 V^1 \beta^1 + \varepsilon_1, \cdots, \tilde{v}_{test}^J = \Phi_J V^J \beta^J + \varepsilon_J \tag{12}$$

The rationale behind the DRP-JSR method is that the multiple measurements are highly correlated; thus, they tend to be represented by the same set of atoms. However, as aforementioned, due to the variation of environment and imperfection of the measurement process, all the J sensors are not exactly the same. Therefore, it is more reasonable to represent them with respect to the same set of atoms but weigh them with different coefficient values.

In order to seek for this row-sparse matrix with common sparse support as equation (12), an efficient algorithm for simultaneous sparse linear-regression of multiple related signals is required to that take into account this precious piece of sparsity as a prior information. We found the algorithms based on hierarchical Bayesian model [11] for this problem. A shared prior is placed across all of the J sensors. Under this hierarchical Bayesian modeling, data from all J sensors contribute toward inferring a posterior on the hyerparameters, and once the shared prior is thereby inferred, the data from each of the J individual sensors is then employed to estimate the sensor-dependent sparse coefficients. In the practice of activity recognition, when the sensors to be learned share some common latent factors, it may be beneficial to take into this relation into account. When applied to sparse learning, joint sparsity is always taken into account for multi-task learning.

After recovering the spare representation coefficient matrix, we can estimate the class label. Similar to the single task case, where minimal reconstruction residual vector criteria are used, we make a decision based on the lowest total reconstruction error accumulated from all the sensors.

$$\hat{i} = argmin \sum_{j=1}^{J} \left\| \tilde{v}_{test}^j - \tilde{V}^j \delta_i^j (\hat{\beta})^j \right\|_2 \tag{13}$$

Where $\delta_i(.)$ denotes the operation of preserving the rows of matrix $\hat{\beta}^j$ corresponding to class i and setting all others to be zero.

4   Experiment Results

4.1   WARD Dataset

For this work, we used the wearable action recognition database (WARD), which is implemented by Yang et al. of University of California, Berkeley[12]. The five sensor nodes (J=5) contain a 3-axis accelerometer and a 2-axis gyroscope, placed at different locations on the bodyone on the waist, two on the wrists, and two on the ankles. The sampling rates for both accelerometer and gyroscope are set to 20Hz. The dataset has been made publicly available, and consists of data recorded from 20 participants with different gender, age, height, and weight, for 13action categories: 1. Stand (ST). 2. Sit (SI). 3. Lie down (LI). 4. Walk forward (WF). 5. Walk left-circle (WL). 6. Walk right-circle (WR). 7. Turn left (TL). 8. Turn right (TR). 9. Go upstairs (UP). 10. Go downstairs (DO). 11. Jog (JO). 12. Jump (JU). 13. Push wheelchair (PU). Each participant performs five trials for each action. In total, there are 1300 examples.

We currently process all data offline in MATLAB. Our experiments use Sparse Bayesian Learning toolbox[10]. For each motion sequence in the WARD database, we randomly sample an action segment of length h in time. In the experiment, we choose $h=40$ as a short action duration, which corresponds to 2 seconds given the 20Hz sampling rate. The raw sensor sampled data are filtered using a five-point moving average to reduce high frequency noise. The training sets and the test sets are designed as follows. During the test, we employ a leave-one-subject-out validation approach to examine the subject-independence classification performance on a test sequence. This validation process was repeated for all twenty subjects. The number of samples in training sets from 19 subjects is 1235, i.e. $n=1235$.

4.2   Recognition Accuracy under RP

The Gaussian random projection matrices were chosen in our experiments. For each kind of random matrices, the validation process was repeated 10 times, a group of RP matrices were generated randomly every time. Each group of RP matrices consists of five random matrices Φ_j, in which each matrix corresponds to one sensor node respectively.

To investigate the robustness of the proposed SRC-RP algorithm for dimensionality reduction by RP, we set five different compression ratios of 0, 0.3, 0.5, 0.7 and 0.9. Compression ratio is defined as $(N\text{-}M)/N$. Table 1 gives the mean and standard deviation for recognition accuracies of the three approach with various compression ratios, the first column indicates the ratio of compression.

As shown in Table 1, with the increase of compression ratios, the mean recognition accuracies of three classifiers degrade slightly while the standard deviations of the recognition accuracies arise. It is observed that DRP-JSR method outperform the other method under the same compression ratio, which shows the superior classification performance of the joint-sparsity-based classification methods.

Table 1. Activity recognition accuracies (meanstandard $\pm$ deviation)of the three different sparsity models

Compression ratio	DRP-JSR	SRC-S	SRC-A
0	88.77	85.46	83
0.3	87.50±2.01	84.60±2.36	83.55±2.47
0.5	87.22±2.16	84.27±2.64	83.08±2.48
0.7	87.05±2.19	83.94±2.73	82.94±2.49
0.9	83.74±3.25	79.56±3.43	80.45±3.76

4.3   Compared with other Classification Methods

To further validate the performance of the proposed method, four common classifiers were carried out to recognize human activities on the WARD. The classifiers were nearest neighbor (NN) classifier, nearest subspace (NS), Bayesian Networks, and SVM. Bayesian Network was implemented under WEKA environment, and SVM was implemented under MATLAB environment by using LIBSVM toolbox. The average recognition accuracies of subject-independent for three classifiers are given in Table 2. As listed in Table 2, the DRP-JSR method achieved higher accuracy under the same compression ratio.

Table 2. Activity recognition accuracies (meanstandard $\pm$ deviation)of the common classifiers

Compression ratio	DRP-JSR	NS	NN	Bayes Net	SVM
0	88.77	83.2	81.0	87.8	87.9
0.3	87.50±2.01	82.85±1.66	79.38±1.89	83.22±1.66	83.29±1.65
0.5	87.22±2.16	82.20±1.83	79.27±2.18	83.57±1.59	83.02±1.52
0.7	87.05±2.19	81.66±2.13	78.51±2.58	82.05±1.36	82.51±1.58
0.9	83.74±3.25	78.75±5.29	76.40±3.61	77.87±1.83	80.01±1.63

5   Conclusion

In this paper, we generalize SRC to handle the multi-sensor classification problem with distributed random projection and joint sparsity priors. By exploiting the structural information across the multiple sparse representation vectors for the multiple sensors, we can reduce the number of measurements required for proper model estimation and improve the accuracy of classification. Several different models are investigated in this paper. 1) Separate sparse representation and their sparse patterns may be quite different. 2) All the representation vectors have equal values. 3) sparse coefficient vectors share similar patterns (selecting the same set of atoms), but with different coefficient values. We exploit the data correlation both temporally and spatially. The projections of the signal measurements are performed at each source node, only taking into account the temporal correlation of the sensor readings. The spatial correlation is then exploited at the sink through a joint sparsity model able to characterize different types of signals.

In the future, we would like to progress this work. With the development of compressive sensing and solution, we will find the analytical relationship between the RIP constants and the action recognition results and give a strong foundation to decide the number of projections required to get robust recognition results.

References

1. Seeger, C., Buchmann, A., Laerhoven, K.V.: MyHealthAssistant: A phone-based Body sensor network that captures the wearer's exercises throughout the Day. In: 6th IEEE International Conference on Body Area Networks, pp. 181–189. IEEE Press, New York (2011)
2. Yang, C.C., Hsu, Y.L.: A review of acclerometry-based wearable motion detector for physical activity monitoring. Sensors 10, 7772–7788 (2010)
3. Reichardt, D., Miglietta, M., Moretti, L., Morsink, P., Schulz, W.C.: CarTALK 2000: safe and comfortable driving based upon inter-vehicle-communication. In: IEEE Intelligent Vehicle Symposium, pp. 545–550. IEEE Press, Piscataway (2002)
4. Ghasemzadeh, H., Jarari, R.: Physical movement monitoring using body sensor networks: a phonological approach to construct spatial decision trees. IEEE Transactions on Industrial Informatics 7(1), 66–77 (2011)
5. Donoho, D.L.: Compressed sensing. IEEE Trans. on Information Theory 52(4), 1289–1306 (2006)
6. Barson, D., Wakin, M.B., Duate, M.F., Sarvotham, S., Baraniuk, R.G.: Distributed compressed sensing (November 2005) (preprint)
7. Wright, J., Yang, A., Ganesh, A., Sastry, S.S., Ma, Y.: Robust face recognition via sparse representation. IEEE Trans. on Pattern Anal. Mach. Intell. 31(2), 210–227 (2009)
8. Yuan, X.P., Liu, X., Yan, S.: Visual classification with multitask joint sparse representation. IEEE Trans. on Image Processing 21(10), 4349–4360 (2012)
9. Zhang, H., Nasrabadi, N.M., Zhang, Y., Huang, T.S.: Joint dynamic sparse representation for multi-view face recognition. Pattern Recognition 45, 1290–1298 (2012)
10. Baraniuk, R., Davenport, M., Devore, R., Wakin, M.: A simple proof of the restricted isometry property for random matrices. Constr. Approx. 28(3), 253–263 (2008)
11. Ji, S., Dunson, D., Carin, L.: Multitask compressive sensing. IEEE Trans. on Signal Processing 57(1), 92–106 (2009)
12. Yang, A., Kuryloski, P., Bajcsy, R.: WARD: a wearable action recognition database (2009), http://www.eecs.berkeley.edu/~yang/software/WAR/

Construction of Lightweight Certificate-Based Signature and Application in Cloud Computing

Shaohui Wang and Suqin Chang

[1] College of Computer, Nanjing University of Posts and Telecommunications,
Nanjing 210023, China
[2] Jiangsu High Technology Research Key Laboratory for Wireless Sensor Networks,
Nanjing 210003, China
[3] Network and Data Security Key Laboratory of Sichuan Province
wangshaohui@njupt.edu.cn

Abstract. Certificate-based signature (CBS) scheme preserves advantages of certificate-based encryption, such as implicit certification and no private key escrow problem. In this paper, we propose a new short and efficient CBS scheme in the random oracle model based on the Schnorr signature scheme. The short signature length and efficient computation make it particularly useful in power and bandwidth limited environment. In addition, we present the new application of CBS scheme to the Single Sign-On(SSO) problem in the cloud computing environment, which allows users to sign on only once and have their identities automatically verified by each application or service they want to access. Based on our new CBS scheme construction, the new SSO solution is much more efficient than the one based on proxy signature scheme.

Keywords: Certificate-based Signature, Lightweight, Proxy Signature, Single Sign-On, Cloud Computing.

1 Introduction

In a traditional public key cryptography(PKC), a certificate, which is generated by a trusted party called the Certificate Authority(CA), provides an unforgeable signature and trusted link between the public key and the identity of the user. And there is a hierarchical framework that is called public key infrastructure(PKI) to issue and manage certificates. This approach seems inefficient, in particular when the number of users is very large, because in the point of view of a verifier, it takes two verification steps for independent signatures.

Identity-based cryptography(IBC), invented by Shamir[1] in 1984, solves the aforementioned problem by using the identity (or email address) as the public key while the corresponding private key is a result of some mathematical operation of user's identity and the master secret key of a trusted authority, named "Private Key Generator(PKG)". Now the certificate is implicitly provided and the explicit authentication of public key is no longer required. Recently Boneh and Franklin[2] propose a practical ID-based encryption(IBE) scheme based

L. Sun, H. Ma, and F. Hong (Eds.): CWSN 2013, CCIS 418, pp. 61–70, 2014.

on bilinear maps. The main disadvantage of identity-based cryptography is an unconditional trust to the PKG, because PKG can impersonate any user, or decrypt any ciphertext. Hence, IBC is only suitable for a closed organization where the PKG is completely trusted by everyone in the group.

To integrate the merits of IBC into PKI, Gentry[3] introduced the concept of certificate-based encryption(CBE). A CBE scheme combines a public key encryption scheme and an identity based encryption scheme between a certifier and a user. Each user generates his/her own private and public key and requests a certificate from the CA, and CA uses the key generation algorithm of an IBE scheme to generate the certificate. The certificate is implicitly used as part of the user's decryption keys, which are composed of the user-generated private key and the certificate. Although CA knows the certificate, it does not have the user's private key. Thus it cannot decrypt any ciphertext. The corresponding notion of certificate-based signature(CBS) is first suggested by Kang et.al.[4]. However, one of their proposed schemes is found insecure against key replacement attack, as pointed out by Li et al.[5]. In parallel to their constructions, Liu et.al.[6] propose two CBS schemes, one of which is constructed without random oracle and the other without pairings, and Au et.al.[7] propose a certificate-based ring signature scheme. Recently, Bao et.al.[8] presente the most efficient CBS scheme among the schemes based on pairings, which requires two pairing operations for the verification algorithm.

Cloud computing has been envisioned as the next generation information technology architecture for enterprises, due to its long list of unprecedented advantages in the IT history: on demand self-service, ubiquitous network access, location independent resource pooling, rapid resource elasticity, usage-based pricing and transference of risk[9]. The proliferation of different remote applications and services makes it impractical for large corporations to manage each separate authentication system, which raises the need for centralized user authentication solutions, i.e. secure single sign-on(SSO for short). In most current SSO architectures[10,11], the user receives "ticket" after he successfully signs on the identity provider. When the user tries to access some service, it is then required to contact the identity provider in order to authenticate the "ticket" presented. In [12], a new method to solve SSO problem is presented based on proxy signature[13], which does not require direct communication between the user and the identity provider. The user himself proves that he has been authenticated by trusted identity provider.

In this paper, we propose a new lightweight CBS scheme without pairings based on the Schnorr signature scheme. The security of the scheme is presented in the random oracle model. The efficiency and the short signature length make the scheme particularly useful in power and bandwidth limited environment. In addition, we discuss the application of CBS scheme to the SSO problem in cloud computing, and our new method is much more efficient than the one presented in [12] based on proxy signature.

The rest of the paper is organized as follows. In section 2, we review some preliminaries required in this paper. In section 3, we propose a lightweight CBS

scheme, and security proof is presented. The application to the SSO problem in cloud computing is presented in section 4, and we conclude the paper in section 5.

2 Preliminaries

Notation: Let k denote the security parameter, which will be an implicit input to the algorithm. For a function $f : N \rightarrow R^+$, if for every positive number α, there exists a positive integer l_0 such that for every integer $l > l_0$, it holds $f(l) < l^{-\alpha}$, f is said to be negligible.

2.1 Computational Assumptions

Here we present the usually used problems that are difficult to solve, including Discrete Logarithm, Computational Diffie-Hellman, Decisional Diffie-Hellman problem. Here, G_1 is a group with the prime order p, $g \in G_1$ is a generator, and $a, b \in Z_p^*$:

Discrete Logarithm(DL) Problem: Given the pair (g, g^a), compute and output a. We say that the algorithm A solves the DL problem with the advantage ϵ if $Pr(A(g, g^\alpha) = a) = \epsilon$.

Computational Diffie-Hellman (CDH) Problem: Given the tuple (g, g^a, g^b), compute and output g^{ab}. We say that the algorithm A solves the CDH problem with the advantage ϵ if $Pr(A(g, g^a, g^b) = g^{ab}) = \epsilon$.

Decisional Diffie-Hellman (DDH) Problem: Given the tuple (g, g^a, g^b) and $h \in G_1$, decide whether $h = g^{ab}$. We say that A solves the DDH problem with the advantage ϵ if $|Pr(A(g, g^a, g^b, g^{ab}) = 1) - Pr(A(g, g^a, g^b, h) = 1)| = \epsilon$.

2.2 Certificate-Based Signature and Security Model

Definition 2.1 Certificate-based Signature(CBS) Scheme. A CBS scheme is denoted by five algorithms as (Setup, UserKeyGen, Certify, Sign, Verify), of which Setup, UserKeyGen, Certify, Sign algorithms are probabilistic algorithms, and Verify is deterministic:

· Setup is usually run by CA. Taking as input a security parameter, it returns the certifier's master key msk and public parameters $params$.

· UserKeyGen takes $params$ as input. When run by a client, it returns user's public key PK and secret key usk.

· Certify. This algorithm is run by CA. Taking $(msk, params, PK, ID)$ as input, where ID is a binary string representing the user information, it returns $cert$ to the client.

· Sign takes $(params, cert, usk)$ and message m as input, and it outputs a signature σ.

· Verify takes $(params, PK, ID, m, \sigma)$ as input, and it returns either valid indicating the signature is valid, or the special symbol $\perp$ indicating invalid.

The security requirements of a CBS scheme include completeness and existential unforgeability.

Definition 2.2 Completeness. The property requires that if σ is the result of applying algorithm Sign with input $(params, cert, usk, m)$ and (usk, PK) is a valid key-pair, then valid is the result of applying algorithm Verify on input $(params, PK, ID, m, \sigma)$, where $cert$ is the output of Certify algorithm on input $(msk, params, PK, ID)$.

Roughly speaking, as to the security of existential unforgeability, two different types of attacks respectively by an uncertified user and by the certifier are concerned. The security is defined by two different games and the adversary chooses which game to play. In Game 1, the adversary essentially assumes the role of an uncertified user, while in Game 2, the adversary essentially assumes the role of the certifier which has the secret key msk.

Game 1: The challenger runs Setup, and gives $params$ to the adversary. The adversary then issues the following queries:

Userkeygen Query (ID): If ID has already been created, nothing is to be carried out. Otherwise, the challenger runs the algorithm UserKeyGen to obtain a secret/public key pair (usk_{ID}, PK_{ID}) and adds them to the list L. In this case, ID is said to be "created". In both cases, PK_{ID} is returned.

Corruption Query (ID): The challenger checks the list L. If ID is there, it returns the corresponding secret key usk_{ID}. Otherwise nothing is returned.

Certification Query (ID): Challenger runs Certify on input $(msk, params, PK, ID)$, and returns $cert$ to the adversary.

Signing Query (ID, PK, m): the challenger generates σ by operating algorithm Sign, and sends it to the adversary.

Finally the adversary outputs a signature σ, a message m and a public key PK with user information ID. The adversary wins the game if

(1) σ is a valid signature on the message m under the public key PK with user information ID, where PK might not be the one returned from Userkeygen Query.

(2) ID has never been submitted to the Certification Query.

(3) (ID, PK, m) has never been submitted to the Signing Query.

Game 2: The challenger runs Setup algorithm, gives $params$ and msk to the adversary A. The adversary interleaves Userkeygen, Corruption, Signing Queries as in Game 1. Finally the adversary outputs a signature σ, a message m and a public key PK with user information ID. The adversary wins the game if

(1) σ is a valid signature on the message m under the public key PK with user information ID.

(2) PK is an output from Userkeygen Query.

(3) ID has never been submitted to the Corruption Query.

(4) (ID, PK, m) has never been submitted to the Signing Query.

Definition 2.3 Existential Unforgeability. Adversary's advantage in the above two games is denoted to be $Adv^i(A) = Pr[A \quad wins \quad Game^{(i)}], i = 1, 2.$ A CBS scheme is said to be secure against existential forgery under adaptively chosen message attacks if no probabilistic polynomial time adversary has non-negligible advantage in either Game 1 or Game 2.

3   A New Lightweight CBS Scheme

In this section, we give a lightweight CBS scheme construction based on Schnorr signature scheme, and security analysis is given in the random oracle model. The idea behind the construction is to use two concatenated Schnorr signature schemes, which have the benefits of efficiency and simplicity.

3.1   Scheme Construction

Roughly speaking, the scheme works as follows. Firstly, using the master secret key, CA produces a Schnorr signature on the identity and the public key of the user as the certificate. Next, the user builds a second Schnorr-like signature on the message, utilizing its private key and the certificate. Construction details are given below.

· Setup. Let G be a multiplicative group with order p, and g is a generator of G. Randomly choose $\alpha \in Z_p$, and set $X = g^\alpha$. Let $H_1, H_2 : \{0,1\}^* \to Z_p^*$ be two cryptographic hash functions. The public parameters and master secret key are given by $params = (G, p, g, X, H_1, H_2)$ and $msk = \alpha$.

· UserKeyGen. User selects a secret value $\beta \in Z_p$ as his secret key usk, and computes his public key PK as g^β.

· Certify. To generate a certificate for the user with public key PK and binary string ID, CA randomly chooses $r \in Z_p$, and sets $y = r + a \cdot h \, mod \, p$, where $h = H_1(g^r, PK, ID)$. The certificate is (y, g^r), and a correctly generated certificate should fulfill the equality: $g^y = g^r X^h$.

· Sign. To sign a message $m \in \{0,1\}^*$, the signer with public key PK, user information ID, certificate (y, g^r) and secret key β, randomly selects $\mu \in Z_p$, and computes

$$z = \mu + (y + \beta)h_1 \, mod \, p$$

where $h_1 = H_2(PK, ID, g^\mu, m)$. The final signature σ is (z, g^μ, g^r).

· Verify. Given a signature σ for a public key PK on a message m, a verifier first computes $h = H_1(g^r, PK, ID)$ and $h_1 = H_2(PK, ID, g^\mu, m)$, and checks whether the equation $g^z = g^\mu (g^r \cdot X^h \cdot PK)^{h_1}$ holds. The verifier outputs valid if it is equal; Otherwise, outputs $\bot$.

3.2   Security Analysis

It is easy to see that the signature scheme satisfies completeness property. To sign a message, the Sign algorithm in our scheme needs 2 modular addition, 1 modular multiplication and 1 modular exponentiation operations, while the scheme in [6] needs 1 modular addition, 2 modular multiplication and 1 modular exponentiation operations. As to Verify algorithm, our scheme needs 3 modular multiplication and 4 modular exponentiation operations, while the scheme [6] needs 4 modular multiplication and 4 modular exponentiation operations. So our scheme is much more efficient than the scheme proposed in [6].

Using the forking lemma, we give the following two theorems to show our new scheme is secure against existential forgery under adaptively chosen message attacks in the random oracle model.

Theorem 3.1 (Unforgeability against Game 1 Adversary). The new CBS scheme is existential unforgeable against Game 1 adversary assuming the Discrete Logarithm assumption holds in group G.

Proof. Assuming there exists an algorithm A can forge valid signatures in Game 1, we construct an algorithm B that makes use of A to solve discrete logarithm problem. B is given a multiplicative group G with generator g, a number $X \in G$, and B is asked to find α such that $X = g^\alpha$. B chooses two hash functions $H_1, H_2 : \{0,1\}^* \to Z_p^*$ as random oracles, assigns (G, p, g, X, H_1, H_2) as the CBS public parameter to A, and answers $A's$ oracle queries as follows:

· UserKeyGen / Corruption Query: B first generates the secret and public key pair according to the CBS scheme, then stores them in the table and outputs the public key. On the corruption query, B returns the corresponding secret key.

· Certification Query: B simulates the oracle to answer $A's$ certification query with public key PK and binary string ID. It randomly chooses $h, b \in Z_p$ and sets

$$y = b, g^r = X^{-h}g^b \, mod \, p, H_1(g^r, PK, ID) = h$$

B outputs (y, g^r) as the query answer, and it is easy to see (y, g^r) satisfies the equality in the Certify algorithm. B stores the value of $(y, g^r, H_1(g^r, PK, ID), PK, ID)$ in the table for consistency.

· Signing Query: A queries the signing oracle for a message m with a public key PK and binary string ID. B checks whether (PK, ID) has been queried for the H_1 random oracle before. If yes, it just gets $(y, g^r, H_1(g^r, PK, ID), PK, ID)$ from the table. B randomly generates $h', d \in Z_p$, and sets

$$z = d, g^\mu = (X^h PK)^{-h'} g^d \, mod \, p, H_2(PK, ID, g^\mu, m) = h'$$

It outputs the signature (z, g^μ, g^r) for the message m and stores the value h'. If (PK, ID) has not been queried, B executes the simulation of the certification oracle and uses the corresponding certificate to sign the message using the above algorithm.

Finally, A outputs a forged signature $\sigma_1^* = (z_1^*, (g^\mu)^*, (g^r)^*)$ on message m^* with public key PK^* and ID^*. B rewinds A to the point it just queries $H_1((g^r)^*, PK^*, ID^*)$ and supplies with a different value, and A outputs another valid signature $\sigma_2^* = (z_2^*, (g^\mu)^*, (g^r)^*)$. We denote c_1, c_2 as the outputs of the random oracle queries $H_1((g^r)^*, PK^*, ID^*)$. Let $\theta = H_2(PK^*, ID^*, (g^\mu)^*, m^*)$, and from the verification equation, we have:

$$z_i = \mu + r\theta + \alpha\theta c_i + \beta\theta \, mod \, p, \quad i = 1, 2$$

In these equations, only μ, r, α, β are unknown to B. B solves for these values from the above 2 linear independent equations, and outputs α as the solution of the discrete logarithm problem.

Theorem 3.2 (Unforgeability against Game 2 Adversary). The new CBS scheme is existential unforgeable against Game 2 adversary assuming the Discrete Logarithm assumption holds in group G.

Proof. Just as the discussion in theorem 3.1, in order to find α such that $Y = g^\alpha$, B randomly chooses $x \in Z_p$, sets $X = g^x$, and assigns (G, p, g, X, H_1, H_2) as the CBS public parameter to A, and answers $A's$ oracle queries as follows:

· UserKeyGen Query: B chooses a particular query ID' and assigns the public key $PK = Y^x$. For the other queries, B generates the secret and public key pair according to the algorithm and stores the values in the table.

· Corruption Query: If the query is not ID', B outputs the corresponding secret key from the table. Otherwise B aborts.

· Signing Query: It can be simulated in the same way as in Game 1, which also does not require the knowledge of the secret key.

Finally, A outputs a forged signature $\sigma_1^* = (z_1^*, (g^\mu)^*, (g^r)^*)$ on message m^* with public key PK^* and ID^*. If $PK^* \neq PK'$, B aborts. Otherwise B rewinds A to the point it just queries $H_2(PK^*, ID^*, (g^\mu)^*, m^*)$ and supplies with a different value. A outputs another two valid signatures σ_2^* and σ_3^*. We denote c_1, c_2, c_3 as the output of the random oracle queries $H_2(PK^*, ID^*, (g^\mu)^*, m^*)$. From the verification equation, we have:

$$z_i = \mu + rc_i + xH_1(g^r, PK^*, ID^*)c_i + \alpha xc_i \, mod \, p, \quad i = 1, 2, 3$$

In these equations, only μ, r, α are unknown to B. B solves for these values from the above 3 linear independent equations, and outputs α as the solution of the discrete logarithm problem.

4   Application to SSO Problem in Cloud Computing

In a single sign-on framework, the user performs a single initial (or primary) sign-on to an identity provider trusted by the applications he wants to access. Later on, each time he wants to access the application, it automatically verifies that he has been properly authenticated by the identity provider without requiring any direct user interaction. A well designed and implemented single sign-on solution will significantly reduce authentication infrastructure and identity management complexity, and it eliminates the need for users to repeatedly prove their identities to different applications and hold different credentials for each applications. Furthermore,

In a secure single sign-on architecture, two main issues are necessary to address: securely establishing the initial sign on and maintaining session state while enforcing access permission. We do not consider the first issue here. After the identity provider verifies the user's identity, the applications should be able to securely verify that the identity provider has recognized the user when he makes an access attempt.

In [12], a new framework is introduced for maintaining session state across the various application servers that trust the identity provider. The user himself proves to each application server that he has been already authenticated by the identity provider. The new framework is based on the proxy signature scheme, a primitive allowing the owner of a private key to delegate to a third party the right to sign certain messages on its behalf, and anyone to verify whether the signature is valid. Now, the most efficient proxy signature scheme is proposed by Boldyreva et.al [14], and it is composed of triple schnorr schemes.

Based on the framework proposed in [12], we give the application of CBS scheme to SSO problem. Using new proposed CBS scheme, which is composed of two schnorr schemes, our method is much more efficient than the scheme in [12]. In the public key based framework, the identity provider, the user and the application servers share their corresponding public keys. The construction has four main components:

1. Access Control List(ACL): The identity provider stores an access control list, which contains unique IDs of the applications a user is allowed to access. For each user, it is denoted by $ACL_{id} = (ID_0, ID_1, ..., ID_n)$.

2. Identity ticket: Identity ticket is a certificate generated by the identity provider. During a session timespan t, it is represented as

$$IDt_{id} = Certify(pk, msk, pk_{id}, ID, t)$$

where ID is user's identity which is listed in the table ACL_{id}, pk_{id} is the public key of the user, and (pk, msk) is the identity provider's key pair.

3. Application ticket: Application ticket is a message containing a given application's unique ID and a CBS signature of ID message generated by a user who using the identity ticket as the $cert$. It is denoted by

$$APPt = (Sign(usk_{id}, IDt_{id}, ID_i, AppID_i), AppID_i)$$

where $ID_i \in ACL_{id}$.

4. Identity broker is an application that helps user to manage identity ticket and application ticket requests.

After identity provider successfully verify the user's identity, it generates the identity ticket and sends it to the user. And the application sign-on procedure is proceeded as follows:

Step a. After storing the identity ticket in the user's computer, the identity broker waits for application sign-on requests.

Step b. When the user wants to access an application, the identity broker receives an application sign-on request from the user. The identity broker generates and sends an application ticket to the application server.

Step c. After receiving the application ticket, the application server verifies its correctness by running $Verify(pk_{id}, pk, APPt)$. If the ticket is valid, it confirms that the identity provider has authenticated the user and that he has the proper access rights. Otherwise, it aborts.

From the unforgeability property of the certificate-based signature scheme, an attacker(including the identity provider) cannot forge an valid application ticket on behalf of the user in order to obtain access to the applications, so the scheme is secure as the one based on proxy signature scheme.

5   Conclusions

In this paper, based on Schnorr signature scheme, we present a new CBS scheme without pairings, which is very efficient and particularly suitable to be implemented in some power-constrained devices, such as wireless sensor networks. In addition, we give a new application of certificate-based signature scheme to the Single sign-on problem, which is of great importance to current distributed application environments such as cloud computing. Based on our new presented CBS scheme, the new SSO method is much more efficient than the one based on proxy signature scheme.

Acknowledgments. This work is supported by the Priority Academic Program Development of Jiangsu Higher Education Institutions(PAPD), the National Information Security 242 Project of China(Grant No.2012A138) and National Natural Science Foundation (NSF) of China (Grant No. 61373006, 61302158).

References

1. Shamir, A.: Identity-Based Cryptosystems and Signature Schemes. In: Blakely, G.R., Chaum, D. (eds.) CRYPTO 1984. LNCS, vol. 196, pp. 47–53. Springer, Heidelberg (1985)
2. Boneh, D., Franklin, M.: Identity-Based Encryption from the Weil Pairing. In: Kilian, J. (ed.) CRYPTO 2001. LNCS, vol. 2139, pp. 213–229. Springer, Heidelberg (2001)
3. Gentry, C.: Certificate-based Encryption and the Certificate Revocation Problem. In: Biham, E. (ed.) EUROCRYPT 2003. LNCS, vol. 2656, pp. 272–293. Springer, Heidelberg (2003)
4. Kang, B.G., Park, J.H., Hahn, S.G.: A certificate-based signature scheme. In: Okamoto, T. (ed.) CT-RSA 2004. LNCS, vol. 2964, pp. 99–111. Springer, Heidelberg (2004)
5. Li, J., Huang, X., Mu, Y., Susilo, W., Wu, Q.: Certificate-based signature: Security model and efficient construction. In: López, J., Samarati, P., Ferrer, J.L. (eds.) EuroPKI 2007. LNCS, vol. 4582, pp. 110–125. Springer, Heidelberg (2007)
6. Liu, J.K., Baek, J., Susilo, W., Zhou, J.: Certificate-Based Signature Schemes without Pairings or Random Oracles. In: Wu, T.-C., Lei, C.-L., Rijmen, V., Lee, D.-T. (eds.) ISC 2008. LNCS, vol. 5222, pp. 285–297. Springer, Heidelberg (2008)
7. Au, M.H., Liu, J.K., Susilo, W., Yuen, T.H.: Certificate based (linkable) ring signature. In: Dawson, E., Wong, D.S. (eds.) ISPEC 2007. LNCS, vol. 4464, pp. 79–92. Springer, Heidelberg (2007)
8. Liu, J., Bao, F., Zhou, J.: Short and Efficient Certificate-Based Signature. Cryptology ePrint Archive, Report 2011/192 (2011), http://eprint.iacr.org/
9. Mell, P., Grance, T.: Draft NIST working definition of cloud computing (2009), http://csrc.nist.gov/groups/SNS/cloud-computing/index.html (referenced on June 3, 2009)

10. De Clercq, J.: Single sign-on architectures. In: Davida, G.I., Frankel, Y., Rees, O. (eds.) InfraSec 2002. LNCS, vol. 2437, pp. 40–58. Springer, Heidelberg (2002)
11. Dodson, B., Sengupta, D., Boneh, D., Lam, M.S.: Secure, consumer-friendly web authentication and payments with a phone. In: Gris, M., Yang, G. (eds.) Mobi-CASE 2010. LNICST, vol. 76, pp. 17–38. Springer, Heidelberg (2012)
12. David, B.M., Tonicelli, R., Nascimento, A., et al.: Secure single sign-on and web authentication. Cryptology ePrint Archive, Report 2011/246, http://eprint.iacr.org/2011/246.pdf
13. Mambo, M., Usuda, K., Okamoto, E.: Proxy signatures for delegating signing operation. In: Proceedings of the 3rd ACM Conference on Computer and Communications Security, CCS 1996, pp. 48–57. ACM, New York (1996)
14. Boldyreva, A., Palacio, A., Warinschi, B.: Secure proxy signature schemes for delegation of signing rights. Journal of Cryptology 25(1), 1–58 (2012)

Information Interaction in Wireless Sensor Networks Based on Socially Aware Computing

Honggang Zhao*, Xiufang Ma, and Chen Shi

Xi'an Communication Institute, Xi'an, 710106, China
`hgz_nwpu@163.com`

Abstract. The integration of pervasive computing and social computing results in a new emerging research field - Socially Aware Computing. This new paradigm makes it possible to study Wireless Sensor Networks (WSN) as a social network, in which the embedded sensors are the main entities as opposed to human beings in a traditional social network. Therefore, the combination of WSN and Socially Aware Computing holds great promise and challenge to use the sensory data to understand human behavior, human mobility, and ultimately to help solve human social problems. In this paper, we propose an information interaction infrastructure in WSN based on Socially Aware Computing, in which the sensory context is used to recognize a broad range of complex human activities and environmental situations. We also present the information interaction challenges for WSN integrated into the Internet and point out the future work in this area.

Keywords: Wireless Sensor Networks, Socially Aware Computing, Internet of Things, Information Interaction.

1 Introduction

Wireless Sensor Networks (WSN) are playing more and more a key role in many application scenarios such as healthcare, agriculture, environment monitoring, and smart metering. It is clear that the potential of WSN paradigm will be fully unleashed once WSN are integrated into the Internet [1, 2], becoming part of the Internet of Things (IoT). However, it is necessary to discuss how to resolve the information interaction problems faced by WSN integrated into Internet, in which sensory data is used to understand human behavior, human mobility, and human activities, and ultimately to help solve human social problems. This is different from the traditional sensor networks [3–6].

While the concept of social awareness has been developed in the field of Computer Supported Cooperative Work for decades, the notion of Socially Aware Computation and Communication has only recently been raised by Alex Pentland [7]. The integration of pervasive computing and social computing results in a new emerging research field in computer science - Socially Aware Computing [8, 9], which aims to leverage the large-scale and diverse sensing devices

---

* Corresponding author.

L. Sun, H. Ma, and F. Hong (Eds.): CWSN 2013, CCIS 418, pp. 71–81, 2014.

that can be deployed in human daily lives to recognize individual behaviors, discover group interaction patterns, and support communication and collaboration [10–12]. Therefore, Socially Aware Computing brings new light to the research of information interaction in WSN integrated into the Internet.

The rest of the paper is organized as follows. Section 2 outlines the information interaction challenges for WSN integrated into the Internet. In Section 3, an information interaction infrastructure in WSN based on Socially Aware Computing is proposed. In section 4, the paper will describe some of the related work that was already done in this new area. Finally, section 5 concludes the paper pointing future research trends in this area.

2   Information Interaction Challenges for WSN Integrated into the Internet

When WSN are integrated into the Internet, more complicated information is collected and mined to understand human behavior and ultimately to help solve human social problems, which brings the new information interaction challenges.

Representation of Heterogeneous Information. When WSN are integrated into the Internet, heterogeneous information is collected from different types of sensor nodes which might measure different data and perform different tasks [22]. The nodes might have different sensors for monitoring the environment [13, 14]. Therefore, multi-source information fusion estimation methods should be given to represent complicated information [23, 24].

Interaction Between Various Sensor Nodes. In traditional sensor networks, all sensor nodes of one type are able to communicate with each other and build a sensor subnet. While in WSN that has been integrated into the Internet, many exiting sensor platforms have different radio modules and are thus not able to communicate with each other [14, 15]. Then the interaction architecture should be provided, thus the sensor nodes in different subnets can interact with necessary information [10, 11], which includes sensor node hardware details (e.g. chip, transceiver), sensor node software details (e.g. operating system versions), and dynamic properties (e.g. battery).

Interpretation of Contextual Information. The sensor node context is the information which is not related to the real human behavior and human activities. This can be location, radio information and its capabilities [24, 25], which can only help to understand more about the sensor and its surroundings. Then data gathering and logical methods for context interpretation should be studied to understand human activities [35, 36].

The new generation of sensor nodes has realized the early vision of context awareness. The next step for WSN should be facilitating real-world impact of more complex recognition, moving toward next-generation opportunistic recognition configurations and large-scale ensembles of sensor nodes interacting with communities of human. When WSN are integrated into the Internet, they will collect and analyze data with an unprecedented breadth and depth and scale.

Socially Aware Computing makes it possible that sensory data can be compiled into comprehensive pictures of both individual and group behavior, with the potential to transform our understanding of our lives, organizations, and societies.

3 Information Interaction Infrastructure in WSN Based on Socially Aware Computing

When WSN are integrated into the Internet, the sensory context is much more than simply used to recognize motion states and location. In this section, an Information Interaction Infrastructure in WSN based on Socially Aware Computing (IIISAC) is proposed, in which the sensory context is used to recognize a broad range of complex human activities and environmental situations.

3.1 Architecture

In order to support a variety of social applications, the IIISAC must meet several requirements. Firstly, it must accept input from diverse sensor nodes and differentiate information based on interaction type and intensity. Exposing relationship type and strength lets applications not only use context-relevant relationships but also compare these relationships. For example, sensor nodes follow the process of overhearing sensor readings of nearby nodes and then comparing them to their local sensor readings. If the remote sensor reading are correlated closely enough with the local sensor readings (they are within a threshold set by decaying the correlation of values based on the distance between the sensor ranges), then the remote sensor reading is considered to be valid.

Secondly, the infrastructure must allow for human-controlled fusion of sensory context. For example, many studies already indicated that cooperative learning can promote learner's interest than learning process purely based on individual competition, so that learners could get more enthusiastic while they can get involved in learning activities. We can utilize wireless sensing technology as a tool to detect learner's interaction by sensing two or more learners' distances in certain amount of time. We can also group students through shared activities and interests. In any case, the choice and relative importance of the relevant sensory information should be personalized and fully under the human's control.

Finally, the infrastructure must include a persistent social knowledge management service, which can be scalable with the number of human communities and the number of sensor nodes. Such a service should support a variety of social requests through a basic API. For example, a researcher might want to know the effect of different irrigation intervals on water saving and grain yield under a new planting technique by asking the research assistants of his partners, who might have conducted these experiments. This query requires access to a neighborhood of distance 2 from the enquiring researcher, making demands on the distribution of the social information on storage nodes and node availability in a decentralized service.

These three requirements correspond loosely to the architectural components that Fig. 1 depicts. When WSN are integrated into the Internet, it is not only possible to obtain fine grain real-time information about the Physical World but also to act upon that information. Context-aware sensor nodes can infer their own readings from knowledge of readings in the neighborhood and their own history. Such WSN is a step toward autonomous reliable networks where sensor nodes not only sense the environment and report their readings, but also perform more sophisticated tasks such as detection of possible outliers, and so forth.

WSN will benefit when sensory information is added to blogs, virtual communities, and social networks applications. This transformation of data derived from sensor networks into a valuable resource for information hungry applications will benefit from techniques being developed for the Cloud Computing and Mobile Agent technologies. Since Cloud Computing provides plenty of application, platforms and infrastructure over the Internet, it might be combined with WSN in the application areas such as environmental monitoring, weather forecasting, transportation business, healthcare, military application etc, in which we can bring various sensor nodes deployed for different applications under one roof and look it as a single virtual WSN entity through Cloud Computing infrastructure. Besides, autonomous intelligent agents can be disseminated to represent various types of actors that interact inside a virtual physical world. Mobile agents can be used to greatly reduce the communication cost, especially over low bandwidth links, by moving the processing function to the data rather than bring the data to a central processor. Human's request can be a task specific executable code traverses the relevant sensor nodes to gather data.

When WSN are combined with Socially Aware Computing, advanced feedbacks can be given by the combination of correlated sensory information, such as fire occurrence (a combination of the following inter-related sensory information: "high temperature" and "presence of carbon monoxide"). When the relation among the sensory information is temporal, ordered correlated events can be interpreted resulting in more advanced feedbacks that go from simple questions, such as "what is the cabin air pressure" to "why did the aircraft window crack". Besides, human behaviors can be interpreted by the gesture analysis of camera signals or by the voice recognition of microphone signals.

IIISAC makes decision support possible to control the physical world around us, such as decision support system for resource-poor farmers. Sensor nodes are placed in comparable fields, where different water conservation measures are used. In this way, comparative readings of soil moisture can be obtained. When human element is introduced into this decision support system, correlation between the recent trend of soil moisture values recorded by sensor nodes and the water requirements for deficit irrigation can be analyzed. Then the farmer can predict the behavior of his crop and use simple water conservation measures.

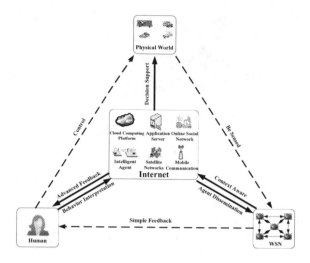

Fig. 1. Information Interaction Infrastructure in WSN Based on Socially Aware Computing

3.2   Usage Scenario

Vehicular transportation is, and it is projected to remain, the most popular way for transporting people and goods among places. With a growing population and continuous development, the widespread use of vehicles has become a real challenge, which requires the combat of the awful side-effects of road traffic. Road transportation is also widely recognized as a significant source of pollution world wide. The problem of air pollution has drastically aggravated in the last few decades, especially the increase in vehicle traffic emissions of sulphur dioxide, carbon dioxide, carbon monoxide, and other pollutants. So the Intelligent Transport Systems (ITS) should be advanced applications which, without embodying intelligence as such, aim to provide innovative services relating to different modes of transport and traffic management, enable various users to be better informed and make smarter use of transport networks, and provide real time information about air pollution to the public. Fig. 3 depicts a detailed usage scenario of ITS, in which modern vehicles can be considered as mobile sensor nodes (Fig. 2).

Modern vehicles can communicate with each other (vehicle-to-vehicle) by the on-board communication devices and form a local sensor subnet, which can be integrated into the Internet through roadside access points (vehicle-to-infrastructure). Then devices fitted to vehicles have the potential to deliver a "social aware environment" where individuals, vehicles and physical world can co-exist and cooperate, thus delivering more knowledge about the transport environment, the state of the network and who indeed is travelling or wishes to travel. Adjacent vehicles can be sensed by radars, location and speed information can be acquired by GPS, the traffic conditions can therefore be inferred by the computing platform. When a traffic accident occurs, drivers can also report

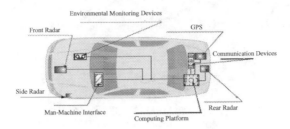

Fig. 2. Modern Vehicle

the accident to the Transport Department through Man-Machine Interface. Air pollution sensory information is collected by environmental monitoring devices.

Because various sensor subnets formed by vehicles have been integrated into the Internet, the Socially Aware Computing can be used to maximize the capacity and to enhance the performance of ITS, which is the warehouse for the collection, processing and dissemination of comprehensive transport information. Optimum driving route search service can be provided for motorists based on options such as distance, time and toll. One-stop portal for a multimodal public transport point-to-point route search service can also be provided for users. Additionally, value-added service providers in the private sector, including telecommunication companies, fleet and freight operators, logistic and IT organizations, can make use of the correlated information for the development of ITS applications such as car navigation, fleet management systems and personalized information services to the public.

ITS can provide dynamic decision support by integrating the control and operation of traffic signals within a district, such as providing better co-ordination of traffic lights at road intersections to help motorists and pedestrians cross roads and junctions safely and efficiently. ITS can also provide the journey time indication service that can provide the estimated journey time, to assist motorists to make an informed route choice.

4   Related Work

WSN have been considered as an integral part of the IoT paradigm [17, 18], in which sensor nodes will be able to dynamically exchange information all over the world in semantically interoperable ways [13–16]. Because of the IPv4 addresses exhaustion, 6LoWPAN protocol [20] has been used in ZigBees Smart Energy 2.0 (SEP2.0) [19] to encapsulate the proprietary ZigBee packet structure within compressed IPv6 packets. As the SEP2.0 is adopted in the Smart Grid, sensors will fully infiltrate our everyday lives. In the meanwhile, the research of Socially Aware Computing [21] has been focused on the large-scale pervasive sensing and search, pattern mining of human communication through phones and instant messaging, group interaction and collaboration. More researchers have realized that WSN and Social Aware Computing can fruitfully interface to strengthen capabilities of WSN and improve our daily lives.

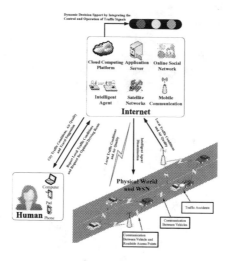

Fig. 3. Intelligent Transport Systems

4.1   Enhanced Sensing Capabilities

Alexis P. et al [11] presented the contribution of social network analysis to sensor networks and gave an example of Vehicular Ad Hoc Networks. Wearable sensor nodes are designed to facilitate group interaction in large meetings and acquire a wide range of data for analyzing social dynamics in [25]. Highly versatile badges are designed in [26], which are equipped with wireless infrared and radio frequency, and a lot of sensor to collect data which can be used to develop features and algorithms aimed at classifying and predicting individual and group behavior. A new scenario is envisioned in [27], where users develop their own participatory urban sensing projects at a large scale through the use of social networks. Consequently, users can participate in campaigns created by other users, according to their sensitivities and interests, exploiting the existing enormous social interconnections offered by existing social networking tools. Literature [28] discusses the key problems which arise in the integration of sensors and social networks. Literature [12] presents the deployment of a wireless sensor network applied to the evaluation of the intensity and the frequency of contacts between tuberculosis infected patients in a particular service unit of a hospital in Paris to track and better understand antimicrobial-resistant bacteria. Literature [36] has pointed out that privacy, security, legal and other related issues may arise from these Wireless Body Area Networks. Some of the interesting research areas are highlighted in [29], where sensors and social networks can fruitfully interface, from sensors providing contextual information in context-aware and personalized social applications, to using social networks as "storage infrastructures" for sensor information. In [35] wireless sensing technology is utilized as a tool to detect learner's interaction by sensing two or more learners' distances in certain amount of time. Based on the mining social interaction, this study claims that social interaction should be considered as an essential factor while formulating cooperative learning groups. A multimedia search engine is designed in [30], which can respond to social queries through integrating social networks with sensor networks. In [34], social-network models are transformed into behavioral feedback displays. These ambient displays, which reflect data on remote and face-to-face interaction gathered by sensor nodes, are intended to raise awareness of social connectedness as a dynamic and controllable aspect of well being.

4.2   Better Network Performance

Kumar P. et al [10] argued that nodes of the sensor networks had their own social life, and based on that assumption, they leveraged ideas from social networks to show how the nodes could communicate in a social networking style to achieve significant efficiency. A selective reprogramming approach is proposed to simplify and automate the process of delivering a code update to a target subset of sensor nodes in [32]. Update dissemination relies on a novel protocol exploiting the social behavior of the monitored individuals. A framework is proposed in [33], which creates an overlay network to create a secure communication passage for dynamic sensory data communication among users belonging to the same community of interest. A. Friggeri et al [31] addressed the challenges of capturing physical proximity and social interaction by means of a wireless network. Alberto Rosi et al [37] explored how social sensing could be integrated into pervasive systems and how sensor networks might utilize social network tools to distribute the sensing responsibilities amongst the networks. A new distributed approach is presented in [38], which establishes reputation-based trust among sensor nodes in order to identify malfunctioning and malicious sensor nodes and minimize their impact on applications. Simulation results show that this approach better than an approach that uses static redundancy levels in terms of reduced energy consumption and longer life of the network. In [39], fusion of information from sensor network nodes that produce different beliefs using particle filters is examined. Strategies for improved inference while saving power on communication are also addressed.

4.3   Typical Applications

SmartSantander [40] proposes a unique in the world city-scale experimental research facility in support of typical applications and services for a smart city. Its EkoBus system deployed in the cities of Belgrade and Pancevo is made available for experimentation on IoT data level. The sytem utilizes public transportation vehicles in the city of Belgrade and the city of Pancevo to monitor a set of environmental parameters (e.g. temperature, humidity) over a large area as well as to provide additional information for the end-user like the location of the buses and estimated arrival times to bus stops. SensorPlanet [41] is a Nokia-initiated cooperation on large-scale wireless sensor networks. The objectives of Sensor-Planet are to make mobile handset-oriented wireless sensor network research easier, allow creation and sharing of large data sets that can be mined by many parties, and accelerate concept innovation for consumer-oriented wireless sensor network research. The UrbanSensing project [42] will bring a new product to the urban design, city planning and urban management market: a platform extracting patterns of use and citizens perceptions related or concerning city spaces, through robust analysis of User Generated Content (UGC) shared by the city users and inhabitants over social networks and digital media. It focuses on developing wireless sensing systems and applying this revolutionary technology to critical scientific and societal pursuits.

5 Conclusions

The combination of WSN and Socially Aware Computing leads to applications that can sense the context of a user in much better ways and thus provides more personalized and detailed solutions. Applications are deeper integrated into the daily life and context-awareness through social network and sensor network data becomes a key enabler for these emerging services. Although some achievements have been made in this new area, a lot of work has to be done.

Multi-objective QoS Protocols. When WSN are integrated into the Internet, Quality of Service (QoS) guarantee is difficult and more challenging due to the fact that the available resources of sensors and the various applications running over these networks have different constraints in their nature and requirements. Therefore, multi-objective QoS protocols (e.g. MAC protocols, routing protocols) should be studied to deal with diverse requirements by different applications under various network constraints.

Evaluation Systems and Experimental Platforms. When WSN are studied as a social network, the sensor nodes resemble individuals in a way that they communicate with their peers, sometimes selectively hiding some information, sometimes selectively exposing some other information, generating or forwarding information, sharing resources, joining or leaving the network. Therefore, we need the evaluation systems and the experimental platforms (e.g. IPv6-enabled WSN platforms) to study how individuals interact with each other.

Applications Led Research. WSN research as a whole suffers a lack of practical application scenarios for which such networks are the best solution. Researchers generally do not emphasize on the application domains they are trying to address. Therefore they cannot accurately assess the efficiency of their proposal because for different application areas there are different technical issues. Socially Aware Computing is a multidisciplinary research area, where efficient implementation of systems requires close collaboration between end users, hardware designers, and software developers. Therefore, the combination of WSN and Socially Aware Computing will benefit from the applications led research.

References

1. Rodrigues, J.J.P.C., Neves, P.A.C.S.: A survey on IP-based wireless sensor network solutions. International Journal of Communication Systems 23(8), 963–981 (2010)
2. IPSO Alliance, http://www.ipso-alliance.org
3. Hu, Y., Sun, Y., Yin, B.: Information Sensing and Interaction Technology in Internet of Things. Chinese Journal of Computers 35(6), 1147–1163 (2012)

4. Demirkol, I., Ersoy, C., Alagoz, F.: MAC protocols for wireless sensor networks: a survey. IEEE Communications Magazine 44(4), 115–121 (2006)
5. Singh, S.K., Singh, M.P., Singh, D.K.: Routing protocols for wireless sensor networks: a survey. International Journal of Computer Science & Engineering Survey (IJCSES) 1(2), 63–83 (2010)
6. Oliveira, L.M.L., Rodrigues, J.J.P.C.: Wireless Sensor Networks: a Survey on Environmental Monitoring. Proceedings of JCM, 143–151 (2011)
7. Pentland, A.: Socially aware computation and communication. IEEE Computer 38(3), 33–40 (2005)
8. Pentland, A., et al.: Computational Social Science. Science 323(5915), 721–723 (2009)
9. Yu, Z., Yu, Z., Zhou, X.: Socially Aware Computing. Chinese Journal of Computers 35(1), 16–26 (2012)
10. Padmanabh, K., Paul, S., Kumar, A.: On Social Behavior of Wireless Sensor Node. In: Proceedings of the 2nd International Conference on Communication Systems and Networks, pp. 429–436 (2010)
11. Papadimitriou, A., Katsaros, D., Manolopoulos, Y.: Social Network Analysis and its Applications in Wireless Sensor and Vehicular Networks. e-Democracy, 411–420 (2009)
12. Fleury, E.: Measuring Social Interactions Using Wireless Sensor Network-Hospital case studies. In: 1st Workshop on Scientific Computing in Health Applications
13. Zuniga, M., Krishnamachari, B.: Integrating future large-scale wireless sensor networks with the internet. USC Computer Science, Tech. Rep. (2003)
14. Mayer, K., Fritsche, W.: IP-enabled wireless sensor networks and their integration into the internet. In: Proceedings of the first International Conference on Integrated Internet Ad Hoc and Sensor Networks, p. 5. ACM (2006)
15. Rodrigues, J.J.P.C., Neves, P.A.C.S.: A survey on IP-based wireless sensor network solutions. International Journal of Communication Systems 23(8), 963–981 (2010)
16. Wang, X.-N., Gao, D.-M.: Research and Design of Next-Generation Full-IP Wireless Sensor Network. Journal of University of Electronic Science and Technology of China 39(6), 924–928 (2010)
17. Roman, R., Lopez, J., Alcaraz, C.: Do Wireless Sensor Networks Need to be Completely Integrated into the Internet? Future Internet of People, Things and Services (IoPTS) eco-Systems, Brussels (December 2, 2009)
18. Zuniga, M., Krishnamachari, B.: Integrating future large-scale wireless sensor networks with the internet. USC Computer Science, Tech. Rep. (2003)
19. http://www.zigbee.org/Standards/Overview.aspx
20. RFC 4919. Pv6 over Low-Power Wireless Personal Area Networks (6LoWPANs): Overview, Assumptions, Problem Statement, and Goals
21. Angulo, C., Godo, L.: Beyond the user: A review of socially aware computing. Artificial Intelligence Research and Development 163, 6–8 (2007)
22. Reddy, S., Shilton, K., Denisov, G., et al.: Biketastic: sensing and mapping for better biking. In: Proceedings of the 28th International Conference on Human Factors in Computing Systems, pp. 1817–1820. ACM (2010)
23. Beale, R.: Supporting social interaction with smart phones. IEEE Pervasive Computing 4(2), 35–41 (2005)
24. Moturu, S.T., Khayal, I., Aharony, N., et al.: Using social sensing to understand the links between sleep, mood, and sociability. In: 2011 IEEE Third International Conference on Privacy, Security, Risk and Trust (Passat) and 2011 IEEE Third International Conference on Social Computing (Socialcom), pp. 208–214. IEEE (2011)

25. Laibowitz, M., Gips, J., Aylward, R., et al.: A sensor network for social dynamics. In: Proceedings of the 5th International Conference on Information Processing in Sensor Networks, pp. 483–491. ACM (2006)
26. Paradiso, J.A., Gips, J., Laibowitz, M., et al.: Identifying and facilitating social interaction with a wearable wireless sensor network. Personal and Ubiquitous Computing 14(2), 137–152 (2010)
27. Krontiris, I., Freiling, F.C.: Integrating people-centric sensing with social networks: A privacy research agenda. In: 2010 8th IEEE International Conference on Pervasive Computing and Communications Workshops (PERCOM Workshops), pp. 620–623. IEEE (2010)
28. Aggarwal, C.C., Abdelzaher, T.: Integrating sensors and social networks. Social Network Data Analytics, 379–412 (2011)
29. John, G., et al.: Integrating Social Networks and Sensor Networks. W3C Workshop on the Future of Social Networking (2009)
30. Soldatos, J., Draief, M., Macdonald, C., et al.: Multimedia search over integrated social and sensor networks. In: Proceedings of the 21st International Conference Companion on World Wide Web, pp. 283–286. ACM (2012)
31. Friggeri, A., Chelius, G., Fleury, E., et al.: Reconstructing social interactions using an unreliable wireless sensor network. Computer Communications 34(5), 609–618 (2011)
32. Pásztor, B., Mottola, L., Mascolo, C., et al.: Selective reprogramming of mobile sensor networks through social community detection. Wireless Sensor Networks, 178–193 (2010)
33. Rahman, M.A., El Saddik, A., Gueaieb, W.: SenseFace: a sensor network overlay for social networks. In: Instrumentation and Measurement Technology Conference, I2MTC 2009, pp. 1031–1036. IEEE (2009)
34. Morris, M.E.: Social networks as health feedback displays. IEEE Internet Computing 9(5), 29–37 (2005)
35. Hsieh, J.C., Chen, C.M., Lin, H.F.: Social Interaction Mining Based on Wireless Sensor Networks for Promoting Cooperative Learning Performance in Classroom Learning Environment. In: 2010 6th IEEE International Conference on Wireless, Mobile and Ubiquitous Technologies in Education (WMUTE), pp. 219–221. IEEE (2010)
36. Al Ameen, M., Kwak, K.: Social Issues in Wireless Sensor Networks with Healthcare Perspective. The International Arab Journal of Information Technology 8(1), 52–58 (2011)
37. Rosi, A., Mamei, M., Zambonelli, F., et al.: Social sensors and pervasive services: Approaches and perspectives. In: 2011 IEEE International Conference on Pervasive Computing and Communications Workshops (PERCOM Workshops), pp. 525–530. IEEE (2011)
38. Probst, M.J., Kasera, S.K.: Statistical trust establishment in wireless sensor networks. In: 2007 International Conference on Parallel and Distributed Systems, vol. 2, pp. 1–8. IEEE (2007)
39. Duric, P.M.: Distributed inference and social learning in wireless sensor networks. IEEE Signal Processing Society (2011)
40. Smart Santander, http://www.smartsantander.eu/
41. Sensorplanet, http://www.sensorplanet.org/
42. Center for embedded networked sensing, http://research.cens.ucla.edu/

A Dynamic Underwater Sensor Network Architecture Based on Physical Clustering and Intra-cluster Autonomy

Hainan Chen[1,2], Xiaoling Wu[1,*], Yanwen Wang[1], Guangcong Liu[2],
Lei Shu[3], and Xiaobo Zhang[2]

[1] Guangzhou Institute of Advanced Technology, Chinese Academy of Sciences, China
[2] Guangdong University of Technology, Guangzhou, China
[3] Guangdong University of Petrochemical Technology, China
xl.wu@giat.ac.cn

Abstract. In this paper, a dynamic architecture is presented for underwater sensor networks based on the physical clustering and intra-cluster autonomy according to the traditional logical clustering theory. In this architecture, the cluster headers eliminate the negative effects of the current and improve the stability of the underwater sensor networks by drawing cluster nodes to do circular motion through cluster cables. This wired communication inside cluster and wireless communication among clusters improve the speed of the data transmission and delivering. On the other hand, in order to solve energy-intensive problem, an energy harvesting technology is considered to provide nodes with sustainable energy. This dynamic underwater sensor network architecture provides a basic model to study the high-performance and reusable underwater sensor networks.

Keywords: underwater sensor network, physical clustering, intra-cluster autonomy, dynamic architecture, energy harvesting.

1   Introduction

UWSNs (Underwater Wireless Sensor Networks) are new type of wireless sensor networks, which are automatically established by the underwater sensor nodes deployed into some specific sea areas, using their self-organized function [1]. It is derived from terrestrial wireless sensor networks technology. In UWSNs, sensors are used for monitoring and gathering real-time data generated from the specific areas. After being processed by using data fusion technique, these data will be sent to the base station which floats on the surface of the water and finally transmit to users.

UWSNs are applied for the underwater scenes. With the impact of the specificity and complexity of the aqueous medium, the UWSNs have lots of difference

---

* Corresponding author.

L. Sun, H. Ma, and F. Hong (Eds.): CWSN 2013, CCIS 418, pp. 82–92, 2014.

from the traditional wireless sensor networks. these differences are mainly reflected on transmission mode and application environment. Firstly, the UWSNs primarily use acoustic communication mode, whose propagation delay is remarkably longer than that of electromagnetic wave, leading to the shorter communication distance and higher density of sensor distribution. On the other hand, the bandwidth of acoustic communication is limited and the bit error rate is higher due to the underwater environment. Another important difference is that current flow and aquatic life have great influence on the movement of underwater sensors, leading to the change of network topology. And then the topology of network would alter. For all the reasons mentioned above, the underwater sensor network applications have been greatly restricted. Therefore, research on the architecture and topology control of UWSNs will have great impact on improving its performance.

In the architecture, Current research is basically focused on three-layer architecture of underwater sensor networks [2]. The base station deployed on the surface of the water is the first layer. This layer is responsible for receiving the data transmitted by the nodes in the sensing area, and delivers these data to the control and analysis center through some efficient transmission mode, for example radio wave transmission. The second layer is composed of many floating nodes which are distributed in the entire monitored space. These nodes are mobile. Their vertical position is adjusted by the node buoy, while horizontal position is determined with the direction of flow changes. In the third layer, the nodes are fixed on the bottom of the water through ropes or chains. We can adjust the length of the anchor chain by changing the node's vertical position. These nodes' position is relatively stable, hence, they can act as the reference nodes. This three-layer's architecture is capable for covering the entire monitored areas. Another famous UWSNs architecture is also based on this three layer's architecture, while several AUVs (Autonomous Underwater Vehicle) are applied to enhance the covering and control ability of the network through their mobility [3]. When monitoring shallow sea, some network model abandons the first and the second layer. In these networks, all nodes are fixed in the water through the anchoring chain, which adjust the node's position. Therefore, when the sea is not too deep, the nodes are able to cover the whole monitoring space [4]. All traditional network models need specific topology control algorithm to maintain the architecture of the network, which result in many problems in practice.

1.1   Problem of Traditional Underwater Sensor Networks

Almost all traditional underwater wireless sensor networks are based on three-layer architecture and accordingly, there are three types of sensor nodes, which are water surface nodes, floating nodes and fixed nodes. In this architecture, nodes are randomly distributed through corresponding topology control and routing algorithms, which are utilized to maintain the networks'architecture and complete the monitoring tasks. Underwater wireless sensor networks cannot be completely applied in reality due to the reasons below: 1) the underwater environment; 2) natural mobile property of aqueous medium; 3) humans are incapable to directly manipulate in underwater environment. Considering the effects cause by underwater wireless sensors and environment, the problems of traditional wireless sensor networks are mainly focused on two parts:

(1) Instability of Network Topology

Underwater wireless sensor networks are designed to monitor the underwater environment, in which the sensor nodes are entirely deployed underwater. The nodes' mobility is inevitable because of the water flow [5], which is a continuous and orientated movement. This flow movement will unavoidably lead to the movement of all wireless topology or more seriously, drives the entire topology out of the monitored area, which results in the failure of monitoring task [6]. Moreover, nodes cannot be precisely localized due to the flow movement, which make it very difficult for nodes localization [7]. Also, water movement and high density distribution of nodes will result in breakdown of the entire UWSNs. Some of the researchers have focused on dealing with the effects caused by the water flow. They have attempted to overcome the uncertainty brought in by nodes' movement via applying some prediction algorithms [8] [9] [10]. Although they have achieved some positive results, the practice of these results is highly limited due to the uncertainty of water movement. Therefore, the research on stability of UWSNs should be further investigated.

(2) Limitation of Energy

Energy consumption has always been considered in WSNs, especially in UWSNs. Both clustering algorithm and power control are designed to improve the energy efficiency. Generally speaking, sensors are incapable to obtain sufficient energy due to the following three reasons: 1) small size of nodes, 2) underwater deployment and 3) can't be directly manipulated by people. Hence, research on traditional architecture and topology control is primarily focused on how to maintain the function and communication quality of the networks with minimal energy cost and extend the nodes' life [11] [12]. In UWSNs, the energy cost of neighbors will dramatically increase if one of the nodes turns into inactive due to the insufficiency of energy. Finally, the whole UWSNs will paralyze. In order to solve this problem, some researchers proposed a new method called "energy harvesting"[13] [14], through which energy consumption problems can be theoretically solved. However in real practice, "energy harvesting"method cannot be completely implemented due to the limited methods of energy gathering and acquiring in underwater environment. Some widely used "energy harvesting"method, such as solar energy source and wind energy source are incapable to use in underwater environment directly, hence, the implementation of underwater "energy harvesting"technology still need long time research and experiment. On the other hand, to accomplish "energy harvesting"technology, the small size and the cost of the nodes are another challenge.

In summary, problem of UWSNs are mainly concentrated on 1) cannot be directly manipulated, 2) inflexible deployment and 3) complex topology. Since all nodes are randomly deployed underwater, the nodes cannot be recycled, which limit the performance of UWSNs and increase the deployment and maintenance cost. In order to solve the problems mentioned above, this paper presents a new UWSNs architecture based on the physical clustering and intra-cluster autonomy.

2 Architecture Model for Dynamic Underwater Sensor Networks

In this paper, a physical clustering method is proposed based on the traditional logical clustering concept. The key point is that cluster nodes are successively connected at equal distance via cable. Nodes with drive engine are regarded as cluster header, which are able to draw other nodes. Energy transmission and data communication are accomplished via cables in the cluster, while communication among clusters is completed through sound wave. The cluster headers manage the whole cluster's energy consumption, and determine the cluster's position through embedded rechargeable battery and solar panel, providing energy to all nodes within the cluster.

2.1 Physical Clustering

Different from logical clustering technique, cables are applied to connect the node, which physically classify the entire network into several clusters. Nodes within clusters communicate with each other via cables, which connect each two adjacent nodes in an equal distance. Cluster headers are capable to move independently through drive engines. Nodes within clusters move in a circle with a fixed center point and a radius which is the half-length of the node's maximal communication distance. These movements are driven by cluster headers with a specific speed, which will stay in a helical status. Fig.1 shows the nodes within a single cluster in steady and kinetic status, respectively.

Using this helical movement, the effects caused by water flow will be counter-acted, which changes the fact happened in traditional UWSNs that nodes move passively along with the water flow moves. According to this circling movement, although nodes still move, as an entity, nodes moves in a cycle, instead of moving some distance in a specific direction, which does not change the position of the entire cluster. More importantly, the position of cluster is able to be controlled since the cluster headers are controllable, resulting in that the entire UWSNs are controllable.

2.2 Intra-cluster Autonomy and Topology Control

Nodes' passive movement can be effectively avoided through this model, hence, this type of UWSNs are considered as immobile overall. The primary goal of this architecture is to maintain the connectivity and coverage of the network. Cluster headers are managed to come out to the surface of the water at times in order to obtain sufficient energy supply.

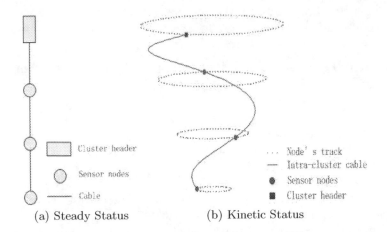

(a) Steady Status   (b) Kinetic Status

Fig. 1. Nodes within a Single Cluster in Steady (a) and Kinetic (b) Status

The cluster header is the brain of the whole cluster, through which nodes within the cluster are able to communicate with each other. Data fusion and nodes' mission allocation are operated by cluster headers. Moreover, the circling speed and radius are also determined by cluster headers. In order to increase the connectivity of the network and reduce collision frequency, nodes within different clusters are incapable to directly communicate with each other. Communications are only available between nodes and cluster headers or between two cluster headers. Data is transmitted from the bottom to the surface of the water, according to which data horizontal transmission between two clusters is avoided. When any node within the cluster is receiving data from a cluster header that belongs to another cluster, this data will be delivered to the cluster header within the same cluster. Then, the header informs other nodes to reject the same data package.

In this dynamic network architecture, cluster header moves in a circle, which overcomes the problem that the horizontal position of underwater nodes is uncontrollable. Although it can increase the flexibility of networks, nodes movements need a lot of energy consumption, which cannot be afforded by traditional UWSNs. Energy supply is necessary in order to support the entire network. Each cluster moves only in vertical direction due to the traction of cluster headers, which come out of the surface according to the hierarchical position and absorb energy via solar panels.

2.3   Dynamic Architecture

Cluster header provides energy for the whole cluster, and can move to some specific area. The entire cluster can be regarded as one logical node, which is controlled by the corresponding cluster header. The entire UWSNs are composed of two main components. The first one is the base station floated on the surface

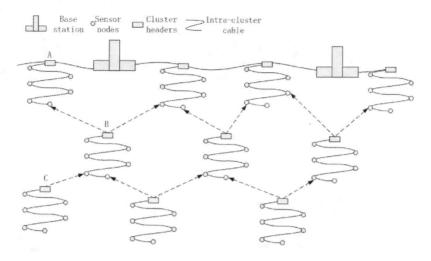

Fig. 2. Dynamic architecture for UWSNs

of the water, which is used to receive data generated by the underwater sensors and to provide energy to the nodes. The second one is the cluster that monitors underwater environment in some specific areas, gathering the corresponding data. This dynamic architecture is shown in Fig. 2.

Base stations float on the surface of the water, continuously gathering energy via solar panel and wind power generator, which is stored in high capacity battery, waiting for the docking among clusters. Base stations start to provide clusters with energy when cluster headers cannot independently gather sufficient energy. At the beginning, sensor nodes are deployed hierarchically measured by the cluster. Clusters in different layers exchange their position in every specific interval in order to maintain the energy collected by the cluster headers, which move out of the surface to gather solar energy. In Fig.2, A, B and C clusters located on different layers come out on to the surface one by one in order to obtain enough energy, which solve the problem that solar energy cannot be gathered in deep water.

3   Performance Analysis

3.1   Coverage Ratio Analysis

The UWSN presented in this paper is a type of dynamic network architecture. Fig.1 (b) shows the status under kinetic model. When the moving speed of cluster headers reaches a certain value, the monitoring gap caused by nodes' movement can be neglected, hence, expand the monitored and covered areas. Fig.3 shows the cross and longitudinal section for a single node's movement and sensing area.

According to the Fig.3, the sensing area generated by the circling movement is a concave sphere, which is shown in Fig.4 (a). For theoretical analysis,

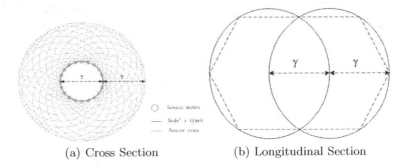

(a) Cross Section   (b) Longitudinal Section

Fig. 3. Cross (a) and Longitudinal (b) Section for a Single Node's Movement and Sensing Area

we extracted an octahedron inside the sphere as an approximate model, which is shown in Fig.4 (b). Therefore, the entire monitored area is shown in Fig.4 (c). Obviously, this analysis is based on traditional UWSNs, in which almost all underwater sensors are incapable to move independently. In order to improve the performance of monitoring, increase the nodes' distribution density becomes the only method. However, in this paper, the entire network is divided into several physical clusters, which are driven via cluster headers, making the entire network maneuverable. In order to increase the experimental accuracy, nodes are deployed in ideal status, which is the same status as in traditional UWSNs. Coverage rate and the number of nodes covered in the same area are also compared in this paper.

For easily analysis and calculation, definition based on the model shown in Fig.4 is:

$$r = \frac{1}{2} \times \gamma \tag{1}$$

where γ is the communication radius and r is the movement radius of cluster headers. This definition is to reduce the monitoring gap.

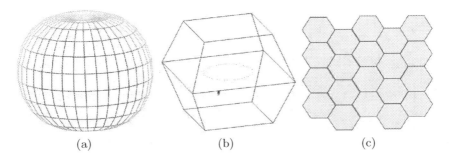

(a)   (b)   (c)

Fig. 4. Nodes' Sensing Area and Deployment Model

The sensing area of a single sensor is determined after communication radius has been determined. In Fig 4. (b), assuming v is the size of sensing area for a single node, and the entire volume dv can be calculated as:

$$dv = 2 \times \frac{(S_1 + S_2 + \sqrt{S_1 \times S_2}) \times h}{3} \tag{2}$$

where, S_1 and S_2 is the top and bottom areas of the model, respectively; h is the height of trapezoid. According to formula(1) and the models mentioned above, we can get:

$$S_1 = 2 \times \gamma^2 \tag{3}$$

$$S_2 = \frac{9}{2} \times \gamma^2 \tag{4}$$

$$h = \frac{\sqrt{3}}{2} \times \gamma \tag{5}$$

In this paper, a $100m \times 100m \times 100m$ area is considered as monitored area, in which coverage rate is calculated and compared with traditional body-centered cube, exploring the relationship between the number of nodes and the coverage ratio. Matlab tool is used in this paper. By observing Fig.5, it is clear that the coverage ratio is improved by this dynamic network architecture.

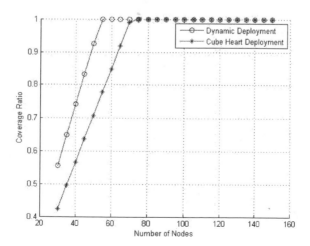

Fig. 5. Relationship between The Number of Nodes and Coverage Rate

3.2   Transmission Delay Analysis

In the architecture proposed in this paper, nodes within a cluster communicate with each other via cables. Compared to the underwater acoustic communications, the communication delay can be neglected if data is transmitted via cables. Moreover, there is no direct communication among nodes, which indirectly exchange data via cluster headers merely. Through this mechanism, data can be transmitted to the surface of the water in a fastest way, which is easy for data collection. In order to calculate the communication delay, we assume that when the cluster header is moving in a circle, the vertical distance between any two neighbor nodes is h:

$$h = \frac{\sqrt{3}}{2} \times \gamma \tag{6}$$

Because nodes within the same cluster connect each other via cables, the monitoring range for a single cluster can be regarded as a series of n vertically center-connected concave sphere areas, where n is the number of node in a cluster. Assume dt is the time of a node completing a circle. When dt is smaller than a threshold value, an event is considered to be sensible only by satisfying the following two conditions:

(1) The horizontal distance between the position of this event and a central axis of any cluster that moves in a circle is smaller than $\frac{\sqrt{3}}{2}\gamma$;
(2) The vertical distance between the position of this event and each sensor node within a cluster is smaller than h.

Once the event is sensed by clusters, data will be directly transmitted to the cluster header, who will send the data to the base station on the surface of the water via multi-hop mechanism. In this paper, an area of $100m \times 100m \times$

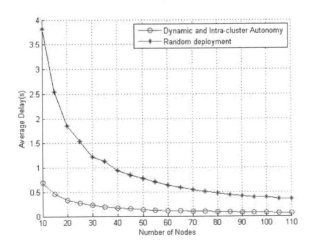

Fig. 6. Comparison of Delay between Two Different Architectures

$100m$ is simulated using Matlab. The relationship between delays of randomly transmitting data under different coverage rate is analyzed and then compared with traditional multi-hop mechanism. Fig. 6 shows this comparison. It is clear that the model presented in is paper has lower delay.

3.3   Energy Consumption

The dynamic autonomy architecture for network presented in this paper can effectively increase the flexibility of the network. It solves the problem that traditional WSNs are incapable to figure out. All these improvements are based on the ability of cluster headers, which need relatively higher energy supplement to overcome the power generated by the water flow. Hence, an energy-harvesting mechanism is proposed to provide the UWSNs with energy, which is based on the autonomous property of wireless sensor nodes. Base stations are also used to afford the entire UWSNs. Therefore, energy supplement can be guaranteed during transmission.

4   Conclusion

In this paper, a dynamic underwater sensor network architecture based on physical clustering and intro-cluster autonomy is presented in order to solve the problems raised by underwater environment. This physical clustering model is autonomous, in which nodes are connected via cables and move in a circle driven by cluster headers. This circular motion can counteract the power caused by the water flow. The entire network is able to be controlled by manipulating the cluster header in each cluster. On the other hand, an energy-harvesting mechanism is proposed to provide the UWSNs with energy. This energy-harvesting mechanism can be easily applied through such dynamic model. Compared to traditional UWSNs, we transfer the nodes' status from passive movements to controllable movements, which expand the covering and monitoring area and increase the flexibility and stability of the network topology. Also, this combination of wired communication within cluster and wireless communication among clusters raises the transmission speed and efficiency. The results show that this dynamic model is advanced compared to traditional UWSNs, especially in transmission delay and coverage rate, which is supposed to be a fundamental model in UWSNs research area in the future.

References

1. Akyildiz, I.F., Pompili, D., Melodia, T.: State of the art in protocol research for underwater acoustic sensor networks. In: Proc. of the 1 st ACM Int Workshop on Underwater Networks, pp. 7–16. ACM, New York (2006)
2. Sun, L.-J.: Overview of Topology Control Techniques in Underwater Acoustic Sensor Networks. Journal of Nanjing University of Posts and Telecommunications (Natural Science) 32(5) (2012)

3. Linfeng, L.: A topology recovery algorithm of underwater wireless sensor networks. In: 12th IEEE International Conference on Communication Technology, ICCT (2010)
4. Liu, L., Wang, R., Xiao, F.: Topology control algorithm for underwater wireless sensor networks using GPS-free mobile sensor nodes. Journal of Network and Computer Applications 35(6), 1953–1963 (2012)
5. Tezcan, H., Cayirci, E., Coskun, V.: A distributed scheme for 3D space coverage in tactical underwater sensor networks. In: Proc. of Military Communications Conf., pp. 697–703. IEEE Press, Monterey (2004)
6. Caruso, A., et al.: The Meandering Current Mobility Model and its Impact on Underwater Mobile Sensor Networks. In: The 27th Conference on Computer Communications, INFOCOM 2008. IEEE (2008)
7. Chandrasekhar, V.: Localization in underwater sensor networks: survey and challenges. In: WUWNet 2006 Proceedings of the 1st ACM International Workshop on Underwater Networks, pp. 33–40 (2006)
8. Zhong, Z., et al.: Scalable Localization with Mobility Prediction for Underwater Sensor Networks. IEEE Transactions on Mobile Computing 10(3), 335–348 (2011)
9. Akbari Torkestani, J.: Mobility prediction in mobile wireless networks. Journal of Network and Computer Applications 35(5), 1633–1645 (2012)
10. Liu, B.: Mobility improves coverage of sensor networks. In: MobiHoc 2005, Proceedings of the 6th ACM International Symposium on Mobile Ad Hoc Networking and Computing, pp. 300–308 (2005)
11. Yu, W., Fan, L., Dahlberg, T.A.: WSN14-1: Power Efficient 3-Dimensional Topology Control for Ad Hoc and Sensor Networks. In: Global Telecommunications Conference, GLOBECOM 2006. IEEE (2006)
12. Ovaliadis, K.: Energy Efficiency in Underwater Sensor Networks: A Research Review. Journal of Engineering Science and Technology Review 3(1), 151–156 (2010)
13. Rezaei, H.F., Kruger, A., Just, C.: An energy harvesting scheme for underwater sensor applications. In: 2012 IEEE International Conference on Electro/Information Technology (EIT), pp. 151–156 (2012)
14. Hormann, L.B., et al.: A wireless sensor node for river monitoring using MSP430 and energy harvesting. In: 2010 4th European Education and Research Conference, EDERC (2010)

Inferring Social Interests in Mobile Networks

Jibing Gong[1], Wenjun Yang[1], Wenyuan Liu[1], and Li Cui[2]

[1] College of Information Science and Engneering,
Yanshan University, Qinhuangdao, China
[2] Institute of Computing Technology, Chinese Academy of Sciences, Beijing, China
gongjibing@gmail.com

Abstract. Social interest refers to a kind of preference that an individual enjoys in social networks. In real world, people's social interests are influenced by various factors such as social relationships, historic social interests and users' private attributes. However, few publications systematically study the problem of social interest inferring in a real mobile network. In this work, we study the extent to which one's social interest can be inferred combining these above factors together, and investigate the Time-Space Probability Factor Graph Model (shortly, TS-FGM). We propose a novel social interest inferring approach based on TS-FGM and transfer the problem into the maximizing problem of the objective function of TS-FGM. In our approach, historic social interests are formalized as time factor, social relationships are formalized as space factor, as well as users' private attributes are formalized as attributes of network nodes. We validate the presented model on an real mobile communication network and find that it is possible to approximately infer 81% of users' social interests.

Keywords: Social Interest Inferring, Factor Graph Model, Mobile Networks.

1 Introduction

Social interest refers to a kind of preference and its related behaviors that an individual enjoys in social networks. Traditional social interest mining aims at web search logs, and is usually utilized for such these applications of search results diversification [1], interests-based recommendation based on interests [2] and scandals preventing [3], et al. However, in social networks, social interest plays an increasingly significant role in the following aspects: 1) dominating users' social behaviors; 2) generating individual tags; 3) containing implicit social ties among users. With the prevalent of social networks, e.g., 900 million Facebook users, 750 million China Mobile users and 500 million Sina Weibo users, social interest mining and analysis has become a hot research issue, and inferring social interests has important theoretical value and broad application prospects.

Inferring social interest is an important task in various social-networks-based applications such as searching product information and rating, recommending advertisement and services, as well as public sentiment surveillance. But, some challenges are still exist:

L. Sun, H. Ma, and F. Hong (Eds.): CWSN 2013, CCIS 418, pp. 93–101, 2014.
© Springer-Verlag Berlin Heidelberg 2014

- how to find the fundamental clues (patterns) that may subtly infer our social interests in the social network;
- during the inferring social interest, how to effectively put the social relationship factor (e.g., relatives, friends and colleagues relationship), historic (social) interest factor and users' private attributes (e.g., location) together;
- how accurate can we infer individuals' (social) interests, and how to evaluate merits of the proposed approach in a real mobile network.

To address these challenges, we try to systematically investigate the problem of social interest inferring in a real mobile network. Specifically, we first engage in some high-level investigation of how different factors correlate with individuals' interests, and formalize the problem of social interest inferring; based on Time-Space Probability Factor Graph Model (TS-FGM) [4], we then combine social relationships, historic social interest factor and users' private attributes together to build a unified model for the network; next, we propose a novel approach for users' social interests inferring; at last, we study on what influence on inferring accuracies of social interest these above factors will have in a real-world experimental data set.

2 Our Approach

2.1 Problem Definition

Traditionally, A mobile social network can be represented as $G = (V, E)$, where V is the set of $|V| = N$ users and $E \subset V \times V$ is the set of directed/undirected links between users. Given this, we can describe the other related definitions as follows.

Definition 1. *Social interest: A social interest h user u_i has at time t refers to certain interest or several related topics. It can be represented as a triple (h, u_i, t) (or shortly h_i^t). Let H^t be the set of social interests of all users at time t. Further we denote all users' social interests as the social interest $\boldsymbol{H} = \{(y, u_i, t)\}_{i,t}$.*

Without loss of generality, we first consider the binary social interest, that is $h_i^t \in \{0, 1\}$, where $h_i^t = 1$ indicates that user u_i had a social interest at time t, and $h_i^t = 0$ means that the user did not have the social interest. Such a social interest log can be available from many online social network systems. Further, we assume that each user is associated with a number of attributes (e.g., location, call time, call duration and messages) and thus have the following definitions.

Definition 2. *User attribute matrix: Let D^t be a $N \times w$ matrix that represents values of user attributes at time t, where each row d_i includes all attributes of user u_i, each column includes all values of these attributes. An element d_{ij} represent the jth attribute value of user u_i.*

The attribute matrix describes user-specific characteristics, and can be defined in different ways. Thus, we can define the input of our problem, a set of attribute augmented networks.

Definition 3. *Attribute augmented network: The attribute augmented network is denoted as $G^t = (U^t, E^t, D^t, H^t)$, where U^t is the set of users and E^t is the set of links between users at time t, and D^t represents the attribute matrix of all users in the network at time t, and H^t represents the set of social interests of all users at time t.*

Based on the above concepts, we can define the problem of inferring social interests in Mobile Networks. Given a series of T time-space-dependent attribute augmented networks, the goal is to learn a model that can best fit the relationships between the various factors and the user social interest. More precisely,

Problem 1. **Inferring Social Interests in Mobile Networks.** Given a series of T time-space-dependent attribute augmented networks $\{G^t = (U^t, E^t, D^t, H^t)\}$, where $t \in \{1, \cdots, T\}$, the goal of inferring social interests in Mobile Networks to learn a mapping function

$$f : (\{G^1, \ldots, G^{T-1}\}, U^T, E^T, D^T) \to H^T$$

Note that in this general formulation, we allow the graph structure to evolve over time and also arbitrary dependency from the past. To have a social interest inferring problem to work with, we model the time-space-dependency by introducing a social interest for each user. More specifically, users' social interests at time t are influenced by their private attributes, their own social interests at time $t-1$ and their neighbors' social interests at both time t and $t-1$. And their social interests are dependent on their neighbors' social interests at time t and $t-1$.

2.2 Time-Space Factor Graph Model (TS-FGM)

Considering several influence factors (e.g., social relationships) on social interest inferring together, we build the Time-Space Factor Graph Model(TS-FGM) of Mobile Network as: Given T time-continuous attribute augmented network $G = G^t = (U^t, E^t, D^t, H^t)$, where $t \in 1, \cdots, T$, $U = U^1 \cup U^2 \cup \cdots \cup U^T$, $|U| = N$. And then we define joint distribution of H, all social interests in G, as in (1).

$$p(H|G) = \prod_{t=1}^{T} \prod_{i=1}^{N} f(h_i^t|s_i^t) f(s_i^t|s_{\sim u_i}^{t-1}) f(s_i^t|s_{\sim u_i}^t, d_i^t) \qquad (1)$$

where $\sim u_i$ represents neighbors of u_i in the network. The following important factors should be considered when designing the model: (1) the social interest of user u_i at time t will be affected by social interests of his friends at time t; (2) the social interest of user u_i at time t has close relations with his own previous social interests($time < t$); (3) in the same social relationship, social interests of user u_i will perform certain correlations.

Objective function to maximize the Time-Space Factor Graph mode of Mobile Networks is formalized, as in (2).

$$p(H|G) = \frac{1}{F} \exp\{f_h(\cdot) + f_s(\cdot) + f_m(\cdot) + f_d(\cdot)\} \qquad (2)$$

where $F = (2\pi\sigma^2)^{\frac{N \times T}{2}} F_1 F_2$,

$$f_h(\cdot) = \sum_{t=1}^{T} \sum_{i=1}^{N} \frac{(h_i^t - s_i^t)^2}{2\delta^2} \tag{3}$$

$$f_s(\cdot) = \sum_{t=1}^{T} \sum_{i=1}^{N} \sum_{j=1}^{N} \lambda_{ij} m_{ji}^{t-1} p(s_i^t, s_j^{t-1}) \tag{4}$$

$$f_m(\cdot) = \sum_{t=1}^{T} \sum_{i=1}^{N} \sum_{j=1}^{N} \beta_{ij} m_{ij}^t q_{ij}(s_i^t, s_j^t) \tag{5}$$

$$f_d(\cdot) = \sum_{t=1}^{T} \sum_{i=1}^{N} \sum_{k=1}^{w} \alpha_k q_k(s_i^t, d_{ik}^t) \tag{6}$$

Learning TS-FGM is to estimate a parameter configuration $\psi = (\{s_i\}, \{\alpha_k\}, \{\beta_{ij}\}, \{\lambda_{ij}\})$ from a given historic social interest log $\mathbf{H}$, that maximizes the log-likelihood objective function $\mathcal{O}(\psi) = \log p_\psi(\mathbf{Y}|\mathbf{G})$, i.e., $\psi^\star = \arg \max \mathcal{O}(\psi)$. This function is derived through combining social interest bias factor and social interest correlations of users together.

3   Experiments

3.1   Experimental Setup

Data Set. Our experiments are performed on the data set which was generated by a mobile social network (MSN).In the MSN data set, we have collected all-day communication (by SMS and call), individual interest, activity, GPS location and calendar information from some volunteers of a university from May to July, 2010. This data represents over 36,000 hours of continuous data on human activity and rating label.

Baseline Method. We use SVMLight [17] as the baseline algorithm to evaluate our social interests inferring. It uses users-associated attributes as well as historic interests of their neighbor to train a classification model and then employs the classification model to infer users' social interests.

Evaluation Measures. We evaluate the proposed model in terms of Precision and F1-Measure, and compare with the baseline methods to validate the effectiveness of the proposed model.

Environment. The basic learning algorithm is implemented using C++ and the SVM experiment is implemented by Matlab R2006a. Both of them are performed on a server running Microsoft Windows 2k Enterprise with a AMD Phenom(tm) 9650 Quad-Core Processor (2.3GHz) and 8GB memory.

3.2   Inferring Performance

While we analyze what contribution different factors could make, in the model (TS-FGM), the two following factors are considered: social relationship and historical social interest. Specifically, each of these factors is removed one by one. The social relationship factor is first to be deleted and history/time factor is second. And then, we train TS-FGM model and perform social interest inferring using it. Fig. 1 displays F1-Measure values after respectively removing each factor from TS-FGM model. In Fig. 1, TS-FGM-S indicates the results neglecting social relationship factor, namely space factor, and $\lambda = 0$. TS-FGM-T historical social interest factor, namely time factor, and $\beta = 0$. TS-FGM-TS both social relationship and history/time factors, as well as $\lambda = 0$ and $\beta = 0$. From this figure, we can see that inferring performance in the above cases gradually decline. This shows that our method combining these factors together is reasonable and achieves the better social interest inferring effect. Simultaneously, the conclusion can also be drawn that different factors have different effects on the model.

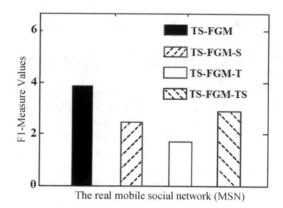

Fig. 1. Contributions given by factors on F1-Measure in our TS-FGM model

3.3   Comparasion with Baseline Algorithm

We select SVMLight [17] as the baseline algorithm. It first uses both users' related attributes and social interests of their neighbors as the classifier for training. And then take advantage of this classifier to infer users' social interests. We adopt RBF kernel function as learning algorithm of SVMLight and use Jackknife and Holdout method to validate inferring accuracies. Comparative results are shown in Table 1 and tell that our inferring effects are better than the baseline method of SVMLight.

Table 1. Comparasion with the baseline algorithm (Precision)

Interests	SVMLight	TS-FGM
Shopping	60.3% (Jackknife)	81.6%
Play	71.0% (Holdout)	86.4%
Eat	73.8% (Jackknife)	74.5%

4 Related Work

Some key technologies related to social interest inferring include social ties inferring across Heterogeneous Networks [5] and Influence mining in Large Social Networks [6]. Traditional approaches to social interests inferring aim at web search logs. Recently, some researchers have reported their methods. For example, Ref. [1] propose a novel search results diversification technique that combines mined social interest from query logs with a probabilistic model, and present a random walk with restart algorithm on the query-URL bipartite graphs using both semantic relevance and social interest in order to meet both the relevance and the diversity requirements in the ranking of search results. To prevent further scandals, Ref. [3] presents a method that utilizes the viewers' behaviors to analyze social interests. Dabi Ahn et al. [8], closest to our work, explores how to formulate a method of inferring user interests by combining both familiarity and topic similarity with social neighbors. For this, it first investigates the degree of familiarity with each social neighbor based on the tendency of social interaction. Then, it obtain two topic distributions in terms of social activities and interest descriptions, respectively by using Latent Dirichlet Allocation (LDA), a generative probabilistic model to uncover the topic structure of the contents. Finally, it quantifys the degree of interest based on the familiarity with each social neighbor and the similarity between two topic distributions.

A closely related research topic is user interest detection from viewing activities on web pages or OSNs, such as text classification techniques[12], ExpertRank algorithm [14] and users' related documents classification [13]. White et al. [9] devised a method to predict user interests by defining five contexts of URL such as interaction, collection, task, historic, and social context on the Web. Sharma and Cosley [10] proposed an recommendation application (called PopCore) in Facebook that uses several network-centric algorithms based on popularity, similarity and strength with social neighbors. But, they did not take into account semantics in the contents of OSN communication. Campbell et al. in Ref. [15] utilized the e-mail contents and social network pattern in e-mail communications to discover interested users in particular topics. Unsupervised clustering of email text messages used to detect interests. They compared the content-based only approach and the graphbased approach that take into consideration both text content and communication patterns. Kardan and others in Ref. [16] proposed a new ranking algorithm "SNPageRank" for finding the interests model in Friendfeed Social Network, the proposed algorithm utilized updated version of PageRank algorithm, instead of web pages, people in Social Networks and the connections between them are used as hyper links, and the connections between nodes are weighted. This algorithm works fine in determining users with high contribution in the Social Network without determining in which field they are interested or experts. From our point of view, confidence correlation assumption between profile data and documents in this research may perform well in organizational level but not in the the case of SNS.

This paper is mainly inspired by the two recent work on interest-based recommending framework [2] and implicit semantic relations discovery [11]. Specifically, Ref. [2] presents an interest based recommending framework for social network, and also gives a formalized model and recommending procedure. The proposed approach for interest-based recommendation can provide different types of interesting recommendations taking into account the current user interaction context; Ref. [11] proposes a technique to discover the implicit semantic relations between entities in text messages, which can infer the interests of a user. The proposed technique based on a semantically enriched graph representation of entities contained in text messages generated by a user, a new algorithm (Root-Path-Degree) is invented and used to find the most representative sub-graph that reflects the semantic implicit interests of the user.

In contrast to all these, our approach analyzes the fundamental clues (patterns) that may subtly reveal our status in the social network, proposes a unified model, based on Time-Space Probability Factor Graph Model (TS-FGM), to combine social relationships, historic interest factor and users' private attributes and transfer social interest inferring problem into the maximizing problem of the objective function of TS-FGM. In TS-FGM, historic social interests are formalized as time factor, social relationships are formalized as space factor as well as users' private attributes are formalized as attributes of nodes.

5 Conclusions

Considering the influence on social interest inferring accuracies from social relationship factor, historic interest factor, and users' private attributes factor, we formalize the problem of social interest inferring in MSNs, present a unified model (TS-FGM) based on Probability Factor Graph Model combining these above factors together and formalized these factors as different factor functions. Our experiments show that these factor functions comply well with user's intuition and observation's results and our proposed approach outperform the baseline algorithm SVMLight. As the future work, it would be interesting to design and implement parallel learning algorithm in order to meet the need of complexity of social network and dealing with large-scale data.

Acknowledgments. This paper is supported in part by the National Basic Research Program of China (973 Program) under Grant No. 2011CB302803, the "Strategic Priority Research Program" of the Chinese Academy of Sciences under Grant No. XDA060307000, the National Natural Science Foundation of China under Grant No. 61003292, the National Natural Science Foundation of

China under Grant No. 61272466, the National Natural Science Foundation of China under Grant No. 61303233, and Qinhuangdao Science and Technology Research and Development of China under Grant No.201001A056.

References

1. Mao, Y.Q., Shen, H.F., Sun, C.Z.: Diversification of Web Search Results through Social Interest Mining. In: 45th Hawaii International Conference on System Science, pp. 3581–3590. IEEE Press, Maui (2012)
2. Agrawal, R., Gollapudi, S., Halverson, A., Ieong, S.: Diversifying Search Results. In: 2nd ACM International Conference on Web Search and Data Mining (WSDM 2009), pp. 5–14. ACM Press, New York (2009)
3. Mitamura, T., Yoshida, K.: Viewers' Side Analysis of Social Interests. In: 12th International Conference on Data Mining Workshops, pp. 301–308. IEEE Press, Brussels (2012)
4. Zhang, Y., Tang, J., Sun, J.M., Chen, Y.R.: MoodCast: Emotion Prediction via Dynamic Continuous Factor Graph Model. In: 10th International Conference on Data Mining (ICDM), Sydney, NSW, pp. 1193–1198. IEEE Press (2010)
5. Tang, J., Lou, T.C., Kleinberg, J.: Inferring Social Ties across Heterogeneous Networks. In: 5th ACM International Conference on Web Search and Data Mining (WSDM 2012), Seattle, Washington, USA, pp. 743–752. ACM Press (February 2012)
6. Tang, J., Wu, S., Sun, J.M.: Confluence: Conformity Influence in Large Social Networks. In: 9th ACM SIGKDD International Conference on Knowledge Discovery and Data Mining (KDD 2013), Chicago, USA, pp. 1–9. ACM Press (2013)
7. Bookstein, A.: Information Retrieval: A Sequential Learning Process. Journal of the American Society for Information Sciences (ASIS) 34(5), 331–342 (1983)
8. Ahn, D., Kim, T., Hyun, S.J., Lee, D.: Inferring User Interest using Familiarity and Topic Similarity with Social Neighbors in Facebook. In: IEEE/WIC/ACM International Conferences on Web Intelligence and Intelligent Agent Technology (WI-IAT), pp. 196–200. IEEE/ACM Press, Macau (2012)
9. Liu, Y., Bian, J., Agichtein, E.: Predicting Information Seeker Satisfaction in Community Question Answering. In: 32nd Annual ACM SIGIR Conference, Boston, USA, pp. 483–490 (2009)
10. Liu, Y., Huang, J., An, A., Yu, X.: ARSA: A Sentiment-aware Model for Predicting Sales Performance using Blogs. In: 30th Annual International ACM SIGIR Conference, Amsterdam, Holland, pp. 607–614 (2007)
11. Al-Kouz, A., Albayrak, S.: An Interests Discovery Approach in Social Networks Based on Semantically Enriched Graphs. In: 2012 International Conference on Advances in Social Networks Analysis and Mining, Istanbul, Turkey, pp. 1272–1277 (2012)
12. Al-Kouz, A., Luca, E.W.D., Albayrak, S.: Latent Semantic Social Graph Model for Expert Discovery in Facebook. In: 11th International Conference on Innovative Internet Community Systems, ICSC, Berlin, Germany, pp. 1–11. Springer Press (2011)
13. Metze, F., Bauckhage, C., Alpcan, T., Dobbrott, K., Clemens, C.: The "Spree" Expert Finding System. In: Proceedings of International Conference on Semantic Computing, ICSC, Irven, CA, pp. 551–558. Springer Press (2007)

14. Jiao, J., Yan, J., Zhao, H., Fan, W.: Expertrank: An Expert User Ranking Algorithm in Online Communities. In: Proceedings of International Conference on New Trends in Information and Service Science, NISS 2009, Beijing, China, pp. 674–679. Springer Press (2009)

15. Campbell, C.S., Maglio, P.P., Cozzi, A., Dom, B.: Expertise Identification using Email Communications. In: 12th International Conference on Information and Knowledge Management, New Orleans, LA, USA, pp. 1–4. Springer Press (2003)

16. Ahmad, K., Amin, O., Farzad, F.: Expert Finding on Social Network with Link Analysis Approach. In: 19th Iranian Conference on Electrical Engineering, ICEE 2011, Tehran, Iran, pp. 1–6. Springer Press (2011)

17. Joachims, T.: Training Linear SVMs in Linear Time. In: 12th ACM SIGKDD International Conference on Knowledge Discovery and Data Mining, pp. 217–226. ACM Press, New York (2006)

Link Quality Based Orthogonal Sniffing Movement Algorithm towards Mobile Sink*

Jian Shu, Xiaotian Geng, Gang Hu, Di Luo, and Linlan Liu

Internet of Things Technology Institute
Nanchang Hang Kong University, Nanchang, Jiangxi, P.R. China

Abstract. Wireless sensor networks (WSNs) have been widely used in many applications. However, in some particular situations such as battlefield communication and disaster monitoring, fixed sink nodes have shown their shortage on deployment, energy balance and connectivity. Also, most of the related works on mobile sink ignored packet loss and data collection coverage. In this paper, we propose a movement strategy for mobile sink based on the link quality: Orthogonal Sniffing Movement Algorithm (OSM). The movement strategy is carefully designed by analyzing the relationship between the route of sink node and link quality to achieve high data collection coverage. The movement of the mobile sink is determined dynamically by the evaluation results of link quality with sensor nodes. The simulation results reveal that OSM achieves high data collection coverage compared to other movement strategies.

Keywords: movement strategy, Mobile Sink, OSM, WSNs.

1 Introduction

Wireless Sensor Network (WSN) is a complex of sensor technology, embedded computing, wireless communications and distributed information processing [1]. It has emerged as a key technology for many monitoring applications [2]. Generally, a WSN is a three-level network system consisting of sensor nodes, sink nodes and management nodes. Sink nodes are designed to collect and transmit data from sensor areas to a base station. In some particular applications such as battlefield communication and disaster monitoring, a complete wireless sensor network is often divided into several small separated subnets connected by a main route which consists of many sink nodes. However, problems often occur when using fixed sink in such applications: Restricted by energy, geographical conditions and other factors, deploying sink nodes is more difficult than sensor nodes, and it is hard to repair if a sink node is out of energy; Sensing data cannot transmit to sink nodes by a single hop; Multi-hop mechanism and the construction of main route has brought the Hotspots problem; Also, redundant nodes have to be used if subnets have bad connectivity, which increases costs.

---

* This work is supported by The National Natural Science Foundation of China under grant NO.61262020 and Aeronautical Science Foundation of China under grant ON.2010ZC56008.

Part of the problems are rooted in fixed sink nodes. Since the micro UAVs are well improved in both autonomous control and environment mapping [3], mobile nodes such as quadcopter [4] received a widespread concern. Mobile sink can reduce energy consumption and increase network life cycle while ensuring tolerable data delivery latency [5], that's why it also attracts a large number of researches on movement strategy of mobile sink. In [6], Data Collection Scheme with Regular track (DCSR) has been proposed as a movement strategy for mobile sink. It selected a number of collection sites at the first place according to the sensor distribution, and then a quantum genetic algorithm was performed to calculate the shortest loop across the sites. The sink node would travel along that loop periodically and collect data at each site. This strategy achieves high throughput of the network and low energy consumption, but it increases data delivery latency. In [7], an optimization model named min-energy min-distance (MEMD) of mobile sink's moving path was introduced. It has a monotonic decrease of data delivery latency for greater limits on the energy consumption, but it doesn't take the packet loss and the collection coverage as a consideration. In [8], an energy balanced routing algorithm: EBRAMS has been proposed. It distributes energy dissipation throughout the sensors and lengthen network lifetime compared with the LEACH and PEGASIS. In [9], the author described a Partition-based Nearest Job Next data collection scheme using mobile sink. It clusters the sensor nodes by partitioning the sensing field into grids, and schedules the data collection carried out by the mobile sink. This scheme decreases the delivery latency but doesn't mention the packet loss results. In [10], authors proposed a heuristic framework using multiple orbits for the sinks' trajectories. Design of the framework is aimed at very large WSNs and it also takes the lifetime and delay as its main consideration. [11] recommended an improved energy-efficient PEGASIS-based routing protocol (MIEEPB), which could achieve proficient energy utilization of wireless sensors.

Most of the related researches focus on the trade-off between network lifetime and delivery latency [12] [13] [14] [15] [16] [17] [18] [19] [20] [21]. However, with the increasing speed of mobile sink and the larger scale of sensor nodes, data

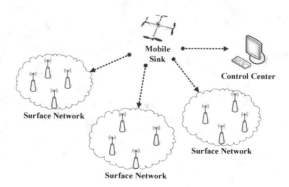

Fig. 1. Battlefield communication network

in some of the sensing areas may not be collected completely because of low link quality, which will lead to a serious information loss. Just as shown in Figure 1, apply to battlefield communication network in which each information would be extremely important, low collection coverage would have serious consequences. For this reason, we propose a high data collection coverage algorithm based on link quality: Orthogonal Sniffing Movement Algorithm (OSM) which is carefully designed by analyzing the relationship between the route of sink node and link quality to reduce the packet loss.

2   Network Model

Towards the scenarios such as UAV battlefield communication network, we build a network model using a mobile sink. When the mobile sink starts the mission and begins to collect data, it will visit every sensing area that does not connected with each other. How to visit each area efficiently can be seen as the traveling salesman problem which is an NP-Complete problem. But, when the mobile sink entered into each area, as shown in Figure 2, the collection coverage of sink node (Sc) cannot include the whole sensing area (Sa). Since Sc is a irregular region, we consider it a square with a side length of l, which can be easily obtained from formula (1) as

$$l = \sqrt{2} \times (h \times tan\frac{\theta}{2}) \tag{1}$$

where h is the flight altitude of the mobile sink and θ is the beam radiation angle of the directional antenna. The mobile sink travels through each grid according to the travel pattern shown in Figure 3. Other travel patterns are also possible. As shown in Figure 2, the initial coordinate of the sink node is $(l/2, l/2)$ and the direction is along the X axis. Denote the assemblage of cluster-head nodes which can be detected by the sink node at the same time as $U_N = Sa \cap Sc(N \in N_1, N_2...N_i)$.

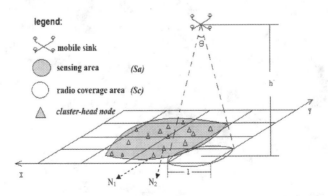

Fig. 2. Network Model

After a while, when the sink node move to $(3l/2, l/2)$, $U_N = \{N_1, N_2\}$. As shown in Figure 2, the node N_2 is located on the edge of sink collection coverage. There is a high probability that the link quality between sink node and N_2 is too bad which may lead to a consequence that the data saved by N_2 cannot be collected completely. Thus, the problem is how to adjust the collecting position to ensure a complete collection from the cluster-head nodes like N_2.

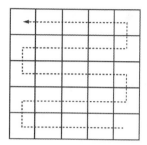

Fig. 3. A simple travel pattern

3 Orthogonal Sniffing Movement Algorithm (OSM)

The core algorithm of the movement strategy is carefully designed based on three aspects: the research of link quality between sink node and sensor node, analysis of link parameters, and experiments that evaluate the performance of the algorithm. First, we will describe the methods of obtaining the link quality parameter and then introduce the key data structure we designed for the algorithm. At last, we will show the detail of the algorithm step by step.

3.1 Link Quality Parameter

In this paper we propose Link Quality Parameter (LQP) as the decisive argument to evaluate the link quality. As intermediate results, Packet Delivery Rate (PDR) and Channel Quality (CQ) are used. PDR is obtained by measuring the Packet Receive Rate (PRR) and filtering by the $WMEWMA$ algorithm. Regard the sink node as the sender and the cluster-head nodes as the receiver, calculate the PRR and express the result as a floating-point number that is greater than 0 and less than 1. In order to reduce interference caused by abnormal measurement data, the PDR is obtained by:

$$PDR = \alpha \bullet WMEWMA + (1 - \alpha) \bullet PPR_i' \tag{2}$$

where PRR_i' is the current measured value, α is weight and $\alpha \in [0, 1]$, the smaller α is, the more significant PRR is. The Channel Quality (CQ) is represented for recognition clarity of RF signal, and obtained by measuring the Signal to Noise Ratio (SNR). According to $IEEE802.15.4$, Received Signal Strength Indication

$(RSSI)$ has been recorded in each successful received packet by which we can obtain the SNR conveniently:

$$SNR = \frac{RSSI_r}{RSSI_v} \qquad (3)$$

where $RSSI_r$ is the $RSSI$ measured when the node is receiving data, and $RSSI_v$ is when the node is idle. After adjusted by the Link Quality Indicator (LQI), which is also recorded in the packet, the CQ can be obtained. Finally, after processing each node, the PDR_{N_i} and the CQ_{N_i} are calculated. The Link Quality Parameter of each node can be obtained as follows:

$$LQP_{N_i} = \lambda \bullet \frac{PDR_{N_i}}{PDR_t} + (1 - \lambda) \bullet \frac{CQ_{N_i}}{CQ_t} \qquad (4)$$

where the PDR_t is the threshold of the PDR, the CQ_t is the threshold of the CQ and λ is weight. The greater λ, the more LQP relies on PDR.

3.2 Cluster-Head Nodes Status Table

In order to keep and utilize the parameters and the status of cluster-head nodes, a carefully designed table as shown in Table 1 is required.

Table 1. Cluster-head Nodes Status Table

Node ID	LQP	Collection Status
N_1	0.8933	1
N_2	0.1501	0
N_3	0.6715	1
	......	

In Table 1, the first column $NodeID$ is designed to keep the identifiers of the cluster-head nodes which were detected by the sink node. The second column keeps the Link Quality Parameters for each node and values in the last column represent whether the cluster-head node has been collected or not. If it has been collected, the value should be 1 and if it has not, the value should be 0.

3.3 Algorithm Description

Step 1: Table Initialization. When the sink node entered the sensing area as shown in Figure 2, it would be hovering at the coordinate of $(3l/2, l/2)$ and be ready to collect data from the cluster-head nodes. Meanwhile, link-quality-testing packets would be broadcast by the sink node. Each cluster-head node who received the packet would send an ACK packet back, in which contained its PRR, $RSSI$ and LQI. Sink node would calculate the LQP for each cluster-head node and fill up the table. The Collection Status of such nodes would be set to 0.

Step 2: Data Collection. The mobile sink would send data collection command packet after the status table had been initialized. Each cluster-head node who received the command would send the sensing data to the sink and finish its own task. Then the mobile sink would fill up the status table according to the sensing data, set the Collection Status to 1 when the node finished collecting.

Step 3: Orthogonal Sniffing. Check the cluster-head node status table if there are nodes whose collection status remains 0, such as the node N2 shown in Table 1. In order to ensure a complete collection from N2, the sink node should adjust its collecting position as follows:

1) Record the current LQP for node N_2 as LQP_0, and then move forward (direction is insignificant). Test the LQP of N_2 while moving forward and the second column will keep changing.

2) After Δt of unit-time, sink record a new LQP value for N_2 and after 5 times, sink will stop moving and we can obtain a LQP vector:

$$\overrightarrow{LQP} = (LQP_1, LQP_2...LQP_5) \tag{5}$$

3) Calculate the difference vector:

$$\overrightarrow{\Delta LQP} = (\Delta LQP_1, \Delta LQP_2...\Delta LQP_5) \tag{6}$$

where:

$$\Delta LQP_i = LQP_i - LQP_0 \tag{7}$$

and then the maximum value of the difference vector ΔLQP_{max} is easy to obtain:

$$\Delta LQP_{max} = max(\Delta LQP_1, \Delta LQP_2..:\Delta LQP_5) \tag{8}$$

Denote n as the index of ΔLQP_{max}. For example, if $\Delta LQP_{max} = \Delta LQP_2$, then $n = 2$.

4) Now the situation should be considered in three cases:

A. $n = 1$:

In this case, as shown in Figure 4(a), the LQP of N_2 was getting lower during the 5 Δt of unit-times which means the link quality between mobile sink and N_2 was getting worse. So the mobile sink should turn 180 degrees and proceed through step 1) to step 4).

B. $n = 5$:

In this case, as shown in Figure 4(b), the LQP of N_2 was getting higher during the 5 Δt of unit-times which means the link quality between mobile sink and N_2 was getting better, and the mobile sink was approaching the perfect collecting location. First, the sink checks the latest LQP if it is above the threshold. If it is, proceed to step 5) directly; If it's not, proceed through step 1) to step 4).

C. $1 < n < 5$:

In this case, as shown in Figure 4(c), the LQP of N_2 was getting higher at the first place and getting lower in the end. First, the mobile sink should go backwards for $(5 - n) \times \Delta t$ of unit-times. Then turn 90 degrees (direction is insignificant) and proceed through step 1) to step 4).

5) Sniff over. Recollect the data from N_2. Check the cluster-head node status table again if there are still some nodes whose collection status remains 0, and if so, proceed through step 1) to step 5) until all of the collection status are marked with 1.

Step 4: Move Forward. Move forward to the other grids and proceed through step 1 to step 4 repeatedly until the collection of the sensing area is accomplished.

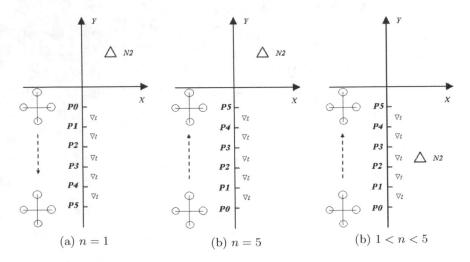

(a) $n = 1$ (b) $n = 5$ (b) $1 < n < 5$

Fig. 4. Orthogonal Sniffing

4   Simulation and Results

4.1   Experiment Parameters

In this paper, we implemented the OSM algorithm in NS2 environment and compared it with Stationary, Random and DCSR to analyze the performance. Among the four strategies, Stationary submit data in active mode, which needs to be supported by a routing protocol. In this paper we use the Flooding protocol. Experiment parameters are shown in Table 2. Four indicators were considered in the simulation:

Collection coverage: The ratio of the number of nodes which are collected completely by the sink node divided by the total number of nodes in the network.

Table 2. Experiment Parameters

Parameter	Values
Nodes distribution range	$200m \times 200m$
The total number of nodes	$100, 200, 300, 400$
The speed of mobile sink	Stationary: $0m/s$
	Others: $3m/s, 10m/s$
Initial energy for each node	$4.0J$

Throughput: The ratio of the data contained in the network divided by the time mobile sink completed the mission.

Data collection efficiency: The ratio of the sensing data collected by the mobile sink divided by the total sensing data sensed in the whole network.

Energy remaining: The remaining energy after the mobile sink completion.

4.2   Simulation Results

1) Collection Coverage. The collection coverage is shown in Figure 5. In Figure 5(a), mobile sink moves at a speed of $3m/s$, and in 5(b) it moves at $10m/s$. In Stationary, the sink node is fixed, the same below.

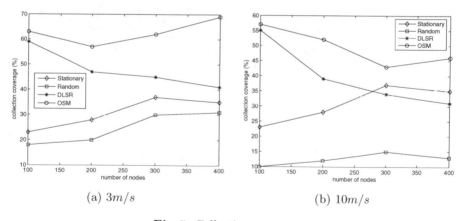

(a) $3m/s$ (b) $10m/s$

Fig. 5. Collection coverage

Figure 5 shows that, the Stationary strategy has a low coverage due to data confliction and packet loss; the Random strategy has a lower coverage because of the unreasonable path planning; although the DCSR strategy has a well planned path, packet loss still frequently exist; the OSM strategy has a higher collection coverage because of the sniffing to nodes which have an unacceptable link quality.

2) Throughput. Throughput is one of the most important indicators to measure the performance of the network. As shown in Figure 6, the throughput of the OSM is higher than Stationary and Random due to the stable collection and high coverage. But it extended the moving path while sniffing so it is a little lower than the DCSR.

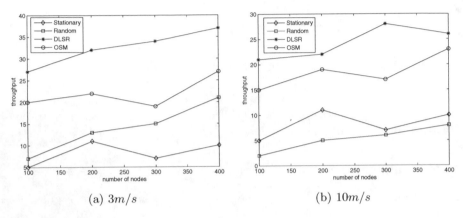

(a) $3m/s$ (b) $10m/s$

Fig. 6. Throughput

3) Data Collection Efficiency. As shown in Figure 7, the OSM strategy has the highest data collection efficiency because of its high coverage. Mobile sink can collect more data during the same mission.

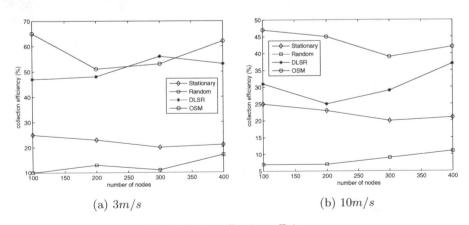

(a) $3m/s$ (b) $10m/s$

Fig. 7. Data collection efficiency

4) Energy Remaining. The energy remaining results are shown in Figure 8. The Random strategy has the highest record not because of good performance, the reason is that most of the cluster-head nodes have not been detected; Network using Stationary strategy has a large number of routing information, combined with the Hotspots problem, the energy cost is increased; The DCSR has the lowest energy cost because of the well planned path; The OSM strategy cost extra energy during evaluating the link quality, but the result remains tolerable.

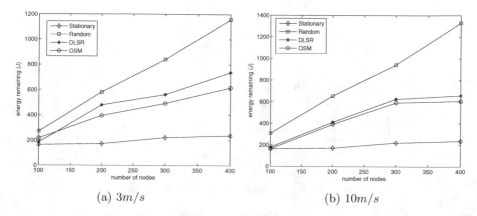

(a) 3m/s   (b) 10m/s

Fig. 8. Energy remaining

5   Conclusions

In this paper, OSM, a high coverage movement strategy for mobile sink in wireless sensor networks is proposed. The algorithm is carefully designed base on analyzing the link quality between the mobile sink and the cluster-head nodes. Those nodes which are located on the edge of the sensing area can be sniffed and covered by mobile sink using OSM so that the collection coverage is increased. Simulation results demonstrate that the proposed strategy is collection-efficient and provides higher collection coverage.

References

1. Cui, L., Ju, H., Miao, Y., et al.: Overview of Wireless Sensor Networks. Journal of Computer Research and Development 42(1), 163–174 (2005)
2. Ren, X., Liang, W.: Delay-Tolerant Data Gathering in Energy Harvesting Sensor Networks With a Mobile Sink. In: Globecom 2012 - Ad Hoc and Sensor Networking Symposium (2012)
3. Kumar, V., Michael, N.: Opportunities and challenges with autonomous micro aerial vehicles. The International Journal of Robotics Research 31(11), 1279–1291 (2012)

4. Achtelik, M., Zhang, T., Kuhnlenz, K., et al.: Visual tracking and control of a quadcopter using a stereo camera system and inertial sensors. In: International Conference on Mechatronics and Automation, ICMA 2009, pp. 2863–2869. IEEE (2009)

5. Gupta, M.R.K., Saxena, M.S., Singh, S., et al.: An Comparison and Evaluation for Data Gathering and Sharing with Inter Node Communication in Mobile-Sink. International Journal (2012)

6. Guo, J., Sun, L.-J., Xu, W.-J., et al.: Mobile sink-based data collection scheme for wireless sensor networks. Journal on Communications 9, 023 (2012)

7. Zhang, X.-W., Shen, L., Jiang, Y.-F.: Optimizing path selection of mobile Sink nodes in mobility-assistant WSN. Journal on Communications (2) (2013)

8. Guan, J., Sun, D., Wang, A., et al.: Energy Balanced Routing Algorithm Based on Mobile Sink for Wireless Sensor Networks. Journal of Computational Information Systems 8(2), 603–613 (2012)

9. Ahmadi, M., He, L., Pan, J., et al.: A Partition-based data collection scheme for wireless sensor networks with a mobile sink. In: 2012 IEEE International Conference on Communications (ICC), pp. 503–507. IEEE (2012)

10. Poe, W.Y., Beck, M., Schmitt, J.B.: Achieving high lifetime and low delay in very large sensors networks using mobile sinks. In: 2012 IEEE 8th International Conference on Distributed Computing in Sensor Systems (DCOSS), pp. 17–24. IEEE (2012)

11. Jafri, M.R., Javaid, N., Javaid, A., et al.: Maximizing the Lifetime of Multi-Chain PEGASIS Using Sink Mobility. World Applied Sciences Journal 21(9), 1283–1289 (2013)

12. Pazzi, R.W.N., Boukerche, A.: Mobile data collector strategy for delay-sensitive applications over wireless sensor networks. Computer Communications 31(5), 1028–1039 (2008)

13. Bi, Y., Sun, L., Ma, J., et al.: HUMS: an autonomous moving strategy for mobile sinks in data-gathering sensor networks. EURASIP Journal on Wireless Communications and Networking (2007)

14. Xu, Z., Liang, W., Xu, Y.: Network Lifetime Maximization in Delay-Tolerant Sensor Networks with a Mobile Sink. In: 2012 IEEE 8th International Conference on Distributed Computing in Sensor Systems (DCOSS), pp. 9–16. IEEE (2012)

15. Behdani, B., Smith, J.C., Xia, Y.: The Lifetime Maximization Problem in Wireless Sensor Networks with a Mobile Sink: MIP Formulations and Algorithms. IIE Transactions (2013)

16. Javaid, N., Khan, A.A., Akbar, M., et al.: SRP-MS: A New Routing Protocol for Delay Tolerant Wireless Sensor Networks. arXiv preprint arXiv:1303.6518 (2013)

17. Wankhade, S.R., Chavhan, N.A.: A Review on Data Collection Method with Sink Node in Wireless Sensor Network. International Journal 4 (2013)

18. Waghole, D.S., Deshpande, V.S.: Reducing Delay Data Dissemination Using Mobile Sink in Wireless Sensor Networks. International Journal of Soft Computing and Engineering 3 (2013)

19. Zhang, X., Kang, G., Zhang, P., et al.: Game Theoretic Clustering Scheme for Mobile Sink WSN. Journal of Information & Computational Science 10(3), 869–881 (2013)

20. Zhang, L., Zhang, K., Song, J.: Mobile Sink-Based Data Gathering Algorithm in Wireless Sensor Networks. Chinese Journal of Sensors and Actuators 5, 024 (2012)

21. Shanmugam, D.B., Anitha, G., Kumar, K.V., et al.: A Design Approach for Data Collection in Wireless Sensor Networks with a Mobile Base Station. International Journal 2(12) (2012)

Fast Neighbor Discovery Protocol Based on MANET-RTLS*

Kejian Xia, Fei Liu, Jie Zou, and Jie He**

University of Science and Technology Beijing, Computer and Communication
Engineering, Beijing100083, China
bjxkj@vip.163.com, happy326111@sina.cn,
{zoujie1987,hejie1983}@gmail.com

Abstract. In order to satisfy the requirements of rapidly neighbor discovery in Mobile Ad-hoc Networks based Real Time Location System (MANET-RTLS), this paper proposed a Slot-Divide Round Protocol Based on CSMA Neighbor Discover (SDRBC). The protocol could reduce the unnecessary transmission and improve the channel utilization efficiency. The performance of SDRBC is simulated with OMNET++, the results indicate that the SDRBC reduces more than 30 percent time consumption of neighbor discovery, compared to other existing protocols.

Keywords: Mobile Ad-hoc Networks (MANET), Neighbor discover, Carrier Sense Multiple Access protocol (CSMA), Medium Access Control (MAC).

1 Introduction

The principle of the Real-time positioning system is that the target node measures distances or angles with a number of base stations. And then the localization algorithm calculates the target node coordinates based on the measured distances/angles and the coordinates of the corresponding base stations. In general real time location system, base stations are deployed in determined locations and their coordinates are measured manually. However, in emergency scenarios, time cost of deployment and manually measurement is subject to greater constraints. Thus, the manually measured way cannot be applied to these emergency scenarios. Mobile Ad-hoc Networks based Real Time Location System (MANET-RTLS) is a kind of short-range wireless communication network which combines the real-time positioning technology with mobile ad hoc network technology. In MANET-RTLS, the locations and topology of the base stations are no longer a known quantity. MANET technology enables the base stations measure distances/angles mutually, build base station topology and calculate the relative

---

* This work has been performed under the National Natural Science Found-ation of China (Grants No. 61302065 and No. 61172049) and Doctoral Fund of Ministry of Education of China (Grant No. 20100006110015).
** Corresponding author.

L. Sun, H. Ma, and F. Hong (Eds.): CWSN 2013, CCIS 418, pp. 113–121, 2014.

coordinates of the base stations. Therefore, MANET-RTLS can overcome the shortcomings of manually measurement and can be applied to the emergent scenarios, such as fire scene and field operations[1][2][3].

In MANET-RTLS, neighbor node discovery, which is processed between base station placement and distance measurements among base stations, is a key step of building MANET-RTLS system. The existing node discovery protocols can be divided into the following categories: Birthday protocol[9], Random protocol[10], Multi-channel protocol [11][12], Directional antenna protocol[13]. Birthday protocol is used for static self-organizing network. Because Birthday protocol does not take the channel conflict and transmission delays into account, it causes lower channel utilization efficiency and the time consumption is difficult to estimate. Random protocol, which is developed based on ALOHA, is suitable for asynchronous node discovery. The advantage of Random protocol is that it does not require clock synchronization. In literature [11], the authors propose a solution based on the control channel synchronous multichannel. In literature [12], the authors propose an asynchronous multi-channel programs that network communication range by node clustering, each cluster elect cluster head node and the cluster head node is responsible for collecting neighbors and their channel sets. Based on the information collected, the cluster head select a common channel and broadcast to other nodes for node discovery. In literature [13], authors propose a protocol based on directional antenna. In the protocol Nodes using directional antennas transmit and receive signals and directional antennas divided the discovered nodes into fan-shaped area to reduce conflict.Though all these protocols can be used in mobile networks, the time consumption is not acceptable when they are used in large scale networks.

In this paper, we proposed Slot-Divide Round Base On CSMA Neighbor Discover Protocol(SDRBC). In our protocol, time is divided into units of slots and each time slot is further divided into four min-slots to reduce unnecessary transmission. It achieves the purpose of reducing the node discovery time. The rest of this paper is structured as follows: section 2 describes the proposed protocol including the basic assumptions and the protocol description, section 3 introduces the protocol time performance analysis, section 4 introduces the protocol simulation results and analysis, section 5 Conclusions and future work.

2   Slot-Divide Round Base on CSMA Neighbor Discover Protocol

2.1   Basic Assumptions

Foundation of short-range wireless location is wireless geometric measurement techniques, which includes Receive Signal Strength Indicator(RSSI)[4], Time of Arrival(TOA)[5], Time Difference of Arrival(TDOA)[6], Angle of Arrival(AOA)[7]. This paper use TOA to launched research of MANET-RTLS base topology construction protocol. In the localization system based on TOA, the target node measures distances with at least three base stations to calculate the position. In MANET-RTLS, the position of base station node is unknown. The relative topology of base stations can be obtained by measuring the distance between the Anchors[8].Figure 1 is a typical topology of MANET-RTLS which contains a SINK node for collecting information, Anchor node as a TAG positioning reference and TAG distributed among at least three ranges Anchor in the network.

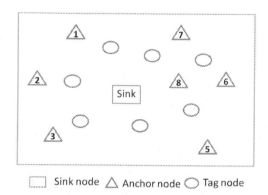

Fig. 1. A kind of MANET-RTLS topology

The proposed SDRBC protocol has following basic assumptions:
(1) Anchor: Its location does not change until the completion of the neighbor discovery. (2) SINK: Its transmission range is large enough to synchronize all Anchor nodes by broadcasting.

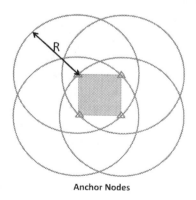

Fig. 2. Anchor Coverage

In MANET-RTLS, Anchors and Sink are the infrastructure, which are similar to the base stations in classical localization system. Figure 2 shows a square area which constitutes of four Anchors with communication range R. And all Tags in the square area can be localized by measuring distances with these four Anchors. To prevent topology changing which is caused by Anchor mobility, we could run SDRBC periodically to rebuild the topology.

2.2   Protocol Description

As shown in Figure 1, SDRBC protocol network topology: a SINK node is responsible for clock synchronization, data acquisition, slot allocation. Anchors and TAGs random layout at the initial stage in the network. SDRBC is used for searching Anchor without consideration for TAG.

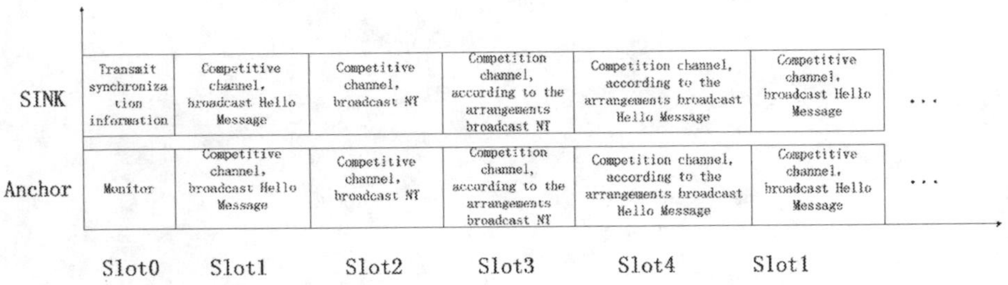

	Transmit synchroniza tion information	Competitive channel, broadcast Hello Message	Competitive channel, broadcast NT	Competition channel, according to the arrangements broadcast NT	Competition channel, according to the arrangements broadcast Hello Message	Competitive channel, broadcast Hello Message	
SINK							...
Anchor	Monitor	Competitive channel, broadcast Hello Message	Competitive channel, broadcast NT	Competition channel, according to the arrangements broadcast NT	Competition channel, according to the arrangements broadcast Hello Message	Competitive channel, broadcast Hello Message	...
	Slot0	Slot1	Slot2	Slot3	Slot4	Slot1	

Fig. 3. Protocol timing diagram

SDRBC uses CSMA protocol for collision avoidance and divides time into time slots. Figure 3 shows a protocol timing diagram. Each Slot is organized as follows:

Slot0: It is the initial stage of the protocol and clock synchronization occurs.

Slot1: After receiving clock synchronization message, Anchor node selected random delay $t_i(t_i \in \omega - \delta, \omega$ is length of Slot and δ is transmission delay of node)in Slot1 and listen to the channel until t_i then broadcasting Hello Message to inform other nodes in CSMA way. Hello Message packet format is shown in Figure 4. Anchor gathers neighbors' Hello Message.

Slot2: Anchor node selects random delay, then broadcasts their neighbor list (NT) in CSMA way. Format of NT packet is shown in Figure 5.

Anchor receives neighbor node NT and then checks whether the transmitter is in its own NT. If not, add it into its own NT and in slot3 broadcast its own NT again. Check whether the received NT contains itself, and if not, then in slot4 broadcast its own NT.

Slot3: If it is needed, Anchor broadcast NT in the CSMA way after random delay t_i. When the Node receives a new NT, it will check whether itself is in the NT. If it is, it will cancel the broadcast. If it is not, it continues broadcasting on demand.

Slot4: If the node needs to broadcast NT at this slot, the actions in Slot 3 are repeated.

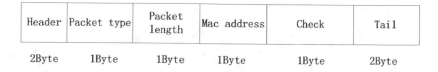

Header	Packet type	Packet length	Mac address	Check	Tail
2Byte	1Byte	1Byte	1Byte	1Byte	2Byte

Fig. 4. Hello Message packet format

Header	Packet type	Packet length	Mac address	NT List	Check	Tail
2Byte	1Byte	1Byte	1Byte	Average 8Byte	1Byte	2Byte

Fig. 5. Contains NT data packet format

3 Performance Analysis

In slot1, SDRBC protocol uses CSMA way to broadcast Hello Message. It makes the channel utilization higher than the Birthday protocol and Random protocol. In slot2, it broadcasts its NT in CSMA way. We assuming that, Anchor uses 802.15.4 physical layer and data transfer rate is 250kb / s. Hello Message transmission time:

$$t_h = 8*8/250000 = 0.256ms \tag{1}$$

NT average packet transfer times:

$$t_{nt} = 16*8/250000 = 0.512ms \tag{2}$$

In MANET-RTLS, Anchor's average node degree is 8 and time cost of transmitting a NT packet is 2 twice of transmitting a Hello Message. In slot2, it will compare its own NT and received NT. If the receiver's NT does not contain the transmitter then the receiver broadcasts NT packet in slot3 and if the transmitter's NT does not contain the receiver, then the receiver arranged for broadcasting Hello Message in Slot4. The purpose of this arrangement is to reduce unwanted broadcast transmission in the channel. And in Slot3,we continue to judge arrangement of Slot4 to makes this goal more explicit.

The node retracted time unit is 320 in CSMA way. When for the first time backoff, BE = 2, maximum backoff time is $(2^{BE} - 1) * 320 = 960$ and when for the second time backoff, BE = 3, maximum backoff time is $(2^{BE} - 1) * 320 = 2.24ms$. The sum of the twice longest backoff time is 3.2ms. So length of Slot1 time can be set to 4ms. In slot2, broadcast transmission NT requires twice time as slot1, Slot2 can be set to 6ms. Slot4 and Slot3 are under the arrangement, they were set to 3ms and 4ms.

4   Simulation

The proposed protocol has been simulated with OMNET++ software. In the simulation process, N Anchor nodes are distributed in a square area of 1000m * 1000m. Each Anchor node has a maximum coverage of 100m.

4.1   Uniform Distribution

First, a uniform layout is selected to make the average node degree of each individual node is 8. SINK and the Anchor topology is shown as Figure 6.

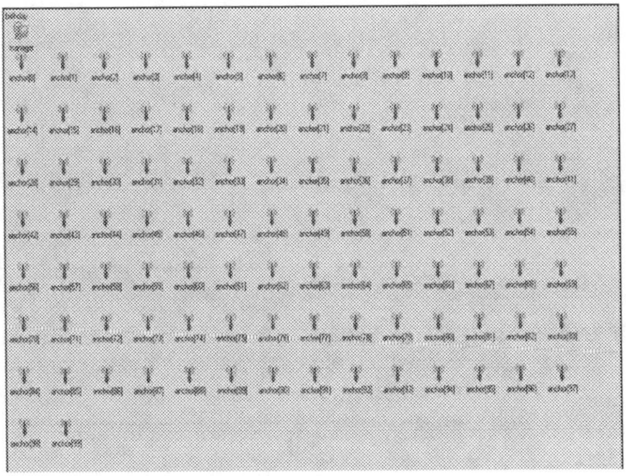

Fig. 6. Uniform layout node topology

In the cases that the node number is 0,50,100,150,200, we record 10 sets of data of each case and calculate the average time. The recorded data is used to compare the average node discovery time with other protocols including Birthday, Random and SDRBC. Related parameters are set as follows: In Birthday protocol, for a specific node, the probability of transmission mode is 0.4 while the probability of listening mode is 0.6. And the length of the slot is 1ms. As for Random protocol, slot period ω is 3ms. In SDRBC protocol, slot1 is 4ms, slot2 is 6ms, slot3 is 4ms, slot4 is 3ms. The comparison of simulation results is shown in Figure 7. When the Anchor node number is around 10,the node discovery time of three protocols are almost the same. When the node number is 50, the discovery time of three protocols time start to show some difference.

In Birthday protocol, node discovery time is 610ms, while the time cost of Random and SDRBC protocol are 69ms and 54ms respectively. The time cose of node discovery time of SDRBC protocol is the shortest. When the number of nodes is 100, the discovery time keep increasing. The discovery time of SDRBC is still the shortest. When the number of nodes is 450, node discovery time of

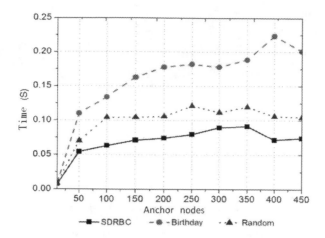

Fig. 7. Comparison of uniform layout

Birthday protocol is 200ms while node discovery time of Random and SDRBC protocol is same as 100 nodes. Node discovery time of Random protocol is 100ms-110ms and node discovery time of SDRBC protocol is stabilized at 70ms. The average node discovery time of SDRBC is 30 percent shorter then Random protocol.

4.2 Random Distribution

Another scenario is random distribution. In this simulation, the nodes are randomly placed without limitation of the average node degree and the parameters are same to the previous case. The comparison of simulation results is shown in Figure 8. Node discovery time of Birthday protocol is close to Random and SDRBC when the number of nodes is less than 50, When the number of nodes is greater than 50, node discovery time rises rapidly. When the number of node is 150, the node discovery time is as high as 2.5s, while Random goes up to 64ms and SDRBC is only 34ms. When the number of nodes is 450, the node discovery time of Random protocol is 1.34s and the node discovery time of SDRBC is only 0.34s, which is only 25.4 percent of the node discovery time of Random protocol. The mean discovery time of SDRDB is only 49 percent of the mean time of Random protocol.

5   Conclusions and Future Work

In order to improve the real-time characteristic of MANET-RTLS, this paper proposed a SDRBC protocol based on CSMA. Compared with Birthday protocol and Random protocol, this protocol reduces the possibility of channel conflict and improves the channel's utilization rate. Moreover, it significantly reduces

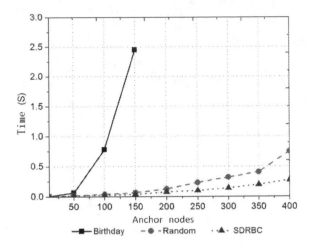

Fig. 8. Comparison of random layout

the time for node discovery. In random distribution, SDRBC protocol reduced 99 percent node discovery time compared with Birthday and 50 percent compared with Random protocol. Therefore, SDRBC is a fast neighbor discovery protocol,which can accelerate the node discovery in MANET-RTLS. In order to obtain better performance, future work will focus on the optimization of the length of each time slot and apply the protocol to a real network.

References

1. Li, C., Wang, G.: IEEE802.15.4 MAC protocol research in wireless sensor network. Computer Science (01), 34 (2007)
2. Pahlavan, K., Levesque, A.: Wireless Information Networks, 2nd edn. John Wiley and Sons, New York (2005)
3. Guillemette, M.G., Fontaine, I., Caron, C.: Hybrid RFID-GPS Real-TimeLocation System for Human Resources: Development, Impacts and Perspectives. In: Pro. of the 41st Hawaii International Conference on System Sciences, USA, pp. 1530–1605 (2008)
4. Geng, Y., Chen, J., Pahlavan, K.: Motion Detection Using RF Signals for the First Responder in Emergency Operations. In: Proceedings of the 24th Annual IEEE International Symposium on Personal, Indoor and Mobile Radio Communications (PIMRC), London (September 2013)
5. Geng, Y., He, J., Deng, H., Pahlavan, K.: Modeling the Effect of Human Body on TOA Ranging for Indoor Human Tracking with Wrist Mounted Sensor. In: 16th International Symposium on Wireless Personal Multimedia Communications (WPMC), Atlantic City, NJ (June 2013)
6. Mensing, C., Plass, S.: Positioning algorithms for cellular networks using TDOA. In: 2006 IEEE International Conference on Acoustics, Speech, and Signal Processing, Toulouse, p. IV (2006)

7. Tian, H., Wang, S., Xie, H.: Localization using Cooperative AOA Approach. In: Wireless Communications, Networking and Mobile Computing, Shanghai, pp. 2416–2419 (2007)
8. Youssef, A., Agrawala, A., Younis, M.: Accurate anchor-free node localization in wireless sensor networks. In: Performance, Computing, and Communications Conference, New York, pp. 465–470 (2005)
9. Luo, J., Guo, D.: Neighbor discovery in wireless ad hoc networks based on group testing. In: Forty-Sixth Annual Allerton Conference on Communication, Control, and Computing, Urbana-Champaign, pp. 791–797 (2008)
10. Hamida, E.B., Chelius, G., Fleury, E.: Revisiting neighbor discovery with interference consideration. In: 3rd ACM International Workshop on Performance Evaluation of Wireless Ad Hoc, Sensor and Ubiquitous Networks, New York, pp. 74–78 (2006)
11. Thoppian, M., et al.: MAC-Layer Scheduling in Cognitive Radio based Multi-Hop Wireless Networks. Presented at the Proceedings of the 2006 International Symposium on World of Wireless, Mobile and Multimedia Networks (2006)
12. Arachchige, C.J.L., et al.: An Asynchronous Neighbor Discovery Algorithm for Cognitive Radio Networks. In: New Frontiers in Dynamic Spectrum Access Networks, Chicago, pp. 1–5 (2008)
13. Vasudevan, S., et al.: On neighbor discovery in wireless networks with directional antennas. In: 24th Annual Joint Conference of the IEEE Computer and Communications Societies, pp. 2502–2512. IEEE Press, USA (2005)

Congestion Control Based on Multi-priority Data for Opportunistic Routing*

Ning Zhang, Nan Ding, and Xiaopeng Hu

Department of Computer Science and Technology
Dalian University of Technology
Dalian 116024, P.R. China
zhangning1989625@gmail.com, dingnan@dlut.edu.cn

Abstract. In order to effectively satisfy the latency requirements of the multi-priority data transmission in wireless sensor network, this paper proposes a congestion control algorithm based on multi-priority data for opportunistic routing. By means of introducing the node queue model of multi-priority data and studying the next-hop node selection strategy based on the traditional opportunistic routing, the new algorithm CEDOP working on the multi-priority data is developed, which pays attention to the shortest path, residual energy of nodes and congestion control. The simulation results demonstrate that the scheme can effectively solve the latency issue of the high-priority data transmission in wireless sensor network under the situation of low latency and network load balance.

Keywords: wireless sensor network(WSN), multi-priority data, congestion control, opportunistic routing.

1 Introduction

As the rapid development of mobile communication technology, embedded computing technology and sensing technology, wireless sensor network(WSN) has been considered to be one of the most convenient and economical solution in a lot of important fields. In practice, once an emergency occurs, such as a node breaks down or is about to run out of the energy, WSN expects the node can immediately take the action to send an emergent alarm packet to the monitoring center, which makes the network more reliable and efficient. How to develop an appropriate routing strategy, which does not diminish the capability of network, to make sure the emergent alarm packet transmission to the destination as soon as possible is an urgent problem in wireless sensor network. Opportunistic routing is a new dynamic multi-hop routing algorithm which is put forward in recent years. Afterwards, how to choose the next-hop node is the main challenge

* Foundation Items: National Natural Science Foundation of China under Grant No.61272523; Nation 12th Five-Year Science and Technology Major Project Topic (No. 2011ZX05039-003-004); and the Fundamental Research Funds for the Central Universities (DUT12JS01).

L. Sun, H. Ma, and F. Hong (Eds.): CWSN 2013, CCIS 418, pp. 122–132, 2014.

when designing an opportunistic routing algorithm. So far, the algorithms have been developed mainly consider two aspects for the designing: distance and energy, which can effectively reduce the data transmission latency and increase the lifetime of network at the same time.

However, current researches on opportunistic routing algorithm in wireless sensor network are lack of consideration of transmission latency requirements when transmitting different data. Hence, the latency of the real-time and rapid transmission of the high-priority packets are unacceptable to some extent, however, it is particularly significant application in the real world. Consider the following scenario: we deploy a wireless sensor network with some image and temperature sensors in an area, whose main functions are intrusion detection and temperature monitoring. When it detects an unidentified object run into the network area, the image packets generated by the image sensors should be immediately sent to the monitoring center so that we can judge the category and the movement of the unidentified object rapidly. Differ with image packets, the temperature packets will be delayed for a period of time. At this time, an opportunistic routing algorithm is needed, which assigns different priorities to image packets and temperature packets. Once image packets with high-priority need to be sent, the node will send image packets firstly, which can make sure the high-priority data packet reaches the monitoring center as soon as possible.

Focusing on these problems, in order to meet the latency requirements of data transmissions with different priorities and the real-time delivery rate for high-priority packets, we propose a congestion control algorithm based on opportunistic routing for multi-priority data in this paper, called CEDOP. Combined with traditional routing algorithm, with the consideration of the shortest path and residual energy of nodes, a multi-priority queue node model is put forward, which would dynamically choose the next-hop node according to the priority of the packets being transmitted. The simulation results show that the CEDOP algorithm which is different from the traditional routing algorithms has the advantages that not only effectively reduce the transmission latency, improve the network throughput and balance the energy consumption, but also obviously reduce the transmission latency of the high-priority packets, thus making the network more reliable.

The paper is organized as follows: section 1 presents the introduction; section 2 describes the system model adopted in the paper and related works; section 3 details the opportunistic routing algorithm CEDOP proposed in this paper; section 4 demonstrates the simulation experiment which shows a much better performance; conclusion is summarized in section 5.

2 System Models and Related Works

2.1 Network Model

The CEDOP algorithm proposed in this paper assumes that all nodes in the network are distributed randomly in a rectangular area. The network model has the following properties: (1) within a specific network, there is only one sink node, which is deployed in the middle of the rectangular area, and the rest of the nodes are deployed randomly; (2) all the deployed of nodes will no longer be moved, and the geographic location information of each node will not be obtained; (3) each node has a unique id; (4) each node is in the same communication domain, and can only communicate with other neighbor nodes in the same domain; (5) all of the nodes send packets in accordance with a specific frequency, and here we assume that all of the nodes in the model generate and transmit a packet in a unit time; (6) all of the nodes are equal, and have the same computation and communication ability as well as the same initial energy. The energy of each node cannot be replenished, therefore, when the energy is used up, the node will stop working. Integrating the assumptions above, we present some definitions of the network model as follows:

Definition 1. Network Model. The wireless sensor network is described using an undirected graph structure, noting for $G = (U, E)$, where U is the node set; E is the undirected edge set which links nodes among the node set. If node $u_i(u_i \in U)$ is in the communication domain of node u_j, there exists $e(u_i, u_j) \in E$. We assume that the radiuses of different communication domains of nodes are equal with each other.

Definition 2. Node Depth. Sink node uses the flooding way to determine the depth of each node. The depth of the sink node is defined as 0; the depth of node with one hop to the sink node is defined as 1; the depth of node with two hops to the sink node is defined as 2; the depth of the rest nodes can be defined in the same manner. So, the max depth of network is the maximum depth of all the nodes, note for D_{Max}.

Definition 3. Network Lifetime. The network lifetime can be defined as the total number of hops in all the packets transmission process in the network from the beginning of the network until parts of the nodes run out of energy.

Definition 4. Transmission Efficiency. The total number of packets received by the sink node from the beginning of the network when the energy of some nodes is exhausted is defined as the transmission efficiency.

2.2   Multi-priority Queue Node Model

The CEDOP opportunistic routing algorithm is proposed to solve the multi-priority packets transmission problem in wireless sensor network. Before choosing the next-hop node for packet forwarding, the routing scheme need to temporarily cache the received packets with different priorities in the local cache queues; and it need to ensure the high-priority packets could reach the sink node as soon as possible in the data transmission.

Assume that the network has only two kinds of packets, one is high priority and the other is low priority. Then, each node in the network is equipped with two cache queues which are used to store the forwarding packets: one is a high-priority cache queue Q_H, which is used to cache the high-priority data; another is a low-priority cache queue Q_L, which is used to cache the low-priority data. When the high-priority queue contains the cached data, it tends to forward the high-priority packets firstly. Only when the high-priority queue is empty, it begins to forward the data with low priority.

2.3   The Shortest Path Prediction

The network model proposed in this paper assumes that all of the deployed nodes will no longer move, so the depth of each node is also fixed. The routing scheme is based on the shortest path when choosing the next-hop node, that is, it will choose the nodes which are nearest to the destination in the path. Therefore, while designing the opportunistic routing, packets can be forwarded along the shortest path based on the depth of nodes, which can effectively improve the network throughput and reduce the transmission latency.

In the graph G, the path between node s and destination d is defined as $(s, u_1, u_2, \ldots, u_n, d)$, in order to transmit the packets quickly along the direction near to the target node, this paper proposes a method to select the next-hop node in the neighbor node set:

$$DP_i = D_i/D_{\max} \tag{1}$$

In equation (1), D_i is the depth of node u_i, D_{Max} is the maximum depth of all the nodes in the network, DP_i is the normalized shortest path prediction. When choosing the next-hop node, it will select the node with the minimum path prediction as a next-hop one for data forwarding by calculating the shortest distance prediction of the node's neighbor set.

2.4   Energy Problem

In this paper we make some assumption described as follows: (1) the initial energy of each node in network model is equal; (2) energy consumption consists of two parts: energy consumption for transmitting packets and receiving packets respectively; (3) it is a fixed value for energy consumption of each node when transmitting and receiving one bit data. So the energy consumption is independent of the transmission distance between adjacent nodes. Accordingly, we adopt the following energy model to calculate the energy consumption:

$$E_c = e \times (K_r + K_t) \tag{2}$$

Where E_c denotes the total energy consumption of a node for receiving k_r bits data and transmitting k_t bits; e is a factor indicating the consumption per bit at the transfer and receiver circuit. So residual energy of the node is:

$$E_{left} = E_{init} - \sum E_c \tag{3}$$

Where E_{left} denotes the residual energy and E_{init} is the initial energy. In opportunistic routing algorithm based on energy consumption, the residual energy of the adjacent nodes will be calculated firstly, and then the node with the maximum residual energy will be selected as the next-hop node for data forwarding. In this way, the algorithm can effectively balance energy consumption among nodes and achieve obvious improvement on network lifetime.

2.5   Congestion Analysis

For the multi-priority queue node model proposed in this paper, the node congestion situation can be determined according to the usage of the priority queues. When one node need to forward data packets, the decision of selecting a next-hop node can be made in the line with the node congestion status, which improve the network throughput and reduce the data transmission delay.

While describing the node congestion situation, for the high-priority packets, the congestion of the forwarding node only considers the current usage of the node high-priority queue; but for the low-priority packets, the congestion of the next-hop node not only considers the usage of the low-priority queue, but also need to consider the usage of the high-priority queue at the same time. It is mainly because that only when the high priority queue is empty, the packets in the low-priority queue could be forwarded to the next-hop.

For the packets with high-priority, the congestion factor is defined as:

$$C_{Hi} = \sum_{i=1}^{N_H} LH_i \bigg/ Buf_H \qquad (4)$$

Where N_H is the number of the packets in the high-priority queue, LH_i is the size of the high-priority packet (bit), and Buf_H is the cache size of the high-priority queue (bit).

For the packets with low-priority, the congestion factor is defined as:

$$C_{Li} = \left(\sum_{i=1}^{N_H} LH_i + \sum_{i=1}^{N_L} LL_i \right) \bigg/ Buf_L \qquad (5)$$

Where N_H denotes the number of the packets in the high-priority queue, LH_i is the size of the high-priority packet (bit), N_L denotes the number of the packets in the low-priority queue, LL_i is the size of the low-priority packet (bit), and Buf_L is the cache size of the low-priority queue (bit).

3   Opportunistic Routing Algorithm CEDOP

In order to meet the demand of different priorities data transmission, and guarantee the data with high-priority is transmitted on time, we consider the shortest path prediction, residual energy of nodes and congestion control at the same time. Then we define and model the node Delivery Utility in this paper, which serves as a theoretical basis for selecting routing path dynamically in opportunistic routing.

Definition 5. Delivery Utility (DU_i). It represents the degree or grade of excellence that one node serving as the next-hop node itself when it forwards data packets associated with different priorities. The node delivery utility is in connection with the shortest path prediction, residual energy and congestion control.

DU_i is obtained according to equation (6) below:

$$DU_i = W_1 \times C_i + W_2 \times E_i + W_1 \times DP_i \tag{6}$$

$$DU_i = W_1 \times C_i + W_2 \times \frac{(E_{init} - E_{left})}{E_{init}} + W_1 \times D_i/DP_i \tag{7}$$

Where C_i is the congestion factor of the forwarding node, E_i stands for the effectiveness factor of the residual energy, and E_{init} is the initial energy; E_{left} is the residual energy of a forwarding node; D_i is the depth of forwarding node; D_{Max} is the Maximum depth of nodes in the network; W_1, W_2 and W_3 weight the index of congestion, energy and distance which impact on the delivery utility respectively, and meet the formula $W_1 + W_2 + W_3 = 1$. In this paper, we set $W_1 = W_2 = W_3 = 1/3$, which are equal with each other for convenient consideration. The computing of Delivery Utility is normalized as it showed in equation (6) and (7), which combines the shortest path prediction, residual energy and congestion control with different priority data forwarding.

It will select the node with low delivery utility value as the next-hop node, when forwarding different priorities packets by using CEDOP opportunistic routing protocol in WSN. In another word, the lower the value DU_i of the node displays, the larger the opportunity that the node is selected as the next-hop forwarding node will be.

4 Simulation Experiments and Analysis

4.1 Simulation Environment

The proposed CEDOP opportunistic routing algorithm is experimented through the simulation, which is based on the NS-2 software. The parameters are set as table1. According to the assumption of network model, the simulation chooses the node located in the center of the network as the sink node.

4.2 Analysis and Evaluation

The simulation applies both the proposed CEDOP opportunistic routing algorithm and other two traditional opportunistic routing algorithms to the Multi-Priority Queues node model, which aims at realizing the performance on multi-priority data transmission. We compare the performances of different network aspects as follows: (1) According to the depth of nodes included by a specific communication domain, we select the minimum one (the nearest node towards the sink node) as the next-hop node, which is based on the shortest path routing

Table 1. Parameters of the experiment

Parameters	Value
Size of network area	$25m * 25m$
The number of nodes	300
Node initial energy	50J
Location of the sink node	(12,12)
Energy consumption for data receiving	10^1 J/bit
Energy consumption for data sending	10^1 J/bit
Node communication domain	1m

algorithm; (2) It is based on the energy consumption routing algorithm, which choosing the node with most residual energy as the next-hop node through calculating the residual energy of each node within the scope of the communication domain.

The multi-priority data packet transmission task is conducted in the same simulation environment and topological structure using the node model we proposed in this paper. According to the definition of network lifetime we present in section 2, the simulation is stopped when there is no energy remained of a node in the network.

4.2.1 Network Lifetime Comparison

Based on the CEDOP opportunistic routing algorithm we proposed and two traditional opportunistic routing algorithms mentioned above, we repeat this experiment 100 times until the simulation stops automatically. The average statistical results of network lifetime are listed in figure1:

As we have seen in figure1, the shortest path routing algorithm results in the energy of the node in the critical path consuming too fast in the procedure of packet transmission, which selects the nearest node towards the sink node as

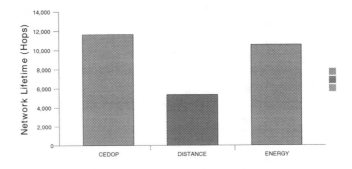

Fig. 1. The average lifetime of the network

the next-hop node. Therefore, its network lifetime is the shortest. The energy consumption routing algorithm chooses the node with the most energy remained as the data forwarding node based on computing the residual energy of each node in the communication domain. So it can guarantee the balance of network energy consumption, and prolong network lifetime largely. However, the network lifetime of the two algorithms achieved is much lower than the CEDOP opportunistic routing algorithm we proposed.

4.2.2   Transmission Efficiency Comparison

In order to analyze the transmission efficiency, we record the total number of the data packets the sink node received successfully as the representation of transmission efficiency. The experiment based on the CEDOP opportunistic routing algorithm we proposed and two traditional opportunistic routing algorithms as before repeat 100 times until the simulation stops. Figure2 shows the simulation results.

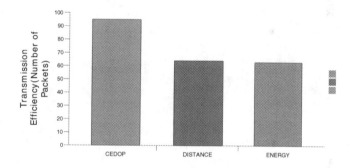

Fig. 2. The average transmission efficiency of the network

From Figure2 we can see that the algorithms based on the shortest path routing and the energy consumption routing are optimized in terms of distance and energy respectively when selecting the next-hop node, which improves the transmission efficiency to some extent. However, our CEDOP opportunistic routing algorithm not only considers the distance and residual energy problems, but also takes the congestion status of a node into account, thus achieving an obvious improvement on the transmission efficiency comparing with other routing algorithms.

4.2.3   The Residual Energy Distribution Comparison

The simulation is conducted for 100 times to compare the distribution of the residual energy of nodes. As we can see from figure3, the horizontal axis stands for the ranges of the node's residual energy distribution, and the vertical axis shows the average number of nodes within each range.

This experiment aims at calculating the residual energy of each node and obtaining the distribution of nodes based on the energy remained. It only considers

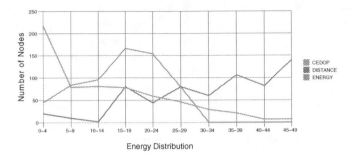

Fig. 3. The left energy distribution

the shortest distance in the shortest path routing algorithm, so the residual energy of nodes is extremely little in the critical path while data transmission, which lead to the energy consumption mainly concentrating on very part of the nodes. The figure shows that only 10% nodes' residual energy is below 30%, which demonstrates that the algorithm causes imbalance of the residual energy of nodes. Both the energy consumption routing algorithm and our CEDOP opportunistic routing algorithm are designed to take the residual energy of nodes into consideration, which balances the network energy consumption. We can also conclude that our CEDOP opportunistic routing algorithm balances the network energy consumption very well and making the nodes with 30% residual energy less than initial energy are above 70% from figure3.

4.2.4   High-Priority Data Transmission Latency Comparison

The proposed CEDOP opportunistic routing algorithm and the traditional opportunistic routing algorithm are compared in the three simulations explained above. Through analysis we can conclude that our CEDOP opportunistic routing algorithm outperforms in prolonging network lifetime, improving network transmission efficiency and balancing the network energy consumption against other opportunistic routing algorithms.

The target of this experiment is to prove the proposed CEDOP opportunistic routing algorithm can optimize the high priority data transmission latency problem to some extent. Hence, we manually set the congestion status of current network as $10\%, 20\%, \ldots, 90\%$ before the experiments and then send a high-priority data packet from the farthest node against sink node to observe. The transmission path of the packet is tracked, and the latency when it reaches the sink node is recorded as well. To facilitate the comparison, different models are applying to select the next-hop node when the data is transmitted, which is listed below: (1) The proposed multi-priority queue node model in this paper takes the congestion status of nodes into account; (2) The multi-priority queue node model without regard to the congestion situation of nodes; (3) The model without the multi-priority queue. We experiment for 100 times on the three situations respectively and log the average latency. The results are shown in figure 4:

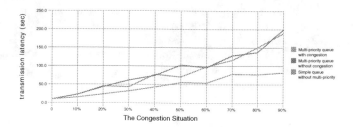

Fig. 4. The compare of the transmission delay

The CEDOP presented in this paper is mainly based on the multi-priority queue node model, which merges the shortest path, the residual energy of nodes and the congestion control at the same time. As we have seen in figure 4, the curve of the high priority data transmission latency is relatively flat when we use the multi-priority queue node model with the congestion status considered. What's more, we can find out that the transmission latency is lower than other two situations in the case of relatively serious congestion status. In conclusion, the proposed CEDOP opportunistic routing algorithm meets the demand of different priority data transmission latency, and achieves relatively good performance.

5   Conclusion

In this paper, based on the analysis of the existing opportunistic routing algorithm, we have presented a congestion control algorithm based on opportunistic routing for multi-priority data to satisfy the multi-priority data transmission latency in the practical application of WSN, which takes the shortest path, residual energy of nodes and congestion control under the multi-priority queue model into account at the same time. Based on the CEDOP algorithm, in the process of the data packet transmission, it will choose the node with the minimum delivery utility as the forwarding node when dynamically selecting next-hop node for the data packets with different priorities. Finally, the simulation results demonstrate that the proposed algorithm can effectively improve the efficiency of the data transmission, and make high-priority packets' delivery on time being a guarantee.

References

1. Poonguzharselvi, B., Vetriselvi, V.: Survey on routing algorithms in opportunistic networks. In: 2013 International Conference on Computer Communication and Informatics (ICCCI), pp. 1–5. IEEE (2013)
2. Biswas, S., Morris, R.: Opportunistic routing in multi-hop wireless networks. ACM SIGCOMM Computer Communication Review 34(1), 69–74 (2004)

3. Paquereau, L., Helvik, B.E.: Opportunistic ant-based path management for wireless mesh networks. In: Dorigo, M., et al. (eds.) ANTS 2010. LNCS, vol. 6234, pp. 480–487. Springer, Heidelberg (2010)
4. Vahdat, A., Becker, D.: Epidemic routing for partially connected ad hoc networks. Technical Report CS-200006, Duke University (2000)
5. Thanayankizil, L.V., Kailas, A., Ingram, M.A.: Two energy-saving schemes for cooperative transmission with opportunistic large arrays. In: IEEE Global Telecommunications Conference, GLOBECOM 2007, pp. 1038–1042. IEEE (2007)
6. Camilo, T., Carreto, C., Silva, J.S., Boavida, F.: An energy-efficient ant-based routing algorithm for wireless sensor networks. In: Dorigo, M., Gambardella, L.M., Birattari, M., Martinoli, A., Poli, R., Stützle, T. (eds.) ANTS 2006. LNCS, vol. 4150, pp. 49–59. Springer, Heidelberg (2006)
7. Rodoplu, V., Meng, T.H.: Minimum energy mobile wireless networks. IEEE Journal on Selected Areas in Communications 17(8), 1333–1344 (1999)
8. Lee, J.W., Lee, J.J.: Ant-colony-based scheduling algorithm for energy-efficient coverage of WSN. IEEE Sensors Journal 12(10), 3036–3046 (2012)
9. Orda, A., Rom, R.: Shortest-path and minimum-delay algorithms in networks with time-dependent edge-length. Journal of the ACM (JACM) 37(3), 607–625 (1990)
10. Pelusi, L., Passarella, A., Conti, M.: Opportunistic networking: data forwarding in disconnected mobile ad hoc networks. IEEE Communications Magazine 44(11), 134–141 (2006)
11. Zhong, Z., Wang, J., Nelakuditi, S.: Opportunistic any-path forwarding in multi-hop wireless mesh networks. University of South Carolina (2006)
12. Lo, S.C., Lu, C.L.: A Dynamic Congestion Control based Routing for Delay-Tolerant Networks. In: 2012 9th International Conference on Fuzzy Systems and Knowledge Discovery (FSKD). IEEE (2051)
13. Yuan, Q., Cardei, I., Wu, J.: An efficient prediction-based routing in disruption-tolerant networks. IEEE Transactions on Parallel and Distributed Systems 23(1), 19–31 (2012)
14. Diana, R., Lochin, E.: Modelling the delay distribution of binary spray and wait routing protocol. In: 2012 IEEE International Symposium on a World of Wireless, Mobile and Multimedia Networks (WoWMoM), pp. 1–6. IEEE (2012)
15. Massri, K., Vernata, A., Vitaletti, A.: Routing protocols for delay tolerant networks: a quantitative evaluation. In: Proceedings of the 7th ACM Workshop on Performance Monitoring and Measurement of Heterogeneous Wireless and Wired Networks, pp. 107–114. ACM (2012)
16. Zeng, K., Lou, W., Zhai, H.: Capacity of opportunistic routing in multi-rate and multi-hop wireless networks. IEEE Transactions on Wireless Communications 7(12), 5118–5128 (2008)
17. Darehshoorzadeh, A., Cerda-Alabern, L.: Distance progress based opportunistic routing for wireless mesh networks. In: 2012 8th International Wireless Communications and Mobile Computing Conference (IWCMC), pp. 179–184. IEEE (2012)
18. Jin, Z., Deng, W., Yan, N., et al.: A study of Multi-Priority Opportunistic Directional Routing for VANET. In: 2010 International Conference on Wireless Communications and Signal Processing (WCSP), pp. 1–4. IEEE (2010)

A Survey on Sensor Deployment in Underwater Sensor Networks

Dewen Zeng[1], Xiaoling Wu[1,*], Yanwen Wang[1], Hainan Chen[1,2], Kangkang Liang[1,2], and Lei Shu[3]

[1] Guangzhou Institute of Advanced Technology, Chinese Academy of Sciences, China
[2] Guangdong University of Technology, Guangzhou, China
[3] Guangdong University of Petrochemical Technology, China
xl.wu@giat.ac.cn

Abstract. Underwater sensor networks are becoming a new field, mainly applied for ocean data collection, ocean sampling, environmental and pollution monitoring, etc. Similar to terrestrial sensor networks, it is essential to provide communication coverage in such a way that the whole monitoring area is covered by the sensor nodes in UWSN. Many important deployment strategies for terrestrial sensor networks have been proposed, most of which cannot be directly applied to UWSN due to its unique 3D characteristics. This paper surveys the different deployment algorithms that can be applied to the domain of UWSN, classified into 3D underwater sensor networks, 2D underwater sensor networks and gateway node deployment. Different schemes are compared and their advantages and disadvantages are discussed.

Keywords: survey, physical clustering, deployment, UWSN.

1 Introduction

Underwater Sensor Networks (UWSNs) recently attracts a growing interest from the network researchers[1,2]. The underwater context offers to the researchers the possibility to design and to imagine new applications. Potential applications domain includes military surveillance (e.g. leak detection), ecology (e.g. water quality and biological monitoring) and public safety (e.g. seismic and tsunami monitoring), etc[3,4]. However, UWSNs are deployed in 3-D environment which introduce new challenges in terms of connectivity, coverage and mobility[5]. Although a lot of researches have been done for node deployment and self-organization in terrestrial WSNs, underwater sensor networks deployment is still a new field. Underwater sensor networks are quite different from terrestrial sensor networks, as shown in Table 1. Suitable deployment of underwater sensors for efficient monitoring is one of these crucial issues[6,7].

Just as the electromagnetic wave on the land, acoustic communication is the most promising communication medium in underwater sensor networks. However, there are also some disadvantages such as low bandwidth, high propagation delay, variable speed of sound, non-negligible node mobility and high bit

---

* Corresponding author.

L. Sun, H. Ma, and F. Hong (Eds.): CWSN 2013, CCIS 418, pp. 133–143, 2014.
© Springer-Verlag Berlin Heidelberg 2014

error rate in acoustic communication [8]. Many previous deployment solutions assume that mobile sensors, redeployment of nodes, and particular deployment grid structures may not be feasible for the underwater environment. Moreover, energy consumption is also a big problem for the source of energy because a node in a sensor network is often attached with a battery cell which is limited by its size[9-12]. Hence, some researchers begin to design new deployment algorithms that are suitable to the underwater environment.

Table 1. Comparison between Underwater and Terrestrial Wireless Sensor Networks

	Sensor	Energy	Communication Module	Speed	Communication signals	Manner of working	Hardware Configuration	Cost
UWSN	Pressure, Ray, acoustical, magnetic sensor	Battery, solar energy, tidal energy	Sound MODEM	slow	Acoustical signal	Reactive	Higher order and Path overhead	Relatively expensive
Terrestrial Sensor Networks	Light, Temperature, Humidity, Shock sensor	Solar energy, Wind energy source, electricity	Radio frequency module	fast	Electromagnetic wave, RF, Acoustical Signal	Proactive	Low	Relatively low

2   State of Art Analysis

In this paper, we provide a survey of some deployment strategies specifically designed for UWSNs.

At first, we introduce two common concepts: gateway node and surface station. Gateway is a network device functioning as a relay station, which is in charge of transmitting data from the underwater sensor nodes. It is equipped with a long-range vertical transceiver to relay data to a surface station, a horizontal transceiver to communicate with the sensor nodes to send commands and configuration data, and to collect monitored data [13].

The surface station receives and then processes multiple data from the underwater gateways via acoustic transceiver. Meanwhile, with a long-range radio transmitter and/or a satellite transmitter, it's in charge of transmitting data from an onshore sink to a surface sink.

The work done in [13] is considered as the pioneering effort towards the deployment of sensor nodes for underwater environment. The authors divide the deployment in UWSN into two communication architectures, i.e., two-dimensional and three-dimensional architecture. In two-dimensional architecture, sensor nodes are anchored at the bottom or a certain layer under the surface of ocean where these nodes and gateway nodes can be organized by means of acoustic links. The underwater gateways are responsible for relaying data from ocean bottom to surface sink. In three-dimensional architecture, sensor nodes float at different depth levels covering the entire volume monitored region. The sensors attached with surface buoys through wires whose lengths can be regulated in order to adjust the depth of these nodes.

Literature [7] proposes an energy-efficient self-organizing technique based on fuzzy logic systems (FLSs) to enhance the coverage of a UWSN after an initial random placement of sensors. In the algorithm, after an initial random deployment, each node detects the number and location of its neighbor nodes and its own battery level and evaluates its next-step shift distance using the FLSs. However, this algorithm cannot guarantee the full coverage. In [5], a localized sensor self-deployment algorithm named Greedy- Rotation-Greedy (GRG) is proposed to guarantee maximal coverage radius. The OGRG drives sensors with a localized manner to move from vertex to vertex over an equilateral triangle tessellation to surround the target point in a greedy-rotation alternate fashion. However, both of these two algorithms require either mobile sensor nodes or redeployment of nodes, which may not be feasible for UWSN.

For sensor deployment, topology plays a crucial role in issues like communication performance, power consumption, network reliability and fault tolerance capabilities. Efficient deployment of multiple radio-enabled surface sinks can enhance the performance of network in many aspects. On the basis of this fact, some deployment techniques are proposed to maximize the efficiency of the network by choosing proper locations for gateway placement. Therefore, the gateway deployment strategy becomes the focus aimed to remove the gap between topological architecture and randomly deployment. Meanwhile, by proposing an adaptive topology for UWSN, it 's easy to extend the lifetime of UWSNs which is helpful for protocol designers.

3   The Research Issues and Directions

3.1   Deployment Strategy in 2D Underwater Sensor Networks

An important factor in the deployment issue is the sensor detection capabilities [14,15]. Depending on the employed technology, sensing model can be divided into two types. The first one is called binary model. The sensor is supposed to be able to detect a target if and only if the distance between the sensor and the target is less than a particular sensing range. This model was mainly considered in research works addressing area coverage problems, such as target detection or k-coverage problem.

Since the binary model communication architecture in the terrestrial network is very similar to the one in the UWSN, both of the two deployment strategies are also similar.

Literature [13] proposes the triangular-grid deployment and derives useful geometric properties. Consider the common case of sensors with same sensing range r, the optimal deployment strategy to cover a two dimensional rectangular area using the minimum number of sensors is to deploy each sensor at the vertex of the grid of equilateral triangles, as shown in Fig. 1. With this configuration, by adjusting the distance d among sensors, i.e., the side of the equilateral triangles, it is possible to increase the coverage rate (by reducing the uncovered areas), even to achieve full coverage (i.e., the uncover areas is zero). As it is mathematically proven, when $d = \sqrt{3}r$, the uncovered areas are zero, the overlapping areas are minimized and the full coverage of a target area can be achieved. However, it requires relatively higher number of sensors; hence, they pay attention to find a trade-off between the number of deployed sensors and the achievable sensing coverage. They formulated a function to find the minimum number of sensors that need to be deployed to guarantee a target sensing coverage, which is dictated by the application requirements.

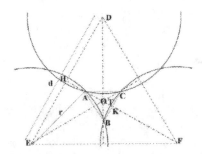

Fig. 1. The Optimal Deployment Strategy

Meanwhile, literature [13] provides an estimate of the number of redundant sensor nodes to be deployed to compensate for possible failures. However, it does not show how to deploy the redundant sensors and which sensors are redundant.

In literature [7], the authors propose another deployment strategy. Based on the consideration of mobile sensor nodes' localization and maximizing the surveillance area, they arrange the nodes in two rows along the coastline in order to provide a rectangular surveillance area with the property that any point within this area is within communication range of at least three nodes. The distance between two nodes in the same row is equal to R, where R is the underwater communication range of the nodes. Assume that the first row is fixed, we can calculate the location of the second row, i.e. the increment d_x, d_y, to maximize the surveillance area. The deployment strategy is scalable. Much more nodes can be deployed on x axis and y axis to increase the surveillance area. It will increase $\frac{R}{2}$ in length when deploying every one node on x axis and increase d_y in width when deploying every node on y axis.

The second model assumes that sensing ability diminishes as the distance to the monitored target increases. In this model, a confident and maximum sensor monitoring circle is defined. If any target occurs within the confident circle, then target detection sensitivity is considered as 1. If the target occurs out of the confident circle but within the maximum circle, then the detection sensitivity decreases as the distance increases. Finally, when the distance is larger than the radius of the maximum circle, the target is no longer detected.

Literature [1] proposed an optimal model to evaluate the effectiveness of a deployment. To each $P(x, y)$, there is a required minimum sensitivity threshold, denoted as r_{xy}. Ideally, a good UWSN deployment should lead to full coverage, i.e. the measured sensitivity of that point is larger than r_{xy}. In this work, the sensitivity in a point is estimated by all the sensors in its vicinity. The sensitivity of the point $P(x, y)$, which they denote as $S(s, p(xy))$ is estimated by all the sensors available in the monitored area.

$$S(s, p(xy)) = max\{S(s_i, P(x, y))\} \tag{1}$$

where s_i is the ith sensor in the monitored area. Of course, it is possible to obtain a deployment in which $S(s, p(xy)) > r_{xy}$ at any point in the target region. Therefore, in addition to the satisfaction of the minimum sensitivity thresholds requirement, they introduce a new metric: the overall sensitivity quadratic error. To formally express this metric, they denote each surface unit defined by its coordinates (x, y), the difference between the desired and the obtained (after deployment) sensitivities values is described as $d_{xy} = r_{xy} - S(s, p(xy))$. The overall sensitivity quadratic error, denoted Q, is given by the following formula:

$$Q = \sum d_{xy} \tag{2}$$

The sensitivity quadratic error represents the average difference (computed over all points of the monitored area) between the minimum sensitivity threshold and the sensitivity obtained after-deployment.

Then, the second step is to find a heuristic approach to address the problem of sensor deployment. They propose a geometric method inspired from the image processing and 3D modeling field, namely, mesh representation. The algorithm is named as Differentiated Deployment Algorithm (DDA). The basic idea is to permit progressive meshes division as long as it is considered to be beneficial. Mesh division can be considered to be beneficial when quadratic error (Q) decreases. Otherwise, the division is not permitted, and the mesh is marked. At last, we can find the most effective deployment in which the overall sensitivity quadratic error is minimal.

3.2   Deployment Strategy in 3D Underwater Sensor Networks

Three-dimensional underwater networks are often used to detect and observe phenomena that cannot be adequately observed by means of submarine sensor nodes, i.e., to perform cooperative sampling of the 3D ocean environment[16,17]. In this architecture, sensors float at different depths to observe a given phenomenon. There are some methods to adjust the depth of the underwater sensor node, for example, there is a kind of sensor devices which are anchored to the bottom of ocean in such a way that they cannot drift with currents. Some sensor devices are equipped with a floating buoy that can be inflated by a pump via an electronically controlled engine that embedded on the sensor.

Literature [13] proposed some deployment strategies in UWSN such as the simplest deployment strategy which does not require any form of coordination from the surface station. Sensors are randomly deployed on the bottom of the $3D$ volume, where they are anchored. Then, each sensor randomly chooses its depth, and, by adjusting the length of the wire that connects it to the anchor, it floats to the selected depth. Finally, each sensor informs the surface station about its final position. The main disadvantage is that the $3D$-random scheme cannot guarantee the coverage rate. Therefore, the second deployment strategy is proposed that the surface station calculates the depth for each sensor in order to achieve the target 1-coverage ratio. Finally, each sensor's target depth is assigned and it floats to the desired position. The third deployment strategy, called bottom-grid, needs to be assisted by one or multiple AUVs, which deploy the underwater sensors to a predefined target locations to obtain a grid deployment on the bottom of the ocean. Each sensor is also assigned a desired depth by the AUVs and accordingly floats to achieve the target coverage ratio.

Just as the probability model in 2-dimension, literature [3] proposes a probability model in 3-dimension to estimate the sensor coverage rate and node degree. Nodes are deployed into a volume of size $l \times m \times n$. Let the location of node i be represented by Cartesian coordinates (X_i, Y_i, Z_i), where $0 \geq X_i \geq l$, $0 \geq Y_i \geq m$ and $0 \geq Z_i \geq n$. We assume sensor nodes are uniformly distributed; each sensor node has equal likelihood of being at any location in the deployment region. Then, the analytical probability can be computed that two distinct nodes i and j have a common link.

Let (k, r, l, m, n) represent a network with k nodes, each with a communication range r, deployed in a region of dimensions $l \times m \times n$. In a network (k, r, l, m, n), the occurrence probability p of link (i, j) between any two distinct nodes i and j is:

$$p = \frac{1}{l^2 m^2 n^2}\left(-\frac{1}{6}r^6 + \frac{8}{15}r^5(l + m + n)\right) - \frac{1}{2}\pi r^4(ml + nl + mn) + \frac{4}{3}\pi r^3 lmn) \quad (3)$$

The expected coverage volume of a single node is:

$$\emptyset = \frac{1}{lmn}\left(-\frac{1}{6}r^6 + \frac{8}{15}r^5(l + m + n)\right) - \frac{1}{2}\pi r^4(ml + nl + mn) + \frac{4}{3}\pi r^3 lmn) \quad (4)$$

Let C_k be the expected volume covered by k nodes, V is the coverage volume. C_k can computed:

$$C_K = \left[1 - \left(1 - \frac{\emptyset}{v}\right)^k\right]v \quad (5)$$

This paper provides us a method to calculate the coverage rate in underwater environment; however, we cannot attain any practical deployment strategy.

Literature [4] proposes a practical deployment strategy in $3D$ underwater sensor networks. They assume that the nodes are initially deployed at the bottom of the water and can only move in vertical direction in 3-D space, and the nodes can adjust themselves at different depths based on the certain deployment strategy. Since the main purpose is to maximize the coverage rate by the minimum number of the sensor nodes, the adjustment of the topology is to reduce the sensing overlaps among the neighboring nodes. The nodes continue to adjust their depths until there is no room for improving their coverage. In [4], they formulated the deployment problem that determine the coverage overlaps among the sensors and group them (i.e., assigning new depths) based on such overlaps to the graph coloring problem where each node (i.e., vertex) in a graph is assigned a different color to its 1-hop neighbors. This problem is known as NP-Hard. Therefore, the graph will be formed based on the sensing ranges of the sensor nodes and the groups will correspond to colors in order to assign a unique group ID to a node which will be different to its 1-hop neighbors. After this processing, each node determines its new depth by using the depth of the ocean/water and the total number of colors. Finally, the nodes strive to move further in order to reduce the coverage overlaps that exist even after the last round of movement.

There are four phases in proposed distributed algorithm: (1) Clustering; (2) Grouping; (3) Depth assignment; (4) Additional rounds. In the clustering phase, they cluster the nodes in 2-D at the bottom of the ocean based on their node IDs. The basic idea is that each node in a neighborhood picks the highest ID in that neighborhood as its cluster ID (CID) (as it is shown in Fig. 2 and Fig. 3). In grouping phase, the coloring is performed within each cluster by the certain distributed algorithm. In the depth assignment phase, the leader of each cluster will assign the nodes within the cluster to move to a certain depth while the coverage overlaps in 2-D will be reduced in 3-D (Fig. 4). Finally, in the additional rounds phase, the nodes will move further away from each other in order to reduce the coverage overlaps that exist even after the initial round of movement.

In this paper, deployment strategies for two-dimensional and three-dimensional underwater sensor networks architectures are categorized, and the analysis is provided. The comparison of UWSNs' deployment algorithms are shown in Table. 2.

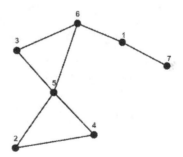

Fig. 2. Initial network

4   Gateway Node Deployment

In ground base WSN, several topologies concerning with pre-configured sensors, such as Mesh, Hexagonal, Pyranet or Bruijn, were proposed by some researchers. The common flaws among them are that the number of neighbors a node could have, has a significant effect on fault-tolerance capabilities and network throughput. Furthermore, a longer network diameter often introduces a considerable transmission delay. However, because of limitations we do not have any preconfigured topology for UWSNs so far. There is a gap between topological architecture and sensor deployment for UWSN[18-21].

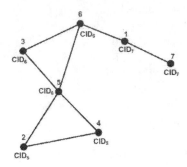

Fig. 3. Clustering of sensor nodes based on node IDs

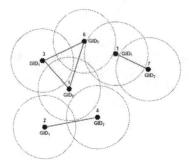

Fig. 4. Grouping of the nodes based on sensing coverage overlaps

Literature [2] presents an enhanced clustering algorithm to build a topological architecture named as ToWs, which formulates the problem as an optimization problem. That is to say, the gateway deployment is expected to have minimal delay and minimal energy consumption by finding the locations of underwater gateway nodes.

Assume that the sensors are expected to be deployed randomly in the area of interest by a relatively uncontrolled means. In ToWs, sensor nodes are firstly deployed as a Tree model, then, the children connect to each other like a wheel with virtual links but multi-hop channel. In each wheel, they select their CH by using ranking algorithm. A ToWs consists of the amplitude M and level L denoted by a ToWs (K, L, M). For example, a ToWs $(K, 1, 2)$ is a tree that its children are connected to each other like a Ring and besides, they have a center node (CN) that they are connected to.

Each CN with its brothers is one cluster. M is the number of nodes in the circumference. Thus, number of nodes within each cluster equals to $M + 1$. (For instance, ToWs $(4, 1, 4)$ has 21 nodes like a normal tree with 4 children). Network degree (ND) of this topology is 9, because each CN has M extra edges to its inter cluster's nodes. More than that, each CN with 1 channel is connected to its father from outer cluster's node and is similarly connected to its children (in contrast with normal Tree that each node is just connected to its father and

Table 2. Comparison of UWSNs' Deployment Algorithms

	Methods Adopted	Literature	Coverage	Node Number	Network Lifetime	Energy Consumption
2-D	Random deployment strategy	8	low	more	short	high
	The gateway deployment strategy models	8	high	No change	long	low
	Sensors are anchored to the bottom of the ocean	13	low	more	short	high
	Triangular-grid deployment pattern	8	high	less	long	low
	Fuzzy logic systems	7	high	less	long	low
	Reducing MAC contention	5	high	less	long	low
3-D	To adjust the depth of each sensor node	13	high	less	long	low
	3D-random	13	low	more	short	high
	Bottom-random	13	low	No change	short	high
	Bottom-grid	13	low	No change	short	high
	A geometric method	1	high	less	long	high
	Optical Sensor Networks	16	⋆	⋆	⋆	⋆

children). Each node in ToWs (K, L, M) is labeled with three variable parameters $(K, LandM)$. Similarly, each ToWs (K, L, M) has k sub networks ToWs $(K, L - 1, M)$, which are labeled with C index, where $2 < C < L$. Therefore, with these three parameters such as (x, y, z), each node has unique address. They can be constructed by grouping basic building blocks. For larger networks and in order to have more distributed networks, the number of K can be increased. In this gateway architecture, fault-tolerance capabilities and network throughput will be improved.

Meanwhile, some researchers pay attention to maximize the network lifetime through some certain deployment algorithm (UDA) for underwater sensor networks in ocean environment. For example, the paper [6] proposes the UDA algorithm which can determine and select the best cluster shape, then partition the space into layers and clusters while maintaining full coverage and full connectivity. In addition, nodes closer to sinks are possible to bear a heavier data-relaying mission. UDA sets different node deployment densities at different layers in response to the potential relay discrepancy.

In order to alleviate the burdens of high propagation delay and high error probability during transmission, literature [9] proposes a kind of surface-level gateways deployment method, in which a prediction assisted dynamic surface gateway placement algorithm for mobile underwater sensor networks, called PADP, intends to maximize the coverage within a specific period of time. PADP applies a tracking scheme to predict sensor nodes' positions, adopting branch-and-cut to solve the optimization problem, and employing a disjoint-set data structure to handle connectivity.

5   Conclusion

Generally speaking, the deployment in UWSN is mainly in theoretical research and far from the practical application because of the unique characteristics such as the variable speed of sound and the non-negligible node mobility due to water currents. So, on one side, we expect the appearance of some new technology to solve those problems in UWSN, and on the other side, there are many challenges that need to be explored when the field of underwater sensor networks is rapidly growing.

References

1. Aitsaadi, N., Achir, N., Boussetta, K., Pujolle, G.: Differentiated Underwater Sensor Network Deployment. In: OCEANS 2007 – Europe, pp. 1–6 (2007)
2. Hamidzadeh, M., Forghani, N., Movaghar, A.: A new hierarchical and scalable architecture for performance enhancement of large scale underwater sensor networks. In: 2011 IEEE Symposium on Computers & Informatics (ISCI), pp. 520–525 (2011)
3. Li, X., Frey, H., Santoro, N., Stojmenovic, I.: Localized Sensor Self-Deployment for Guaranteed Coverage Radius Maximization. In: IEEE International Conference on Communications, ICC 2009, June 14-18 (2009)
4. Akkaya, K., Newell, A.: Self-deployment of sensors for maximized coverage in underwater acoustic sensor networks. Computer Communications (2009)
5. Vieira, L.F.M., Almiron, M.G., Loureiro, A.A.F.: 3D MANETs: Link Probability, Node Degree, Network Coverage and applications. In: 2011 IEEE Wireless Communications and Networking Conference (WCNC), pp. 2042–2047 (2011)
6. Heidemann, J., Ye, W., Wills, J., Syed, A., Li, Y.: Research Challenges and Applications for Underwater Sensor Networking. In: Wireless Communications and Networking Conference, WCNC 2006. IEEE (2006)
7. Mathur, R., Sharma, M.K., Misra, A., Baveja, D.: Energy-Efficient Deployment of Distributed Mobile Sensor Networks Using Fuzzy Logic Systems. In: Advances in Computing, Control & Telecommunication Technologies, ACT 2009 (2009)
8. Zhang, Y., Li, X., Fang, S.: Deployment analysis in two-dimensional Underwater Acoustic Wireless Sensor Networks. In: 2011 IEEE International Conference on Signal Processing, Communications and Computing, ICSPCC (2011)
9. Liu, J., Han, X., Al-Bzoor, M., Zuba, M., Cui, J.-H., Ammar, M.A., Rajasekaran, S.: PADP: Prediction assisted dynamic surface gateway placement for mobile underwater networks. In: IEEE Symposium on Computers and Communications, ISCC (2012)
10. Ayaz, M., Baig, I., Abdullah, A., Faye, I.: A survey on routing techniques in underwater wireless sensor networks. Journal of Network and Computer Applications 34, 1908–1927 (2011)
11. Tan, H.-P., Diamant, R., Seah, W.K.G., Waldmeyer, M.: A survey of techniques and challenges in underwater localization. Ocean Engineering 38, 1663–1676 (2011)
12. Zhou, Z., Cui, J.-H., Zhou, S.: Efficient localization for large-scale underwater sensor networks. Ad Hoc Networks 8, 267–279 (2010)
13. Pompili, D., Melodia, T., Akyildiz, I.F.: Three-dimensional and two-dimensional deployment analysis for underwater acoustic sensor networks. Ad Hoc Networks 7(4), 778–790 (2009)
14. Guo, Y., Liu, Y.: Localization for anchor-free underwater sensor networks. Computers and Electrical Engineering (2013)
15. Gu, X., Yang, Y., Hu, R.: Analyzing the Performance of Channel in Underwater Wireless Sensor Networks (UWSN). Procedia Engineering 15, 95–99 (2011)

16. Reza, A., Harms, J.: Robust Grid-based Deployment Schemes for Underwater Optical Sensor Networks. In: 2009 IEEE 34th Conference on Local Computer Networks (LCN 2009), Zurich, Switzerland, October 20-23 (2009)
17. Golen, E.F., Mishra, S., Shenoy, N.: An underwater sensor allocation scheme for a range dependent environment. Computer Networks 54, 404–415 (2010)
18. Guo, Z., Wang, B., Cui, J.-H.: Generic prediction assisted single-copy routing in underwater delay tolerant sensor networks. Ad Hoc Networks 11, 1136–1149 (2013)
19. Domingo, M.C., Prior, R.: Energy analysis of routing protocols for underwater wireless sensor networks. Computer Communications 31, 1227–1238 (2008)
20. Grasso, R., Cococcioni, M., Mourre, B., Osler, J., Chiggiato, J.: A decision support system for optimal deployment of sonobuoy networks based on sea current forecasts and multi-objective evolutionary optimization. Expert Systems with Applications 40, 3886–3899 (2013)
21. Chen, B., Pompili, D.: Team formation and steering algorithms for underwater gliders using acoustic communications. Computer Communications 35, 1017–1028 (2012)

Energy Management and Optimization in Wireless Multimedia Sensor Networks*

Yong Fu[1], Qiang Guo[2], Changying Chen[3], Ming Yang[1], and Yinglong Wang[4]

[1] Shandong Province Key Laboratory of Computer Network, Shandong Computer Science Center, Shandong, China
[2] School of Management Science and Engineering, Shandong University of Finance and Economics, Shandong, China
[3] Information Research Institute of Shandong Academy of Sciences, Shandong, China
[4] Shandong Academy of Sciences, Shandong, China
yongfu0976@gmail.com,
{guoq,chenchy,yangm,wangyl}@sdas.org

Abstract. Combining wireless sensor networks and video/voice communication for multi-data hybrid wireless network suggests possible applications in numerous fields. However multimedia data and sensor data have significant differences in data characteristics and communications. Especially multimedia codec and processing would consume a lot of energy, meanwhile high-speed massive real-time voice data processing poses challenges for wireless channel management, hardware design and energy management. In this paper, we present a wireless audio sensor network platform A-LNT, study and discuss key elements for energy management design and implementation: hybrid MAC protocol design based on super frame, multimedia codec and processing, wireless address filtering, efficient power management unit, and so on. Furthermore, we adopt experiment measurement and simulation methods, discuss and analyze these energy management strategies and optimization methods in detail. The study will provide useful advice and reference for low power design in future wireless multimedia sensor network and internet of things research.

Keywords: Wireless Multimedia Sensor Networks, MAC Protocol, Energy Management, Internet of Things.

1   Introduction

Research of Wireless Multimedia Sensor Networks(WMSN) [1] draw attention to scientists and engineers in the last few years, with the rapid development of Internet of Things(IOT) and mobile internet [2],[3]. Combing multimedia communication and wireless sensor networks(WSN)[4] suggests possible applications

* This paper is supported by the Shandong Provincial Foundation for Outstanding Yong Scientist (Grant No. BS2012DX035, BS2011DX031), the Science and Technology Development Foundation of Shandong Academy of Sciences (Grant No. KJH201110).

L. Sun, H. Ma, and F. Hong (Eds.): CWSN 2013, CCIS 418, pp. 144–154, 2014.
© Springer-Verlag Berlin Heidelberg 2014

in health care systems, dispatch and communication in WSN applications, emergency communications, etc. However, multimedia data and WSN data are Significant different in transmission features; moreover multimedia data processing and encoding/decoding would use lots of energy; furthermore, frequent high-speed real-time transmission of multimedia data poses challenges for WSN channel management, protocol design, hardware design and energy management.

Energy consuming is a key basic issue in WSNS, it is also a core issue of restricting the WMSN development. researchers have undertaken considerable work on energy saving, such as routing protocol design[5], QOS-based MAC protocol research and cross-layer protocol design[6], low-power multimedia codec algorithm[7], distributed compression codec algorithm[8], multimedia key feature extraction[9], energy harvesting[10]. However, these studies often only consider performance optimization on one aspect and ignore the other aspects. In this paper, we summarize the energy management strategy in WMSN on the base of our previous Wireless Audio Sensor Network(WASN) research, adopt experimental method and simulation method to study and analyze these energy saving/optimizing methods. In details, we discusses the transmission features of multimedia data and WSN data at first; then we propose a dynamic channel distribution method and MAC protocol based on super-frame for multimedia transmission, this protocol is realized and discussed on our WASN platform A-LNT; Further, we discuss the energy saving strategy by using micro controller /wireless chip hardware resources and embedded software; high-efficient power management resolution for optimizing battery energy conversion efficiency is simulated and studied at last.

1.1   MAC Protocol Design

Most WSN nodes are battery-powered, and periodic sleeping and wake-up are widely applied in MAC protocol design to reduce energy consumption, such as S-MAC[11], T-MAC[12] and Diff-MAC[13]. While multimedia transmissions would occupy wireless channels until the end of the communication. WMSN MAC protocol design must taking into account the WSN and multimedia communication requirements, and these operations are Significantly different in following areas: (1) multimedia are delay-sensitive, while WSN requires high data-reliability. (2) multimedia data are burst and would generate large amount of data transmission, while there are small amount of data transmissions in WSN and there is little change in data traffic in most cases. (3) multimedia transmissions require precise synchronization, while WSN has much lower requirements on clock-synchronization. In WSN, reply mechanism and data retransmission are applied to make sure data transmission reliability, but it would cause transmission delay. multimedia communications are real-time and require synchronous in transmitter and receiver. Meanwhile data stream encodings are popular in Wireless multimedia communication, some error rate is acceptable. Taking CVSD codec as an example, even the error rate reaches 10%, the MOS is greater than 3. Frequent confirms in wireless multimedia communications increase network burden but the QoS improving is limited, in addition WSN data is useless for WSN nodes and network management, and frequent wake-up from sleeping would rapid deplete node power. Letting senor keep in sleeping when there are multimedia transmission could prevent energy lost effectively and extend nodes's lifetime.

Moreover, multimedia nodes require higher main frequency for complex codec and data processing. Furthermore WMSN system would assign more wireless channel to multimedia communications and restrict sensor nodes data transmission to reduce conflicts and congestion. Although wireless channel would be occupied in multimedia communications, the channel would be in idle for a long time, so high main frequency is not needed any more, and wireless channels should be redistributed to network management and senor data transmission.

In a word, In order to meet the requirements of multimedia communications and keep low power consumption, MAC protocol should be clock synchronous and could adjust channel allocation with network changing. We designed our MAC protocol as shown in Fig. 1.

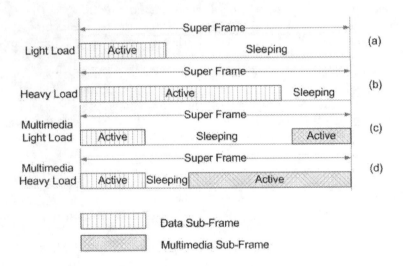

Fig. 1. Hybrid channel dynamic allocating mechanism

This mechanism is consists of four key components: (1) The network adopts a low time synchronization accuracy and reduce node main frequency to reduce energy consumption. the data sub-frame times are automatic adjusted with network loads and CSMA mechanism is adopted to manage wireless channels. (2) When there are multimedia data transmissions, node's main frequency is increased to work in full-speed mode and adopts high-precise time synchronization, reduce data sub-frame time while ensuring network performance. (3) Sensor nodes listen channel and send data only in data sub-frame. (4) Channels are allocated by Center node using TDMA mechanism in multimedia sub-frame.

Taking A-LNT as an example, A-LNT is consists of 1 center node(CNODE), up to 16 audio nodes(ANODE) and 64 sensor nodes(DNODE), it supports three communication modes: peer-2-peer mode(P2P), CNODE forwarding mode(PCP) and voice conference mode(VCF). this platform supports three P2P voice communication most or a VCF including all ANODES. the super-frame T is 20.48ms and high main frequency is 16MHz, the super-frame is divided into 1 data sub-frame (t0=6.04ms) and 6 multimedia sub-frame(t1-t6=3.4ms). 32T compose a management cycle TT, T0 is CNODE slot for network management. T1-T16 are DNODE slots. Every 65.5s(3200T) CNODE sends a spooling packet, all nodes should send reply packet in specified slot, if there are sensor data need to upload the node sends them simultaneously. nodes No.1 -No.16 reply in first management period TT1, nodes No.17-No.32 reply in TT2, and all replies should be finished in TT4. If CNODE didn't receive reply from one node for three successive, CNODE would delete the node. Priority design rules are as follows: CNODE has the highest priority, DNODES have highest priority in allocated slot, other data are sent sequentially according to the priority within the data sub-frame. The high-speed crystal is shutdown when ther is no voice communication, and the node's main clock reduces to about 2MHz, TT increases to 655s (i.e. 32000T). All nodes wake up in T0 when the cycle is CNODE spooling cycle and go to sleep until it's time to send reply packet. when new nodes appear, they compete channel through CSMA/CA mechanism. This adaptive hybrid channel allocation method is an effective solution to the contradiction between multimedia communications and system power consumption.

2 Energy Management and Optimization: Hardware-Related

WSNS are highly experimental researches. The system powerconsumption could be further reduced by using microcontroller resources and hardware design. We will discuss energy management optimization measures from audio data processing, wireless address filtering and efficient power management in follwoing sections.

2.1 Multimedia Encoding/Decoding and Data Processing

Selection of multimedia codecs has great impact for system performance and power consumption. In general, the high compression ratio algorithm is complexity, and high power consumption. Low compression ratio algorithm is low-power, but has high code rate and bandwidth-intensive. General data processing of multimedia data packet is packaged centrally, in order not to affect the new multimedia data processing the data forwarding and receiving must be completed within a very short time, which requires a high processor clock speed. Processing multimedia codec data in the form of data stream in interrupt could reduce main frequency requirements greatly. In A-LNT, the voice codec chip for the CMX649, using CVSD coding, data rate is 15.625Kbps, typical power consumption is 2.4ma@3V. In order to reduce hardware requirement and guarantee communication quality, we introduce 4 data buffers, 2 for storing received audio data and 2 for storing encoded audio data. In sampling periods, cross access to buffers are used to ensure audio contents complicity and correction. The processing step is carried out simultaneously with wireless packet processing.

2.2   Addressing Filtering

In wireless network, all active nodes listen radio channel, in most cases only one node is the target node, other nodes receive useless packet and waste time to unpack and handle it. Address filtering is introduced to reduce wireless data processing time, which means the wireless packet is unpacked and handled when address is matched, otherwise the packet is abandoned. Address filtering can reduce processing time of that complete reception. In order to get precise time, the packet process time model is introduced:

$$
\begin{cases}
T_{send} = T_s + T_w + \frac{N_p + N_a}{B} \\
\\
T_{rev} = T_r + T_m + \frac{N_p + N_a}{B}
\end{cases}
\tag{1}
$$

Where T_{send} is the sending packet processing time, T_{rev} is the receiving packet processing time, T_s is the transmitter MCU processing time, T_w is the wireless sending time, T_m is the receiver MCU processing time, T_r is the wireless receiving time, N_p is the packet payload length in bits, N_a is the preamble bits, sync word and other data inserted automatically by CC2500, B is wireless transmission speed. The processing times of different packet lengths are measured as shown below:

Table 1. Processing times of different packet lengths and hardwares

Time (us)	Address match?	MCLK (MHz)	SPI Speed (Kbps)	Payload Length(Bytes)
45	No	16	4000	5
900	Yes	2	500	5
160	No	2	500	5
350	Yes	16	4000	12
45	No	16	4000	12
1500	Yes	2	500	12
160	No	2	500	12
1050	Yes	16	4000	46
45	No	16	4000	46

The timing accuracy is 5us in above measures. The total processing time saving with parameters of Table.1 VS No. of nodes are shown in Fig. 2.

Where B means bytes, HS means high speed and LS means low speed. It can be seen from above graph, the processing time of all active nodes in WSN is

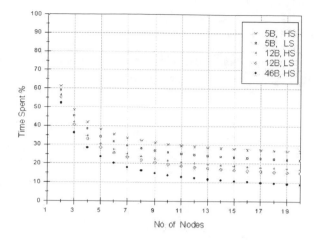

Fig. 2. Time spent VS No. of nodes

reducing with the nodes number increasing and packet length increasing. Even there are only 2 nodes, the processing time is reduced by 38%. When the No. of ANODE reaches 6, the time spent is reduced to 20% of that without Address filtering. It is an efficient method to reduce network power consumption.

We have discussed energy management methods by protocol design,using hardware resources and embedded software optimization. Fig. 3 is A-LNT channel assignment and address filtering diagram. The system could reduce conflict by the greatest degree and improve the utilization of the radio channel.

3   Efficient Power Management

We have established and tested the experimental platform. The operation currents are shown in table 2. Audio codec and audio amplifier has high requirements

Table 2. Current Summary

Node Type	Tx(mA)	Rx(mA)	Audio(mA)	Average Current(mA)	Sleep Mode(mA)
CNODE	21.4	19.6	27	53	3.2
ANODE	21.4	19.6	27	52	0.9
DNODE	21.4	19.6	-	22	0.6

for power supply, so a high Power Supply Rejection Ratio(PSRR) Low Dropout Regulator(LDO) is necessary. However, directly connecting a LDO to batteries will Increase current consumption and reduce available battery capacity. A high performance step down DC-DC converter TPS62203 is added to the circuit in

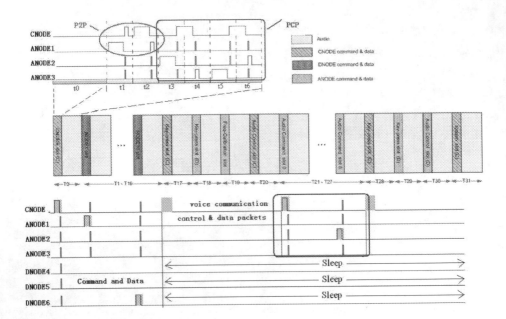

Fig. 3. A-LNT channel allocation and address filtering diagram

order to improve efficiency. The power management circuit schematic is seen in Fig. 4. We have studied the batteries lifetime in theory.

In order to simplify calculation we assume the battery maintains OCV(constant open circuit voltage) 1.5V and RI(the internal resistance) is $150m\Omega$. Battery capacity Q is 2300mAh. The batteries are three alkaline batteries in series. The ANODE currents vary with operation mode: TX, RX, Sleep, and Audio. Average TX time tTX is 2ms/1000T, the RX time tRX is 3ms/1000T.For boards with only LDO, the battery lifetime is:

$$T_{days} = \frac{Q \times 3600}{I_{auido} \times taudio + I_{rx} \times tRX + I_{sleep} \times tsleep + 3600 \times 24 \times Ildo} \quad (2)$$

Where Ildo is supply current of LDO, the LDO is XC6204B30 in the design and Ildo is 70uA. For boards with DC/DC converters, battery lifetime is:

$$T_{days} = \frac{Q \times 3600}{I'_{auido} \times taudio + I'_{rx} \times tRX + I'_{sleep} \times tsleep + 3600 \times 24 \times Ildo'} \quad (3)$$

Where

$$I'_i = \frac{Ii \times V_{out}}{(OCV - RI \times Ii') \times \eta} \quad (4)$$

And V_{out}=3.3V, η=95%. The calculation results are shown in Fig. 5. It can be seen that the DC/DC converter extend battery life time by greater than 29%.

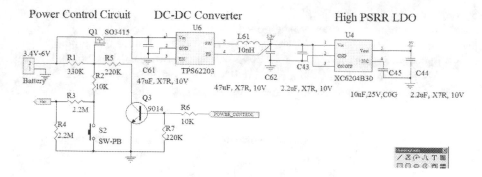

Fig. 4. Power management circuit

If voice communication time is 30 minutes per day, ANODES could work for more than 60 days without changing batteries. Its also possible to serial more batteries or use high voltage batteries extending node working time.

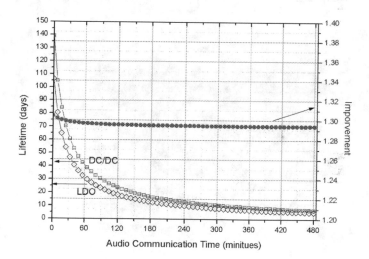

Fig. 5. Battery life time VS voice communiction time

The minimum input voltage is calculated by following equations:

$$Vin_{min} = Vout_{max} + IL_{max} \times (r_{ds}(ON)_{max} + RL) \tag{5}$$

$$IL_{max} = Iout_{max} + \frac{Vout \times \left(1 - \frac{V_{out}}{V_{in}}\right) / (L \times f)}{2} \tag{6}$$

Where: $Iout_{max} = 53mA$; $V_{out} = 3.3V = 3.3V$; $L = 10\mu H$; $f = 1MHz$; $r_{ds}(ON)_{max} = 670m\Omega$; the power inductance is CDRH5D28NP-100N from

Sumida and RL=$RL = 65m\Omega$ .The result shows that is V_{in} less than 3.4V, for three alkaline batteries in series, the board could extract almost all the energy. In practical application, users may want to turn off the terminal equipment when they finish their works. We use a low VCEsat(BISS) transistor PBSS5320T from NXP semiconductors and a small signal PNP transistor 9014 to design a load switch(Fig. 6). Although P-channel MosFet(PMOS) Transistors are popular in load switch designs, we chose a BISS transistor because it is ESD insensitive and has a constant VBE about 650mV. So the voltage measurement circuit is easy to realize. The power control circuit work-flow is as follows: When the batteries are connected to the board, the BISS transistor is off, when the tact switch S2 is pressed, the BISS transistor is ON, then the MCU turn on Q3, the board works normally, and the MCU monitors voltage between R4 and R5. When the S2 pressed again or Batteries voltage is lower than threshold voltage for 30 seconds, the MCU turn off Q2, the board is powered down and the quiescent current is only 2.21uA.

the simulation circuit diagram in TINA-Ti 9.0 is as shown in Fig. 7, and The simulation results are shown in Fig. 8. The current consumption of BISS transistor is about 255uA and the VBEsat is about 50mV when the load current is 50mA.

Fig. 6. Audio node test-board

It can be seen that the load current change detection voltage is kept constant, while the load switch when the differential pressure at full load is less than 50mV, current consumption is about 250uA. Node node shutdown current consumption is only 2.21uA. The power management circuitry has virtually no impact on the node power consumption.

3.1   Conclusion

Introducing multimedia communication to WSN would extend WSN applications, and it has very broad application prospects, at the same time more

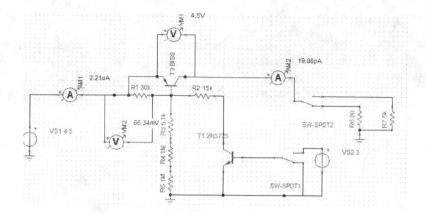

Fig. 7. Power control circuit simulation diagram in TINA-Ti 9.0

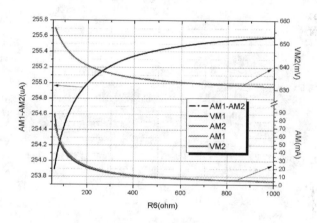

Fig. 8. Voltages and currents VS loads

stringent low power design requirement is posed. In this paper, we have studied and discussed key elements for energy management design and implementation by taking A-LNT as an example: adaptive dynamic channel allocation method, multimedia encoding/decoding and processing, wireless address filtering and efficient power management and optimizing. Furthermore, we adopted experiment measurement and simulation methods, discuss and analyze these energy management strategies and optimization methods in detail from protocol design, embedded software programming and hardware design. The study will provide useful advice and reference for low power design in future wireless multimedia sensor network and internet of things research.

References

1. Melodia, T., Akyildiz, I.F.: Research Challenges for Wireless Multimedia Sensor Networks. Distributed Video Sensor Networks 4, 233–246 (2011)
2. Ma, H.D.: Internet of things: Objectives and scientific challenges. Journal of Computer Science and Technology 26, 919–924 (2011)
3. Yick, J., Mukherjee, B., Ghosal, D.: Key Technologies and Applications of Internet of Things. Computer Science 37, 1–4 (2010) (in Chinese)
4. Yick, J., Mukherjee, B., Ghosal, D.: Wireless sensor network survey. Computer Networks 52, 2292–2330 (2008)
5. Cao, X., Wang, R.C., Huang, H.P., Sun, L.J., Xiao, F.: Multi-Path Routing Algorithm for Video Stream in Wireless Multimedia Sensor Networks. Journal of Software 23, 108–121 (2012) (in Chinese)
6. Li, R.F., Li, R.F., Luo, J.: Survey of MAC protocol in wireless multimedia sensor networks. Journal on Communications 29, 111–123 (2008) (in Chinese)
7. Sha, C., Wang, R.C., Huang, H.P., Sun, L.J.: An Energy Saving Strategy Based on Coverage Optimization and Compression Cost Estimation for Wireless Multimedia Sensor Networks. Acta Electronica Sinica 39, 2353–2358 (2011) (in Chinese)
8. Chia, W.C., Chew, L.W., Ang, L.M., Seng, K.P.: Low memory image stitching and compression for WMSN using strip-based processing. International Journal of Sensor Networks 11, 22–32 (2012)
9. Molina, J., Mora-Merchan, J.M., Barbancho, J., Leon, C.: Wireless Sensor Networks: Application-Centric Design. InTech (2010)
10. Koulali, M.-A., Kobbane, A., El Koutbi, M., Tembine, H., Ben-Othman, J.: Dynamic power control for energy harvesting wireless multimedia sensor networks. EURASIP Journal on Wireless Communications and Networking, 1–8 (2012)
11. Ye, W., Heidemann, J., Estrin, D.: An energy-efficient MAC protocol for wireless sensor networks. In: IEEE INFOCOM 2002, pp. 1567–1576. IEEE Press, New York (2001)
12. Van Dam, T., Langendoen, K.: An adaptive energy-efficient MAC protocol for wireless sensor networks. In: 1st International Conference on Embedded Networked Sensor Systems ACM, pp. 171–180. ACM Press, New York (2003)
13. Yigitel, M.A., Incel, O.D., Ersoy, C.: Design and implementation of a QoS-aware MAC protocol for Wireless Multimedia Sensor Networks. Computer Communications 34, 1991–2001 (2011)

Maximizing the Network Lifetime by Using PACO Routing Algorithm in Wireless Sensor Networks

Yuhan Su, Jinxiu Li, Zhenquan Qin, Lei Wang, and Wenzhe Zhang

School of Software, Dalian University of Technology,
Dalian, 116020, China
{ksmartinsun,jinxiu2216,zhqqin33,hansonzheg}@gmail.com,
lei.wang@dlut.edu.cn

Abstract. The network lifetime is a fundamental criterion for evaluating WSNs. Receiving and sending data packets consume energy so judicious routing strategies can effectively extend operational time. The ant colony optimization algorithm, known as ACO, is a probabilistic technique for solving computational problems. In this paper, an ACO-based routing algorithm called PACO is proposed. We take three factors into consideration. First of all, the hops are to be minimized. Additionally, energy distance is defined and needs minimizing. We also define the popularity of the sensors given the necessity to avoid those nodes that are used too often while routing. The definition of the lifetime and energy model is discussed as well. By conducting the simulation, it is proved that PACO outperforms other ACO routing algorithms, indicating that PACO is a promising routing algorithm for prolonging the lifetime of WSNs.

Keywords: WSN, ACO, network lifetime, routing algorithm, popularity.

1 Introduction

The advance of electronics and communication technology has made real-time monitoring possible. Wireless sensor networks (WSNs) are often used in this field. They have gained world-wide attention, particularly with the proliferation in Micro-Electro-Mechanical Systems technology which has facilitated the development of smart sensors. WSNs present unique characteristics mainly due to their component devices, the sensor nodes. They contain signal-processing circuits, micro-controllers and a wireless transmitter/receiver antenna. Resources are always limited such as low memory, reduced power battery and limited processing capabilities.

WSNs have great potential for many applications in scenarios [1] such as military target tracking and surveillance, natural disaster relief and biomedical health monitoring. Their quality of services is strongly dependent on the network performance. The network lifetime is a fundamental criterion for evaluating a

L. Sun, H. Ma, and F. Hong (Eds.): CWSN 2013, CCIS 418, pp. 155–165, 2014.

WSN. Since most nodes of WSNs are powered by nonrenewable batteries, the study of prolonging the network lifetime has become one of the most important issues in WSNs. Due to the characteristics of WSNs, the routing protocol has to be different from those traditional ones. First of all, the routing algorithm must be energy-efficient since the resource of energy is valuable in WSNs. Second, it should be adapted to the expandability of WSNs. Additionally, the algorithm ought to have good robustness and fault tolerance, which means one node's failure cannot affect the whole network. These requirements have posed a big challenge for designing a routing algorithm in WSNs. It is necessary to design a routing algorithm which is both distance-aware and energy-efficient.

Several methods have been proposed for routing in WSN, which will be discussed in the next section. However, few of them take both distance, namely hops, and energy into consideration. Among all the modern heuristics, the ant colony optimization algorithm, known as ACO [2], is special for its effectiveness and distributed parallel computing mechanism. Additionally, with strong robustness, ACO can be easily combined with other techniques. In this paper, we propose a routing algorithm based on classic ACO, which takes both physical distance and energy consumption into consideration in order to maximize the lifetime of WSN. We also define the popularity of a node to make the routing algorithm avoid those nodes which are too popular when choosing the route. This will help to prolong the lifetime of the popular nodes, thus improving lifetime of the whole network. We call this kind of routing algorithm as PACO.

The remainder of this paper is organized as follows: Section 2 shows some of the related work in this field. Section 3 describes the basic model and ideas of our algorithm. Section 4 proposes PACO and all the useful equations are showed. Section 5 presents the simulation of the algorithm and makes some comparison. Conclusions and further work are presented in the last section.

2   Related Work

Lots of routing algorithms and techniques have been proposed for prolonging the lifetime of WSNs, some of which are reviewed in [3].

The work in [4] designed a distributed energy balancing routing protocol, which decentralizes the data traffic in the network in a way that prolongs the lifetime of the network. The algorithm makes a tradeoff between packet delay and energy balance. Despite the applicability of the algorithm in many WSN scenarios, it assumes that each SN can communicate directly with the sink, which is not always feasible for multi-hop routing.

Tang et al. [5] proposed an energy-efficient multicast routing scheme named extended multicast routing scheme with pruning and energy balancing (E-MPEB). E-MPEB uses pruning and energy balancing algorithms to save energy and balance load. Especially, it supports multisource multicast and multiple multicast tasks. However, this research was based on static networks. They did not consider mobile networks and other network models.

A type of bio-inspired network called swarm intelligence (SI) [6], defines a new set of rules that can be adapted for WSNs in terms of gathering food and communications among species such as ants, bees and birds. These SIs have to be adjusted to develop new protocols for optimizing and managing sensor networks. Among them, ACO has been used by some researchers.

AntHocNet is an ant based routing protocol proposed by Di Caro [7] in the effort to combine the advantages from AntNet. AntHocNet reactively finds a route to the destination on demand, and proactively maintains and improves the existing routes or explore better paths. In AntHocNet, ant maintains a list of nodes it has visited to detect cycles. The source node sends out forward ants and when it receives all the backward ants, one generation is completed.

Camilo et al. [8] designed a routing algorithm based on ant colony optimization. They look for paths between the sensor nodes and a destination node, that are at the same time short in length and energy-efficient, contributing to maximize the lifetime of the WSN. However, there are some mathematical problems in the algorithm.

An ACO-based approach that can maximize the lifetime of heterogeneous WSNs has been proposed by [9]. The methodology is based on finding the maximum number of disjoint connected covers that satisfy both sensing coverage and network connectivity. A construction graph is designed with each vertex denoting the assignment of a device in a subset. Based on pheromone and heuristic information, the ants seek an optimal path on the construction graph to maximize the number of connected covers.

The above algorithms have their own special ideas and some of them tend to have good performance. However, none of them considered the necessity to avoid those nodes that are used too often while routing. The lifetime can be prolonged if the nodes can live longer. Also, it is important to take both physical distance and residual energy into account while routing. That is what we focus on in this paper.

3   System Model and Considerations

3.1   Lifetime of WSNs

In the literature, we can find a great number of relevant publications that address the problem of sensor network lifetime. Some papers employ network lifetime as a criterion that needs to be maximized, but never exactly define the term network lifetime. However, the majority of authors do state how net-work lifetime is defined in the context of their work. Obviously, this leads to a strong diversity of coexistent definitions.

The definition found most frequently in the literature is n-of-n lifetime. In this definition, the network lifetime T_n^n ends as soon as the first node fails, thus

$$T_n^n = \min_{v \in V} T_v \tag{1}$$

With T_v being the lifetime of node v. However, in most cases the lifetime calculated by this metric will be far too short for meaningful evaluation of sensor network applications. The T_n^n metric is also not adequate for evaluating scenarios that consider hardware failures, because randomly distributed hardware failures might occur very early and thus distort the lifetime measure considerably.

In this paper, we define the lifetime as T_n^k, the time during which at least k out of n nodes are alive. In another word, the network is alive until $n - k$ sensors dies.

3.2   Energy Consumption

Generally, sensors consume energy when they sense, receive and transmit data. Communication characteristics and energy consumption models affect the advantages and performance of protocol. In this paper, we give each sensor an initial energy E_0. Receiving a packet and sending a packet consumes the same amount of energy ε, which is showed as below:

$$E_{TX} = E_{RX} = \varepsilon \tag{2}$$

3.3   Factors of PACO

When maximizing lifetime of WSNs, we have to take both physical distance and remainder energy of the nodes into account. The popularity of sensors is also important as discussed above. In a word, there are three important factors in our routing algorithm PACO.

(1) Hops

A routing algorithm has to consider the physical distance, namely hops in WSNs. Hops refer to the number of nodes that a packet has visited from the source to the destination. Receiving and forwarding a packet consumes much energy for sensor nodes, whose energy resource is scarce. To prolong the lifetime of WSN, it is necessary to minimize the hops that a data packet travels so that the energy consumed can be decreased. The ant cooperation mechanism in ACO has been used in solving traveling salesman problem, so it is not a difficult task for PACO to find a path with less hops.

(2) Energy

Energy resource is the scantiest and most valuable resource of WSNs. WSNs have great potential for many applications in various scenarios but the problem of energy consumption poses a big challenge for researchers. People want to make full use of the energy of all sensor nodes thus we can attain more information from the sensors. PACO takes the residual energy of sensors into consideration while routing. We will define energy distance in the next section so that PACO can choose the nodes that have relatively more energy than others to form the path.

(3) Popularity

In this paper we introduce the concept of popularity of the nodes, which will be defined in the next section. It is often the case that the node which has sent many data before may send more data afterwards. This kind of nodes may have a large energy consumption which may make the load unbalanced, thus decreasing the lifetime of WSNs. Therefore we define popularity of a node in WSNs. The bigger the popularity is, the smaller the possibility of the node to be chosen is. In this case, we can decrease the energy consumed by those popular nodes and transfer the consumption to those nodes which are relatively unpopular. Then we can balance the load and thus increase the lifetime of WSNs.

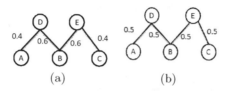

(a)   (b)

Fig. 1. An example of the popularity

An example is showed as Fig. 1. Node D is neighbour to A and B, which means A and B are within the transmission range of D. Node E is neighbour to B and C. We assume that in modified ACO, the possibility of ant that is in D to choose A, namely p(DA), is 0.4. Similarly, p(DB)=0.6, p(EB)=0.6 and p(EC)=0.4, which is showed as Fig. 1(a). According to the values of the possibility, it is apparent the energy of B is the highest. After several routing based on modified ACO, obviously the energy consumption of B is much larger than other nodes. Then the possibility is changed like this: p(DA)=0.5, p(DB)=0.5, p(EB)=0.5 and p(EC)=0.5, which is showed as Fig. 1(b). Although the possibility of the ant in D to choose A is the same with that to choose B, we hope that D can choose A instead of B because B has consumed too much energy and this is not good for balancing the load and prolonging the lifetime. If we design an algorithm which can avoid nodes like B while routing, the overall energy consumption will decline so the lifetime can be prolonged. Based on this, we define popularity to decrease the possibility of popular nodes.

4   PACO Routing Algorithm

We propose PACO to find the best route in WSN which maximizes the lifetime of the network. We introduce the new concept called the popularity of a node, which is calculated as:

$$pop_i(t) = \frac{T_i}{T} \tag{3}$$

where T_i shows the times of the node i that has been used in the previous routing before the moment t and T represents the total times of use among nodes in the network. The bigger pop is, the more popular the node is. To use the popularity in our algorithm, we define δ as the popularity factor which is defined as:

$$\delta_i(t) = \begin{cases} \log [pop_i(t)]^{-1} & pop_i \neq 0, 1 \\ 1 & pop_i = 0, 1 \end{cases} \quad (4)$$

It shows the frequency of use of node i in the previous routing before the moment t. The smaller δ is, the more popular the node is, which means the possibility to use it should be decreased relatively in the next routing.

After defining popularity, we can create other equations. In our algorithm, we take both the distance and the energy into consideration when we choose the next node during routing. In this case, we define the energy distance as follows:

$$e_{ij} = \frac{1}{E_i} + \frac{1}{E_j} \quad (5)$$

where E_i shows the residual energy of node i.

In PACO, we use the following formula to compute the possibility when choosing the next node:

$$p_{ij}^k(t) = \begin{cases} \dfrac{[\tau_{ij}(t)]^\alpha \cdot [\eta_{ij}(t)]^\beta \cdot [\delta_j(t)]^\gamma}{\sum\limits_{s \in allowed_k} [\tau_{is}(t)]^\alpha \cdot [\eta_{is}(t)]^\beta \cdot [\delta_s(t)]^\gamma} & if j \in allowed_k, \\ 0 & otherwise. \end{cases} \quad (6)$$

where $allowed_k$ is the set of feasible components; that is, edges (i, s) where s is a city not yet visited by the ant k. The parameters α, β, γ control the relative importance of the pheromone the heuristic information η_{ij} and the popularity. η_{ij} is given by

$$\eta_{ij} = \frac{1}{(d_{ij})^{w_1} \cdot (e_{ij})^{w_2}} \quad (7)$$

the parameters w_1 and w_2 control the relative importance of the physical distance versus the energy distance. In WSNs, we just have to consider the number of nodes that a packet has visited. In another word, d_{ij} should be 1 in the above formula at any time. So its final form is as follows:

$$\eta_{ij} = \frac{1}{e_{ij}} \quad (8)$$

The pheromone τ_{ij}, associated with the edge joining cities i and j, is updated as follows:

$$\tau_{ij} = (1 - \rho) \cdot \tau_{ij} + \sum_{k=1}^{m} \Delta\tau_{ij}^k \quad (9)$$

where ρ is the evaporation rate, m is the number of ants, and $\Delta\tau_{ij}^k$ is the quantity of pheromone laid on edge (i, j) by ant k:

$$\Delta\tau_{ij}^k = \begin{cases} \dfrac{Q}{(h_k)^{w_1} \cdot (\varepsilon_k)^{w_2}} & if \ ant \ k \ used \ edge \ (i,j) \\ 0 & otherwise \end{cases} \quad (10)$$

where Q is a constant that can affect the speed of convergence. h_k is the hops that the ant k has went through and ε_k is the energy distance the ant has passed.

In PACO, an ant chooses the next node based on the following construction rule:

$$i = roulette\_wheel\_select(\overrightarrow{P}) \tag{11}$$

where i is the index of selected by the roulette wheel selection [10] based on the probability distribution given by (6). The probability distribution is recorded as $\overrightarrow{P}$. In this case, our algorithm PACO has been proposed. We use this algorithm for routing in WSNs to maximize the lifetime of the network. The whole process of the routing is showed by Algorithm 1.

Algorithm 1. PACO ROUTING ALGORITHM

1: **for** $i \leftarrow 1$ **to** $maxGeneration$ **do**
2: **for** $j \leftarrow 1$ **to** $numberAnts$ **do**
3:   **for** $s \leftarrow 1$ **to** $numberNodes$ **do**
4:    clear $tour$;
5:    add $beginNode$ to $tour$;
6:    **for** $t \leftarrow 1$ **to** $numberNodes$ **do**
7:     $sum \leftarrow 0.0$;
8:     **if** t in $allowedNodes$ and t is $neighbour$ to $currentNode$ **then**
9:      $sum+ = power(pheromone[currentNode][t], \alpha) *$
       $power(1.0/\, distance[currentNode][t], \beta) * \log(1.0 *$
       $sumPopu/\, popu[t])$;
10:    **end if**
11:   **end for**
12:   **for** $t \leftarrow 1$ **to** $numberNodes$ **do**
13:    **if** t in $allowedNodes$ and t is neighbour to $currentNode$ **then**
14:     $p[t] = (power(pheromone[currentNode][t], \alpha) *$
       $power(1.0 * sumPopu/distance[currentNode][t], \beta) *$
       $\log(1.0 * sumPopu/popu[t]))/sum$;
15:    **end if**
16:   **end for**
17:   $nextNode =$ rouletteWheelSelect(p);
18:   delete $nextNode$ from $allowedNodes$;
19:   $currentNode = nextNode$;
20:   add $currentNode$ to $tour$;
21:   **if** $currentNode = end$ **then**
22:    break;
23:   **end if**
24:   **if** $ants[j].getTotalEnergy() * ants[j].getTotalHops() < bestTotal$ **then**
25:    $bestTotal = ants[j].getTotalEnergy() * ants[j].getTotalHops()$;
26:   **end if**
27:   **end for**
28: **end for**
29: updatePheromone();
30: updateDistance();
31: **end for**

---

5   Simulation and Comparison

We implement PACO routing algorithm and make some simulation. We give each sensor 100 energy units. Receiving and sending a data packet cost each sensor 2 energy units. We distribute different numbers of sensors in the area. The lifetime of the whole network is measured by the product of a constant time interval Δt and the numbers of packets that the whole network can pass, which means:

$$T = \Delta t * N_{packet} \tag{12}$$

Algorithm 2. PROCEDURE OF SIMULATION

---

1   Randomly distribute n sensors in the area;
2   Initialize the data;
3   **do**
4   **do** Randomly choose one source node and one
             destination node;
5   Simulate packet routing with PACO algorithm;
6   PacketNumber ++;
7   **until** $n - k$ sensors die
8   Output the lifetime;

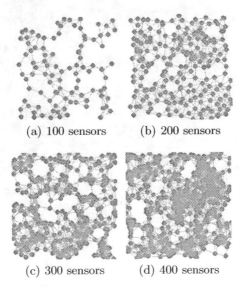

(a) 100 sensors   (b) 200 sensors

(c) 300 sensors   (d) 400 sensors

Fig. 2. The four scenarios of the simulation

We make simulation with different scenarios, where the number of sensors is 100, 200, 300 and 400. The procedure of our simulation is showed as Algorithm 2. The graphs of the network in our simulation are showed as Fig. 2. There are many parameters in PACO algorithm, the values of which are showed as Table 1.

In every scenario, we conduct five experiments and use the average of the lifetime as the final result. For example, the five experiments of PACO when there are 400 sensors is showed as Table 2.

Table 1. The values of the parameters in PACO

Parameters	Value
Initial Energy	100
Energy consumption per packet	2
Number of sensors	400,300,200,100
Lifetime parameter k	360,270,180,90
Area of the region	$300*300m^2$
Times of iterations	20
Number of ants	40
Weight α	1
Weight β	5
Weight γ	1
Time interval Δt	10s

Table 2. The values of the parameters in PACO

Experiment Number	Lifetime/s
1	11860
2	11920
3	12250
4	12020
5	11980

Therefore, the average lifetime of PACO when there are 400 sensors is 12006s.

We use some other algorithms to make comparison with PACO. The contrast algorithms are classic ACO considering hops(HACO) and classic ACO considering energy(EACO). The results are showed as Fig. 3.

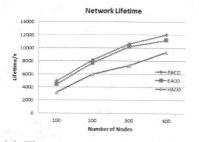
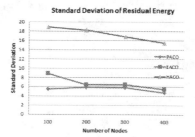

(a) The comparison of the lifetime by different algorithms

(b) The comparison of the standard deviation by different algorithms

Fig. 3. The four scenarios of the simulation

We can see from the graph that the lifetime improved by PACO is the largest among the three algorithms. The result of EACO is near to the PACO but is apparently not so good as that of PACO. The reason lies in the popularity which can elude the nodes that are too popular in the routing. Fig. 4 shows the standard deviation of the residual energy of all the sensors. According to the figure, it is obvious that the standard deviation of the sensors in PACO is the smallest, which means the popularity is beneficial to balance the load of sensors. The standard deviation of the HACO is the largest because it simply considers the hops. As a result of this, HACO is not good at balancing the load as well as improving the lifetime.

Therefore, we can draw the conclusion that PACO outperformed others in terms of maximizing the lifetime of WSNs. Hops, energy and popularity are the three factors that help to find the best route in order to improve the lifetime.

6   Conclusion

With the objective of maximizing the lifetime of WSNs, this paper proposes an ACO-based routing algorithm PACO. PACO takes both the hops and residual energy into account and the popularity of sensors is considered as well. The algorithm tries to find a path where the energy is rich and avoid those nodes that are too popular. The cooperation mechanism of ants ensures the effectiveness. By conducting the simulation, it is proved that the PACO algorithm manages to maximize the network lifetime. The result is better than other contrast algorithms, indicating that PACO is a promising routing algorithm for prolonging lifetime of WSNs.

PACO is a routing algorithm with popularity. There is room for improvement of the definition of sensors' popularity. Additionally, the details of applying PACO to a specific routing protocol remain to be considered for further work.

Acknowledgement. This work is supported by Natural Science Foundation of China under Grants No. 61070181, No. 61272524 and No. 61202442. Lei Shu's research work in this paper is supported by the Guangdong University of Petrochemical Technologys Internal Project No. 2012RC0106.

References

1. Simon, G., Maroti, M., Ledeczi, A., Balogh, G., Kusy, B., Nadas, A., Pap, G., Sallai, J., Frampton, K.: Sensor network-based countersniper system. In: Proceedings of the Second International Conference on Embedded Networked Sensor Systems (Sensys), Baltimore, MD (2004)
2. Dorigo, M., Birattari, M., Stutzle, T.: Ant Colony Optimization. IEEE Computational Intelligence Magazine, 28–39 (November 2006)
3. Saleh, S., et al.: A survey on energy awareness mechanisms in routing protocols for wireless sensor networks using optimization methods. Transactions on Emerging Telecommunications Technologies (2013)

4. Ok, C.-S., et al.: Distributed energy balanced routing for wireless sensor networks. Computers & Industrial Engineering 57(1), 125–135 (2009)
5. Tang, X., et al.: Energy - efficient multicast routing scheme for wireless sensor networks. Transactions on Emerging Telecommunications Technologies (2013)
6. Saleem, M., Di Caro, G.A., Farooq, M.: Swarm intelligence based routing protocol for wireless sensor networks: Survey and future directions. Information Sciences 181(20), 4597–4624 (2011)
7. Di Caro, G., Ducatelle, F., Gambardella, L.M.: AntHocNet: an adaptive nature inspired algorithm for routing in mobile ad hoc networks. European Transactions on Telecommunications 16(2) (2005)
8. Camilo, T., Carreto, C., Silva, J., Boavida, F.: An Energy-Efficient Ant-Based Routing Algorithm for Wireless Sensor Networks. In: Dorigo, M., Gambardella, L.M., Birattari, M., Martinoli, A., Poli, R., Stützle, T. (eds.) ANTS 2006. LNCS, vol. 4150, pp. 49–59. Springer, Heidelberg (2006)
9. Lin, Y., et al.: An ant colony optimization approach for maximizing the lifetime of heterogeneous wireless sensor networks. IEEE Transactions on Systems, Man, and Cybernetics, Part C: Applications and Reviews 42(3), 408–420 (2012)
10. Zhong, J., Hu, X., Gu, M., Zhang, J.: Comparison of performance between different selection strategies on simple genetic algorithms. IEEE Computational Intelligence 2 (2005)

J-Divergence Based Decentralized Power Allocation Scheme for Distributed Detection in Wireless Sensor Networks

Xiangyang Liu[1,*], Peisheng Zhu[2], and Donghong Xie[1]

[1] Department of Information Transmission, Xilan Communications Institute,
710106 Xian Shaanxi, China
[2] China Institute of Acoustics, Chinese Academy of Sciences, Beijing, China
liuxiangyangdr@gmail.com
zhups_ioa@126.com

Abstract. In a wireless sensor network with radar-like sensors, the allocation of the limited power of a sensor node between sensing module and communication module should be deliberated. Obviously, the energy consumption of the whole system can be lowered by jointly optimizing the detection performance of the sensor node and the communication performance between the sensor nodes and the fusion center. Therefore, the J-divergence between the distributions of the received local decisions at the fusion center under different hypotheses is used as a performance criterion to optimize the power allocation of sensor node. Numerical simulations shows that the proposed method can strike a good tradeoff between the communication channel quality and the detection quality of local sensor. Although the proposed method is suboptimum, it outperforms the best allocation scheme obtained by the uniform power allocation scheme and the identical symbol error-rate based Power Allocation under the typical fusion rules considered. Besides, the proposed method is independent of specific fusion rule and only needs local processing, which are another two key characteristics.

Keywords: distributed detection, power allocation, signal detection, wireless sensor networks.

1 Introduction

In a wireless sensor network (WSN) with distributed detection application, the objective of system design is to distinguish between two hypotheses, i.e. the absence or presence of a certain target. Such a detection ability is crucial for surveillance scenarios, where the presence or absence of a target is usually determined before its position or velocity is estimated and the sensor units of

---

* The China National Science Foundation under Grant Nos. 61102160 and 61179002 and the project for postgraduates of military science (2010JY0423 -241) support this work.

L. Sun, H. Ma, and F. Hong (Eds.): CWSN 2013, CCIS 418, pp. 166–178, 2014.

the nodes might be based on radar technology [1,2,3,4]. Many authors have analyzed the performance of these distributed detection systems in which transmissions from local sensors to the fusion center (FC for short) are prone to channel fading and noise[5,6,7,8,9], which may render the received decisions at the FC unreliable, especially in resource constrained networks. One prominent feature of a canonical WSN, however, is its limited node energy, which poses many challenges to network design and management. The problem of optimizing detection performance with such imperfect communications brings a new challenge to distributed detection. Considering the scenario of using distributed radar-like sensors to detect the presence of an object through active sensing, Yang et al.[10] formulated the problem of energy-efficient routing for signal detection under the Neyman-Pearson criterion. Moreover, they proposed a distributed and energy-efficient framework that is scalable with respect to the network size, and is able to greatly reduce the dependence on the central FC. Masazade et al.[11] evaluated the sensor thresholds of distributed signal detection system by formulating and solving a multiobjective optimization problem.

Although the literature on energy-efficient communications or signal detection in WSNs is abundant, there is less research on the power allocation between signal detection and communications. In [12], a power allocation approach based on the maximization of the Kullback-Leibler distance is used for the case of object detection. In [13], the bit-error probability of data communications is used to allocate the transmission power and to increase the overall detection probability in UWB signaling systems. Zhang et al.[14] considered the optimization of detection performance with individual and total transmitter power constraints on the sensors and the corresponding power allocation scheme strikes a tradeoff between the communication quality and the local decision quality. But their contribution is based on the additive white Gaussian communication channel and did not consider the optimization of sensing power.

In this paper, we consider a wireless sensor network with radar-like sensor nodes, where a group of sensors transmit their local decisions by Rayleigh fading channel to the FC and then the FC makes a final decision on the presence of a Swerling II target. Our contribution is in the following aspects: (i) we proposed and verified a decentralized power allocation scheme and derive the explicit expression of the J-divergence; (ii) we give conditional probability density function (PDF for short) of the received signal at the FC; (iii) Swerling II fluctuation target and Rayleigh fading communication channels are assumed. The remainder of this paper is organized as follows. In Section 2, the problem of distributed detection in parallel fusion networks with noisy channel was stated, along with the power consumption of sensor nodes, the sensing model, the link model, and the fusion rules. The J-divergence based power allocation strategy is introduced in Section 3. The numerical results are given in Section 4. Finally, Section 5 concludes the paper.

2   Problem Formulation

2.1   Distributed Detection

Let us consider a scenario, where N sensors are scattered over an area to detect the presence of an object, for example people, vehicles, or military targets, using radar-like sensors that emanate specific electromagnetic signals into the region of interest. For the active sensing application, the monitored space is typically divided into many range resolution cells. Each range cell could be probed sequentially to determine the presence of a target by using radar pulses that are possibly launched by directional antennas. Assume the position of the k-th sensor node is (x_k, y_k) . Sensors gathers information pertaining to a target in the position of (x_t, y_t) and makes a decision (for deciding the presence of the target and otherwise) and sends its binary decision to the FC through an unreliable communication channel. In a word, the parallel fusion model is adopted. The position of the FC is assumed to be (x_{fc}, y_{fc}) . Consider the following two hypotheses, the noise-only hypothesis H_0 and the signal plus noise hypothesis H_1 . We assume that the radar and the communication signal use different frequency bandwidth and are uncorrelated to each other.

2.2   Power Consumption of Sensor Nodes

In general, the power consumption of a sensor node can be divided into two kinds, i.e. range-related power consumption and range-free power consumption. Here, consider two kinds of range-related power consumption. One is that consumed by target sensing of the k-th sensor node, which is denoted by $P_{ktot}^{sensing}$. Another is that consumed by the communication between the k-th sensor node and the FC, which is denoted by P_{ktot}^{com} . Except for the range-related power consumption, the other power consumption, for example from low noise amplifier, A/D converter, D/A converter and so on, is range-free. Furthermore, it can be considered fixed or cannot be controlled freely. Besides, to maintain the normal function of a sensor network, sensor node will consume some energy, which may fluctuate. Therefore, the power allocation of sensor node, considered in this paper, is how to share the adjustable power budget by the target sensing power $P_{ktot}^{sensing}$ and communication power P_{ktot}^{com} .

2.3   Sensing Model

Assume that for a Swerling II target with the mean RCS $\bar{\sigma}_{ref}$, located in range R_{ref} from the radar with the peak transmitted power $P_{ref}^{sensing}$, the single-pulse SNR of the output of the square law detector is λ_{ref} . According to the free space radar equation, for a Swerling II target with the mean RCS $\bar{\sigma}$, located at range R_k from the radar with the peak transmitted power $P_{ktot}^{sensing}$, the single-pulse SNR of the output of the square law detector is

$$\lambda_k = R_k^4 P_{ktot}^{sensing} \bar{\sigma} \left(R_{ref}^4 P_{ref}^{sensing} \bar{\sigma}_{ref} \right)^{-1} \lambda_{ref} . \tag{1}$$

The model, therefore, is

$$\begin{cases} H_0: & f_{X_{kj}}(x_{kj}) = \frac{1}{\mu_k} \exp\left[-\frac{x_{kj}}{\mu_k}\right] \\ H_1: & f_{X_{kj}}(x_{kj}) = \frac{1}{\mu_k(1+\lambda_k)} \exp\left[-\frac{x_{kj}}{\mu_k(1+\lambda_k)}\right] \end{cases} \tag{2}$$

where x_{kj} is the signal observed by the k-th sensor, λ_k is the signal-to-noise power ratio (SNR) of the cell under test, and μ_k is the noise power level. In this paper, we assume the local sensors do not communicate with each other, i.e., sensor makes a binary decision $u_k \in \{+1, -1\}$ independently based on its own observation x_{kj} . Let M denote the number of integrated pulses and R that of reference samples. The decision rule of the k-th sensor is

$$u_k = \begin{cases} 1 & , \zeta_k \geq \tau_k \\ -1 & , \zeta_k < \tau_k \end{cases} \tag{3}$$

where $\zeta_k = \left(\sum\limits_{j=1}^{R} y_{kj}\right)^{-1} \sum\limits_{j=1}^{M} x_{kj}$, y_{kj} is the sample of reference cell, and τ_k is decision threshold determined by the false alarm rate P_{lfk} . In this case, the P_{ldk} and P_{lfk} can be calculated as following,

$$P_{ldk} = \Pr(d_k \geq \tau_k | H_1) = \sum_{n=1}^{M} \frac{\tau_k^{n-1}\Gamma(R+n-1)(1+\lambda_k)^R}{\Gamma(R)\Gamma(n)(1+\lambda_k+\tau_k)^{R+n-1}} \tag{4}$$

$$P_{lfk} = \Pr(d_k \geq \tau_k | H_0) = \sum_{n=1}^{M} \frac{T^{n-1}\Gamma(R+n-1)}{\Gamma(R)\Gamma(n)(1+T)^{R+n-1}} \tag{5}$$

Here we assume the sensors have knowledge of their observation quality in terms of P_{ldk} and P_{lfk}.

2.4   Link Model

Assume that the power of the signal radiated into wireless channel by sensor k is denoted by P_{tk}^{com} and total efficiency of power amplifier and antenna is denoted by η_k^{com} , then the power consumed by communication can be denoted by $P_{ktot}^{com} = P_{tk}^{com}(\eta_k^{com})^{-1}$. Considering the path loss incurred during transmission, the power of signal received by the FC and from the k-th sensor is $P_{rk}^{fc} = P_{tk}^{com}/(\varepsilon_k\, d_k^{\alpha_k})$, where ε_k is a constant determined by the antenna characteristics, α_k is the path loss exponent, and d_k is the range from the k-th sensor to the FC. Each local decision is transmitted through a fading Rayleigh channel and the output of the channel for the k-th sensor is given by

$$r_k = \sqrt{P_{rk}^{fc}} h_k u_k + w_k \tag{6}$$

where w_k is zero mean Gaussian noise with variance $\sigma_{w_k}^2$, and h_k is the gain of a real valued Rayleigh fading channel with the PDF given by $f(h_k) = 2h_k e^{-h_k^2}, h_k \geq 0$. The SNR of r_k is

$$\lambda_{ck} = E\left[\left(\sqrt{P_{rk}^{fc}}h_k u_k\right)^2\right]\left(E\left[\left(w_k\right)^2\right]\right)^{-1} = \frac{P_{rk}^{fc}}{\sigma_{w_k}^2}. \tag{7}$$

Given h_k, u_k, P_{rk}^{fc}, the conditional PDF of the received signals r_k at the FC is

$$f\left(r_k/h_k, u_k, P_{rk}^{fc}\right) = \frac{1}{\sqrt{2\pi\sigma_{w_k}^2}}\exp\left[-\frac{1}{2\sigma_{w_k}^2}\left(r_k - \sqrt{P_{rk}^{fc}}h_k u_k\right)^2\right]. \tag{8}$$

The conditional PDF of r_k given the transmitted signal u_k is

$$f_{u_k=1}(r_k) = \frac{\sqrt{2}\sigma_{w_k}e^{-\frac{r_k^2}{2\sigma_{w_k}^2}}}{\sqrt{\pi}\left(2\sigma_{w_k}^2 + P_{rk}^{fc}\right)} + \frac{\left[\text{erf}\left(\frac{r_k\sqrt{P_{rk}^{fc}}}{\sqrt{2}\sigma_{w_k}\sqrt{2\sigma_{w_k}^2 + P_{rk}^{fc}}}\right) + 1\right]r_k\sqrt{P_{rk}^{fc}}}{\left(2\sigma_{w_k}^2 + P_{rk}^{fc}\right)^{3/2}\exp\left(\frac{r_k^2}{2\sigma_{w_k}^2 + P_{rk}^{fc}}\right)} \tag{9}$$

and

$$f_{u_k=-1}(r_k) = \frac{\sqrt{2}\sigma_{w_k}e^{-\frac{r_k^2}{2\sigma_{w_k}^2}}}{\sqrt{\pi}\left(2\sigma_{w_k}^2 + P_{rk}^{fc}\right)} + \frac{\left[\text{erf}\left(\frac{r_k\sqrt{P_{rk}^{fc}}}{\sqrt{2}\sigma_{w_k}\sqrt{2\sigma_{w_k}^2 + P_{rk}^{fc}}}\right) - 1\right]r_k\sqrt{P_{rk}^{fc}}}{\left(2\sigma_{w_k}^2 + P_{rk}^{fc}\right)^{3/2}\exp\left(\frac{r_k^2}{2\sigma_{w_k}^2 + P_{rk}^{fc}}\right)}. \tag{10}$$

The conditional PDF of r_k are given in Eqn.11 and Eqn.12, respectively.

$$f_{H_1}(r_k) = P_{ldk}f_{u_k=1}(r_k) + (1 - P_{ldk})f_{u_k=-1}(r_k)$$

$$= \frac{\sqrt{\frac{2}{\pi}}\sigma_{w_k}e^{-\frac{r_k^2}{2\sigma_{w_k}^2}}}{\left(2\sigma_{w_k}^2 + P_{rk}^{fc}\right)} + (2P_{ldk} - 1)\frac{\sqrt{P_{rk}^{fc}}r_k e^{-\frac{r_k^2}{2\sigma_{w_k}^2 + P_{rk}^{fc}}}}{\left(2\sigma_{w_k}^2 + P_{rk}^{fc}\right)^{3/2}} \tag{11}$$

$$+ \frac{\text{erf}\left(\frac{r_k\sqrt{P_{rk}^{fc}}}{\sqrt{2}\sigma_{w_k}\sqrt{2\sigma_{w_k}^2 + P_{rk}^{fc}}}\right)\sqrt{P_{rk}^{fc}}}{\left(2\sigma_{w_k}^2 + P_{rk}^{fc}\right)^{3/2}}r_k e^{-\frac{r_k^2}{2\sigma_{w_k}^2 + P_{rk}^{fc}}}$$

$$f_{H_0}(r_k) = P_{lfk}f_{u_k=1}(r_k) + (1 - P_{lfk})f_{u_k=-1}(r_k)$$

$$= \frac{\sqrt{2}\sigma_{w_k}}{\sqrt{\pi}\left(2\sigma_{w_k}^2 + P_{rk}^{fc}\right)}e^{-\frac{r_k^2}{2\sigma_{w_k}^2}} + (2P_{lfk} - 1)\frac{\sqrt{P_{rk}^{fc}}r_k e^{-\frac{r_k^2}{2\sigma_{w_k}^2 + P_{rk}^{fc}}}}{\left(2\sigma_{w_k}^2 + P_{rk}^{fc}\right)^{3/2}} + \tag{12}$$

$$\frac{\text{erf}\left(\frac{r_k\sqrt{P_{rk}^{fc}}}{\sqrt{2}\sigma_{w_k}\sqrt{2\sigma_{w_k}^2 + P_{rk}^{fc}}}\right)\sqrt{P_{rk}^{fc}}}{\left(2\sigma_{w_k}^2 + P_{rk}^{fc}\right)^{3/2}}r_k e^{-\frac{r_k^2}{2\sigma_{w_k}^2 + P_{rk}^{fc}}}$$

After the BPSK detected coherently, the probability of error P_{ek}^{sym} that the output u'_k is not equal to u_k is in the form[15] given in

$$P_{ek}^{sym} = \frac{\int_0^{+\infty} f_{u_k=-1}(r_k)\,dr_k + \int_{-\infty}^0 f_{u_k=1}(r_k)\,dr_k}{2} = \frac{1}{2}\left(1 - \sqrt{\frac{\lambda_{ck}}{2+\lambda_{ck}}}\right).$$

$$(13)$$

2.5 Fusion Rules

Here we consider three typical fusion rules. Based on the knowledge of channel statistics and local detection performance indexes, the first fusion rule, i.e. LRT-CS (likelihood ratio test based on channel statistics)[5] , is given by

$$\Lambda_{tot} = \sum_{k=1}^N \log\left\{ \frac{\left[2P_{ldk}-1+\mathrm{erf}\left(\sqrt{\frac{\lambda_{ck}}{2\lambda_{ck}+4}}\frac{r_k}{\sigma_{w_k}}\right)\right]}{\exp\left(-\frac{\lambda_{ck}}{(2\lambda_{ck}+4)}\frac{r_k^2}{\sigma_{w_k}^2}\right)}\frac{r_k}{\sigma_{w_k}}\sqrt{\frac{\pi\lambda_{ck}}{2\lambda_{ck}+4}}+1 }{ \frac{\left[2P_{lfk}-1+\mathrm{erf}\left(\sqrt{\frac{\lambda_{ck}}{2\lambda_{ck}+4}}\frac{r_k}{\sigma_{w_k}}\right)\right]}{\exp\left(-\frac{\lambda_{ck}}{(2\lambda_{ck}+4)}\frac{r_k^2}{\sigma_{w_k}^2}\right)}\frac{r_k}{\sigma_{w_k}}\sqrt{\frac{\pi\lambda_{ck}}{2\lambda_{ck}+4}}+1 }\right\}$$

$$(14)$$

where $\mathrm{erf}(x) = \int_0^x \frac{2}{\sqrt{\pi}}e^{-t^2}\,dt$.

Base on the knowledge of the channel gain, the second fusion rule, i.e. MRC fusion rule, is given as

$$\Lambda_{MRC} = \sum_{k=1}^N (P_{dk} - P_{fk})h_k r_k$$

$$(15)$$

The last is the fusion rule of EGC shown in Eqn.16 that requires the minimum amount of information among the three fusion rules.

$$\Lambda_{EGC} = \frac{1}{N}\sum_{k=1}^N r_k$$

$$(16)$$

3   J-Divergence Based Power Allocation Scheme

In WSNs, a centralized network controller might not be available. Therefore, a decentralized power allocation approach is needed , where each node determines its own power allocation between sensing power and communication power which is in contrast to the centralized approach where the network controller is responsible for calculating the power allocation scheme of every node. Assume that the total power budget of the k-th node is $P_k^{\text{sensing+com}}$ and then $P_{ktot}^{\text{sensing}} + P_{ktot}^{\text{com}} \leq P_k^{\text{sensing+com}}$.

To maximize the detection capability of the total system, the target sensing power and communication power should satisfy the equation $P_{ktot}^{\text{sensing}} + P_{ktot}^{\text{com}} =$

$P_k^{\text{sensing+com}}$. Obviously, detection performance is generally improved if the J-divergence between the distributions of the received local decisions at the fusion center under different hypotheses is maximized. Therefore, we focus on how to intelligently distribute the total power budget $P_k^{\text{sensing+com}}$ of sensor k among sensing and communication, by choosing the proper values of $P_{ktot}^{\text{sensing}}$ and P_{ktot}^{com} , to make the J-divergence of the received signal r_k under H_0 and under H_1 maximum. After some derivation, the J-divergence between $f_{H_1}(r_k)$ and $f_{H_0}(r_k)$ is given by

$$
J_{r_k} \triangleq J\left(f_{H_1}(r_k), f_{H_0}(r_k)\right) = \int \left(f_{H_1}(r_k) - f_{H_0}(r_k)\right) \log \frac{f_{H_1}(r_k)}{f_{H_0}(r_k)} dr_k
$$

$$
= \frac{(P_{ldk} - P_{lfk})}{(1 + \lambda_{ck})} \sqrt{\frac{\lambda_{ck}}{1 + \lambda_{ck}}} \int_{-\infty}^{\infty} r_k e^{-\frac{r_k^2}{2(1+\lambda_{ck})}} \left\{ \log\left(\sqrt{2} + \sqrt{\frac{\pi \lambda_{ck}}{1 + \lambda_{ck}}} \left[2P_{ldk}\right.\right.\right.
$$

(17)

$$
\left.\left. -1 + \operatorname{erf}\left(\frac{r_k}{\sqrt{2}}\sqrt{\frac{\lambda_{ck}}{1 + \lambda_{ck}}}\right)\right] r_k e^{\frac{r_k^2 \lambda_{ck}}{2(1+\lambda_{ck})}}\right) - \log\left[\sqrt{2} + \sqrt{\frac{\pi \lambda_{ck}}{1 + \lambda_{ck}}} \left[2P_{lfk}\right.\right.
$$

$$
\left.\left.\left. -1 + \operatorname{erf}\left(\frac{r_k}{\sqrt{2}}\sqrt{\frac{\lambda_{ck}}{1 + \lambda_{ck}}}\right)\right] \left(r_k e^{\frac{r_k^2 \lambda_{ck}}{2(1+\lambda_{ck})}}\right)\right]\right\} dr_k,
$$

where λ_{ck} is given in Eqn.7. The calculation of Eqn.17 involves the integral of complex function, which is hard to solve. Considering that the J-divergence $J_{u'_k}$ between $f_{H_1}(u'_k)$ and $f_{H_0}(u'_k)$ is also an index of detection performance. So, we use it as the objective function of the optimization of power allocation of a sensors node. After simple derivations, the $J_{u'_k}$ can be denoted as

$$
J_{u'_k} \triangleq J\left(f_{H_1}(u'_k), f_{H_0}(u'_k)\right) = \sum_{u_k=0}^{1} \left(f_{H_1}(u'_k) - f_{H_0}(r_k)\right) \log \frac{f_{H_1}(u'_k)}{f_{H_0}(u'_k)}
$$

$$
= (P_{ldk} - P_{lfk}) \sqrt{\frac{\lambda_{ck}}{2 + \lambda_{ck}}} \left\{ \log \frac{\left[1 - (1 - 2P_{ldk})\sqrt{\frac{\lambda_{ck}}{2+\lambda_{ck}}}\right]}{\left[1 - (1 - 2P_{lfk})\sqrt{\frac{\lambda_{ck}}{2+\lambda_{ck}}}\right]} \right.
$$

(18)

$$
\left. + \log \frac{\left[1 - (2P_{lfk} - 1)\sqrt{\frac{\lambda_{ck}}{2+\lambda_{ck}}}\right]}{\left[1 - (2P_{ldk} - 1)\sqrt{\frac{\lambda_{ck}}{2+\lambda_{ck}}}\right]} \right\} .
$$

4   Numerical Simulation and Results

4.1   Simulation Conditions

In our simulation, we use the WSN configuration described in Section 2. Consider a WSN with 8 sensor nodes and a FC and the system configuration is illustrated in Fig.1. All units of coordinate are meters. The FC is with coordinate (50,450).

The Y-axis coordinates of all the sensors are 0 and their X-axis coordinates of sensor nodes from sensor 1 to sensor 8 are -180, -120, -60, 0, 60, 100, 160, and 220, respectively. Also, assume the target to be detected is located in (100,-150).Assume the false alarm rate of the FC is 0.001. Each radar has the same nominal detection performance. For targets obeying Swerling II fluctuations with average RCS of $5m^2$, a probability of detection 0.5 under false alarm rate 0.01 is obtained at range of 200 meters with the number of integrated pulses $M = 16$ and the number of reference samples per pulse $R = 32$. Assume that the communication system operates at 2.4GHz and adopts the following path loss model given by Shellhammer[16].

$$pl(d) = \begin{cases} 40.2 + 20\log_{10}(d) & d \leq 8m \\ 58.5 + 33\log_{10}\left(\frac{d}{8}\right) & d > 8m \end{cases} \tag{19}$$

Assume that the SNR loss of the practical communication receiver compared with the ideal one is 1dB. Also assume that, for binary symmetric Rayleigh fading channel, a bit error rate 0.001 is required at receiver sensitivity of -90dBm at maximum range of 120 meters with transmitted power 16 dBm. The fading coefficient h_k of the channel between sensors and the FC is Rayleigh distributed with unit mean. Assume that the drain efficiency $\eta_k^{com} = 0.17$ and the total power budget of each sensor node $P^{sensing+com} = 60mW$. Here, we also assume that the communication power of each node lies in a given interval $[P_{min}^{com}, P_{max}^{com}] = [0.01, 59.99]$. For each given power allocation result, 4×10^5 Monte Carlo runs are used to provide the corresponding total probability of detection at the FC.

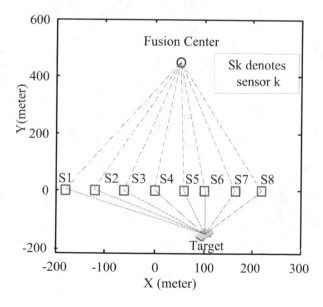

Fig. 1. System configuration

4.2   Two Centralized Power Allocation Schemes for Comparison

To verify the performance of the proposed method given in Section 3, we give two centralized heuristic suboptimal power allocation schemes. The first is a uniform power allocation scheme (UPAS for short). The UPAS assumes that the sensing powers of all the nodes are identical. Also, assume the power budget of each node that can be distributed between sensing and communication is $P^{\text{sensing+com}}$. Assume that the sensing power is $P^{\text{sensing}}_{\text{ktot}} = P^{\text{sensing}}$. Then, the communication power is

$$P^{com}_{ktot} = P^{\text{sensing+com}} - P^{\text{sensing}} \tag{20}$$

A simple method can be used to find a good P^{sensing}. According to the total power budget $P^{\text{sensing+com}}$, determine a sufficiently small power increase ΔP with the relation of $P^{\text{sensing+com}} = L\Delta P$. Let sensing power $P^{\text{sensing}}_{\text{ktot}}$ be ΔP, $2\Delta P,,L\Delta P$ successively and let communication power $P^{com}_{ktot} = P^{\text{sensing+com}} - P^{\text{sensing}}_{\text{ktot}}$. Next, compute the global probability of detection $P_{D,FC}$. The best power allocation scheme is that with the largest global probability of detection. In this method, all the nodes have the identical power allocation scheme. Obviously, the UPAS is simple and does not consider the specific performance of any sensor node.

The second is an identical symbol error-rate based Power Allocation (ISERPA for short) which is based on the following visual thought. Symbol error-rate is a characteristic of communication channel quality. In this scheme, the symbol error rate of the communication between any sensor and the FC is fixed to be P^{sym}_e. Communication power needed for the k-th node can be determined by

$$P^{com}_{ktot} = \frac{2\varepsilon_k d_k^{\alpha_k} \left(1 - 2P^{sym}_e\right)^2}{\eta^{com}_k \left(1 - \left(1 - 2P^{sym}_e\right)^2\right)} \sigma^2_{w_k} \tag{21}$$

The best P^{sym}_e is that corresponds to the largest global probability of detection $P_{D,FC}$ at the FC, which can be found by the exhaustive searching in an interval $[P^{sym}_{e\,\min}, P^{sym}_{e\,\max}]$, where $P^{sym}_{e\,\min}$ can be determined by the minimum of the symbol error rate achieved by all the sensor and the $P^{sym}_{e\,\max}$ is the correspondingly maximum value.

4.3   Simulation Results

Fig.2 shows the variation of the J-divergence $J_{u'_k}$ versus the sensing power of each node. Because both the distances between sensor nodes and the target and the distances between sensor nodes and the FC are different, the maximum J-divergence obtained at each sensor node is different from one another. The optimum sensing power obtained is given in a power vector $\zeta_{\text{sensing}} = [P^{sensing}_{1tot}, P^{sensing}_{2tot}, \ldots, P^{sensing}_{Ntot}]$ $= [45.52, 47.63, 47.93, 42.81, 34.37, 31.96, 36.48, 44.92]$. From the power values, we can find that the proposed method is a geographically adaptive allocation scheme.

The best sensing powers obtained by UPAS under the LRT-CS, MRC and EGC are 36.48mW, 38.29mW, and 47.93mW, respectively. The best sensing

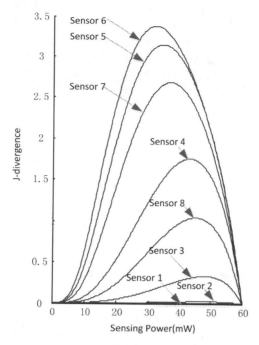

Fig. 2. The plot of J-divergence versus the sensing power of each node

powers obtained by the ISERPA under different fusion rules are given in Fig.3. From it, we can observe that the EGC needs more sensing power than the MRC and the LRT-CS. The results obtained by the J-divergence based power allocation scheme proposed in this paper are also given in Fig.3, where the curve labeled by the Proposed Method corresponds to the optimized sensing powers. Among the eight sensors, sensor 6 needs the least sensing power.

From Fig.1, we can find that the distance between sensor 6 and the target to be detected is shortest among all the eight sensors. Therefore, sensor 6 can consume less sensing power to get better detection performance than the other sensors. Comparing the results obtained under different fusion rules, it can be found that ISERPA and UPAS are both dependent on the fusion rule adopted while the proposed method is independent of specific fusion rule.

For power allocation for signal detection, the aim is to improve the detection performance of the whole system. Next, we consider system-level detection performance under different power allocation schemes. The simulation results are given in Fig.4, which shows that the results obtained by the proposed method are the best under the three fusion rules among the three power allocation schemes. It should be noted that the UPAS and the ISERPA are centralized method which need computing globally the detection probability at the FC while the proposed method is decentralized and only needs local processing. In the proposed method, each sensor node can determine its sensing power independently. More importantly, the power allocation result obtained is independent of the

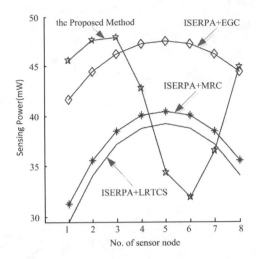

Fig. 3. The best sensing power obtained by different power allocation schemes at different fusion rules

fusion rules, which means the proposed method is a general power allocation scheme.

Finally, we evaluate the differences of detection probabilities using the proposed power allocation scheme and the global optimum power allocation scheme. For convenience, we only consider two sensors, i.e., sensor 6 and sensor 7. The

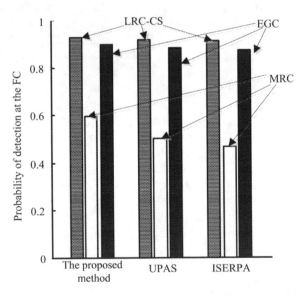

Fig. 4. The best probability of detection achieved by different combinations of power allocation schemes and the fusion rules

FC fuses the results from sensor 6 and sensor 7 by the LRT-CS fusion rule to make a global decision. The optimum power allocation is found by a brute-force grid search in a two dimensional space of all possible power allocations. The obtained power allocation for sensor 6 and sensor 7 are 31.88mW and 36.54mW, respectively and the corresponding probability of detection is 0.57. In this case, the sensing powers by the proposed method remain unchanged and the practical probability of detection is 0.56, which is slightly less than the detection performance obtained by the optimum power allocation scheme.

5   Conclusion

The WSN with distributed detection application is a specialized target detection network and the communications in this network are served for signal detection. As an effective metric of detection information, J-divergence is used as the optimization criterion for global power allocation for signaling in wireless sensor networks in literature, but in contrast in this paper J-divergence is served as an optimization criterion for power allocation of local sensor node between sensing and signaling. The effectiveness of the proposed method was verified by Monte Carlo simulation. Although the proposed method is a suboptimum, it outperforms the best allocation scheme obtained by the uniform power allocation scheme (UPAS) and the identical symbol error-rate based power allocation (ISERPA) under the typical fusion rules considered. In a word, the proposed method is high-performance, independent of specific fusion rule and decentralized. In the future, we will extend the work to more practical cases to design adaptively decentralized power allocation scheme.

References

1. Yang, Y., Blum, R.S., Sadler, B.M.: Distributed Energy-Efficient Scheduling for Radar Signal Detection in Sensor Networks. In: Proc. IEEE Int. Radar Conf., pp. 1094–1099 (2010)
2. Xu, L., Liang, Q.: Radar Sensor Network Using a Set of New Ternary Codes: Theory and Application. IEEE Sensors Journal 11(2), 439–450 (2011)
3. Liang, J., Liang, Q.: Design and Analysis of Distributed Radar Sensor Networks. IEEE Transactions on Parallel and Distributed Systems 22(11), 1926–1933 (2011)
4. Ren, Q.: Energy Detection Performance Analysis for UWB Radar Sensor Networks. EURASIP Journal on Wireless Communications and Networking, Article ID 709723, 1–12 (2010)
5. Niu, R., Chen, B., Varshney, P.K.: Fusion of decisions transmitted over Rayleigh fading channels in wireless sensor networks. IEEE Trans. on Signal Processing 54(3), 1018–1027 (2006)
6. Chen, B., Tong, L., Varshney, P.K.: Channel-aware distributed detection in wireless sensor networks. IEEE Signal Processing Magazine 23(4), 16–26 (2006)
7. Kanchumarthy, V.R., Viswanathan, R., Madishetty, M.: Impact of Channel Errors on Decentralized Detection Performance of Wireless Sensor Networks: A Study of Binary Modulations, Rayleigh-Fading and Nonfading Channels, and Fusion-Combiner. IEEE Trans. on Signal Processing 56(5), 1761–1769 (2008)

8. Wu, J.-Y., Wu, C.-W., Wang, T.-Y.: Channel-Aware Decision Fusion With Unknown Local Sensor Detection Probability. IEEE Trans. on Signal Processing 58(3), 1457–1463 (2010)
9. Lai, K.-C., Yang, Y.-L., Jia, J.-J.: Fusion of Decisions Transmitted Over Flat Fading Channels Via Maximizing the Deflection Coefficient. IEEE Trans. on Vehicular Technology 59(7), 3634–3640 (2010)
10. Yang, Y., Blum, R.S., Sadler, B.M.: Energy-Efficient Routing for Signal Detection in Wireless Sensor Networks. IEEE Trans. on Signal Processing 57(6), 2050–2063 (2009)
11. Masazade, E., Rajagopalan, R., Varshney, P.K., et al.: A multiobjective optimization approach to obtain decision thresholds for distributed detection in wireless sensor networks. IEEE Trans. on Systems, Man, and Cybernetics, Part B: Cybernetics 40(2), 444–457 (2010)
12. Bielefeld, D., Fabeck, G., Zivkovic, M., et al.: Optimization of cooperative spectrum sensing and implementation on software defined radios. In: Proc. Int. Workshop Cognitive Radio Advanced Spectr Management, CogART, pp. 1–5 (2010)
13. Alirezaei, G.: Channel capacity related power allocation for ultra-wide bandwidth sensor networks with application in object detection. In: Proc. IEEE ICUWB. Syracuse, NY (2012)
14. Zhang, X., Poor, H.V., Chiang, M.: Optimal Power Allocation for Distributed Detection Over MIMO Channels in Wireless Sensor Networks. IEEE Trans. on Signal Processing 56(9), 4124–4140 (2008)
15. Proakis, J.G., Salehi, M.: Digital Communications. McGraw-Hill Higher Education, New York (2008)
16. Shellhammer, S.J.: Estimation of Packet Error Rate Caused by Interference using Analytic Techniques. A Coexistence Assurance Methodology. IEEE 80219-05/0028r1 (2005)

Random Graph Model for Opportunistic Sensor Networks Based on Divided Area*

Jian Shu, Linxin Zeng, and Linlan Liu

Internet of Things Technology Institute
Nanchang Hang Kong University, Nanchang, Jiangxi, P.R. China

Abstract. Opportunistic Sensor Network (OSN) is different from traditional networks because it frequently splits into several parts and connections are characterized by their opportunistic nature. To re-describe the connectivity of OSN, Divided Area Random Graph (DARG) model is introduced according to the opportunistic nature of connections. DARG divides the radio communication area of each node into three parts: communication area, probabilistic communication area and none-communication area. After calculating the communication probability of each area, total probability formula is adopted to calculate the direct communication probability between nodes. Then, Probabilistic Path Matrix (PPM) is employed to capture the communication probability caused by "Storing-Carrying-Forwarding" communication pattern which is very typical in OSN. Finally, based on PPM, Network Connection Mean Probability (NCMP) is defined to determine how well the network is connected. It is helpful for many applications to characterize how well the network is connected based on this model. Theoretical analyses and simulations results show that DARG is more practical than conventional random graphs and NCMP can describe OSN connectivity better.

Keywords: Opportunistic Sensor Network (OSN), Connectivity, Opportunity, Divided Area Random Graph (DARG), Probabilistic Path Matrix (PPM), Network Connection Mean Probability (NCMP).

1 Introduction

Opportunistic Sensor Network (OSN) [1], consisting of nodes which move randomly or with regular patterns to realize the data collection in target areas, shares the basic features with Opportunistic Network (OpporNet) [2] and Delay Tolerant Network (DTN) [3], which are intermittent connection and frequent separation. Compared with largely deployed static sensor network, OSN is capable of sensing large area with lower power consumption, and it's more economical and versatile than the existing fixed stationary sensor network.

* This work is supported by The National Natural Science Foundation of China under grant NO.61262020 and Aeronautical Science Foundation of China under grant ON.2010ZC56008.

L. Sun, H. Ma, and F. Hong (Eds.): CWSN 2013, CCIS 418, pp. 179–190, 2014.
© Springer-Verlag Berlin Heidelberg 2014

Topology in OSN constantly evolves due to nodes' movement, randomly shut-down of radio devices, as well as environmental noises on wireless link. This leads to the non-existence of completely static paths between majorities of node pairs. For the sake of accomplishing information transportation, nodes have to make full use of communication opportunities created by the nodes' movement. This kind of communication pattern reveals the opportunistic nature of connection between nodes. But this opportunistic nature poses a big challenge to network operations, such as real-time sending of commands from sink to sensor nodes and real-time reporting of senor data from sensor nodes to sink. These operations can be tough to be done. The connectivity of network, if can be obtained, could be useful for the design of data disseminations mechanisms, and be helpful for the nodes' selection of routing protocols to forward data. So, it is meaningful for many applications to determine how well the network is connected.

However, conventional definition of connectivity, which just has two states: zero or one, could not describe all connection states in OSN preferably. In wire-less local area network with infrastructure, mobile terminals are able to com-municate with others as long as they can connect to at least one of the access points. Whereas in mobile Ad hoc network, only the fully connected network gives a guarantee of successful data delivery by multi-hops. As opposed to these networks, OSN frequently separates into several parts, this causes disconnection of network. So it is significant to re-describe the connectivity in OSN.

When describing the connectivity, deterministic method which concentrate too much on details and structures of network is unsuitable to describe connec-tivity of OSN due to its constantly evolving topology [4]. Therefore, numbers of scholars adopted statistical techniques and probability theory to describe and analyse this kind of network, in which, random graph theory and percolation theory analyse network's characteristics by studying the statistics properties of network components. [4] pointed out that by introducing the probabilistic rules, random graph theory is competent for describing the complexity of networks. So numbers of scholars [5–7,9–11] adopted random graph theory to analyse con-nectivity.

How to suitably characterize how well the network is connected in OSN against the opportunistic nature of connection is meaningful. Section 2 reports the re-lated work about the using of random graph to investigate the connectivity, and in section 3 we propose a random graph model named Divided Area Random Graphs to analyse the direct and indirect communication probability between nodes. In section 4 Network Connection Mean Probability is defined to charac-terize how well the network is connected, and conclusion is in section 5.

2   Related Work

In conventional random graphs like the Erdos-Renyi graph, the link probability between nodes was same to all links, which made it inappropriate to be directly used in realistic networks modelling. By introducing the arbitrary dependen-cies between different links, Random Network model was proposed based on the combination of conventional random graph model and the theory of Kolmogorov complexity. Simulations showed it was possible to construct a randomized distributed algorithm which provided connectivity with high probability [5].

In wireless Ad hoc networks, each node should transmit message with enough power to guarantee the connectivity of networks. Toward this end, random graph theory was used to prove that if n nodes were placed on the disk of unit area of two dimensions and each node transmitted at a power level so as to cover an area of $\pi r^2 = \frac{\log n + c(n)}{n}$, then the network was connected with probability one if and only if $c(n) \to \infty$, and the network was disconnected if $\lim_{n \to \infty} \sup c(n) < \infty$ [6]. However, this result is constrained to the dense networks. Given the number of nodes was n and communication radius was r_0, [7] conducted the connectivity analysis from three viewpoints, that were the number of neighbours, the path probability between any two nodes and the probability of connected network existence. In order to guarantee an approximate connected networks, the critical threshold pair (n, r_0) was given out through approximation of no isolated nodes.

Conventional random graphs theory did no allow the dependencies between nodes' links [8]. While in Fixed Radius model [9] link probability was one if the distance between nodes was less than fixed radius. And this model was used to analyse the phase transition of network when nodes' transmit power were less than the critical power level. Similar phase transition phenomenon happens on the message propagation in vehicular networks. An analytical model for bi-directional linear network of vehicles was developed in [10], based on which, both upper and lower bounds of the average message propagation speed were derived by exploiting a connection with the classical pattern matching problem in probability theory. When below the lower bound which was a function of the traffic density in each direction, the average message speed was the same as the average vehicle speed. On the other hand, when above the upper bound, the average message speed quickly increased as a function of traffic density and approached radio speed.

Range-limited Graphs model [11] was proposed by improving the Fixed Radius model. In this model, the link probability is a constant value $p \in [0, 1]$ if the distance between nodes is less than fixed radius, and the communication probability is $p(2c - c^2)$, where $c = \sqrt{r^2 - \left(\frac{i-j}{n+1}\right)^2}$. However, there was little explanation about the setting for value of p.

The [5–7,9–11] mentioned above were based on boolean communication model which assumed there existed no environmental noises. However this assumption is too ideal. In realistic scenarios, signal interferences, shadow fading and multiple path shadow effects constantly exist which lead to the uncertainty of link [12]. And this is beyond what boolean communication model can analyse, which just has two states: communication with probability one and communication with probability zero. While the probabilistic communication model [13] is capable of handling it with the consideration of the uncertainty of link, it determines the link existence in the way of probability. So the probabilistic communication model is more practical. To investigate connectivity in OSN, our random graph model will be constructed based on probabilistic communication model.

3   DARG Model

In probabilistic communication model,communication probability between nodes is analysed under the impact of the uncertainty of link. Based this model, DARG model is constructed to give out the direct and indirect communication probability.

In probabilistic communication model, when the Euclidean distance between nodes is less than r, the direct communication probability between nodes is one; when the Euclidean distance between nodes is more than R, the direct communication probability between nodes is zero; when the Euclidean distance between nodes falls into range $[r, R]$, then the direct communication probability between nodes is

$$p = e^{\frac{-w(d_{ij}-r)}{R-r}} > 0 \tag{1}$$

When the Euclidean distance between nodes falls into range $[r, R]$, the direct communication probability between nodes is not only influenced by distance, but the environmental noises as well. This is the reason for the uncertainty of link.

3.1   Direct Connectivity Probability

DARG (as shown in Fig.1) divides the radio communication area of each node into three parts: communication area, probabilistic communication area and non-communication area. In which, the probabilistic communication area is corresponding to the situation that the Euclidean distance between nodes falls into range $[r, R]$. This kind of division is helpful for the analysing of uncertainty of link.

DARG is constructed as following. In the network area D, choose node i randomly from node set as the centre of two circles $C1$ and $C2$ with r_1 and r_2 as radiuses ($r_1 < r_2$) respectively. These two circles divide D into three parts, $D(ic)$ as communication area, $D(ip)$ as probabilistic communication area and $D(in)$

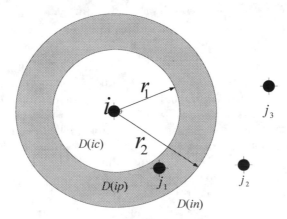

Fig. 1. DARG model

as non-communication area. Set $E0$, $E1$ and $E2$ as the event which will happen when node j falls into $D(ic)$, $D(ip)$ and $D(in)$ respectively, and set $EC0$, $EC1$ and $EC2$ as the event which will happen when node j is able to communicate with node i after the node j falls into $D(ic)$, $D(ip)$ and $D(in)$ respectively.

With DARG model, we can get theorem 1 as following.

Theorem 1. In DARG model, the direct communication probability between nodes i and j is

$$p_{ij} = p(E0) * p(EC0) + p(E1) * p(EC1) + p(E2) * p(EC2) \tag{2}$$

Proof. According to definition, $E0$ is the event which will happen when node j falls into $D(ic)$, and $EC0$ is the event which will happen when node j is able to communicate with node i after the node j falls into $D(ic)$, so $E0$ is the condition for $EC0$ to happen. It is the same as $E1$ for $EC1$ and $E2$ for $EC2$. By total probability formula, p_{ij} is the direct communication probability between nodes i and j.

The random deployment makes the distances between nodes can't be determined, when node j falls into $D(ic)$, the communication probabilities change with the distances changing. In order to get the communication probability when node j falls into $D(ic)$, (1) is modified by DARG model as following.

$$pe = \frac{\int_{r_1}^{r_2} e^{\frac{-w(d_{ij} - r_1)}{r_2 - r_1}} d(d_{ij})}{r_2 - r_1} \tag{3}$$

By definition, each node is located at a point defined by two random variables: x and y coordinates. x and y are normalized into $[0, 1]$. Sort nodes by the x coordinate value (or y). Rank statistics is used to estimate the probability that two given nodes i and j can communicate with each other [11]. n is the number of nodes. For a uniform distribution, in terms of the rank statistics, expected value of the sth largest value of sorted x is calculated as $\frac{s}{n+1}$. When node j falls into $D(ip)$, (4) holds.

$$(x_i - x_j)^2 + (y_i - y_j)^2 < r_2^2$$
$$(x_i - x_j)^2 + (y_i - y_j)^2 > r_1^2 \tag{4}$$

Replace with expected value of x, this becomes

$$(y_i - y_j)^2 < r_2^2 - (\frac{i}{n+1} - \frac{j}{n+1})^2$$
$$(y_i - y_j)^2 > r_1^2 - (\frac{i}{n+1} - \frac{j}{n+1})^2 \tag{5}$$

Define right part of (5) as constant values c_2^2, c_1^2, this becomes

$$(y_i - y_j)^2 < c_2^2$$
$$(y_i - y_j)^2 > c_1^2 \tag{6}$$

As shown in Fig.2, Smaller triangle (dark region) in the lower right-hand corner is the region that does not satisfy $(y_j - y_i) < c_2$, when $y_i = 0$, $y_j < c_2$, so the base of the triangle is $1 - c_2$; Smaller triangle in the upper left-hand corner is the region that does not satisfy $(y_i - y_j) < c_2$, when $y_j = 0$, $y_i < c_2$, so the altitude of the triangle is $1 - c_2$, and the area of a single smaller triangle is $\frac{(1-c_2)^2}{2}$. In the similar way, the area of a single bigger triangle (gray region) is $\frac{(1-c_1)^2}{2}$. So the likelihood that node j falls into $D(ip)$ is

$$p(E1) = (1 - c_1)^2 - (1 - c_2)^2 \tag{7}$$

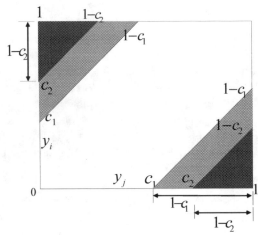

Fig. 2. The probability of node j falls into probabilistic communication area

In a similar way

$$p(E0) = 1 - (1 - c_1)^2 \tag{8}$$

$$p(E2) = (1 - c_2)^2 \tag{9}$$

Combining (2),(3),(7),(8)and(9),the direct communication probability p_{ij} between nodes i and j can be obtained.

3.2   Simulation and Comparison

Probability Connectivity Matrix (PCM) [11] is adopted to describe the probabilities that nodes can communicate with others. In PCM, the element at i^{th} row and j^{th} column is the communication probability between node i and node j. Set $n = 7, r_1 = 0.3, r_2 = 0.5$ and $w = 3$, simulations are conducted in Matlab7.0 and the PCM of DARG model is given as following.

$$\mathbf{PCM} = \begin{bmatrix} 1.0000 & 0.5543 & 0.4227 & 0.1749 & 0 & 0 & 0 \\ 0.5543 & 1.0000 & 0.5543 & 0.4227 & 0.1749 & 0 & 0 \\ 0.4227 & 0.5543 & 1.0000 & 0.5543 & 0.4227 & 0.1749 & 0 \\ 0.1749 & 0.4227 & 0.5543 & 1.0000 & 0.5543 & 0.4227 & 0.1749 \\ 0 & 0.1749 & 0.4227 & 0.5543 & 1.0000 & 0.5543 & 0.4227 \\ 0 & 0 & 0.1749 & 0.4227 & 0.5543 & 1.0000 & 0.5543 \\ 0 & 0 & 0 & 0.1749 & 0.4227 & 0.5543 & 1.0000 \end{bmatrix} \tag{10}$$

In Erdos-Renyi graph, the same probability was used to construct links between any nodes, this is inappropriate for the realistic scenarios in which dependencies between links exist. With rank statistics, DARG model makes nodes nearby communicate with higher probabilities. The dependencies between links are reflected in matrix (10), in which the values of direct communication probability get higher if they are closer to diagonal of PCM.

Set parameters $n = 40$, $r_1 = 0.3$, $r_2 = 0.5$ and $w = 3$, a 3-D plot of PCM generated by DARG is shown as below intuitively.

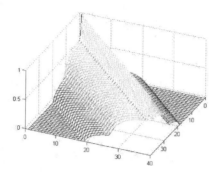

Fig. 3. A 3D-plot of probability connectivity matrix

In Range-limited Graphs model, the link probability between nodes is a constant value $p \in [0, 1]$ if the distance is less than fixed radius, and the communication probability is $p(2c - c^2)$, where $c = \sqrt{r^2 - (\frac{i-j}{n+1})^2}$ [11]. However, little explanation about the setting for value of p was given in [11]. Simulation of the Range-limited Graphs model is conducted in Matlab7.0 with $n = 7$, $r = 0.5$, $p = 1$ and get the result as below.

$$\mathbf{PCM} = \begin{bmatrix} 0 & 0.7339 & 0.6785 & 0.5521 & 0 & 0 & 0 \\ 0.7339 & 0 & 0.7339 & 0.6785 & 0.5521 & 0 & 0 \\ 0.6785 & 0.7339 & 0 & 0.7339 & 0.6785 & 0.5521 & 0 \\ 0.5521 & 0.6785 & 0.7339 & 0 & 0.7339 & 0.6785 & 0.5521 \\ 0 & 0.5521 & 0.6785 & 0.7339 & 0 & 0.7339 & 0.6785 \\ 0 & 0 & 0.5521 & 0.6785 & 0.7339 & 0 & 0.7339 \\ 0 & 0 & 0 & 0.5521 & 0.6785 & 0.7339 & 0 \end{bmatrix} \quad (11)$$

Compared with the elements in matrix (10), elements in matrix (11) are bigger (diagonal elements of matrix are ignored), except the zero elements. Because of the setting for $p = 1$ in the simulation, it causes all nodes within range of communication can communicate with each other with probability one. In fact, it is not always true, even though nodes are within range of communication, there is no guarantee they can communicate with each other with probability one, as the communication is influenced by the signal interferences and shadow fading.

It is important to notice that when $r_1 = r_2$, the probabilistic communication model is degraded into boolean communication model, and DARG model become the same as Range-limited Graph model when its p is set to 1. On the other hand, when $r_1 \neq r_2$, DARG model adopts probabilistic communication model to analyse the environmental noises. This kind of analysis was overlooked by Range-limited Graph model.

3.3   The Indirect Connectivity Probability

DARG model gives the direct connectivity probability between nodes. By multiplying the probability matrix, the multi-hops paths probabilities between nodes also can be deduced.

Definition 1 [14].   Probability matrix multiplication. Matrix A and B with dimension $n \times n$, $C = A \otimes B$ is the product of A and B, when $i \neq j$, $C_{ij} = 1 - \prod_{k \neq i,j}(1 - A_{ik} * B_{kj})$, When $i = j$, $C_{ij} = 1$, C_{ij} is the element of C which gives the probability that there exists at least one path from node i to node j through relay node k.

Theorem 2.   The probability that there exists at least one path with h hops from node i to node j is PCM_{ij}^h, which is the element of PCM^h, $PCM^h = PCM^{h-1} \otimes PCM(h > 1)$.

Proof.   When $h = 2$, $PCM^2 = PCM \otimes PCM$, by definition 1, it is straightforward to be proved.

Assume theorem 2 holds when $h = N - 1$, the probability that there exists a path of $N - 1$ hops from node i to node k is PCM_{ik}^{N-1}.

When $h = N$, it takes two steps to reach the node j from node i: the first step takes $N - 1$ hops to reach node k, and the second step takes one hop to reach node j. And the probability of existing at least one path of N hops from node i to node j is element of the product of PCM^{N-1} and PCM, that is $PCM_{ij}^N = 1 - \prod_{k \neq i,j}(1 - PCM_{ik}^{N-1} * PCM_{kj})$. So $PCM^N = PCM^{N-1} \otimes PCM$ holds. So theorem 2 holds for all h ($h > 1$).

Through theorem 2, PCM^2, PCM^3 can be deduced from PCM in matrix(10) as following.

$$\mathbf{PCM^2} = \begin{bmatrix} 1.0000 & 0.2909 & 0.2426 & 0.2409 & 0.2619 & 0.2648 & 0.2732 \\ 0.2909 & 1.0000 & 0.3781 & 0.3225 & 0.3100 & 0.3321 & 0.3310 \\ 0.3744 & 0.4381 & 1.0000 & 0.4601 & 0.3788 & 0.3636 & 0.3833 \\ 0.4137 & 0.5179 & 0.5829 & 1.0000 & 0.5140 & 0.4201 & 0.3995 \\ 0.3302 & 0.5210 & 0.6172 & 0.6573 & 1.0000 & 0.5067 & 0.3635 \\ 0.1424 & 0.3831 & 0.5660 & 0.6492 & 0.6521 & 1.0000 & 0.3579 \\ 0.0306 & 0.1569 & 0.3964 & 0.5752 & 0.6180 & 0.5369 & 1.0000 \end{bmatrix} \quad (12)$$

$$\mathbf{PCM^3} = \begin{bmatrix} 1.0000 & 0.2582 & 0.3703 & 0.4882 & 0.5567 & 0.5645 & 0.5195 \\ 0.2072 & 1.0000 & 0.3867 & 0.4922 & 0.5731 & 0.5886 & 0.5334 \\ 0.3037 & 0.3745 & 1.0000 & 0.5028 & 0.5490 & 0.5686 & 0.5204 \\ 0.4627 & 0.5420 & 0.5919 & 1.0000 & 0.5673 & 0.5215 & 0.4595 \\ 0.5348 & 0.6657 & 0.7171 & 0.7112 & 1.0000 & 0.5116 & 0.3727 \\ 0.4688 & 0.6735 & 0.7670 & 0.7740 & 0.7111 & 1.0000 & 0.3953 \\ 0.3164 & 0.5656 & 0.7288 & 0.7823 & 0.7520 & 0.6594 & 1.0000 \end{bmatrix} \quad (13)$$

Matrix (12) and (13) show the probabilities of paths with 2 and 3 hops between any nodes. Comparing the values of corresponding elements of matrix (12) and (13), it is easy to find that even the hops in a path is increasing, the probability of a path existence may still getting higher.

4   Network Connectivity Probability

For the sake of better characterizing how well the network is connected in OSN, this section first proposes Probabilistic Path Matrix to calculate the probability that nodes can communicate with others through any paths. Based on it, the Network Connection Mean Probability is defined to achieve this goal.

4.1   Probabilistic Path Matrix

Theorem 3.   Probabilistic Path Matrix (PPM) can achieve the probability that there exists at least one path between any two nodes. That is

$$PPM_{ij} = \begin{Bmatrix} 1 & i = j \text{ or } sum_{ij} >= 1 \\ sum_{ij} & i \neq j \text{ and } sum_{ij} < 1 \end{Bmatrix}. \quad (14)$$

in which, $sum_{ij} = PCM_{ij} + PCM_{ij}^2 + ... + PCM_{ij}^{n-1}$.

Proof.   PCM gives the direct connectivity probabilities between any two nodes, and PCM^2 gives the probabilities that there exists at least one path of 2 hops. Since the maximum hops in a path is $n-1$ (without loops), $PCM^h (h \in [2, n-1])$ gives the probabilities that nodes are connected through intermediate nodes. Therefore, PPM gives the probabilities that there exists at least one path between any nodes.

Through theorem 3, PPM can be deduced from PCM in matrix (10) as following.

$$\mathbf{PCM} = \begin{bmatrix} 1 & 1 & 1 & 1 & 1 & 1 & 1 \\ 1 & 1 & 1 & 1 & 1 & 1 & 1 \\ 1 & 1 & 1 & 1 & 1 & 1 & 1 \\ 1 & 1 & 1 & 1 & 1 & 1 & 1 \\ 1 & 1 & 1 & 1 & 1 & 1 & 1 \\ 1 & 1 & 1 & 1 & 1 & 1 & 1 \\ 1 & 1 & 1 & 1 & 1 & 1 & 1 \end{bmatrix} \quad (15)$$

Comparing the value of elements in matrix (10) and matrix (15), where $PCM_{74} = 0.1749$ and $PPM_{74} = 1$, the indirect connectivity probability is 0.8251, which is the connectivity probability caused by the "Storing-Carrying-Forwarding" communication pattern in OSN.

4.2   Network Connection Mean Probability

Even though PPM can give out the communication probabilities between any two nodes through any paths, we still want to acquire how well the network is connected from network perspective instead of node perspective. Network Connection Mean Probability is defined to fulfill this mission.

Definition 2. The Network Connection Mean Probability (NCMP) is the mean of the sum of all elements except the diagonal element in PPM. That is

$$NCMP = \frac{\sum_{i=1}^{n} \sum_{j=1,i\neq j}^{n} PPM_{ij}}{n^2 - n} \tag{16}$$

Just as the definition 2 stated, with the consideration of communication probabilities between any pair of nodes, NCMP should be capable of characterizing how well the network is connected. And in this way, the connectivity of network can be reflected.

In realistic scenarios, connectivity of network increases with the communication radius increasing, and decreases with environmental noises getting stronger. In DARG model, communication radius is reflected as r_1 and r_2, and environmental noise is reflected as path loss index w. If there exists the same law between NCMP and r_1, r_2 as well as w respectively, namely NCMP increases with r_1 and r_2 increasing, and decreases with w increasing, then NCMP is able to describe the connectivity preferably. In order to validate this, the following simulations are conducted to check whether there exists the law between r_1, r_2, w and NCMP.

Fig.4 and 5 show how NCMP changes with r_1 and r_2 respectively. In Fig.4, as $r_2 = 0.6$ which is relatively high, NCMP increases rapidly with r_1 increasing

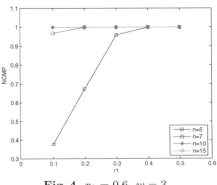

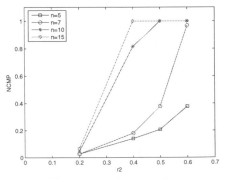

Fig. 4. $r_2 = 0.6$, $w = 3$ **Fig. 5.** $r_1 = 0.1$, $w = 3$

and soon reach to 1 when the number of nodes is more than 7. In Fig.5, NCMP increases with r_2 increasing when $r_1 = 0.1$, more specifically, NCMP reach to 0.8 rapidly when r_2 is more than 0.4 and the number of nodes is more than 10, and NCMP increases rapidly when r_2 is more than 0.5 and the number of nodes is less than 7.

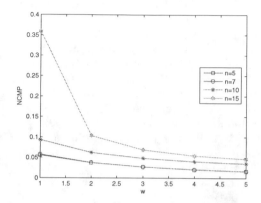

Fig. 6. The effect of w on NCMP ($r_1 = 0.1, r_2 = 0.2$)

Fig.6 shows that NCMP decreases with w increasing when r_1 and r_2 are both fixed, and this kind of decreasing is more obvious when the number of nodes get more. So there exists the law between r_1, r_2, w and NCMP, and NCMP is able to describe the connectivity of network preferably.

Fig.4, 5 and 6 show the law that the changes of NCMP with r_1, r_2 and w respectively to different n is different, which illustrate the role of n. As the area is fixed, the more nodes can achieve higher connectivity, and other factors such as communication radius and environmental noises can cause more obvious effect on connectivity.

5 Conclusion

This paper proposed a DARG model to analyse the connectivity in OSN with the consideration of uncertainty of links. As opposed to other random graph, DARG model adopted probabilistic communication model to analyse the uncertainty of links, this made DARG more practical. Based on DARG, PPM was introduced to capture the communication probability caused by "Storing-Carrying-Forwarding" communication pattern, and NCMP was defined to characterize how well the network is connected, and it was preferable to describe connectivity in OSN as validated by simulations. The further work is trying to use mobile nodes to construct the realistic scenarios of OSN and validate the effect of our approach.

References

1. Eisenman, S.B., Lane, N.D., Campbell, A.T.: Techniques for improving opportunistic sensor networking performance. In: Nikoletseas, S.E., Chlebus, B.S., Johnson, D.B., Krishnamachari, B. (eds.) DCOSS 2008. LNCS, vol. 5067, pp. 157–175. Springer, Heidelberg (2008)
2. Pan, D.R., Cao, W., Liu, X., Sun, J.J., Shi, X.J.: A performance-guarantee routing algorithm in complex distributed opportunistic networks. The Journal of China Universities of Posts and Telecommunications 19, 87–93 (2012)
3. Li, Q., Gao, W., Zhu, S., Cao, G.: A routing protocol for socially selfish delay tolerant networks. Ad Hoc Networks 10(8), 1619–1632 (2012)
4. van der Hofstad, R.: Random graphs and complex networks. Lecture notes (2011), http://www.win.tue.nl/~rhofstad/NotesRGCN2011.pdf
5. Chlamtac, I., Faragó, A.: A new approach to the design and analysis of peer-to-peer mobile networks. Wireless Networks 5(3), 149–156 (1999)
6. Gupta, P., Kumar, P.R.: Critical power for asymptotic connectivity in wireless networks. In: Stochastic Analysis, Control, Optimization and Applications, pp. 547–566. Springer, Birkhäuser Boston (1998)
7. Bettstetter, C.: On the connectivity of ad hoc networks. The Computer Journal 47(4), 432–447 (2004)
8. Ellis, R.B., Martin, J.L., Yan, C.: Random geometric graph diameter in the unit ball. Algorithmica 47(4), 421–438 (2007)
9. Krishnamachari, B., Wicker, S.B., Bejar, R.: Phase transition phenomena in wireless ad hoc networks. In: IEEE Global Telecommunications Conference, GLOBECOM 2001, vol. 5, pp. 2921–2925. IEEE Press (2001)
10. Agarwal, A., Starobinski, D., Little, T.D.: Phase Transition of Message Propagation Speed in Delay-Tolerant Vehicular Networks. IEEE Transactions on Intelligent Transportation Systems 13(1), 249–263 (2012)
11. Brooks, R.R., Pillai, B., Racunas, S., Rai, S.: Mobile network analysis using probabilistic connectivity matrices. IEEE Transactions on Systems, Man, and Cybernetics, Part C: Applications and Reviews 37(4), 694–702 (2007)
12. Baccour, N., Koubaa, A., Mottola, L., Zuniga, M.A., Youssef, H., Boano, C.A., Alves, M.: Radio link quality estimation in wireless sensor networks: a survey. ACM Transactions on Sensor Networks (TOSN) 8(4), 34 (2012)
13. De Gennaro, M.C., Jadbabaie, A.: Decentralized control of connectivity for multi-agent systems. In: 2006 45th IEEE Conference on Decision and Control, pp. 3628–3633. IEEE Press (2006)
14. Haenggi, M., Andrews, J.G., Baccelli, F., Dousse, O., Franceschetti, M.: Stochastic geometry and random graphs for the analysis and design of wireless networks. IEEE Journal on Selected Areas in Communications 27(7), 1029–1046 (2009)

A Multi-resolution Task Distribution Method in Mobile Sensing System

Jun Liu and Siwang Zhou

College of Information Science and Engineering
Hunan University, Changsha, China

Abstract. With the popularity of mobile phones, mobile sensing system has become an important research area in wireless sensor network. In this paper, a multi-resolution task distribution method for mobile sensing system is presented. First, a task map of sensing area is defined according to its physical map. Then a set of of information parameters are designed, and the task map is encoded. Thus the mobile nodes are capable of downloading the task map using parametric encoding map. In our proposed method, mobile nodes can stop receiving task map at any time, and a task map with suitable resolution is obtained. Through experiment about error rate of parametric encoding, multi-resolution receiving method and encoded information size, we can conclude that parametric encoding and multi-resolution receiving are suitable for mobile sensing system.

Keywords: Mobile Sensor Network, Task Map, Parametric Encoding, Multi-resolution.

1 Introduction

Mobile sensor network [1] is a special kind of wireless sensor network made of mobile node with mobility, which has become a research hot topic along with popularity of smart phones embedded with sensory device. Mobile sensor has been widely applied in fields such as environmental monitoring [2], healthcare [3], noise monitoring, etc.

Existing research about mobile sensing system mainly focuses on how to obtain sensor data effectively [4] [5]. We can use smart phones embedded sensing devices to collect sensor data within certain mobile sensing area. We can share information with the help of data memorizer [6] to exchange data among different mobile nodes. Mobile sensor data can also be used for Opportunity Network [7] and Routing problems. Sometimes we are not able to obtain sensor data. As mobile devices are not controlled by sensing system but owned by individuals. We can take some measures [8] to incentive individual mobile node to provide sensor data. To maximize data utility, a systematic sensing structure is needed. System server would be able to control the mobile node to perform interaction and data exchanging so as to maximize the use of sensor data.

In a typical mobile sensing system, task distribution is a potential research direction. Some preliminary research has been done about task distribution,

L. Sun, H. Ma, and F. Hong (Eds.): CWSN 2013, CCIS 418, pp. 191–200, 2014.

such as Zoom's[9] sensing framework. The main purpose of this system is to provide concise and efficient support for mixed equipment and unstructured mobile network. Its main idea is to encode a task map according to physical map, then use this map to control mobile node to conduct certain task within certain area. Each pixel value in task map represents a grid area, corresponding to the actual square region of the physical map. We can choose suitable sensor group to perform specified sensing tasks according to information received.

Zoom put forward the first mobile sensing framework based on map. Encoded map information includes coordinate information as well as the type of Task (Task ID). However, Zoom does not provide encoding method for subarea of the sensing area, this made mobile node choosing task area freely impossible. What's more, mobile nodes may not have enough resource to decode the entire map. On the other hand, multi-resolution encoding in Zoom is determined by the server but not the mobile node.

This paper puts forward a solution to Zoom's framework. Mobile node can choose to receive task map selectively through parameters passing and perform the corresponding tasks. Meanwhile, mobile node can terminate receiving task map at any time, get the corresponding resolution, execute the task of selected area.

2   Parametric Encoding and Multi-resolution Map Receiving Process

2.1   Location Based Task Distribution Framework

We define a task to be a set of operations which one or more mobile nodes need to perform to accomplish a high-level objective. For example: a task is to collect the noise pollution data in an area, and feedback to predefined base station. A task map is used to represent geographical regions and the corresponding sensing tasks, task map can be viewed as an image overlaid on top of the physical map. For each task there is a unique Task ID, a node can receive task map from sensing system and get the Task ID.

In this paper, we assume that sensor nodes know their own location, which can be obtained from GPS receivers, and there exist protocols to disseminate task information, in the network and for a node to download the task from sensing system. This assumption is reasonable for mobile devices have reasonable networking capability.

Fig. 1 shows a location-based task distribution framework which consists of three main components: parameter transmission, task encoding, task receiving and decoding. For parameter transmission, mobile nodes transport parameters to system server according to the task. For task encoding, the server and terminal machine encode certain region into task map according to these parameters. For task receiving and decoding, mobile nodes receive the encoded task map, calculate its image pixel values, get its location information and the Task ID, then mobile nodes compare new Task ID with the original Task ID to decide whether to perform a new task.

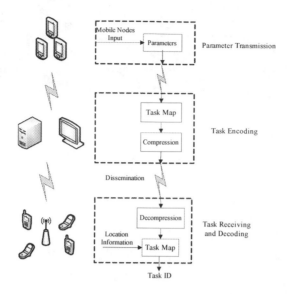

Fig. 1. Location based task distribution framework

Fig. 2 illustrates how mobile sensing system works. Fig. 2(a) is the physical map of a city. The server decides to measure light in the left area and to measure noise in the right area. The server defines the regions (e.g.marked region on the map) by pixel to arrange the corresponding tasks. We use STIF encoding techniques which is similar to GIF to encode the task map. The encoded task map is shown in Fig. 2(b). Mobile nodes receive the task map and obtain the corresponding Task ID to perform the task.

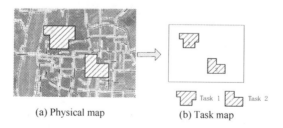

(a) Physical map   (b) Task map

Fig. 2. Physical map and Task map

Suppose the two regions overlap. Then nodes in the overlapping area must perform both tasks. The overlapping area is assigned a new Task ID, which in turn includes both the two given tasks. The complexity of this operation is handled at the back end. Hence, the nodes themselves do not have to implement complex algorithms to interpret multiple tasks.

Mobile nodes in the sensing system only need for parameter passing and task map decoding. The complexity of the encoding is done by operation at the back end, which minimizes the resource consumption of mobile nodes.

2.2 Parametric Encoding

Mobile node cannot understand complex physical map. We encode physical map into task map, which is helpful for mobile node to grab the information. However, it is impossible to decode the entire task map since its computing, storage, energy resources are limited. So we have to figure out a way to select certain region to encode and decode.

Parametric encoding refers to the server selects and encodes the corresponding physical map into task map according to map information, such as city name, street name. Map information is stored in database as a form of raster data. Raster data is a kind data structure based on grid model. The space is divided into grid units. By given the corresponding attribute value to each grid unit, we can use this data structure to represent the geographical entities. The table which created by the server is used to store the street information. Encoded task map is sent to the sensing system through the server.

Fig. 3 shows the structure of parametric encoding. Fig. 3 shows a diagram for a 3x3 grid data. The server can interpret each raster data according to the name of the city and the street. For example city name is: A1, A2, A3, street name is: B1, B2, B3. As shown in the figure bellow:(A1,B1)shows the city name and the street name is A1,B1. We can obtain specific data according to arbitrary parameters, such as information named street B2 (the third column). We can also obtain the required raster date according to multiple parameters, such as the city name, street name is A2,B3(the second line of the second column).

Parameter	Value
City name	A1,A2,A3...
Street name	B1,B2,B3...
⋮	⋮

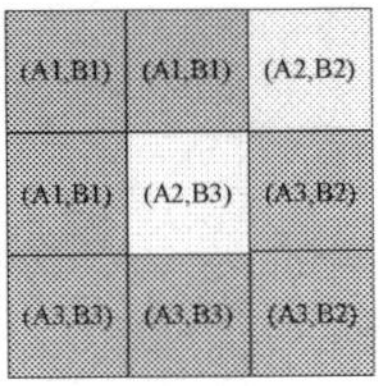

(A1,B1)	(A1,B1)	(A2,B2)
(A1,B1)	(A2,B3)	(A3,B2)
(A3,B3)	(A3,B3)	(A3,B2)

Fig. 3. Structure of parametric encoding

Fig. 4 illustrates process of the parametric encoding.

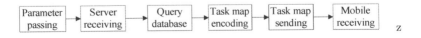

Parameter passing	→	Server receiving	→	Query database	→	Task map encoding	→	Task map sending	→	Mobile receiving

z

Fig. 4. Process of the parametric encoding

Fig. 5 illustrates the principle of the parametric encoding. (1) Mobile nodes in sensing system interact with the server, and send the parameter to the server. (2) The server receives the parameters,which as a query condition. (3) The server connects database to get the sensing data. The corresponding query results are sent to the server. (4) The server sends the results to the terminal machine. The terminal machine decodes the selected area according to the received query data, and sends the decoded map to the server. (5) The task map is sent to the sensing area by server. (6) Mobile nodes in the sensing area receive the encoded task map, decode it, get the Task ID and then perform a sensing task.

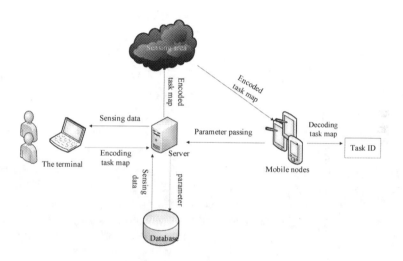

Fig. 5. Principle of the parametric encoding

Mobile nodes can choose a given area to decode, thus save a lot of time. Meanwhile the encoded task map size is far less than physical map, thus energy needed by mobile node is reduced as well.

2.3   Multi-resolution Task Map Receiving

Mobile nodes in the sensing region can choose specific area to decode, and terminate receiving task map at any time. Mobile nodes can select any resolution of the task map which is sent by the server, decode the task map and get information about sensing area. That means mobile nodes can choose the appropriate resolution according to the need of the task.

In traditional image receiving process, we are unable to open the map while the download is not completed. In this paper, we propose multi-resolution task map. Mobile node can open the map as well as it receives the task map. The longer the receiving time, the higher the resolution, until the node receives the same resolution as the server sending (server sends the highest resolution map).

The major concept of multi-resolution task map receiving is bit-plane encoding. For images whose gray value presented by multiple bits. Each bit stands for a binary plane, also known as bit-plane. For example, here is a vector[2,0,3,1], transferred into a binary is[10,00,11,01]. You can use two bit-plane to present this vector:[1,0,1,0], [0,0,1,1]. The first plane is composed of the higher bit of the vector, while the second is the lower bit in the vector. Again, respectively, the results of the two bit-plane encoding can show the original vector. This process is called bit plane encoding.

The receiving process of the multi-resolution task map is show in Fig. 6:

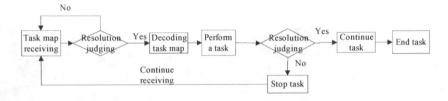

Fig. 6. Process of multi-resolution task map receiving

Fig. 7 and Fig. 8 illustrate the principle of multi-resolution receiving. Mobile nodes in the sensing system select a area to perform a specific task. The server sends encoded task map to sensing area. Mobile nodes select to receive the encoded task map. Firstly, the raster data of the received task map is shown in Fig. 7, which is made up of unit 1,(2),3,(4). (2) and (4)are divided as a example later. The resolution of the received task map is very low. The corresponding street is shown in Fig. 8(a), the original city map is made up of multiple street, however, the received map could only shows one main street due to the low resolution. If mobile nodes choose to receive sensing data continually. The resolution of the received map become higher. Each raster data received is shown in Fig. 7, which is made up of unit 5,6,7,8, decomposed by grid unit(2). Because the resolution of the received task map becomes higher, the corresponding city map becomes clear. The corresponding street is shown in Fig. 8(b). Some street branch can already be seen in city map. Mobile nodes keep receiving. The received raster data is shown in Fig. 7, which is made up of unit 13,14,15,16, decomposed by grid unit(9). The corresponding street is shown in Fig. 8(c). As the received task map becomes more and more clear, the resolution of the task map become higher and higher, until mobile nodes receive the highest resolution task map. The corresponding street is shown in Fig. 8(d), which is the same as the city map in a small square shown in Fig. 8(e).

Mobile nodes decode the task map and get Task ID of physical area after receiving task map. Nodes can interact with the server and change the resolution of the map in the process of performing a task. For a specific area, the nodes may need higher resolution map(for example, nodes may need to decide whether a task is outside or inside a building). The nodes can stop performing the task, continue to receive the encoded task map and get a higher resolution.

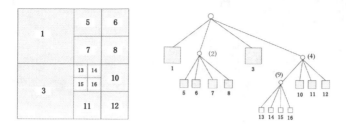

Fig. 7. Raster data of the multi-resolution

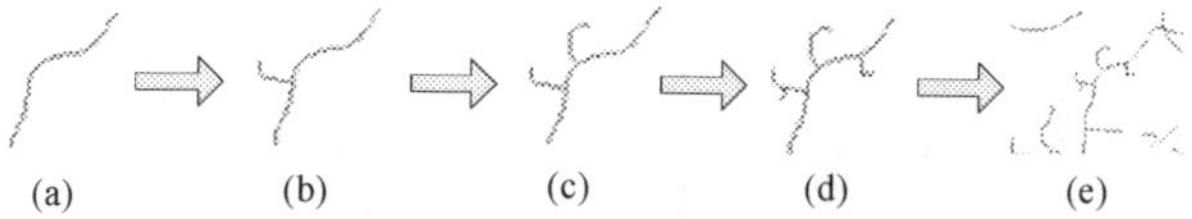

Fig. 8. Street message of the multi-resolution

3 Analysis of Experimental Results

In order to test the error rate of parametric encoding, image display and encoded information size under different resolution, we extract the GIS shapefile [10] for Portland and its nearby suburbs from the latitude and longitude coordinates of (7586981.563, 649562.086) to (7702365.364, 710230.26). The shapefile is available at the US Census Bureau website and contains several recodes. Parametric encoding error rate means measure the probability error occur during inquire database and perform a task.

Fig. 9 shows the error rate of different resolution. The higher resolution of the task map, the lower the error rate. When the resolution is 685x429, the error rate is 4.9%. When the resolution is 4913x3473, the error rate is almost 0. This is because a lower resolution means less street information. Some streets in the map may overlapped. So if we use street name as a parameter to inquire the database, errors may appear. The error rate of parametric encoding method is always below 5%. So the parametric encoding is suitable for mobile sensing system.

Fig. 10 shows task map encoded in this paper. Fig. 11 shows the multi-resolution encoded task map in Zoom.

Analysis: For Zoom's multi-resolution map, pixel values under different resolution means different size of physical area. A higher resolution map represents a smaller physical area, while the encoded task map is larger. This paper presents multi-resolution map. More detail raster data received means higher resolution of the map. But the size of different resolution map is equal. Compared with Zoom, a pixel value in this method represents an unchanged square of the physical map.

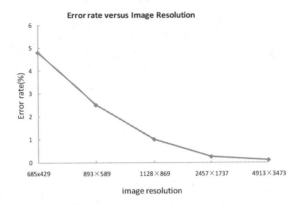

Fig. 9. Error rate of different image resolution

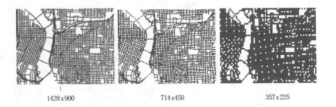

Fig. 10. Multi-resolution map in this paper

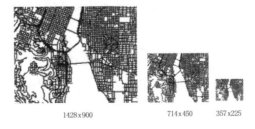

Fig. 11. Multi-resolution map in zoom

Therefore, the mobile nodes can select different resolution while performing a task. Mobile node can continue an unfinished task for the size of the received task map does not change.

Fig. 12 compares the encoded information size between the parametric encoding in this paper and encode region with method in Zoom. With the increment of resolution, encoded map size in both the parametric encoding and Zoom will gradually increase. For the same resolution, parametric encoding only chooses to encode a specific area, and the map size is less Compared with Zoom. Parametric encoding saves the energy of the mobile nodes.

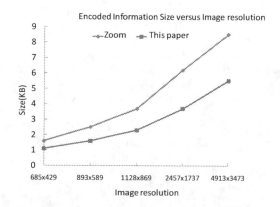

Fig. 12. Encoded information size of different resolution

4   Conclusion

This paper puts forward mobile sensing framework based on parametric encoding and multi-resolution task map receiving. Mobile nodes can choose physical area of sensor network accordingly. Mobile nodes send parameters to the server. Server sends the encoded task map to the sensing system. Parametric encoding increases the flexibility of mobile nodes and simplifies the working process of the mobile node as well. The complex task encoding process is conducted by the server, thus save computing resource of the mobile nodes. A Multi-resolution task map receiving method is proposed in this paper. Mobile nodes can choose to receive and decode map of any resolution, then perform the corresponding sensing tasks. Through experiments, we conclude that parametric encoding and multi-resolution task map receiving method are suitable for mobile sensing system. Compared with Zoom, the flexibility of mobile node increased and more energy consumption has been saved.

References

1. Howard, A., Matarić, M.J., Sukhatme, G.S.: Mobile sensor network deployment using potential fields: A distributed, scalable solution to the area coverage problem. In: Proc of International Symposium on Distributed Autonomous Robotics Systems, pp. 299–303 (2002)
2. Mun, M., et al.: Peir, the Personal Environmental Impact Report, as a Platform for Participatory Sensing Systems Research. In: Proc. 7th ACM MobiSys, pp. 55–68 (2009)
3. Thiagarajan, A., et al.: VTrack: Accurate, Energy-Aware Traffic Delay Estimation Using Mobile Phones. In: Proc. 7th ACM SenSys, Berkeley, CA (November 2009)
4. Bao, X., Roy Choudhury, R.: Movi: mobile phone based video highlights via collaborative sensing. In: Proc. 8th International Conference on Mobile Systems, Applications, and Services, MobiSys 2010, pp. 357–370. ACM, New York (2010)
5. Oliver, N., Mangas, F.F.: Healthgear: Automatic sleep apnea detection and monitoring with a mobile phone. Journal of Communications (March 2007)
6. Ngai, E., Huang, H., Liu, J., Srivastava, M.: OppSense: Information sharing for mobile phones in sensing field with data repositories. In: Proc. of SECON (June 2011)
7. Rana, R., Chou, C., Kanhere, S., Bulusu, N., Hu, W.: Ear-phone: an end-to-end participatory urban noise mapping system. In: Proc. of ACM/IEEE IPSN 2010, pp. 105–116 (2008)
8. Burke, J., Estrin, D., Hansen, M., Parker, A., Ramanathan, N., Reddy, S., Srivastava, M.B.: Participatory sensing. In: Workshop on World-Sensor-Web (WSW 2006), pp. 117–134 (2006)
9. Dang, T., Feng, W., Bulusu, N.: Zoom: A multi-resolution tasking framework for crowdsourced geo-spatial sensing. In: Proc. of IEEE Infocom, pp. 501–505 (2011)
10. Xia, K., Wei, C.: Study on Real-Time Navigation Data Model Based on ESRI Shapefile. In: Proc. of IEEE Infocom, pp. 174–178 (2008)

EBRP: An Energy Balance Routing Protocol for Wireless Sensor Network with Intermittent Connectivity

Yulao Han[1,2], Dingyi Fang[1,*], Xiaojiang Chen[1], Xiaoyan Yin[1], and Chen Liu[1]

[1] Department of Information and Technology,
Northwest University, Xi'an 710127, China
[2] Department of Mathematics and Computer,
PanZhiHua University, PanZhiHua 617000, China
ylhan2008@126.com, {dyf,xjchen,yinxy,chenliu}@nwu.edu.cn

Abstract. Wireless sensor network commonly used to monitor wild environments with sparse events. In this application, the primary concern is how to maximize the network lifetime. In order to save energy, the intermittent connected wireless sensor network(ICWSN) is formed by putting nodes into sleeping state for a long time. In the paper, we propose a link metric which considers both link quality and residual energy of nodes for delivering packets on wireless links and presents a routing protocol called EBRP based on the link metric in ICWSN. Using data packet retransmission mechanism based on predicting active time slots of nodes solves the problem of data transmission failure due to unreliable links. Simulation shows that the proposed protocol achieves a good balance between reliability and real-time, as well as the maximum network lifetime.

Keywords: wireless sensor network, network lifetime, link metric.

1 Introduction

Environmental monitoring[1–4] is a relatively common wireless sensor network application scenario, such as the deformation monitoring of soil sites of the Great Wall [4]. In the application, considering the fact that occurrence of interesting events has sparse characteristics, in order to maximize network lifetime, it is an effective practice to let nodes sleep for most of the time, which forms intermittent connected wireless sensor network(ICWSN)[5] and brings a great delay for data collection. Traditionally data packet is always transmitted along a predetermined path to destination node in the wired network or wireless network with better connectivity. At present, one of the hot topics is how to provide network lifetime maximization while reliability and real-time of communications can satisfy certain requirements in ICWSN[5–8, 11, 12].

---

[*] Corresponding author.

L. Sun, H. Ma, and F. Hong (Eds.): CWSN 2013, CCIS 418, pp. 201–211, 2014.
© Springer-Verlag Berlin Heidelberg 2014

In recent years, we have witnessed some major advances[6–8] in designing data collection in order to guarantee the strict quality-of-service requirements in ICWSN. However, these advances exist a series of problems. In particular, routing tree is proposed to collect data in [6], where nodes are assigned staggered active/sleep schedules based on the depth of nodes in the tree, which greatly reduces transmission delay, but increases the delay caused by the failure of data transmission due to unreliability of wireless links. In [7], opportunistic routing which takes advantage of the broadcast nature of wireless network is combined with ICWSN. It relies on routing performance to determine a unique forwarding set among the receiving nodes, so the way can improve reliability of data transmission and can reduce delay of data transmission. However, the strength of opportunistic routing always is comes from the diversity of the candidates forwarder's links. Therefore, if nodes are in intermittent work mode and have low-density deployment, then relatively few nodes will simultaneously be in active state in a time slot, so the performance of opportunistic routing will become very low. In [8], the author proposes a robust multi-pipeline scheduling protocol (RMS) and proves that it can guarantee reliability and real-time of data transmission effectively. In RMS protocol, each node is assigned optimized time slot and packets can be switched among multiple pipelines when failure is encountered in previous pipeline forwarding. However, each node is assigned optimized time slot at the cost of communication and calculation which can consume more energy of nodes. This is hard to be accepted because WSN applications demand for high energy efficiency. Moreover, RMS determines forwarding set simply based on link quality regardless of node's residual energy. Consequently, some nodes with higher link quality tend to be used frequently, while others seldom are used, unbalanced use of nodes makes some nodes disabled quickly, and greatly reduces network lifetime.

In this paper, we give a link metric called the Sum of Link Quality and Energy(SLQE) and present an Energy Balancing Routing Protocol(EBRP) for ICWSN, a novel routing technique that balances energy consumption among next-hop nodes by jointly considering link quality and residual energy. Moreover, EBRP exploits active time slot prediction based retransmission mechanism to ensure timeliness and reliability of data transmission.

2   Network Model and Relevant Hypothesis

Suppose all nodes except sink in ICWSN is homogeneous with the same transmitting power, communication radius and initial energy. Moreover, we also assume that network is locally synchronized by using a MAC layer time stamping technique, as described in [9]. In this paper, the multi-hop wireless sensor network is modeled as a communication graph G (V, E, P, W), where V refers to the set of sensor nodes, E stands for the set of radio links between the nodes in V, an edge (i, j) belongs to E if and only if node j is in the transmission range of node i, P is a set of all links' weighs, each link (i, j) has a weight, denoted by $p_{i,j}$, which is the link quality for link(i, j) and can be obtained by using probe message[10], for simplicity, we assume that link quality for all links is now known, W is the set of work scheduling of sensor nodes which can be achieved by our proposed scheduling model, the detailed scheduling model will be described below.

Work Scheduling Model: Sink is in active state for all the time, while other nodes are in the intermittent work mode in which sensor nodes activate very shortly and stay in sleeping state for a very long period of time. Let T denote sensor nodes' working period and T is divided into a number of time slots with equal length π, a time slot π can only transmit one packet. For clarity, we represent work scheduling of a node such as i with a finite binary string w_i in which 1 denotes the active state and 0 denotes the sleeping state. we will assign work scheduling to each sensor node by (1).

$$X_{n+1} = (X_n + C)mod(\frac{T}{\pi}) \qquad n = 0, 1, 2, \cdots, \frac{T}{\pi * C} . \tag{1}$$

Where X_0 is a node's ID and denotes the first active time slot of the node, X_n denotes the $(n + 1)^{th}$ active time slot, $\frac{T}{\pi}$ is the sum of time slots in a work period T, C controls duty cycle which is the ratio of the number of active time slots to the number of all time slots in a work period T. For instance, suppose C=5, $\frac{T}{\pi} = 20$, then work scheduling w_3 for the node labeled as 3 can be computed as (00100001000010000100) by (1). Obviously, the node's duty cycle can be calculated as 20%.

3   Overall Design

In this section, we first introduce a new link metric for ICWSN. We then elaborate on the main idea of our proposed EBRP protocol based on the link metric.

3.1   SLQE Link Metric

In previous work, link metric is mostly based on link quality, always does not consider node's residual energy. The link metric quickly makes nodes with high link quality invalid because large data forwarding task mainly relies on these nodes. In comparison, we provide the link metric SLQE which combines link quality with residual energy of next-hop node. As a result, it can balance node's energy consumption and thus increases the network lifetime. In this case, SLQE metric for link (i, j) denoted as $SLQE_{i,j}$ can be written as:

$$SLQE_{i,j} = \beta * p_{i,j} + (1 - \beta) * \frac{E_j}{E_{max}} \qquad j \in N_i . \tag{2}$$

where $p_{i,j}$ is link quality for link (i, j), N_i is the set of next-hop nodes of node i, E_j is residual energy of node j, E_{max} is initial energy of all nodes, β is a predefined parameter in range [0, 1] which is a good tradeoff between link quality and residual energy.

3.2 EBRP Protocol Description

In this subsection, we introduce our proposed protocol which consists of three parts, namely, network initialization, routing process and updating residual energy of nodes.

Network Initialization: In the following, we sketch the network initialization three steps of EBRP protocol: formation of nodes layer, constructing next-hop neighbor table and constructing forwarding set.

(1) Formation of nodes layer: In the step of network initialization, all nodes are in an active state and find out its layer number which represents its shortest hop count away from the sink. First the sink starts to broadcast a control message CM containing a hop count c initialized to 0. On the way, the hop count is incremented. After each node receives CM, it waits for a while for more copies of CM to arrive, then it picks the CM with the smallest hop count and regards the smallest hop count as its layer number. In this way, layer number of the sink is defined as L0 and the nodes nearest to the sink is L1. the further the node is to the sink, the larger its layer number can be. Fig. 1 shows final generated network layer.

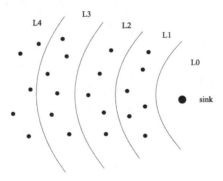

Fig. 1. Network layer

(2) Constructing next-hop neighbor table: In this step, to collect next-hop neighbor node's information, each node broadcasts a message containing its own ID, residual energy and hop count to sink. If node i has received message from node j and hop count of node i is bigger than that of node j, then node i's neighbor table will record node j's ID and residual energy information, then SLQE metric for link (i, j), $SLQE_{i,j}$, can be computed by (2) and work scheduling w_j for node j can be computed by (1). For node i, its next-hop neighbor table is showed as follows in table 1.

(3) Constructing forwarding set: The number of all nodes' biggest forwarding k is the same and is predefined in the network initialization. After step 2 is carried

Table 1. The next-hop neighbor table for node i

Node ID	Residual Energy	Work Scheduling	Link Quality	SLQE Metric
2	E_2	w_2	$p_{i,2}$	$SLQE_{i,2}$
5	E_5	w_5	$p_{i,5}$	$SLQE_{i,5}$
101	E_{101}	w_{101}	$p_{i,101}$	$SLQE_{i,101}$

out, each node has known its next-hop neighbor table, then the table is sorted in descending order of their SLQE metrics and node i obtains the forwarding set, denoted by $F_{i,k}$, consisting of the first k nodes in the sorted neighbor table.

Routing Process: Routing process can be finished by forwarding layer by layer. We now take Fig. 2 as an example for introducing forwarding process of data packet. All nodes in the forwarding set have different work scheduling, when a node such as D has data packet to transmit in time slot t=4, the forwarding sequence of these forwarding nodes of the node depends on their active time slots. The closer time slot of a node is to t, the higher forwarding priority the node has. The forwarding process is repeated until node D have received a ACK from any node in its forwarding set or the number of transmitting packets have exceeded k. Or to be more precise, node D's forwarding set consists of two nodes, node F and node H. D first attempts to transmit the data packet to H because active slot 6 of node H is more priority than that of F, if node D failures to transmit the data packet to node H, then it will transmit the data packet to F in time slot 7 once more. At last, if node D still failures to transmit and if the maximum forwarding number k is set to 2, node D will discard the data packet and terminates the forwarding process.

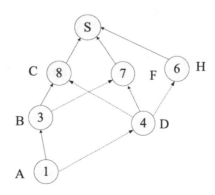

Fig. 2. Intermittent network topology

Updating Residual Energy of Nodes: With the running time of network increased, network lifetime can be greatly reduced if we overlook the fact that residual energy of all nodes is gradually decreasing. Therefore each node should support real-time update on its neighbor node's residual energy. One way of doing so is that an ACK message containing residual energy of the current node i can be returned to node j when node i receives a data packet from j. In one case, residual energy of some nodes may not be updated because these nodes failure to transmit data packet to receiving node, but the factor has less impacts on network performance in some network environments where interesting events are very sparse. If necessary, all nodes can carry out neighborhood discovery mechanism to update their residual energy at regular interval.

4   Discussion about Forwarding Ratio and Delay

As in the previous, we have obtained forwarding set of node i denoted as $F_{i,k}$. We now calculate one-hop forwarding ratio and forwarding delay based on link quality and work scheduling. $EDR(i, F_{i,k})$ which is one-hop forwarding ratio from i to at least one node of forwarding set can be calculated as follows:

$$EDR(i, F_{i,k}) = p_{i,1} + \sum_{m=2}^{k} \prod_{j=1}^{m-1} (1 - p_{i,j}) * p_{i,m} . \tag{3}$$

We now give some discussions on how to increase one-hop forwarding ratio based on (3). A way to do so is to add the maximal forwarding number k, but the way further exacerbates energy consumption of transmitting nodes. Another idea is to adjust parameter β in (2). Suppose average link quality of all links in ICWSN is 0.6 and maximal forwarding number k is 3, then one-hop forwarding ratio is more than 80% computed by (3). Furthermore, we assume that all nodes are evenly distributed on the plane such that each one-hop forwarding ratio is approximately identical. As a result, end-to-end forwarding ratio is no less than 88% when maximal hop count in ICWSN is no more than 5. Thus, k is set to 3 in our simulations.

Similarly, $EDT(i, F_{i,k})$ which is one-hop forwarding delay from i to at least one node of forwarding set can be expressed as follows:

$$EDT(i, F_{i,k}) = \sum_{j=1}^{k} \pi * \delta_{i,j} * p(i, j) . \tag{4}$$

$$p(i, j) = \frac{\prod_{m=1}^{m-1} (1 - p_{i,m}) * p_{i,j}}{1 - \prod_{m=1}^{k} p_{i,m}} . \tag{5}$$

Where $\delta_{i,j}$ is the number of intervals between active slot of node i and active slot of the jth node in i's forwarding set, p(i, j) is the probability that a packet transmission by node i failures at the first j-1 times while is successful at the jth attempt under the condition that the data packet can be transmitted successfully within j attempts. From (4), we can easily find that one-hop forwarding delay can be reduced as k and β increase. Furthermore, that also reduce end-to-end data transmission delay.

5   Simulations and Analysis

We compare our proposed EBRP with traditional FLOOD protocol and RMS protocol in [8] using a self-written simulator in java language and make further performance analysis and evaluation. Evaluation criteria is comprised of data packet forwarding ratio, network lifetime and end-to-end forwarding delay. In our simulations, nodes are randomly deployed in a 200 m × 200 m area. The number of nodes varies from 300 to 600 with a step of 50 and the sink is placed in the center of the field. In each time slot, we randomly choose a sensor to generate a new data packet and let it send the data packet to the sink. Each result is averaged over 20 random network topologies. Here we assume $\beta = 0.9$, k=3 and let all nodes' duty cycle be 20% in our EBRP protocol. To be fair, the size of forwarding set in RMS also is set to 3. We compare network performance of above three protocols under network configurations with different node density.

Fig. 3 shows the line chart of data packet forwarding ratio. From the chart, we can see that forward ratio would increase for these three protocols as the number of nodes increases. For FLOOD protocol, the reason is that as the number of nodes increases, the fixed deployment area means each node has more active state's neighbor nodes, which can increase data packet forwarding ratio. Moreover, RMS and EBRP protocol can select better performance's link for data packet forwarding. We can also observe that FLOOD protocol always outperforms EBRP and RMS protocols under different node density. The reason is that FLOOD protocol always transmits a data packet to all nodes around the transmitting node regardless of each node's position, which greatly helps the data packet to get more chances to be delivered to the sink. EBRP and RMS protocol achieve approximately increase in forwarding ratio, but RMS protocol is a little higher than EBRP protocol. This is because RMS protocol could attempt to select next-hop forwarding node with the best link quality, while for EBRP, it might also try worse links because $\beta = 0.9$ is a tradeoff between link quality and residual energy to choose next-hop forwarding node, so EBRP actually reduces forwarding ratio by balancing energy consumption among forwarding set. We also note that forwarding ratio can maintain above 85% for all three protocols.

Next, Fig. 4 reports the end-to-end forwarding delay for RMS and other two baseline protocol. Note that the end-to-end forwarding delay would decrease as the number of nodes increases for all three protocols. For FLOOD protocol, this is because as the number of nodes increases, each node has more active state's neighbors, in this case, more active nodes can provide opportunities for forwarding data packet. Moreover, when a node has more neighbor nodes, RMS and EBRP protocol can select better performance's links for data packet forwarding and thus reduces the number of retransmission. Forwarding delay in FLOOD is much lower than that of other two protocols. The reason is the same as the

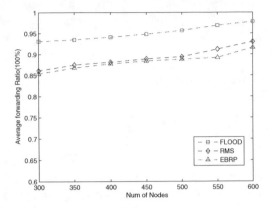

Fig. 3. Num of nodes vs. average forwarding ratio

relation of above-mentioned data packet forwarding ratio among three protocols. Due to space limitations, we won't list them here. The end-to-end forwarding delay's line chart for EBRP and RMS protocol are basically similar, but RMS protocol is slightly lower than EBRP protocol. The reason mainly results from two aspects: RMS 1) could assign time slot to each node in optimized way, but EBRP protocol gives each node's time slot according to its own ID; 2)selects nodes with high link quality as forwarding set, thus reduces retransmission times and forwarding delay.

Finally, we study how average network lifetime changes, the result is plotted in Fig. 5. We can see that average network lifetime for EBRP and RMS is higher than that of FLOOD. One reason is that the number of nodes in forwarding set

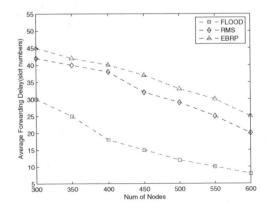

Fig. 4. Num of nodes vs. average forwarding delay

is set to 3 in EBRP and RMS, while for FLOOD, one node which has received a data packet will transmit it to all nodes, that is, its forwarding set consists of all neighbor nodes. As a result, it takes much more energy to finish a data packet's forwarding task. Another reason is that FLOOD results in exist of multiple copies of the same data packet. Moreover, Fig. 5 also shows a very interesting phenomena that network lifetime gradually decreases with increasing of the number of nodes in FLOOD, this is because that as the number of nodes increases, active state neighbors of each node will become more and more, so if a node require to transmit a data packet, all active neighbor nodes of the node will participate in the data packet forwarding. Overall, EBRP have higher network lifetime than RMS, the reason mainly is two aspects: 1) at the beginning of RMS, each node is assigned optimized time slot to reduce data packet forwarding delay at the cost of communication and calculations, especially increasing of traffic can greatly increase node's energy consumption, while EBRP protocol gives each node available time slot according to its own ID without any communicating overhead. 2) EBRP chooses next-hop forwarding node based on parameter $\beta = 0.9$ which considers residual energy of next-hop node and balances energy consumption.

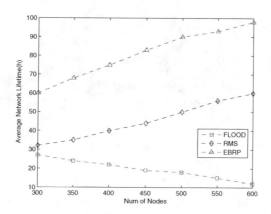

Fig. 5. Num of nodes vs. average network lifetime

6   Conclusion

This paper presents EBRP, an energy balancing routing protocol for ICWSN. The simulation results show the proposed protocol has higher comprehensive performance and can greatly prolong network lifetime compared with FLOOD and RMS protocol. Therefore the proposed protocol will be suitable for a class of application such as long-last deformation monitoring for field soil sites, where network lifetime must last for a long time such as several years while packet forwarding ratio and transmission delay must be able to satisfy certain requirements.

Acknowledgments. This work was based on Project 2013BAK01B02 supported by the National Key Technology Research and Development Program of the Ministry of Science and Technology of China, Project 61070176, 61272461, 61170218, 61202393 supported by NSFC, Project 2012K06-17, 2011K06-07, 2011K06-09 supported by Science and Technology research project of Shaanxi province, China, Project 211181 supported by the Key Project of Chinese Ministry of Education, Project 12JK0936 supported by Special Education Natural Science Foundation of Shaanxi province, China, Project 20106101110018 supported by Research Fund for the Doctoral Program of Higher Education of China, Project 2013BAK01B02 supported by National Key Technology R&D Program, Project YZZ12094 supported by Northwest university Graduate Student's Innovative Talent Training Project, Project 2013KW01-02 supported by International Cooperation Foundation of Shaanxi Province, China.

References

1. Brooke, T., Burrell, J.: From ethnography to design in a vineyard. In: Conference on Designing for user Experiences, pp. 1–4. IEEE Press, ACM Press, New York (2003)
2. Tiano, P., Pardini, C.: Book of Proceedings of the International Workshop SMW 2008, Florence, pp. 817–191 (2008)
3. Beutel, J., Gruber, S., Gubler, S., Hasler, A., Keller, M., Lim, R., Talzi, I., Thiele, L., Tschudin, C., Yuecel, M.: The PermaSense Remote Monitoring Infrastructure. In: ISSW 2009 Europe, Switzerland, pp. 817–191 (2009)
4. Chen, X., Fang, D.: PDHP: An Efficient WSN Routing Protocol Used in the Micro-Environment Monitoring for the Prototection of Solid Relics. Journal of Computer Research and Development, 223–229 (2011)
5. Tie, X., Venkataramani, A., Balasubramanian, A.: R3: robust replication routing in wireless networks with diverse connectivity character-istics. In: The ACM Special Interest Group on Data Communication (ACM SIGCOMM). ACM Press, Toronto (2011)
6. Lu, G., Krishnamachari, B., Raghavendra, C.S.: An Adaptive Energy Efficient and Low Latency MAC for Data Gathering in Wireless Sensor Networks. In: Proceedings of the 18th International Parallel and Distributed Processing Symposium, IPDPS (2004)
7. Landsiedel, O., Ghadimi, E., Duquennoy, S., Johansson, M.: Low Power, Low Delay: Opportunistic Routing meets Duty Cycling. In: 11th ACM/IEEE International Conference on Information Processing in Sensor Networks (IPSN). ACM/IEEE Press, Beijing (2012)
8. Cao, Y., Guo, S., He, T.: Robust multi-pipeline scheduling in low-duty-cycle wireless sensor networks. In: 31st IEEE International Conference on Computer Communications (IEEE INFOCOM 2011). IEEE Press (2011)
9. Maroti, M., Kusy, B., Simon, G., Ledeczi, A.: The Flooding Time Synchronization Protocol. In: 2nd ACM Conference on Embedded Networked Sensor Systems (ACM SenSys). ACM Press, Maryland (2004)

10. Fonseca, R., Gnawali, O., Jamieson, K., Levis, P.: Four Bit Wireless Link Estimation. In: HotNets: Proc. of the Workshop on Hot Topics in Networks (2007)
11. Gu, Y., He, T.: Data forwarding in extremely low duty-cycle sensor networks with unreliable communication links. In: 5th ACM Conference on Embedded Networked Sensor Systems (ACM SenSys), pp. 321–334. ACM Press, Sydney (2007)
12. Xiong, S., Li, J., Li, M., Wang, J., Liu, Y.: Multiple task scheduling for Low-duty-cycled wireless sensor networks. In: 30th IEEE International Conference on Computer Communications (IEEE INFOCOM 2011), pp. 1323–1331. IEEE Press, Shanghai (2011)

Researches on Wireless Embedded Middleware for Service Sharing

Juan Luo, Feng Wu, Feng Zhou, and Renfa Li

School of Information Science and Engineering,
Hunan University, Changsha 410082, China
juanluo@hnu.edu.cn

Abstract. With the rapid development of Internet of Things, more and more embedded devices are involved in it. But application and sensing devices are serious coupled, which makes development processes quite difficult and complicated. This paper designs a service oriented embedded middleware for IoT, called OSGi based distributed service sharing middleware. This embedded middleware abstract application service firstly, process related data and operate with each other. Under the premise of using the OSGi dynamic modular to lower the coupling degree of embedded sensing devices in sensing layer, then a service- oriented programming platform is proposedfor the upper Internet applications, which makes the development of the application system more convenient and fast. The simulation results show that the middleware is more efficient for service use and depend less on computing resources.

Keywords: embedded middleware, OSGi, service, distributed.

1 Introduction

A large number of heterogeneous embedded sensors are distributed in the sensing layer of the Internet of Things, which can accurately sense and efficiently control the objective world[1]. Due to the heterogeneities of the intelligent embedded devices in the sensing layer from several aspects, such as quantity scale, hardware platform, communication protocols, and software environment, the application of the Internet of Things must directly face the underlying structure[2], which leads to a series of problems, for instance, the excessive coupling between the Internet of things application system and the sensing layer including the sensing devices in it, which is lack of flexibility and expansibility in the process of their application.

To solve the problems mentioned above, the conception Internet of Things Middleware is introduced. Broadly defined, Middleware is a type of software that is between the operating system and applications, providing heterogeneities from various perspectives like API, the shielding device communication protocol, network connectivity, operating system, etc., thus realizing the transparent uniform access to heterogeneous devices and resources[3]. The Internet of Things Middleware is located in various sensing nodes, which is a layer of software under

L. Sun, H. Ma, and F. Hong (Eds.): CWSN 2013, CCIS 418, pp. 212–220, 2014.
© Springer-Verlag Berlin Heidelberg 2014

the Internet of things application system. however, currently there is no unified model of the overall architecture of middleware, most studies are conducted on the foundation of the RFID middleware and wireless sensor network middleware, and the design of the middleware structure is carried out according to the traditional mode of application service center. Application service middleware[4] put middleware structure above the background server, so vast amounts of data processing, redundancy compression, redundant operations, and expedited forwarding heavily rely on applications service middleware. The dynamics, diversity, and interoperability of services that sensing layer provides and the transition from Internet of things terminal application to tiny, handheld intelligent terminals brings about some constraints in several aspects of the operation of application software middleware, such as automated management, dynamic service matching and so on.

With the purpose of resolving the problems and reducing the defects during the process of using the application service middleware model, this thesis provides a distributed embedded service middleware model by putting the hierarchical structure of middleware in the Internet of things on the intelligent embedded sensors in the sensing layer.

2   Related Research

Service Oriented Architecture (SOA)[5] is a very popular software design framework, which divides the whole application system into a series of independent functional units, namely, services. Services call each other through a good interface constraint, while the build-ins of service units are completely hidden without mutual interference.

OSGi framework, defined as The Dynamic Module System for Java, is a kind of micro kernel middleware platform which implements an elegant, full and dynamic component model[6]. The application program (bundle) can be dynamically installed, started, stopped, and uninstalled in the form of a plug-in at run time, and each bundle can provide one or more services (exposed interfaces), other applications are just required to access to services according to the interface description without paying attention to the service provider and the service internal running mechanism.

Distributed OSGi has realized the mutual information interaction among multiple OSGi frameworks. Literature[7] proposed that the extension of distributed OSGi can be realized by using Jini (Java Intelligent Network Infrastructure) technology, the introduction of Jini technology, however, is highly invasive for the original OSGi programming model. Apache CXF D-OSGi[8] is a reference implementation of distributed OSGi specification, and bundles running in a single JVM can be deployed to different JVMs through Apache CXF D-OSGi, while D-OSGi exposed bundles and the implementation of local stub is realized through the Http service, the performance overhead of which, compared with embedded sensors, is very large for either the Http service launch or the SOAP protocol transmission. StarOSGi[9] is a type of distributed extension model specific to

CORBA system that is proposed by researchers in National University of Defense Technology. StarOSGi design conforms to the RFC119 specification, and holds the original OSGi programming model, however, it mainly aims at the application of CORBA interoperable extensions, which is not universal. R-OSGi[10], as a set of distributed communication components of the OSGi framework, is rather popular. It allows to call the service from the outer OSGi framework in the local OSGi framework, however, R-OSGi is invasive on the OSGi programming model to some extent.

3   Design of the DssOSGi Framework

The design of the frame of Distributed Service Sharing OSGi (DssOSGi) is shown in Fig.1.

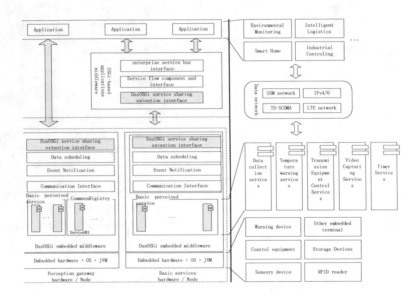

Fig. 1. The overall application architecture of DssOSGi

DssOSGi, combined with the connection characteristics of sensory equipment in the sensing layer and referred to the requirements of distributed OSGi design in RFC 119 specification, sets up the common shared service registry in the gateway node of the sensing layer (or SINK node). All the intelligent embedded sensing devices distributed in the sensing layer will run DssOSGi middleware, and embedded sensors, based on their respective functions or network roles, will encapsulate the basic services that they provide in the corresponding bundles and register to the local OSGi framework. DssOSGi can dynamically register the basic services that embedded sensors provide to the CommonRegistry

(If and only if the services are identified as access to other equipment or upper application).

DssOSGi manages the OSGi framework and the basic services that it provides in sensing network through this centralized approach which have certain defects like single point of failure. The centralized approach, compared with fully distributed service management, however, has a lot of merits on the perspective of network synchronization flow, information interaction efficiency,etc. In order to reduce the additional overhead brought about by synchronization services in the sensing network.

All sensors in the network can get access to services provided by other sensors and realize service binding and information interaction dynamically through a CommonRegistry, thus complete corresponding collaborative operation or work processes. The application of the upper portion of the Internet of things and the interactions of the sensing layer, such as data interaction, tasks assignment, service management, event notification and so on, can undertake information interaction and get access to service or data through the gateway nodes in the sensing layer.

Enterprise server can be used for the management and operation of large complex Internet applications, which blends distributed service sharing extension modules into basic OSGi framework, and the enterprise bus service (ESB) can be quickly created by taking advantages of the modular merits of the OSGi framework.

While for the Internet of things application which is relatively small and based on mobile intelligent terminal, within the gateway sensing ability, can directly interact with a gateway node for management and processing of the services and data in the sensing network in a more rapid way, can also be more efficient for service, tasks and application updates, etc.

4   Distributed and Shared Service Extension Structure

In order to realize the sharing of distributed services among multiple OSGi framework, DssOSGi middleware designs several core modules, including RemoteServiceManager, CommonRegistry, NetworkChannelFactory, TrackManager, Dispatcher.

RemoteServiceManager is the main interface provided by DssOSGi middleware for users or other services to find and get shared services provided by other OSGi frameworks in the entire perception of the network. In order to meet the native OSGi programming style and transparently calling other frameworks services, RemoteServiceManager provides two main methods: getRemoteServiceReference and getRemoteService,which are respectively used to obtain the remote service and remote service instance references that is the local proxy service object.

CommonRegistry is a special gateway deployed in the perception of network for registering shared services provided by each of OSGi framework in the network perception, and responding to their lookup requests. For reducing latency of event notification, once public service registry has received subscription event message, the message will be initiatively pushed to the inner network nodes. In order to allow sensor nodes dynamically join and leave the network, Registry-Discovery in the public registries can find and bind the current network of public service registry.

NetworkChannelFactory class is used to generate local-to-remote or receive remote-to-local data connection request, and then use the resulting network connection for reliable data transmission.

TrackManager can be divided into two parts: SharedServicesTracker and EventSubscriptionsTracker. SharedServicesTracker is used to monitor and capture local OSGi framework services registering, updating or canceling events. EventSubscribeTracker is established for monitoring and capturing local event handler.

Dispatcher is a running bond throughout the extended structure of DssOSGi, which is used for sending or receiving and handling different types of request information. Corresponding function modules will be performed to finish specific operations according to appropriate request type. The completion of local proxy service request forwarding operation is dependent on the Dispatcher.

ProxyFactory is the core component to complete local calling remote shared services. When the service returned from the remote is functioned, it relies on described dynamical information in local service interface to generate remote agent which will be used and registered to the local OSGi framework. Once EventForwardFactory receives local-to-remote event subscriptions message, event transponder will be used to set up local EventHandler according to the corresponding event topics and subscriberUri that is subscriber network positioning address. The local event will be forwarded to the event subscription persons by the use of event handler.

5   Dynamic Service Binding Mechanis

Dynamic service binding is divided into two parts: the process of capturing the publishing local services and the process of acquiring remote services. DssOSGi distributes dynamically local OSGis service registration, updating, cancellation of the event to the public service registry by capturing it, while other OSGi framework obtain a remote service by sending lookup information to the center of registration. Thus services in multiple OSGi frameworks will be shared and a service in a single framework will be extended to the entire network.

Dynamic publishing process of a service is as shown in Fig.2, once a service is registered in local OSGi framework, RemoteServiceTracker started in TrackerManager will capture it.

By monitoring the OSGi frameworks operation of the event subscription services, DssOSGi forward the real-time event subscription request to other nodes within the network framework. Once CommonRegistry receives the topic subscription message, the local copy of corresponding record will be saved and the updated topic subscriptions information will be pushed to all nodes within the current network.

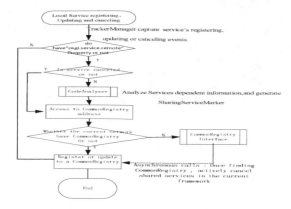

Fig. 2. Process of distributed services publishing

Proxy service operation process is as shown in Fig.3, when the localOSGi framework request remote Shared services, it will produce the local proxy service which gives the examples of the specified service by ProxyFactory, and the generated proxy services will be registered to the local CommonRegistry of the OSGi framework.

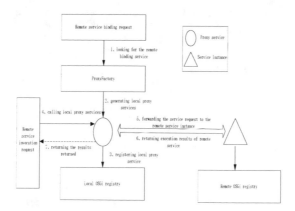

Fig. 3. Schematic diagram of proxy service operating mechanism schematic diagram

When calling request by sending the proxy service, the proxy service will transmit the corresponding requests to the specified Service instance objects. After receiving the call request for proxy service, the distant DssOSGi will capture and call the actual service object via the OSGi framework.

Once a call request is finished ,the DssOSGi will feedback the results to the proxy services, and the proxy service parses returned results and will feedback the result to the caller, thus it complets the calls to the remote service objects. Proxy service mechanism converts the remote service to local services in the OSGi framework transparently, for the corresponding service invoker, proxy service and genuine service object are the same.

6 Experimental Analysis

In view of the service binding time, service call time and service computing degree of resource consumption in the process of the service invocation, there is a comparasion and analysis on both sides of the Apache CXF D-OSGi and DssOSGi. The hardware environment of Performance evaluation is two PC,and by using WiFi wireless network to connect each other, the network average delay is 1 ms.

We provide a unified service interface which is called SampleService for D-OSGi and DssOSGi, and the service interface provides five methods, namely pingInt, pingLong, pingDouble, pingList and pingObject. At the same time, the two frameworks are given the same service implementation, and it will use a for loop within 0   100 in each method for simulation execution process.

In order to avoid the System cache influencing the factors of the service call, every time when binding remote Shared service and circulates and calls all the service method, it will unload the proxy service and use the System.gc() method to perform the collection of JVM garbage. We will sample 100 times to the Service binding and service call in the process of the whole cycle, and then compare the execution results, and record the details about binding time delay, the service invocation time delay, CPU and memory utilization ratio at the process of circulation.

6.1 Time Delay of Service Binding and Call

Fig.4 shows the average time of service binding and service invocation (sampling when circular 100). In the process of generating and binding proxy service,DssOSGi binding takes only about 30ms, and D-OSGi binding reaches around 500ms, it is obvious D-OSGi binding time delay is 15 times than DssOSGi.

Because D-OSGi uses the SOAP protocol based on XML to deal with data interaction, thus the time to parse XML data is the main reason for the relatively

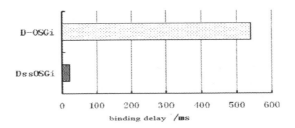

Fig. 4. Time delay ofgenerating and binding proxy service

slowing D-OSGi binding service. In Fig.5, call time delay of all pingXxx method in DssOSGi is better than DCOSGis, and the average call delay is 25 to 30ms.But the method calls of D-OSGi takes around 40 ms in the overall delay, sometimes even up to 50 ms.

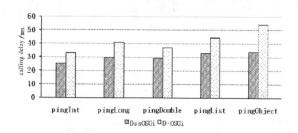

Fig. 5. Methods call time delay between proxy service

6.2   Resource Consumption

In order to accurately capture the consumption of computing resources from DssOSGi and D-OSGi runtime, we use YourKit tool for the sampling record of CPU utilization and memory usage.

Fig.6 shows the CPU utilization between service release and service consumption in the process of sampling circulation, the abscissa is the time line, the ordinate is the percentage of CPU usage.It shows CPU usage ratio at a service consumer side during sampling and calling, and we can see from the diagram DssOSGi and D-OSGi when calling the remote service, overall it is not highly dependent on computing resources, and the average CPU utilization rate takes less than 10 percent.But period of DssOSGi CPU usage is shorter, and it also shows service call delay of DssOSGi is shorter.

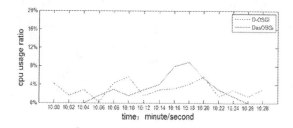

Fig. 6. D-OSGi and DssOSGi service consumer side CPU usage ratio

The simulation results show that the middleware is more efficient for service use and depend less on computing resources.

7   Conclusion

This paper designs a service-oriented middleware structure and realizes the service sharing of embedded distribution based on the OSGi.

This distributed service sharing mechanism overcomes the defect of native OSGi that can't adapt to the distributed system, making the perception layer is able to take advantage of the service-oriented loose coupling to dynamicly publishing and updating basic sensory service, and its service uasage and the extent of depending on computing resources have better performance than the existing distributed platforms. And service composition efficiency of the distributed service-oriented middleware remains to be further research.

Acknowledgment. This work was partially supported by Program for New Century Excellent Talents in University(NCET-12- 0164), Natural Science Foundation of Hunan(13JJ1014).

References

1. Liu, Y.: Introduction of Internet of Things, pp. 9–10. Science Press, BeiJing (2010)
2. Sun, Q.B., Liu, J., Li, S.: Internet of Things: Summarize on Concepts, Architecture and Key Technology Problem. Journal of Beijing University of Posts and Telecommunications, 1–9 (2010)
3. Ibrahim, N.: Orthogonal Classification of Middleware Technologies. In: Third International Conference on Mobile Ubiquitous Computing, Systems, Services and Technologies, pp. 46–51. IEEE Press, Piscataway (2009)
4. Chen, L.: Researches on SOA-based Middleware in Internet of Things, Chang Sha, pp. 12–15 (2012)
5. Hirschheim, R., Welke, R., Schwarz, A.: Service-Oriented Architecture: Myths, Realities and a Maturity Model, pp. 37–48 (2010)
6. Lin, H., Zeng, X.: OSGi Principles and Best Practices, pp. 12–17. Electronic Industry Press, BeiJing (2009) (in Chinese)
7. Lu, Y., Yang, X., Yang, C.: Service Sharing between OSGi-based Residential Gateways in Distributed Network Enviroment. In: IEEE Pervasive Computing, pp. 128–132. IEEE Press, NJ (2009)
8. Alliance A. Apache CXFProject (2013),
   http://cxf.apache.org/distributed-osgi.html
9. Shi, D., Wu, Y., Ding, B.: StaroSGi: A Distributed Extension Middleware for OSGi, 162–165 (2011)
10. Rellermeyer, J.S., Alonso, G., Roscoe, T.: Building, Deploying and Monitoring Distributed Applications with Eclipse and R-OSGi. In: Eclipse Technology Exchange (ETX) Workshop, Montreal (2007)

Indoor Localization Algorithm for Wireless Sensor Network Based on Range-Free

Yubin Chen*, Zhaorong Liu, Yue Li, and Yan Wang

Institute of Software, Nanchang Hangkong University, Nanchang 330063, China

Abstract. Indoor localization of nodes in Wireless Sensor Network(WSN) is impeded by several factors: unreliability of wireless link quality, variety of interference factors, low accuracy of localization. To solve the problem of indoor localization, we propose an range-free algorithm for WSN-based systems. We build several classes of samples that have different similarity by dividing the k-nearest neighbor. Our algorithm are mainly composed of two parts. First, we filter the original samples to remove the noise data out of the original samples. Second, we reduce dimension to overcome the impact of lost packets. The simulation results show that our algorithm can improve the accuracy of localization and the anti-interference capability.

Keywords: Indoor Localization, dimension reduction, anti-interference, KNN.

1 Introduction

Wireless Sensor Network (WSN) is an union of sensor, embedded computing, network and wireless communication, distributed information processing technology. People can access massive information anytime anywhere. This is so-called "Ubiquitous Computing". Localization technology is one of the main supporting technologies of WSN, which plays an important role in extreme environment. Among current localization technologies, such as Global Positioning Systems (GPS) [1], has been the most widely applied. However, in the indoor environments, satellite signal is blocked by building shielding. It turns out to be unavailable. WSNs are a class of distributed computing and communication systems that are an integral part of the physical space they inhabit. Albeit low profile, limited computational power and sparse energy resources, their most interesting feature is the reasoning of and reaction to the world that surrounds them. WSNs have attracted a great deal of research interest during the last few years.

The WSN localization technology mainly includes: Range-based Localization, Range-free Localization . Range-based Localization have to determine the distance between two nodes[2]. This technology often requires additional hardware.Such as Direction-of-Arrival (DoA) localization [3] and Time-of-Arrival

---

* This work is sponsored by Natural Science Foundation of Jiangxi Province, China (No.20122BAB211028) and Supported by Projects of East China Jiaotong University(10RJ02).

L. Sun, H. Ma, and F. Hong (Eds.): CWSN 2013, CCIS 418, pp. 221–230, 2014.

(ToA) localization, which analysis RSS by distance or angle measuring between point-to-point. Since additional hardware is not always available, many Range-free Localization techniques have been proposed. Such as Hop-counting [4] and Fingerprinting [5]. Indoor localization have attracted a great deal of research interest in recent years. It is based on various techniques, ranging from simple RSS [6][7][8] to the more demanding ToA or DoA of the incoming signals. Indoor localization problems are considered much more difficult than outdoor localization problems because GPS signals are not available within buildings or nearby huge structure. Since there are lots of signal interference and signal reflection inside the building, it is even hard to range the signal propagation length using wireless RF signals. Typically in indoor localization, problems of tens-of-meters-long distance or less than ten meters distance are primarily concerns. The main problems of time-based range measurements in indoor environments are errors by multipath and non- line-of-sight (NLOS) measurements.

In the paper, we propose an range-free algorithm for WSN-based indoor localization systems. We first build several classes of samples that have different similarity by dividing the k-nearest neighbor. Our algorithm are mainly composed of two parts. First, we filter the original samples to remove the noise data out of the original samples. Second, we reduce the dimension to overcome the impact of lost packets [9].

The remainder of the paper is organized as follows. We first introduce the basic idea of our algorithm in Sec. 2, and then give the implementation of it. We evaluate the performance of our proposed algorithm in Sec. 3. We conclude the paper in Sec. 4.

2   Algorithm

In this section, we introduce the basic idea of our indoor localization algorithm for *WSN*.

2.1   The Basic Idea

As showed in Fig. 1, the basic idea of the algorithm is to establish a Received Signal Strength Indication (*RSSI*) fingerprint database. Improving the K-nearest neighbor algorithm (*KNN*) with *Kalman Filter* modeling and dimension reduction implement the algorithm:

1. Indoor space is divided into numbered cells according to classification definition, and a large number of experiments indicate that the cell with size of $2 \ m^2$ would be best to distinguish. on the other hand, the space is deployed with N_{rp} Beacons, we ensure that each cell's test position should receive signal of at least 3 Beacons.
2. Fingerprint database Creation: We gather plenty of RSSI eigenvectors from all of Beacon-Nodes' signal to Mobile-Node at the test position ranged in every cell. After being processed together with their category property into $n + 1$ dimension vector,they are stored as fingerprint database.

3. Online Localization: We adopt two critical stages to optimize the *KNN* algorithm. First, the actual received n-dimensional RSSI eigenvectors are smoothed according to *Kalman Filter Model* [10][11]. Second, the improvement by *Dimension Reduction Algorithm* will make the eigenvectors keep on being valid, even if some dimensions fail to receive RSSI eigenvectors caused by the uncertain link quality frequently in *WSN*. At last, we continue to gain the position of Mobile-Node through the output of *KNN Algorithm*.

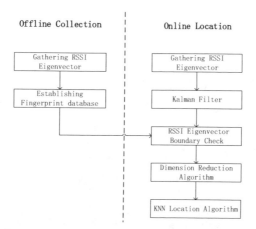

Fig. 1. The Processing of Location Algorithm with Dimension Reduction

2.2   The Implementation

Step one: filter the received n-dimensional RSSI eigenvectors. Establishing *Kalman Filter Model* in WSN node subsystem, we can obtain the optimal estimation of the measurement vector by its recursive, modified and predictable properties. Besides, the algorithm is efficient, accurate to gather the stream of RSSI eigenvectors constantly.

The specific implementation steps for the *Kalman Filter Model*: We order the RSSI values received from different Beacons, and Establish a n-dimensional vector X_n. Namely, the vector component x_i, where $1 \leq i \leq n, i \in N^*$, represents of the RSSI value received from Beacons i.

Considering X_n as a n-dimensional random vector ;we order the RSSI vector received from the same Beacons according to different time; receiving x_n in the sequence. Because the vector component represents from different RSSI values from different Beacons, the X_n random variables are independent, *i.e.*, different components of covariance is zero:

$$cov(x_i, x_j) = 0 \quad (i \neq j, 1 \leq i, j \leq n, i, j \in N^*).$$

Besides the different moments of x_n is independent.

Then we introduce *Kalman Filter Model*, a practical system can be used as follows: the non-stationary sequences vector of x_{k-1} and y_{k-1} was described by the dynamic equations as following:

$$\begin{cases} x_k = \Phi_{k,k-1} x_{k-1} + w_{k-1} \\ \\ y_k = C_k x_k + v_k \end{cases} \quad (k \geq 0)$$

x_k is the state vector, y_k is the observations vector, w_k is the input noise, v_k is the observations noise, $\Phi_{k,k-1}$ is the transition matrix from $k-1$ moment to moment k state , C_k is the process of transfer matrix. We hypothesis:

1. w_k and v_k are zero-mean white noise, which are shown as follows:

$$\begin{cases} E(w_k) = 0 \ Cov[w_k, w_j] = E(w_k w_j^T) = Q_k \delta_{kj} \\ E(v_k) = 0 \ Cov[v_k, v_j] = E(v_k v_j^T) = R_k \delta_{kj} \end{cases}$$

2. w_k and v_k are not related, shown as follows

$$Cov[w_k, v_j] = E(w_k v_j^T) = 0, \quad (\forall k, j)$$

3. the initial state x_0 is a random vector, and not correlated with w_k and v_k, shown as follows:

$$\begin{cases} Cov[x_0, w_k] = E((x_0 - Ex_0) w_k^T) = 0 \\ Cov[x_0, v_k] = E((x_0 - Ex_0) v_k^T) = 0 \end{cases}$$

The Kalman filter recursive formulae are shown as follows:

$$\widehat{x} = \Phi_{k,k-1} \widehat{x}_{k-1} \tag{1}$$

$$P_{k|k-1} = \Phi_{k,k-1} P_{k-1} \Phi_{k,k-1}^T + Q_{k-1} \tag{2}$$

$$K_k = P_{k|k-1} C_k^T [C_k P_{k|k-1} C_k^T + R_k]^{-1} \tag{3}$$

$$\widehat{x}_k = \Phi_{k,k-1} \widehat{x}_{k-1} + K_k(y_k - C_k \Phi_{k,k-1} \widehat{x}_{k-1}) \tag{4}$$

$$P_k = (I - K_k C_k) P_{k|k-1} \tag{5}$$

Hypothesis at k moment and $k-1$ moment, test position from the Beacons of the observed n-dimensional RSSI vector is constant. For the prediction of k moment values is the optimal $k-1$ moment estimation, *i.e*, $\widehat{x}_{k|k-1} = \widehat{x}_{k-1}$. Here the time interval of k moment and $k-1$ moment is measured sample interval (the interval of sending Localization Data Packet from Beacons to Mobile-Node). we only consider noise variable to drive but not controlled variable. So the state transfer matrix and the transfer matrix for the N identity matrix:

$$\Phi_k = C_k = E_n = I_n.$$

And if at any time k, process noise w_k and observation noise v_k ordered by Normal distribution which is zero-mean, valiance are σ_w^2 and σ_v^2, *i.e.*, $w_k \sim N(0, \sigma_w^2), v_k \sim N(0, \sigma_v^2)$. And because the Beacons are independent from the system, so that the w_{ki} and v_{ki} are independent from each other. The covariance matrix:

$$Q_k = \sigma_w^2 E_n, \quad R_k = \sigma_v^2 E_n$$

The $(1) \sim (5)$ recursive formula for:

$$\widehat{x}_{k|k-1} = \widehat{x}_{k-1} \tag{6}$$

$$P_{k|k-1} = P_{k-1} + \sigma_w^2 E_n \tag{7}$$

$$K_k = P_{k|k-1}[P_{k|k-1} + \sigma_v^2 E_n]^{-1} \tag{8}$$

$$\widehat{x}_k = \widehat{x}_{k-1} + K_k(y_k - \widehat{x}_{k-1}) \tag{9}$$

$$P_k = (I - K_k)P_{k|k-1} \tag{10}$$

Here σ_w^2 ,the process noise w_k of covariance matrix $\sigma_w^2 E_n$ coefficient, can be obtained through measurements. And the measurement noise covariance matrix coefficients can be specified manually. In general, if $\sigma_w^2 < \sigma_v^2$, it can be of convergence. We can suppose P_0 freely, but the diagonal elements cannot be equal to 0. For example, $P0$ can be assumed as the diagonal matrix: $P_0 = p_0 E_n$.

According to the measurement of k moment values y_k, the algorithm can be started and infinite recursion continues. Then optimal estimation can draw arbitrary k moment of n-dimensional RSSI observation vectors, efficiently and accurately.

If some dimensions fail to receive RSSI, the algorithm will adopt fixed value to fill it. The filling value will not belong to the defined scope in step 2, so the component will be ignored in step two, but calculate of dimension reduction.

Step 2: after smoothing of the n-dimensional RSSI vector component boundaries and similarity checking, component should belong to a fixed scope, that is RSSI$\in [rssi_{min}, rssi_{max}]$. if Not in the scope ,this dimension will be ignored, And dimension, Required component similarity than the fixed threshold δ that the component shall meet, otherwise the dimension reduction processing. Finally to find the optimal solution, the solution space are obtained.

Dimension reduction of the specific implementation steps as follows:

Two kinds of circumstances Based on RSSI ranging model, and the unknown node and beacon set d section of distance, are: if $d < rssi_{min}$; RSSI is sensitive to be changed; if $d > rssi_{min}$; RSSI is slow to be changed;

This will let localization to be inaccurate, in view of this definition of the upper and lower bounds of the RSSI, that is RSSI$\notin [rssi_{min}, rssi_{max}]$,we use dimension reduction processing and ignore this dimension, otherwise ,the rest of the dimensions for KNN localization would be implemented.

If RSSI$\notin [rssi_{min}, rssi_{max}]$, may be due to causes such as link error or obstacles to receive the RSSI or measure RSSI value anomaly, it will produce serious deviation in localization results. The solution to the problem is defining the similarity threshold δ; Namely, each component x_i of the RSSI vectors X meet (11), can locate through the KNN [12]:

$$|x_i - y_i|^p \leq \delta \quad (\forall i \in N^*, i \leq n) \tag{11}$$

The y_i vector of fingerprint coordinate component, respectively. Only to satisfy the (11) type of fingerprint collection $\{y\|\|x_i - y_i\|^p \le \delta, \quad (\forall i \in N^*, i \le n, \delta > 0, \delta \in R)$ to be located through the KNN. When distance calculation is carried out by using KNN algorithm, to guarantee *Minkowski distance* to be the smallest, at the same time, we should guarantee each component not beyond the component similarity threshold δ.

If the vector does not exist, we carry out the dimension reduction processing. namely, it ignore a certain dimension,Obtained by (11) $|\{y\}|$ cardinality, the largest collection of $\{y\}$ as a fingerprint.

Step 3: in step 2 of the optimal solution space, by using KNN classifier for dimension reduction, after gaining the category from the received n-dimension RSSI vector, we carry on the accurate localization.

The dimension reduction of localization is segmented into specific implementation steps as follows:

First briefly describe KNN principle are:

Assumes that the data set: $\{y_j^{(i)}\}$, $i = 1, 2, \cdots, c$, $j = 1, 2, \cdots, N_i$. When $N(N = \sum_{i=1}^{c} N_i)$ data belong to different category c respectively, In which N_i is the i-th a classification of the number of samples in the w_i. The principle of classification is: for a stay observation vector X, to calculate it with the N category sample distance, then classify it into the nearest class. Based on this classification principle discriminant function of w_i class is:

$$d_i(x) = \min_{j=1,2,\cdots,N_i} \|x - y_j^{(i)}\|, \quad i = 1, \cdots, c$$

Here the distance $\| \, \|$ is *Minkowski distance*, the parameter p of distance is given freely Discriminant rules as follows:

$$x \in \omega_m, \quad m = \arg \min_{i=1,2,\cdots,c} (d_i(x))$$

Because of the above methods according to stay only general mode depends on the category of a recent sample category, so generally called nearest neighbor method or 1-neighbor. In order to overcome a single sample category of accident, thus increasing the reliability of classification, investigation data of k nearest neighbor samples under test, which kind of sample in the k nearest neighbor, most will be x discriminant belong to which category. For example a $k_1, k_2, \cdots, k_c$ samples is x of the k nearest neighbor, $w_1, w_2, \cdots$ Sample of w_c, define w_i class discriminant function is:

$$d_i(x) = k_i, \quad i = 1, 2, \cdots, c$$

Decision rule is:

$$x \in \omega_m, \quad m = \max_{i=1,2,\cdots,c}(d_i(x))$$

We described the data set $\{y_j^{(i)}\}$ is called a fingerprint database, its elements called Fingerprint, in this paper Fingerprint is define as: under the same WSN networks of the RSSI sequence of n-dimensional vector form different Beacon node, they can be gathered from different cell to establish fingerprint database and to be stored. Localization processing is simplified as: matching category position fingerprint with the fingerprint database. using KNN classifier to category fingerprint database classification, it so as to realize the localization process. Dimension reduction is defined, when we caculate *Minkowski distance*, neglect of one m-dimension, but make sure $n - m \geq 3$, then use the rest of the dimensions to caculate the *Minkowski distance* by KNN classifier.

3   Evaluation

We choose laboratory hall with 30 m^2 as simulation experiment area. The WSN is composed of a Mobile-Node, six Beacons and a sink. the details are as follows:

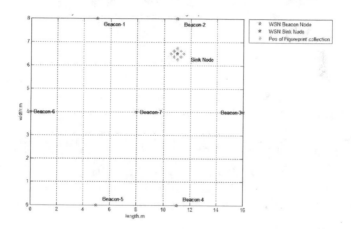

Fig. 2. The Distribution of WSN Becon Node in the grid space

To meet the requirements of WSN communication, namely uniform coverage of WSN signal, experimental experience shows that six beacon nodes will adopt the way of shown in the Fig. 2 can be placed; At the same time to make the Mobile-Node to receive the distinction RSSI from Beacons. The Beacons should be placed in the corner of the hall as scattering as possible; In addition, we deploy all the Beacons on the same plane. What's more, we need make sure that the Mobile-Node receive the signal from at lest 3 Beacons, especially for indoor passage.

The space should be split into several cells with same size, as shown in Fig. 3, which is treated as a category. Here we make cell be split in size of 2 m^2. We gather fingerprint of RSSI value for position in each cell. This process will be repeated by 50 times ever 4 seconds. The black part in Fig. 3 is the area without localization. Our localization system rebuild the space distribution of the laboratory hall. We put eigenvector received from Beacons into fingerprint database. In this experiment,the laboratory hall was split into 25 sub cells.

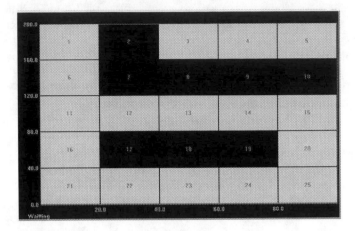

Fig. 3. The indoor positioning system simulation space distribution

3.1   The Impact of *Kalman Filter* and *Dimension Reduction*

Experiments show that the *Kalman Filter* take effect to the localization algorithm as shown in Fig. 4(a). Red dot in figure represent variance results without using *Kalman Filter* technology , otherwise, blue dot represent experimental results based on the method of *Kalman Filter*. It is found that the output fluctuation is better with *Kalman Filter* than without it. In the condition of filter, data fluctuation is small, stable, centralized distribution on both sides. the standard mean is to improve the localization accuracy.

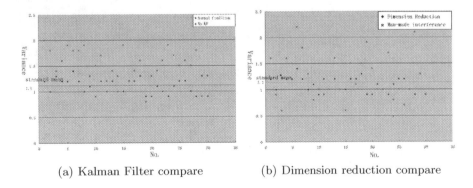

(a) Kalman Filter compare   (b) Dimension reduction compare

Fig. 4. Simulation results

As shown in Fig. 4(b), It represent the different sample results distribution comparing the process with Dimension Reduction to the one without. The red dots represent data gathered without using the dimension reduction, otherwise, the blue dots represent the distribution sample data with using dimension reduction. The experimental results show that dimension reduction make sampling data is not large jitter, excessive dispersion, distribution is relatively steady in the standard mean line. it filter the redundant data and improve the localization accuracy.

Table 1. Network Localization statistic

Conditions \ Data	Receive packets	Failure packets	Success rate
Non KF	200	71	65%
with KF	200	62	69%
Non Dimensionality	200	51	75%
Dimension reduction and KF	200	29	86%

Table. 1 is receiving situation of network nodes, can be intuitive found in using this method to filter, dimension, package rate is greatly increased, and reached the experiment of the desired results.

4   Conclusion

In conclusion, this paper propose a indoor localization algorithm for WSN based on Range-free to improve the accuracy and anti-interference capability. We realize the localization through two stages as follows: Fist, we smooth the eigenvectors by *Kalman Filter Model*, which increase the stability of the RSSI vector; Seconde, we introduce *Dimension Reduction* to make eigenvectors valid even if some RSSI value lost. The modified KNN classifier is efficient, accurate to implement the localization.

References

1. Torres-Solis, J., Falk, T.H., et al.: A review of indoor localization technologies: towards navigational assistance for topographical disorientation. Ambient Intelligence, 51–84 (2010)
2. Mitilineos, S.A., Kyriazanos, D.M., Segou, O.E.: Indoor Localization with Wireless Sensor Networks. Progress in Electromagnetics Research 109, 441–474 (2010)
3. Rohrig, C., Muller, M.: Indoor location tracking in non-line-of-sight environments using a IEEE 802.15. 4a wireless network. In: IEEE/RSJ International Conference on Intelligent Robots and Systems, IROS 2009. IEEE (2009)
4. Nagpal, R., Shrobe, H., Bachrach, J.: Organizing a global coordinate system from local information on an ad hoc sensor network. In: Zhao, F., Guibas, L.J. (eds.) IPSN 2003. LNCS, vol. 2634, pp. 333–348. Springer, Heidelberg (2003)
5. Kjærgaard, M.B.: A taxonomy for radio location fingerprinting. In: Hightower, J., Schiele, B., Strang, T. (eds.) LoCA 2007. LNCS, vol. 4718, pp. 139–156. Springer, Heidelberg (2007)

6. Bahl, P., Padmanabhan, V.N.: RADAR: An in-building RF-based user location and tracking system. In: Proceedings of the IEEE Infocom, Israel (2000)
7. Zhou, G., He, T., Krishnamurthy, S., Stankovic, J.A.: Impact of Radio Irregularity on Wireless Sensor Networks. In: Proceedings of MobiSys 2004, Boston, MA (2004)
8. Elnahraway, E., Li, X., Martin, R.P.: The limits of localization using RSS. In: Proceedings of the 2nd International Conference on Embedded Networked Sensor Systems, Baltimore, MD, USA (2004)
9. Indoor Localization System using Wireless Sensor Networks for Stationary and Moving Target (2009)
10. Welch, G., Bishop, G.: An introduction to the Kalman filter (1995)
11. Paul, A.S., Wan, E.A.: RSSI-based indoor localization and tracking using sigma-point kalman smoothers. IEEE Journal of Selected Topics in Signal Processing 3(5), 860–873 (2009)
12. Guo, G., Wang, H., Bell, D., Bi, Y., Greer, K.: KNN model-based approach in classification. In: Meersman, R., Tari, Z., Schmidt, D.C., et al. (eds.) CoopIS/DOA/ODBASE 2003. LNCS, vol. 2888, pp. 986–996. Springer, Heidelberg (2003)

Hydrodynamic Characteristics Analysis of Expendable BathyThermograph Probe

Zhengbao Li, Libin Du, Jie Liu, and Haijing He

Shandong Provincial Key Laboratory of Ocean Environment Monitoring Technology,
Institute of Oceanographic Instrumentation, Shandong Academy of Sciences,
266001 Qingdao, China
lizhengb@gmail.com, {dulibinhit,liujie0232@163.com},
haijinghe@hotmail.com

Abstract. In this paperthe authors use numerical simulation method to analyze the flow field distribution around the XBT probe and study the impact of hydrodynamic characteristics on the underwater posture stability. The analysis shows that the streamlined structure design of probe can effectively reduce the resistance of the probe in water and can maintain the posture stability in the falling process.

Keywords: expendable bathythermographs, hydrodynamic characteristics, numerical simulation, CFD.

1 Introduction

Expendable BathyThermograph(XBT) is a disposable device which can rapidly obtain marine environment data. It can be used for the marine environment forecasting, marine environment monitoring, oceanographic research and military purposes [1].

XBT probe is released by the release device and fall freely in the water. A temperature sensor which is installed on the probe can obtain seawater temperature. The seawater depth is calculated by the fall time of the probe. All the data obtained by sensors is transmitted to the surface receiver via the signal line for analysis and display.

The hydrodynamic characteristics of the XBT probe determine the law of its underwater motion, and therefore have an important investigate significance [2]. In our knowledge, the research about XBT probe hydrodynamic characteristics and underwater motion law rarely reported up to now [3]. In this paper, we focus on the hydrodynamic characteristics analysis of the XBT probe and its external flow field underwater analysis by numerical simulation using the FLU-ENT software. The results of this study can provide a theoretical reference to the structural optimization design and trajectory calculation of XBT probe.

L. Sun, H. Ma, and F. Hong (Eds.): CWSN 2013, CCIS 418, pp. 231–238, 2014.

2   Computational Model and Control Equation

2.1   Computational Model

The shape of XBT probe is shown in Fig. 1. The probes body is streamlined and its rotating tail is asymmetric. Its length is 226mm.

Fig. 1. Illustration of the outline structure of a XBT probe

We create a simulation model based on the structure of the XBT probe by GAMBIT software and meshing. In order to ensure the flow field cans fully develop, we take the calculated field as cylinder region with the axial length is 20 times of the probes length and the diameter is 20 times of its maximum cross-sectional diameter. In order to guarantee the quality of meshing and calculation accuracy, the mesh area around the probe is encrypted partition using split grid painting. The grid number is 610387 after meshing completed. Fig. 2 shows the probe model.

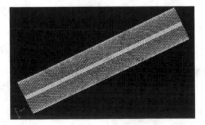 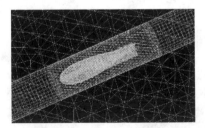

Fig. 2. Schematic grid computing model of XBT probe, the left is a whole map, right is a local map

2.2   Control Equation

FLUENT software is used to calculate the meshed XBT model. The turbulence model chooses three-dimensional $k - \epsilon$ two-equation [4]. The basic control equation is the Navier-Stokes equations:

$$\begin{cases} \rho\frac{Du}{Dt} = \rho X - \frac{\partial p}{\partial x} + \frac{1}{3}\mu\frac{\partial \theta}{\partial x} + \mu\nabla^2 u \\ \rho\frac{Dv}{Dt} = \rho Y - \frac{\partial p}{\partial y} + \frac{1}{3}\mu\frac{\partial \theta}{\partial y} + \mu\nabla^2 v \\ \rho\frac{Dw}{Dt} = \rho Z - \frac{\partial p}{\partial Z} + \frac{1}{3}\mu\frac{\partial \theta}{\partial z} + \mu\nabla^2 w \end{cases} \qquad (1)$$

The calculation model is solved by the implicit finite volume algorithm. The SIMPLEC algorithm is utilized to calculate the coupling of the velocity and pressure. We choose standard algorithm to calculate pressure interpolation, choose second-order upwind mode to calculate Momentum, turbulent kinetic energy and turbulent dissipation rate [5]. In order to prevent divergence and numerical instability in the iterative process, we use underrelaxation algorithm to compute momentum equation and scalar transport equation.

3   Hydrodynamic Characteristic Analysis

3.1   Pressure Analysis

The fluid pressure distribution of probe surface determines its hydrodynamic characteristics. The pressure distribution can reflect the process of fluid flowing through the probe. Fig. 3 is an illustration of surface pressure distribution when the probe is vertically falling.

We can see from Fig. 3, in the case of probes vertical dropping, the pressure distribution around the probe is symmetrical on both sides. Lift and pitching moment is zero, which is conducive to maintaining the probe stability of athletic stance. The fluid is blocked near the probe head when it flows through the probe and the probes speed decreases rapidly. Therefore, stagnation areas from near the head of the probe are partial static pressure higher than stream static pressure. The fluid arranges along the probe head accelerate symmetrically and the pressure decreases rapidly at straight sections of the turning point of the probe pressure reaches the second smallest value (The minimum pressure area appears on the fin dorsal of probe). Hereafter, the pressure becomes higher gradually and on the tail region of the probe, the pressure remains constant. However, there is a high pressure area on the facing flow side of the probe tail and it means the velocity reduced due to block by the probe tail. In the tail side of the back flow, there is an area of low pressure, indicating the flow velocity accelerated. A low-pressure area appeares when the flow through the probe tail and it indicates that the probe tail has a suction effect on the fluid and forms an accelerated procedure. The Fig. 4 shows a schematic of XBT probe surface pressure coefficient.

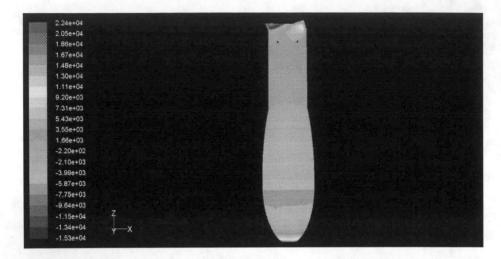

Fig. 3. Illustration of the surface pressure distribution of a XBT probe

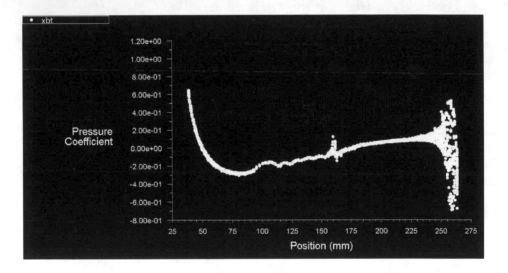

Fig. 4. Illustration of the surface pressure coefficient of a XBT probe

From Fig. 4, we can see that since the flow of fluid hydrostatic shock probe, after the head of the low-speed, the pressure begins to increase gradually until the end of the probe has stabilized, but the fluid through the probe rotating tail appears intense pressure fluctuations, tail side facing the flow pressure liter high, tail lee side pressure decreases. The front position of the probe head has shown as 40mm at the abscissa in Fig. 4 and the position of probe tail shown as 265mm at the abscissa.

3.2   Velocity Analysis

In our simulation, we make the probe as speed reference, set different seawater flow rate, $v = 3.4, 4.0, 4.6, 5.2, 5.8, 6.4m/s$, then we can get the distribution of flow field around the probe in different flow velocity. The results are shown in Fig. 5.

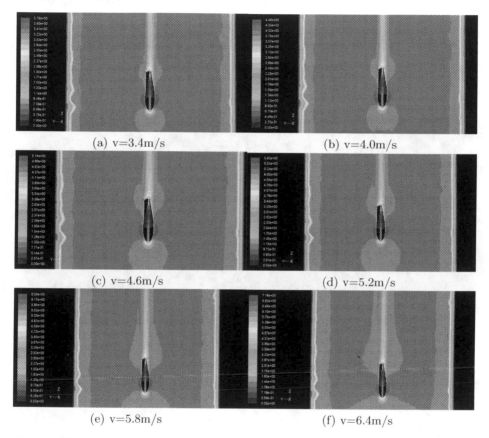

(a) v=3.4m/s   (b) v=4.0m/s

(c) v=4.6m/s   (d) v=5.2m/s

(e) v=5.8m/s   (f) v=6.4m/s

Fig. 5. Velocity profile illustration of section X of a XBT probe under different velocity

From Fig. 5, we can see that the flow field around the XBT probe is similar at different speeds. The flow field is symmetrical and the field flow along the probe attached and does not appear the case of separation. We can determine that the design of XBT probe is reasonable [6]. This is consistent with experience in machinery manufacturing and consistent with K.Shoichis test results [7]. When the fluid flows through the probe, it creates a greater velocity gradient at the probe head and tail area. A velocity field is generated on both sides of the probe when fluid flow through the probe, especially near the head where the speed even greater than the stream velocity. The flow velocity decreases rapidly when fluid flow through the tail, but the flow velocity increases gradually after fluid flow passing the tail. Comparing the distribution of different flow speeds, we can see that the greater of the flow speed, the larger of the probe tail influence on the seawater as shown in Fig. 5 that the variation range of current velocity around the probe tail is larger.

The seaflow velocity is indicated by arrows in Fig. 6, the direction of the arrow represents the direction of velocity and the color of the arrows represents the magnitude of velocity. Arrow density is determined by the grid density in different regions of the calculation model. From the Fig. 6, we can see that a small part of the velocity vector arrows appear disorganized and directionless near the area of the probe head and tail. It means that there is certain intensity turbulence at the two areas.

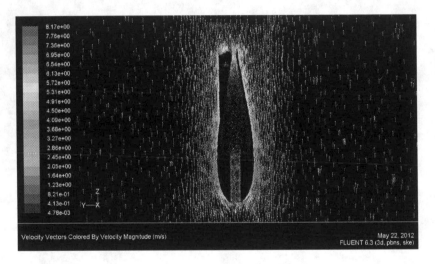

Fig. 6. Vector graphics of seawater speed outside of a XBT probe

3.3   Turbulence Intensity Analysis

Turbulence intensity is the relative standard of the strength of turbulence. In order to analyze tendency of the flow field around the probe better, we simulate the turbulence intensity distribution around the XBT probe and get the turbulence intensity vector distribution (Fig. 7).

We can see that the turbulence intensity focused on region of the front of the probe head and tail and turbulence intensity in the tail area is more intense. This is caused by the tail agitated seawater ceaseless in the falling process of the probe. The turbulence can affect the flow field around the XBT probe to a certain degree and then affect the movement posture of the probe. However, it can be seen in Fig. 7, the turbulence area and intensity is very limited which generated in the falling process of the probe, so the impact on the flow field around the

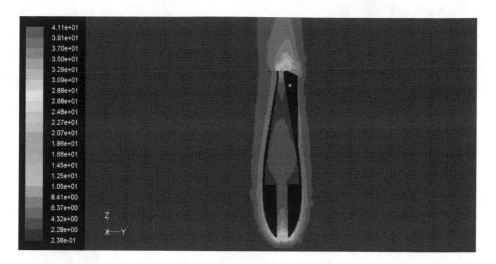

Fig. 7. Illustration of the turbulence intensity distribution around XBT probe

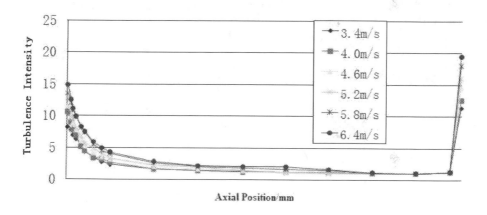

Fig. 8. Turbulence intensity curve with the axial position of the probe

probe is also very limited which can be ignored. This also explains XBT probe streamlined design is very reasonable. Processing the data of Fig. 7, we can get the turbulence intensity curve with the axial position of the probe in different flow speeds as shown in Fig. 8. It can be seen in Fig. 8, when the seawater impact the probe in different velocity, at the front area of the probe less than 25mm, the turbulence is intense relatively, and then, the turbulence leveling out, however, at the end of the probe tail, the turbulence intensity sharply increased. It can be predicted that fluid change from the laminar boundary layer into a turbulent boundary layer in less than 50mm at the front end of the probe head and the tail end of the probe at greater than 220mm, and this is consistent with the results of Lancasters wind tunnel tests [8].

4   Conclusion

According to the hydrodynamic characteristics analysis of the XBT probe, we get the flow field distribution around the probe when it falling in the seawater. Through analysis shows, there are a certain intensity turbulence areas around the probe head and tail and the presence of turbulence can affect the posture stability of the probe underwater, however, due to the reasonable streamlined structural design of the probe, the scope and intensity of the turbulence region are limited, and the affect of turbulence to the underwater posture stability of probe is negligible. The velocity flow field distribution and pressure flow field distribution around the probe are symmetrical which conducive to maintaining the posture stability of the probe in the seawater. In this paper, the hydrodynamic characteristics analysis can provides a research foundation for the further study of the XBT probes underwater movement and its posture stability analysis.

Acknowledgments. This work was supported by the National High-Tech Research and Development Plan of China under Grant No. 2012AA091904, 2013AA09A411, the Public science and technology research funds projects of ocean under Grant Nos. 201105030, 201305026, the Shandong Provincial Natural Science Foundation under Grant No. ZR2012FL14.

References

1. Liu, M., Chen, W., Liu, J.: CFD based flowfield analysis of an expendable bathythermographs probe. Shandong Science 25(5), 22–24 (2012)
2. Xiao, H., Liu, C., Tao, J.: Numerical Simulation of Drag Coefficient for CTD Probes and its Experimental Vertification. Ocean Technology (3), 35–37 (2006)
3. Chen, W., Zhang, R., Liu, N.: Numerical Simulation the Flow Field of Expendable Current Profiler. Review Science and Technology 28(20), 62–65 (2010)
4. Chow, C.-Y.: An introduction to computational fluid dynamics. Shanghai Jiaotong University Press, Shanghai (1987)
5. Wang, F.-J.: Calculation Hydrodynamic Analysis. Tsinghua University Press, Beijing (2004)
6. Qu, B.: The shape of the object head effect on hydrodynamic characteristics. Ship Science and Technology 3, 27–35 (1988)
7. Shoichi, K., Hiroji, O., Toshio, S., et al.: Evaluation of the fall rates of the present and developmental XCTDs. Deep Sea Research Part I: Oceanographic Research Papers 55(4), 571–586 (2008)
8. Lancaster, R.W.: Brief Report on Wind Tunnel Testing of Present and New XCP. Bodies Sippican Ocean Systems 18, 2–3 (1982)

Application Framework for Marine Environment Information System with Spatiotemporal Sensor Data

Feifei Shen[1], Qing Liu[2], Keyong Hu[1], and Yongguo Jiang[1]

[1] Department of Computer Science Ocean University of China, 266100, Qingdao, China
[2] Ocean University of China Library, 266100, Qingdao, China
shenfeifei@ouc.edu.cn

Abstract. Sensor based marine environment monitoring system is widely adopted to collect, store and distribute marine environment data. Unfortunately, there is no unified framework existing to apply for the development process, which results in poor software quality and data integration problems. This paper presents a common system framework which supports marine environment in-situ data and model outputs integration and appliance development. The framework presented is consisted of flexible database architecture, scalable data loader, data cooperation service, reusable component and plug-in, configuration and security tools. A practical project is carried out to validate the usability of framework. The result shows that the framework is feasible and efficient.

Keywords: marine environment data, application framework, sensor data, database, component.

1 Introduction

Sensors are becoming more and more ubiquitous and can be found that they are used in a vast range of environments including the ocean observation domain [1]. Marine environment spatiotemporal sensor data is the fundamental knowledge for humans to improve the understanding of oceans. It is important in various fields of oceanographic research, such as climate change, national security and public health risks. With the improvement of science and technology, more and more methods for ocean observing have been applied [2–4]. Shore stations, inshore ocean observation buoys, underwater observation platforms, research ships, drifting buoys and ocean satellites, a large number of marine environment data is acquired gradually. Correspondingly, lots of Marine Environment Information Systems (MEIS) are designed for managing and applying these data, which achieve better results in specific scenario [5–10]. However, most MEIS are developed and deployed independently in order to satisfy local business requirements or scientific research, which are heterogeneous and lack of systemic extensibility such as not supporting new sensor dataset collected with stationary storage

L. Sun, H. Ma, and F. Hong (Eds.): CWSN 2013, CCIS 418, pp. 239–250, 2014.

model, system interoperation and module's reusing, resulting in software duplication, marine data exchange, integration difficulty and low software development efficiency.

There are multiple web applications for spatiotemporal sensor data in marine field [11–13], and they are developed for storing, disseminating, and managing ocean data. They are very useful data sites for domain researchers and distributing large amounts of data. There are two main problems. First, the data sources are document-based. Related data such as same project, same research institute or same variable is stored in the same dataset with additional metadata [14] (for example netCDF, csv) and these datasets are relatively small, which lead that a large number of small files are hosted in the data server and detailed data query and acquired are not supported. Naturally, data mining, data fusion and other data analysis are also difficult to be achieved. Therefore, constructing database system and mapping marine dataset into database table are essential. Second, data integration and system interoperation are not implemented because that cross-platform data programming interfaces are not constructed and data consumers have no means to download interesting data for programing. In practice, we propose a software framework for in-situ data based on sensor and ocean model outputs on the basis of ocean data characteristics and requirements analysis. Common database schema is researched and applied to the practice system; also integration interfaces named data cooperation-service and reusable components are designed. Based on the framework, MEIS can be developed quickly and effectively to satisfy most application requirements. Programming efforts of researchers will be reduced, as well as software quality will be improved . To verify its feasibility and efficiency, a marine environment information system is developed based on the application framework.

Specifically, our main contributions are as follows. First, a flexible data storage model is crucial for the application system. Common database schema for in-situ data and ocean model outputs are designed in this paper, and ocean data is loaded into database through data loader. Data loader is configurable and scalable for different ocean dataset. Second, data cooperation-service interface specification based on web service are proposed which make the data accessing and system integration consistent and easy. Third, reusable components can be produced through component factory, which encapsulates the functional modules in marine environment data analysis, visualization and can be configured for managing and displaying data. Also component factory is scalable to accommodate new components so that the application can be extended cost-efficiently. The rest of this paper is organized as follows. Section 2 describes the whole framework. The design details and main implementation approaches are illustrated in Section 3. Section 6 presents application case. Finally, conclusions and future work are given in Section 5.

2   Framework Overview

Application framework defines the whole system skeleton. Figure 1 shows the whole system framework of the MEIS, which is mainly composed of data collection, data management, data service, business, component, service management, configuration and security tools. Marine environment in-situ data are multi-source and diverse sensor data because of a variety of observing instrument and so many observing elements. They are usually collected, transmitted and processed in file form due to environmental factors, which makes different datasets need to have a corresponding data load dirve. Data collection contains lots of data drives. Through reading configuration information, Data loader call the corresponding data drive to import dataset into database tables, so that users only need to construct corresponding data drive in accordance with drive definition standard, which can reduce programming cost effectively. Data management provides basic maintenance such as query, delete for data cooperation-service. Data cooperation-service provides the data access interfaces for other modules and components. Unified data access interfaces will minimize the cost for application modifying. In this work, the service-oriented architecture is employed, which is an evolution of distributed computing based on the request/response design paradigm for synchronous and asynchronous applications. Data cooperation service provides data access through web services, which supports local application and remote application integration. We have designed several web service interfaces to retrieve data crossed platform and integrate separated applications in this application framework. Through service management we can accomplish data maintenance, service registry, application integration and so on.

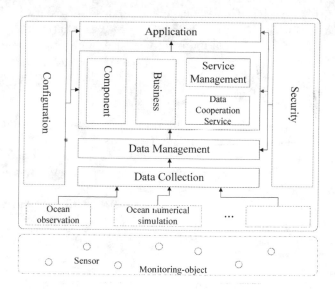

Fig. 1. Application framework

For the common system functions, they are implemented as the components which are relative independent units. Component integrates components developed, which creates the component instance for producing system modules and application. Generally, developed software systems are deployed for specific scenario and solving existing problems. The software framework proposed above supports basic function through components and new components added to component to extend the framework. However, it does not meet all the needs of application. Naturally, business is designed to facilitate the extension of special software function. For different data drive, component relationship and services setting, configuration helps to set parameters according to the requirements. Marine environment data is very important, especially for national security, So system security is an important task. In the application framework, we define a system security standard interface specification, which covers the users, roles, permissions, data encryption and other aspects.

3   Implement of Framework

In this section, all parts of the framework are described one by one.

3.1   Data Storage

The design of database is important to the application framework. The marine environment data collected in different ocean observing system have the same characteristics, but the different focus of scientific research and human factors make its description and format different, resulting in data process and database architecture heterogeneous. The traditional ocean observing software system developed based on different database cannot be reused and dataset files cannot be stored. In this framework, our database architecture can be used to describe and store all of the marine environment data with good flexibility. It includes two types tables: observation tables adn ocean model tables. A detailed description of these tables is provided as follows.

1) Platform. They refer to the description of the ocean observation platform, which standardize the basic observation unit such as research ship, shore station, large buoy, seabed base, underwater experiment platform. Observation platform includes platform identify, platform type, country, investigate organization, investigate project, investigate area, begin date and end date.

2) Station. The Station represents an observation node, in which interested ocean elements are measured. As a basic observation point, observation station should record the station identify, station type, observation platform, location (longitude and latitude), laying date, recycling date and so on.

3) Element. They describe the information of monitored objects such as water temperature, salinity, wave, ccean current. All observation elements are described and configured with same structure containing element identify, element title, element description, observation platform, observation station, instrument, unit, accuracy, error.

4) Instrument. The observation instrument records the parameter of sensor-based measuring device such as instrument identify, title, type, model, manufacturer.

5) Profile. Ocean elements vary in different depth of water, which is with great significance for knowing about ocean discipline. The profile records a vertical path on the interested ocean elements that are observed, which includes profile identify, depth, title, observation platform, observation station, instrument, and section identify.

6) Section. Sectional observation plays an important role in global scope, in which elements in different points and different water depth are monitored. It consists of profile collections observed in different location, including section identify, description.

7) Data. The observation data includes the original data from the data acquisition device and the calculation data based on the original data. It is a series of time data consisting of sample time and sensor values.

8) Dataset. Dataset describes the metadata of model data, which includes identify, title, file format, model, data size and file path.

9) Variable. The variable information in the dataset includes identify, name, data type and dataset identify. 10) Dimension. Similarly, dimension table is correspondence with the dimension of netCDF, which represents the variable's range in space-time and consists of identify, variable identify, dataset identify and length.

11) Attribute. Each variable in a model dataset has some attributes such as unit, standard name, accuracy, and missing value, which are important metadata for understanding the variable data. So the attribute information is necessary. The attribute table has the fields of attribute name, value, data type, variable identify linked to the variable and dataset identify linked to Dataset.

12) Value. Value stores the model data, including identify, time, water depth, longitude, latitude, value and variable identify linked to variable.

Each table described above except Data has a field named ExpansionItem, which stores the additional information in the form of name-value pairs(e.g. "name:value@@name:value") and can satisfy the expansion needs dynamically.

3.2   Data Collection

Generally, the original ocean in-situ data is stored in files, so we designed a ocean data loader to load the ocean dataset into database automatically. Homologous data loader drive is named according to different element category, and the drive is connected to element category through configuration file, so new drive and element can be added easily.Figure 2 shows the structure of Data loader.

3.3   Service Management

Service management plays an important role in application development. UDDI is the most common way for service register, publish and discovery. In this paper, we show the implement of basic function when UDDI server is not deployed. Through dynamic identification technology, new service endpoint can be registered and published, and service calling can be transmitted to service endpoint automatically.

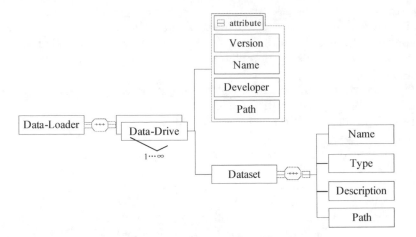

Fig. 2. Data loader configuration

3.4   Data Cooperation-service

The employment of web services can easily achieve interoperability with distributed system. In order to solve all kinds of problems about data integration, service integration and application integration of ocean information system, and achieve collaborative work between different departments, different applications and different hardware and software platforms, ocean information cooperation service interface based on web services with reference to the corresponding service specification is proposed. The main web services are demonstrated as follows.

1) Data Category Service Interface. Based on the ocean data classification and ocean metadata, data category service is used to publish, find and match data resources quickly and easily, and plays an important role in data sharing and data exchange. As shown in Figure 3, seven types of interfaces are included.

2) In-situ Data Access Service Interface. Based on marine environment data category service and basic requirement character, we designed in-situ data access service interface to acquire ocean data through unified and cross-platform ways. Figure 4 shows the basic interfaces.

3) Model Data Access Service Interface. Ocean numerical simulation provides the forecast and hind cast data of ocean elements for researching of ocean variation, and these data are multi-format such as netCDF, HDF. Based on the storage structure of mode data, OGC (Open Geospatial Consortium) proposed WCS (Web Coverage Service) to provide data service [15], but the response result is also based on file. In correspondence with our data storage model, model data service interface is implemented in Figure 5.

4) Security Service Interface. They are used for authorizing, identity authentication, and data encryption. Security service is important for any software system, so we constructs security service interface in the architecture.

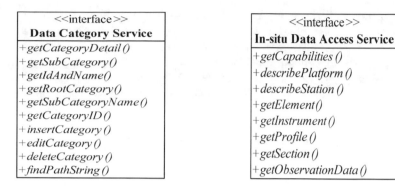

Fig. 3. Data Category-Service interfaces   **Fig. 4.** In-situ Data Access-Service interfaces

<<interface>>
File Data Access Service
+ *GetCapabilities ()*
+ *DescribeVariable ()*
+ *DescribeAttribute ()*
+ *DescribeDemension()*
+ *GetValue()*
+ *DescribeDataset ()*

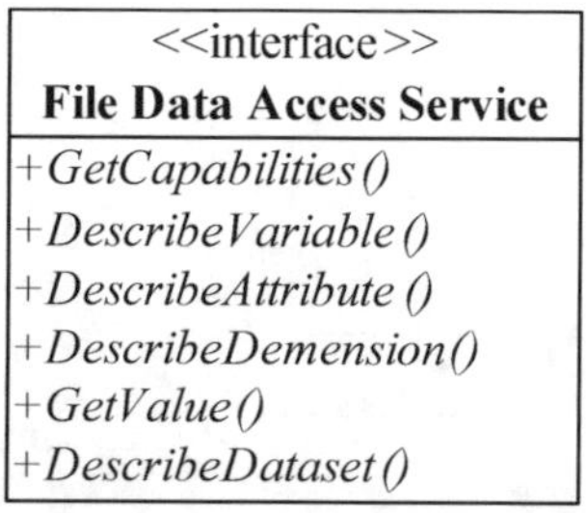

Fig. 5. Model Data Access-Service interfaces

As integrated components, data cooperation service and application can be deployed on different computers in a network in order to build large-scale distributed system. Also the standardization of service interface can achieve unified call of the web services and lay the foundations of constructing a universal access client.

3.5   Component

We have designed several types of reusable components for MEIS to improve the efficiency of development. All of them are configurable and called uniformly through the unified interfaces. Generally, the following components are necessary for MEIS such as 2D vector graphic, 2D scalar graphic , Element curve trend, Geospatial Map, Station map, Data query and Data export.

3.6   Business

Generally speaking, software systems are deployed for specific scenario and requirement to solve existing problems. The software framework proposed above supports basic function to extend the framework through components. However, it does not meet all the needs of application. Naturally, business is designed to facilitate the extension of special software function. Based on plug-in mechanism, business provides interface assembly which defines interfaces to be implemented by the software plug-in for function extension. Any plug-in based on the assembly interfaces can be integrated and called automatically. Figure 6 describes the structure of business. Every plug-in implements the interfaces and is verified, registered, discovered, called through plug-in manager, while plugin library stored all plug-ins integrated in the system. Plug-in includes the assemble and description document based on xml. Figure 7 shows the scheme of description document.

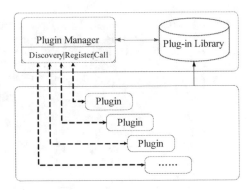

Fig. 6. Business plug-in

3.7   Configuration

Configuration includes three types of configuration information. First, our framework can be extended on the new observing platform without impacts to the existing system due to the common database schema and the adoption of web services. The parameters of new observing platform are add to database by using the configuration, including the observing platform description, observing station, observing instrument, observing element and so on. Second, giving the ocean dataset and data-drive from an observing platform or data model, we can further specify the detailed configuration parameters for loading them into database. The configuration information mainly includes the dataset and data-drive shown in Figure 2. All data loading configuration information are stored in one configuration document, which will be stored in the database and can be described in an XML schema. Third, according to the framework, applications are constructed through the components and plug-ins, and application interfaces are a series of components and plug-ins with corresponding relationship. Application configuration configure application interfaces.

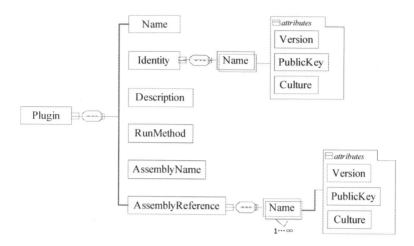

Fig. 7. Plug-in description

3.8   Security

In the application framework, we define a system security standard of interface specification, which covers the users, roles, permissions, data encryption and other aspects. By adding permission items, each item can be assigned to the appropriate authority roles and users to achieve dynamic security management. Security is logically independent of the software system, which manages the users and roles permission for software system by changing the permission information repository. And it is reusable.

4   Application Example

4.1   Hardware Platform

In order to validate and test the framework, we apply it to the actual marine environment information system of a research project. The system includes marine environment survey data in the past several years, and three ocean observing platforms (GPS wave buoy, ADCP, Automatic Hydrologic Observing System) to monitor the ocean hydrodynamic and meteorological parameters, including wave, ocean current, water temperature, salinity, wind speed, wind direction, air temperature and air pressure. Also numerical simulation for ocean hydrodynamic parameters (wave, ocean current, water temperature, salinity) is conducted. Figure 8 shows the detailed implementation topology.

4.2   Prototype Software

Based on the aforementioned hardware platform, we developed the corresponding prototype system. Data collection system is deployed in workstation for loading

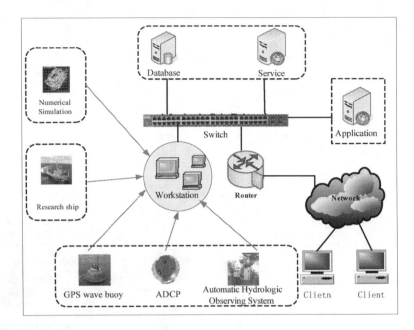

Fig. 8. System topology

the marine survey data, real-time observing data and model data through corresponding data-drive recorded in the configuration document. Database system is hosted in database server with oracle 10g and data cooperation service is published in service server. Application server hosts the main system modules and user interfaces. All of them are connected through a switch in the same local network. Figure 9 and Figure 10 exhibit the main user interfaces of the system. User interfaces are developed through component with parameters configuration. The station map shows the observing stations with geographical information when

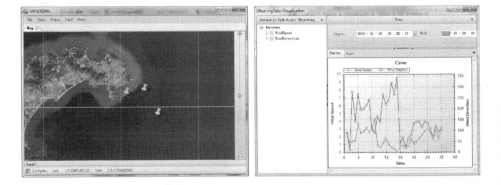

Fig. 9. Station map for user interoperate   **Fig. 10.** Trend curve for user interoperate

user selects the interesting platform. When a station is selected, the associated observation elements are listed. Through selecting the observing element, setting the start and end time, trend curve will be drawn automatically and real-time.

5   Conclusion

In this paper, a application framework for marine environment information system is described, which is suitable for integrating marine environment in-situ data and model outputs, It can offer a universal user interface with rich components, facilitate system integration, and simplify the system development. By means of the prototype system for environment monitoring application, the framework is proved to be feasible and effective. According to the data from practical projects, research on integrating more data and developing application components will also be carried out.

Acknowledgments. This work is supported in part by Major Program of National Ocean Public Benefit Research Foundation under grant No. 200905030 and National Ocean Public Benefit Research Foundation under grant No. 201105030.

References

1. Gross, N.: The Earth will Don an Electronic Skin. BusinessWeek (August 1999)
2. James, R., Robert, H.: In Situ Observations and Satellite Remote Sensing in SEACOOS: Program Development and Lessons Learned. Marine Technology Society 42, 41–54 (2008)
3. Allen, S.: Australia's Integrated Marine Observing System Observation Methods and Technology Review. In: OCEANS 2011 - MTS/IEEE Kona, pp. 1–3 (2011)
4. Moe, K., Smith, S., Prescott, G., Sherwood, R.: Sensor Web Technologies for NASA Earth Science. In: IEEE Aerospace Conference, pp. 1–7 (2008)
5. Fletcher, M., Cleary, J., Cothran, J., Porter, D.: SEACOOS Information Management: Evolution of a Distributed Community System. Marine Technology Society Journal 42, 28–34 (2008)
6. de La Beaujardiere, J., Beegle-Krause, C.J., Bermudez, L., Hankin, S., Hazard, L., Howlett, E., Le, S., Proctor, R., Signell, R.P., Snowden, D., Thomas, J.: Ocean and Coastal Data Management. In: Proceedings of the OceanObs 2009: Sustained Ocean Observations and Information for Society Conference, vol. 2 (2010)
7. Greg, R., Robert, K., Sergey, B., Nikolay, M.: Ocean Data Portal: A Standards Approach to Data Access and Dissemination. In: Proceedings of OceanObs 2009: Sustained Ocean Observations and Information for Society, vol. 2, pp. 21–25 (2009)
8. Rao, E.P., Satyanarayana, B.V., Nayak, S.: Ocean Data and Information System (ODIS) and Web-Based Services. Remote Sensing and Spatial Information Sciences 37(4) (2010)
9. He, Y.-W., Su, F.-Z., Du, Y.-Y., Xiao, R.-L., Su, X.: The Design and Implementation of a Web Services-based Application Framework for Sea Surface Temperature Information. The International Archives of the Photogrammetry, Remote Sensing and Spatial Information Sciences 38, 417–421 (2009)

10. Jing, Y., Li, J., Guo, Z.: Design and Implementation of a Prototype System of Ocean Sensor Web. In: IET International Conference on Wireless Sensor Network, pp. 21–26 (2010)
11. Rudloff, A., Lauterjung, J., Munch, U., Tinti, S.: The GITEWS project (German-Indonesian tsunami early warning system). Nat. Hazards Earth Syst. Sci. 9, 1381–1382 (2009)
12. Taylor, S.M.: Transformative Ocean Science through the VENUS and NEPTUNE Canada Ocean Observing Systems. Nucl. Instrum. Methods Phys. Res., Sect. A 602(1), 63–67 (2009)
13. Proctor, R., Roberts, K., Ward, B.J.: A Data Delivery System for IMOS, the Australian Integrated Marine Observing System. Adv. Geosci. 28, 11–16, doi:10.5194/adgeo-28-11-2010
14. GEO Group. GEOSS Sensor Web Workshop 2009 invitation, May 21-22 (2009)
15. Baumann, P.: OGC WCS 2.0 interface standard-ore. Open Geospatial Consortium Inc., Wayland, MA, USA, OpenGIS Interface Standard OGC (2010)

Weighted Localization for Underwater Sensor Networks

Shaobin Cai, Guangzhi Zhang, and Shilong Liu

College of Computer Science and Technology,
Harbin Engineering University, 150001 Harbin, China
caishaobin@hrbeu.edu.cn

Abstract. ELSN(Efficient Localization for large-scale underwater Sensor Networks) gets the node location by solving equations. However, sometimes the unique solution(no solution or multiple solutions) can not be got from equations because of the measurement error, which leads localization problem. On the basis of ELSN algorithm, a new localization algorithm is proposed. It transforms the process of solving equations into looking for the best point of intersection of the three circles in the plane, and regards the point as the potential location of the node. Firstly, in this algorithm, the node is projected into a two-dimensional plane to reduce the computational complexity of the algorithm. Secondly, every three reference nodes are randomly selected as a combination. That is to say that each triplet of nodes which represents a triplet of equations forms three tangent or intersecting circles. Based on the positional relationship of three circles, an optimal point of intersection is served as a potential location of the target node, and the residuals of each triplet is served as a potential weight. Finally, the weighted results of all potential locations are considered as the final position of the node.

Keywords: Localization, Potential location, Reference node, Residuals, Weight.

As a necessary means of marine monitoring, acoustic sensor networks have a wide spectrum of aquatic applications such as real-time monitoring of the target waters, exploration of marine resources, marine environment monitoring and auxiliary navigation. In order to make sense, the nodes information needs to be combined with its location. So sensor networks node localization technology is one of the key technologies. There are many studies about the wireless sensor network node localization [1-6].

The special features of acoustic channels (high error rate, low bandwidth, and long propagation delay) cause many constraints on the localization schemes for underwater sensor networks. So, how to locate the node in underwater sensor networks is a great challenge.

Literature [7] proposed a localization algorithm, which combines three-dimensional Euclidean distance estimate method [8] and recursion localization estimate method together [9]. But there are still some issues unsolved because of a measurement error. Sometimes it may not be able to solve the equations

L. Sun, H. Ma, and F. Hong (Eds.): CWSN 2013, CCIS 418, pp. 251–260, 2014.

directly which consists of Euclidean formulas to get a unique solution [10]. So some nodes which receive a lot of information can not be located.

Integrating the high weight idea to ELSN algorithm, we propose a scheme called Weighted Localization for Underwater Sensor Networks(WUWSN). It is not to determine the coordinates of the target node by directly solving equations, but to transform the solving equations into finding the best plane intersection point of the circle as a potential position of the node, which takes full advantage of the collected information to locate the node.

1   ELSN Algorithm

ELSN algorithm combines three-dimensional Euclidean distance estimate method and the recursive localization estimate method together. There are several types of nodes, such as reference nodes, non-localized nodes and so on. Reference nodes contain the anchor node and the non-localized node whose confidence value is higher than the stipulated threshold.

In the initialization phase, all the anchor nodes label themselves as reference nodes and set their confidence values to 1. If the confidence value is higher than the threshold value, the non-localized node is added to the reference node set after it is located. There are two types of messages: localization messages and beacon messages. Localization messages are used for information exchange between the non-localized node and the reference node, while beacon messages are designed for distance estimate. During the localization process, each node (including reference nodes and non-localized nodes) broadcast beacon messages periodically which contain its id. And all the neighboring nodes which receive this beacon message can estimate their distances to this node using techniques.

Each non-localized node maintains a counter n, of localization messages it broadcasts. A threshold value K is set to limit the maximum number of localization messages which are sent by each node. each non-localized node also keeps a counter m, of the reference nodes to which it knows the distances. Once the localization process starts, each non-localized node keeps checking m. There are two cases:

(1) When $m < 4$, the non-localized node broadcasts a localization message including the location of the reference node, its estimated distance to the reference node and messages received possibly from other non-localized nodes. Then the node which has received messages can estimate the distances from itself to more non-neighboring reference nodes with the three-dimensional Euclidean distance estimate method. The method above is commonly referred to multi-hop node distance estimate to more non-neighboring reference nodes. m will updated according to the known reference nodes, then the node will return to check m.

(2) When $m \geq 4$, the non-localized node selects four non-collinear reference nodes which have high confidence value. The beacon message includes the coordinates, id number and some other information of the reference node. If the obtained confidence value is higher than the predefined threshold, the confidence value will be calculated after the estimate procedure of the position coordinates.

So this located node will be added to the reference node set. Then, it broadcasts his location messages including its coordinates, id as well as confidence value. It will go back to (1) if the confidence value is higher than the predefined threshold [10].

2   WUWSN

Unlike ELSN, WUWSN does not always check wether $m \geq 4$ to trigger the localization procedure of the target node. Instead it starts Euclidean distance estimate to calculate its own coordinates directly. In this period, the non-localized node generally has collected enough information. So, equations can be formed by Euclidean distance estimate method. WUWSN is not to determine the coordinates of the non-localized node by solving equations directly, but to transform the solving equations to find the best plane intersection point of the circle as a potential position of the node. The basic steps are as follows. Firstly, the three-dimensional problem is transformed into a two-dimensional localization problem. Equations are listed using Euclidean distance estimate method and the unknown elements are eliminated in order to leave the coordinates of target nodes only. Then potential location of the node is sought among circles intersection points. At last, the weighted value of potential locations is regarded as the final result of the node position.

2.1   Euclidean Distance Estimate

The basic idea of Euclidean distance estimate is to estimate the distance between two non-neighboring nodes based on the known one-hop distance. Thus, the non-localized node can estimate the distance between itself and the reference node which might be multiple hops away from it.

This method is illustrated in an example shown in *Figure*1. A non-localized node E wants to estimate its distance to anchor node A, and A is a two-hop neighbor of E. Then node E needs to know the estimated distance to three one-hop neighbor nodes at least. The node A, B, C, D are not co-plane while any three nodes out of the node A, B, C, D, E are not co-line. Node E should have the length information of EB, BA, EC, CA, ED, DA, DB, DC, BC. Three-dimensional Euclidean distance estimate is described as follows. Firstly, node E uses edge BA, CA, BC to construct the basic localization plane while node E knows the length of edge DA, DB, DC. Then node E can estimate the coordinates of node D and node D may have two possible coordinates. Because the lengths of EB, EC and ED are known, node E will have four possible positions correspondingly if node D has two possible positions. Node E can select the possible values of node E after it receives more location information from other reference nodes [10].

This process above can be also illustrated in solving equations equivalently. Coordinates of A, B and C are known, and coordinates of D and E are unknown. Nodes coordinates of D and E are denoted by (x_D, y_D) and (x_E, y_E). Nine equations can be listed based on the known edge distances with the unknown elements

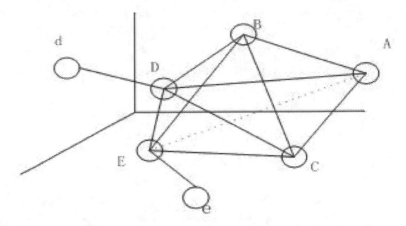

Fig. 1. Three-dimensional Euclidean distance estimate

$(x_D,y_D)$and(x_E,y_E). Then, we can get the equations with the only unknown elements (x_E,y_E) after eliminating unknown elements (x_D,y_D). There will be four possible values corresponding to roots of equations because of the non-sufficient information.

In this case, more information can be gathered to solve equations which have a unique solution. According to the algorithm, the simplest method is to collect the information of neighbor nodes. If node D knows the distance to the node d and node E knows the distance to the reference node e, the equations will have a unique solution. In short, the unknown elements of the equations are the only coordinates of the target non-localized node.

Now we will consider the case that the information just makes equations have a unique solution. Because the presence of underwater measurement error is inevitable, the equations may be no solution. Even if the node has collected enough information, it cannot realize its own localization. Because there are some measurement errors.

Under normal circumstances, the collected information of the node is more than the information which leads to a unique solution. That is to say, the equations is a over-determined system. In fact, measurement errors are inevitable, so the result may deviate from the true value.

2.2   Potential Location

A three-dimensional localization problem is transformed into a two-dimensional localization problem. Each node is equipped with a pressure sensor which can measure the underwater depth accurately. The reference node is projected to the plane where the non-localized node exits. With the help of Euclidean distance estimate method, equations can be formed, and coordinates of non-localized nodes are also contained in the unknown elements of the equations. Then, the unknown elements like coordinates of non-target nodes are eliminated just to retain the coordinate of target node. When the equations just have three entries, there is only a unique solution. The collected information by the node maybe more than the information leading to a unique solution. That is to say, the equations is a over-determined system. So, the entries of the equations about a target node maybe more than three. That is to say, the entries out of equations about a target node are more than three after unknown elements are eliminated. And any triples out of equation system are equivalent with the equation system itself.

$$
\begin{cases}
\sqrt{(x - x_1')^2 + (y - y_1')} = d_{r_1}' \\
\sqrt{(x - x_2')^2 + (y - y_2')} = d_{r_2}' \\
\qquad \vdots \\
\sqrt{(x - x_N')^2 + (y - y_N')} = d_{r_N}'
\end{cases}
\tag{1}
$$

In equations (1), (x, y) is the coordinates of the target non-localized node, and (x_i', y_i') is the projected coordinate of the reference node. N is the number of the reference nodes whose messages are received by the target node and $N \geq 3$. d_{r_i}' is the distance from non-localized node to the i'th reference node.

Each triple (C_N^3) of N equations about one non-localized node corresponds to three reference nodes. Base on the positional relationship of the three circles in the plane, an optimal intersection point is selected to be as a potential location of the non-localized node, and the following cases are some typical examples.

We regard the projected points A_1', A_2', A_3' as the center, the distances from A_1', A_2', A_3' to the non-localized node(red dots in the figure)as radius respectively. And then three circles are formed. Figure 1 shows the position relationship.

1) $Figure2(a)$ shows the case that three circles intersect with one another. As can be seen from the figure, we regard A_1', A_2' as the center respectively, the two circles intersect at two points $P_{12}'(2), P_{12}'(1)$. It may appear that two intersection points are both within the circle A_3' ,or just one intersection point is within it. It may possible that neither of two intersection points is within the circle A_3'. If $P_{12}'(1), P_{12}'(2)$ meet equation (2), $P_{12}'(1)$ is selected to be as the potential position, or $P_{12}'(2)$ will be selected. N refers to the number of the reference nodes whose messages are received by the non-localized node.

$$
\sum_{i=1, i \neq j, k}^{N} \left| \left\| A_i' - P_{jk}(1) \right\| - d_{r_i}' \right| < \sum_{i=1, i \neq j, k}^{N} \left| \left\| A_i' - P_{jk}(2) \right\| - d_{r_i}' \right|
\tag{2}
$$

2) $Figure2(b)$ shows the case that the three circles have a unique intersection point. It is well-reasoned to put the unique intersection point as the estimated position of the non-localized node, and there is no need to participate in the subsequent weight operation.

3) $Figure2(c)$ shows that the two circles do not intersect. In the figure, because the sum of d_{r_1}' and d_{r_3}' is bigger than segment $A_1'A_3'$, the circles A_1' and A_3' have

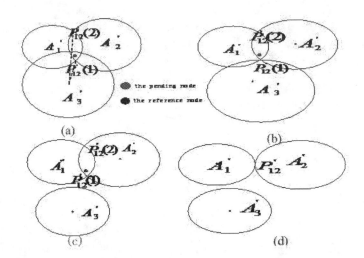

Fig. 2. Intersecting to select potential locations (a) every two circles are intersecting (b) a unique solution (c) no intersection of two circles (d) two circles are tangent

no intersection point. Then $A_1'A_3'$ is divided according to the ratio of $d_{r_1}' : d_{r_3}'$, then the point of demarcation that will participate in the subsequent weight calculation is right the potential location. If A_1' is within A_3' entirely, segment $A_1'A_3'$ will be extended to intersect with circles $A_3'andA_1'$,and the ring $A_3'A_1'$ is divided according to the ratio of $d_{r_1}' : d_{r_3}'$. The intersection point determined by equation (2) will be the potential position of the node and it will be participant in the subsequent weight operation.

4) Figure 2(d) shows the two circles are tangent. Circles $A_1'andA_2'$ tangent at Point P_{12}', so P_{12}' is the potential location determined by the two circles. The potential location is denoted by $P_{jk}(\hat{x}_{jk}, \hat{y}_{jk})$. Subscript jk is used to note which two circles are intersecting and $j \neq k$.

The location of a node can be simply described as the average estimate of the potential locations. However, in order to increase localization accuracy further, the average estimate is replaced by weights related to residuals in this paper.

If $\hat{x}$ is the solution of the equation $f(x) = b$, the residual is defined as $b - f(\hat{x})$. The residual indicates the error between $f(\hat{x})$ and true-value b and the error is $\hat{x} - x$. Not knowing x needed in calculating error, it is a natural choice to calculate the residual instead of the error. The relationship between N residuals and $P_{jk}(\hat{x}_{jk}, \hat{y}_{jk})$ is described as equation (3).

$$\begin{cases} \hat{\varepsilon}_{jk}(1) = |\ \sqrt{(\hat{x}_{jk} - x_1')^2 + (\hat{y}_{jk} - y_1')^2} - d_{r_1}'\ | \\ \hat{\varepsilon}_{jk}(2) = |\ \sqrt{(\hat{x}_{jk} - x_2')^2 + (\hat{y}_{jk} - y_2')^2} - d_{r_2}'\ | \\ \qquad\qquad\qquad\qquad . \\ \qquad\qquad\qquad\qquad . \\ \hat{\varepsilon}_{jk}(N) = |\ \sqrt{(\hat{x}_{jk} - x_N')^2 + (\hat{y}_{jk} - y_N')^2} - d_{r_N}'\ | \end{cases} \qquad (3)$$

The weight of potential position $P_{jk}(\hat{x}_{jk}, \hat{y}_{jk})$ is described as equation (4). The accuracy is inversely proportional to the sum of residuals and the reciprocal of all the residuals represent the weight factor.

$$W_{jk} = \frac{1}{\sum\limits_{i=1}^{N} \hat{\varepsilon}_{jk}(i)} \tag{4}$$

Finally, from the perspective of the weight, the non-localized sensor node is estimated as follows.

$$(x, y) = \frac{\sum\limits_{j=1}^{N-1} \sum\limits_{k=j+1}^{N} W_{jk} * P_{jk}(\hat{x}_{jk}, \hat{y}_{jk})}{\sum\limits_{j=1}^{N-1} \sum\limits_{k=j+1}^{N} W_{jk}} \tag{5}$$

If the number of messages received by the non-localized node is less than three, the method above is not applicable, so other methods should be accepted. If the node gains only two beacon messages, the method is shown as follows. Drawing two circles with A_1', A_2' as the center and d_{r_1}', d_{r_2}' as the radius respectively, the two circles intersect at two points $P_{12}'(2), P_{12}'(1)$. The intersection point $P_{12}'(2), P_{12}'(1)$ will send messages within their own communication radius and the reference node who receives this messages will reply. In this case, between $P_{12}'(2), P_{12}'(1)$, the one who receives more feedback messages will be selected as the estimate location. If the number of messages is less than two, Euclidean distance estimate will be applied directly.

3   Simulation Analysis

MATLAB is used to simulate WUWSNELSN and RECURSIVE [9]. Parameters are set as follows: 1) A 1000m * 1000m * 1000m three-dimensional region which can drift within 20km * 20km area with the water current. 2) The confidence threshold is 0.98. 3)Anchor nodes proportion is from 5% to 35% while the increment interval is 5%. 4) the radius is 200m, the transmitting interval of beacon messages is 100s. The simulation environment is described as follows: the water acoustic channel model uses Rayleigh fading channels model. ToA method is used to measure the distance, and the movement model is Lagrange movement oceanographic models [11-12]. Each simulation experiment is operated 50 times and the 90% of the centralized results interval is set as the experiment result.

3.1   Localization Coverage

*Figure*3 shows the comparison in localization coverage among ELSN, WUWSN and RECUSIVE when the percentage of anchor nodes varies from 5% to 35%. The localization coverage of ELSN is higher than RECUSIVE because Euclidean distance estimate method is used to calculate multi-hop distance in ELSN.

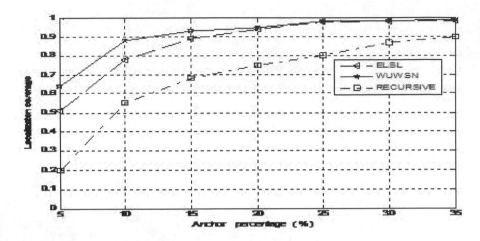

Fig. 3. The comparison chart of ELSN, WUWSN, RECUSIVE in the localization coverage

When the ratio of anchor nodes is small, the localization coverage ratio of ELSN is lower than that of WUWSN, and otherwise the opposite. In the previous case, because of weighted average method, each time WUWSN will be likely to choose the maximum of potential reference nodes affording the location information, so most nodes can receive the appreciate location messages. But sometimes the non-localization node can not get the unique solution of equations. Therefore, the node will not be able to complete the localization procedure. So the localization coverage of WUWSN is higher than that of ELSN. In the latter case, because the information afforded by the anchor nodes is already wealthy, so the reference nodes which are added recursively from ordinary nodes have became non-key factors in this case. So ELSN is close to WUWSN in the localization coverage.

3.2   Localization Error

*Figure*4 shows the comparison in localization error among ELSN, WUWSN and RECUSIVE when the percentage of anchor nodes varies from 5% to 35%. Because of weighted average method, each time WUWSN will likely be able to choose the maximum amount of potential reference nodes affording location information, so localization error of WUWSN is the least. When the anchor node ratio reaches 20%, the three localization error curves begin to reduce, but not so sharply.

3.3   Communication Cost

Now we begin to consider the comparison in the communication cost among ELSN, WUWSN and RECUSIVE when the percentage of anchor nodes varies

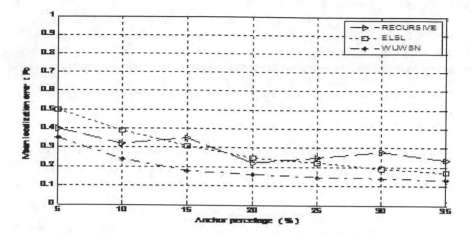

Fig. 4. The comparison chart of ELSN, WUWSN, RECUSIVE in the average localization error

from 5% to 35%. When the proportion of anchor nodes is low, communication cost of RECUSIVE is the lowest. This is because that only a part of nodes send messages in RECUSIVE. But in WUWSN and RECUSIVE, anchor nodes will send beacon messages while some non-localized nodes which do not receive enough beacon messages will also send localization messages. When the proportion of anchor nodes becomes higher, the localization errors play an important factor in communication cost, so the communication costs of ELSN and WUWSN with lower localization errors become low. Because the three-dimensional space is transformed into two-dimensional space, less messages are needed to send. For less messages are needed to send, WUWSN is lower than ELSN in communication cost.

4   Conclusions

WUWSN transforms solving Euclidean equations into finding the best plane intersection point of circles and regards weighted sum of all the potential position as the final position. Compared with ELSN, WUWSN has a obvious advantage that a reasonable estimate location could be found even if there is no enough effective information. The anther advantage is that residuals make location estimate more accurate. The communication traffic becomes less because three-dimensional space is transformed into two-dimensional space. The simulation result shows that compared with ELSN, WUWSN is lower in both of the average localization error and the average communication cost, but is higher in the localization coverage.

Acknowledgements. The work is supported by National Science foundation of China (41176082, 61073182, 40827003, 61073183), the Fundamental Research Funds for the Central Universities (HEUCF1006), and Young backbone teacher project of Heilongjiang province (1155G15).

References

1. Wang, F., Shi, L., Ren, F.: Self-localization systems and algorithms for wireless sensor networks. Journal of Software 5(6), 857–868 (2005) (in Chinese)
2. Wang, S., Yin, J., Cai, Z., Zhang, G.: A RSSI-based self-localization algorithm for wireless sensor networks (45), 385–388 (2008) (in Chinese)
3. Cui, X., Liu, I., Fan, X.: A distributed anchor free localization algorithm in sensor networks. Journal of Computer Research and Development 46(3), 425–433 (2009) (in Chinese)
4. Langendoen, K., Reijers, N.: Distributed Localization In Wireless sensor networks: A quantitative comparison. Computer Networks 42(4), 499–518 (2003)
5. Niculescu, D., Nath, B.: Position and orientation in ad hoc networks. Ad Hoc Networks 2(1), 133–151 (2004)
6. Cai, S., Li, X., Tian, Y., et al.: Alternating combination trilateration based on circle-selection. Journal of Computer Research and Development 46(2), 238–244 (2010) (in Chinese)
7. Zhou, Z., Peng, Z., Cui, J.H., et al.: Scalable Localization with Mobility Prediction for Underwater Sensor Networks. IEEE Transactions on Mobile Computer 10(3), 335–348 (2011)
8. Niculescu, D., Nathi, B.: Ad-hoc localization system(APS). In: Proc. of IEEE GLOBECOM 2001, pp. 2926–2931. IEEE, Piscataway (2001)
9. Albowitz, J., Chen, A., Zhang, L.: Recursive position estimation in sensor networks. In: Proceedings of the IEEE International Conference on Network Protocols (ICNP 2001), CA, Los Angeles, pp. 35–41 (2001)
10. Zhou, Z., Cui, J., Zhou, S.: Efficient localization for large-scale underwater sensor networks. Ad Hoc Networks 8(3), 267–279 (2010)
11. Caruso, A., Paparella, F., Vieira, L., et al.: Meandering current model and its application to underwater sensor networks. In: Proc. of INFOCOM 2008, pp. 221–225. Phoenix, AZ (2008)
12. Bower, A.S.: A simple kinematic mechanism for mixing fluid parcels across a meandering jet. Journal of Physical Oceanography 21(1), 173–180 (1991)

Research on a CPS Real Time Scheduling and Memory Allocation Method Based Reservation

Benhai Zhou

Shenyang Institute of Engineering, Teaching Department of Computer Science,
Shenyang City, Liaoning Province, 110136
13734610@qq.com

Abstract. Cyber and physical system is a deeply embedded distributed real-time systemwhose real time characteristic is the critical property of CPS. In order to improve the real-time performance, most algorithms use the preemptive scheduling model. However, the preemptive scheduling easily leads to task switching frequently, which increases communication overhead. Meanwhile, parallel real time tasks will compete the memory, which affects the timeliness of CPS badly. Aiming at this problem, this paper proposed the real time scheduling and the dynamic memory allocation methods based on reservation, which can maximize the low priority tasks executive time and effectively avoid the memory competition. The experimental results show that the algorithm can effectively reduce the task switching frequency and improve the CPS real-time performance in the limited memory resources.

Keywords: CPS, real time characteristic, scheduling, reservation.

1 Introduction

Today, a pre-cursor generation of cyber-physical systems can be found in areas as diverse as aerospace, automotive, chemical processes, civil infrastructure, energy, healthcare, manufacturing, transportation, entertainment, and consumer appliances. This generation is often referred to as embedded systems. In embedded systems the emphasis tends to be more on the computational elements, and less on an intense link between the computational and physical elements [1].

Cyber-physical systems, the time-critical systems, must finish sending and receiving messages in limited time. The output correctness of the system depends not only on the correctness of the logical result, but also depends on the results of the time. Thus, physical integration of real-time information system, which enhances the ability of identification and handling discrete event in a pre-defined time ranges has great significance.

Node operating system in CPS is a resource constrained systems, and the memory usage and management is more stringent than other systems. Unlike some other desktop operating system (such as Windows, Linux), node CPS provide virtual memory mechanism. Because of the limited resources and cost constraints, node CPS system has not massive management unit. Developers need

L. Sun, H. Ma, and F. Hong (Eds.): CWSN 2013, CCIS 418, pp. 261–270, 2014.

consider the problem of memory allocation and use problem in parallel real-time tasks in sensor networks [2–4].

Therefore, this paper proposes a real-time scheduling and memory allocation method based on the reservation, through the establishment of reservation model, maximizing the low priority task execution time, and reducing the task switching. In addition, the parallel real-time task memory allocation is reserved, as result of reducing memory competition, improving the efficiency of memory usage, and increasing task schedulability of rate. So the new algorithm provides a powerful guarantee for the real time performance of CPS.

2   Background

CPS plays an extremely important role in the medical, intelligent transportation, military and other critical areas, whose typical characteristics of CPS are real-time feature. The CPS must ensure that all real-time tasks need finish before deadline. CPS limits on system resources very strictly. The pure preemptive scheduling problem easily caused by the too much task switches, increases the system overhead, which would seriously affect the real-time performance of the CPS. How to remain the system schedulability under the condition of minimizing the task switches has become a new hot research topic in the CPS environment.

Chen Ying [5] proposed a period tasks ready queue scheduling algorithm, which optimized the preemption number of the dynamic scheduling algorithm. However, the time complexity for dynamic scheduling algorithm is high with heavy system overhead. Evans B G [6] presented a preemption Threshold using in the uncertainty and dynamical priority of the task set. The threshold based on a pro rata [7] is proposed. CHEN etal. [8] take advantages in priority inheritance protocols into preemption threshold scheduling to optimize the worst-case number of task switches. WU [9] gave preemption threshold scheduling algorithm determined by the task characteristic parameters and optimizing the cloud model theory. The DVS preemption threshold algorithm is proposed [10, 11]. However, the threshold value algorithm above failed to solve the system jitter. There are large still numbers of context switches and task deadline miss ratio is relatively high, which affect the real-time performance of the system.

Eswaran [12] put forward the memory protection mechanism, which provides for each task determining the number of pages to limit the interference to other task operation. Maria [13] presents the shared memory and the isolation mechanism for real-time tasks. The shared memory size is fixed, while the memory allocation strategy uses a protection mechanism so that the task memory will not occupied by other tasks.

In this paper, the CPS node real-time scheduling and allocation algorithm are proposed based on reservation by establishing the threshold of protection for maximizing the lower priority task execution time and reserved memory block to parallel real-time tasks, which can improve the real-time task scheduling and memory resource utilization. As a result, the real-time CPS performance is improved.

3   Slack Time Model and Reserved Time Model Description

In a set of schedulable tasks, we use the RM scheduling method for all periodic tasks according to priority from high to low. That is concentrated in the task set τ, the priority of τ_i is higher than $\tau_j (1 \leq i < j \leq n)$. Let the task deadline equal period, and the least common multiple of all task cycle is called a hyper cycle T_H, where each task's period is T_K, i.e. $T_H = lcm(T_k)$, $(1 \leq k \leq n)$. During T_H, all tasks in the system are able to run at least once, and each task can run T_H/T_k times completely. In a hyper cycle, the period of the first m tasks running completely at least once is called $T_m (1 \leq m \leq n)$.

3.1   Slack Time Model

The slack time of a task set is defined as the deadline of high priority task set minus completion time in a hyper period. The deadline of the task set equal to the least common multiple of all task deadlines. The task set completion time means that the sum of the complete execution time of the tasks in a hyper cycle. The task set ordered by priority, The first tasks $p(1 \leq p \leq n)$ consist of a local task set denoted by T_H^P. The slack time of the local set of tasks such as equation (1):

$$S_p = T_H^P \left(1 - \frac{C_1}{T_1} - \frac{C_2}{T_2} \cdots - \frac{C_p}{T_p} \right) \quad (1 \leq p \leq n) \tag{1}$$

After sorting equation (1), we can get equation (2)

$$S_p = T_H^P \left(1 - \sum_1^p \frac{C_p}{T_p} \right) \quad (1 \leq p \leq n) \tag{2}$$

Therefore, if a task set is schedulable, then $S_p \geq 0$, and on the contrary $S_p < 0$.

3.2   Reserved Time Model

In task set τ, arranged by the priority of the task, when the number of tasks is greater than or equal to two, Reserved Time model is showed in formula (3):

$$Threshold_p = MIN(\{S_2 \cdots S_p\}) \tag{3}$$

$Threshold_p$ is the largest execution time of the preempted task. That is, in delay time range $[0, Threshold_p]$ of the high priority, the task set is schedulable.

This paper introduces a test mechanism in preemptive scheduling model. That is, when the high priority task is activated for the ready state, the system test tasks remaining execution time and reserved threshold of low priority tasks. If the remaining execution time of low priority tasks is less than the reserved threshold, then the system can raise the priority of a task to the highest, until the end of the task execution. The task switching times are reduced significantly, at the same time the high priority task set can complete before the deadline. As a result, real-time performance of the system is guaranteed.

3.3   Description of the Reserved Real Time Scheduling Method

According to slack time and reserved model, the algorithm computes the current task slack time, high priority task slack time and its reserved threshold. When the high priority task is ready, the algorithm determines whether the low priority task continue running or not. If the remaining time of the low-priority task is greater than the slack time, the priority will not be raised and the high priority tasks schedule preemptively, while task switching frequency plus 1; On the contrary, the algorithm raises the current task priority to the highest until the completion, the time when the high priority task starts running because of recovering its priority.

---

1. **Initialization** //system Initialization
2. CreateTasks(); //creat task set
3. **Function:** Schedule() //task scheduling
4. {if(τ_p is ready) //the high priority task is ready
5. {Compute($Threshold_p$, S_p, R_i)
6. computing the reserved threshold of high priority, slack time and remaining time.
7. if($R_i < Threshold_p$) //if remaining time less than reserved threshold, the algorithm raises the priority to ceiling, and the high priority task resumes to run.
8. {{rise τ_i priority to CELLPRIO;
9. execute τ_p;}
10. else execute τ_p }}
11. //if the remaining time exceeds the reserved threshold,
12. the high priority task begins to run
13. else execute τ_i;
14. //if there is not high priority task, the current task continue to run.}

3.4   Description of CPS Node Memory Allocation Method

This paper presents a reserved CPS node memory allocation strategy, which provides a new memory allocation method for parallel real-time tasks running on it. When a best effort task in the transmission network, memory resources are extremely limited condition. However, parallel real-time task still maintain real-time and good stability. The algorithm proposed in this paper will be divided into several blocks of memory pages. The block of memory on the node of each parallel real-time tasks can create a private (PMB), and the memory block is not disturbed by other tasks. The shared memory block (SMB), which consistent with the private memory block size servicing for all the parallel real-time applications. The rest is spare memory block (BMB) for all task service.

The new algorithm allocates memory through the page expiring, exchanging and recovering. The specific process is that parallel real-time tasks first access to the private memory block memory pages. If there was no idle private memory block in the page, the algorithm tries to access the shared task reserved memory block. At this time the tasks will be associated with the occurrence of other memory competition.

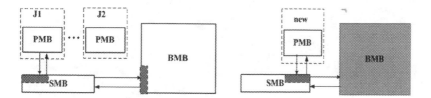

Fig. 1. The switching of memory blocks

If the shared memory block is also no free pages, tasks will return to private memory blocks to find whether there are outdated pages or not. If there are free pages, they will reuse these pages. Finally, if the private memory has not expired pages, based on LRU replacement strategy, the algorithm will replace the active page. Best effort tasks can only access the spare memory block of the memory page. The following is the expiring, exchanging and recovering algorithms described in detail:

```
Step1:create PMB
1.  create_PMB(Ti,size)
2.  {if (BMB is not filled)
3.  Ti.PMB←allocate(BMB,size);
4.  else if (SMB is not filled)
5.  { Ti.PMB←allocate(SMB,size);}
6.  else
7.  {swap out FSB;}}
Step 2: The procedure of getting memory pages;
8.  get_page(Ti,size)
9.  {if(BMB is not filled)
10. Ti.PMB←allocate(PMB,size);
11. else if (SMB is not filled)
12. {if (there are expired pages in PMB)
13. reuse expired pages as free pages;
     else swap out the active pages;}}
```

4 Result and Analysis

4.1 The Experiment of Reserved Real Time Scheduling Method

This paper uses RTSim scheduling simulator testing presented the theoretical method. The simulator can emulate most of the current processor architecture, such as single-processor and multi-processor, CMP and other architecture. Using the simulator, the real-time scheduling algorithm of reserved threshold is compared with RM algorithm. Task sets of the simulation experiment are randomly generated according to the system utilization and the number of tasks, where each task cycle is generated by time range from 1 to 200 units. The WCET of each task is randomly generated from 1 to T_i. And then, it is multiplied by the factor $U/\sum_{i=1}^{n}(C_i/T_i)$ in order to satisfy system utilization. Firstly, let task number is 10, aiming at the different system utilization U, 100 groups of schedulable task set are randomly generated.

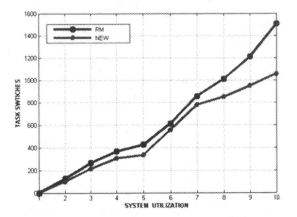

Fig. 2. System Utilization Affecting Task Switches

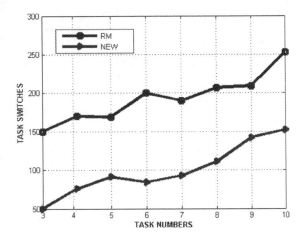

Fig. 3. Tasks Numbers Affecting Task Switches

On RTSIM platform, this paper emulates the RM algorithm and proposed method respectively. Let the execution time be a hyper period and compare the preemptive times. As can be seen in figure 4 and 5, each value in the cartoon is the average of 100 group tasks.

As can be shown from figure 2, in the case of a fixed number of tasks, task switching times of the two algorithms increased with system utilization. Under the assumption of schedulable system, utilization within the range of [0.1, 0.9], the number of task switching is less than RM algorithm, and the average is 19.3% lower than the RM algorithm. Figure 3 shows that, in the case of fixed utilization, task switching frequency of the two algorithms increased with the number of tasks. Under the task number within range of [3, 10], the task switching frequency are lower than the RM algorithm, and the average value is 39.5% less than RM.

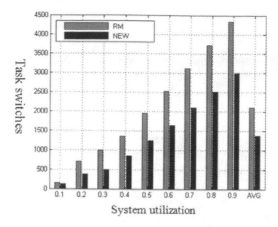

Fig. 4. System Utilization Affecting Task Switches (tasks number = 20)

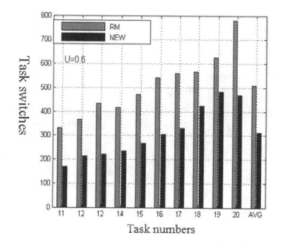

Fig. 5. Tasks Numbers Affecting Task Switches (tasks number = 20)

Let the number of tasks be 20, the experimental results show in Figure 4 and Figure 5.

As can be shown from figure 4, under the assumption of schedulable system, utilization within the range of [0.1, 0.9], the number of task switching is less than RM algorithm, and the average is 28.3% lower than the RM algorithm. Figure 5 shows that, in the case of fixed utilization, under the task number within range of [11, 20], the task switching frequency are lower than the RM algorithm, and the average value is 36.3% less than RM. The results shows that the presented scheduling algorithm based on reserved threshold can effectively reduce the task switching number, which can save system resources and enhance the system reliability and real time performance.

4.2   The Test of Reserved Memory Allocation Method

CPS node selected with 32 bit processor and professional video million pixel processing capability of the codec chip. By using H.264 video compression format making image more clear and convenient for network transmission stream, and save storage space. The network supports the 802.11b/g/n protocol in wireless communication module, which can flexibly set up wireless monitoring environment, supporting for 720P(1280*720), (640×480), (320×240) or (160×120). They can support for various video parameters adjustment so as to adapt a variety of browsing request.

CPS node memory allocation algorithm test compares various memory allocation algorithms in condition that the memory space is limited. The proposed memory allocation algorithm is compared among memory isolation algorithms well as LRU algorithm. We created a best effort task assigned 500MB of heap memory (heap memory mainly stores global variables and static variables). When the task is running, it can fill with the space with limited circles.

Figure 6 shows the four H.264 video applications and for best effort tasks are worked in three different memory allocation algorithms, which displays the result of worst frame rate. As can be seen in Figure 2, four video applications running in the absence of memory pressure, maintained a high and stable frame rate. However, the use of memory allocation algorithm in LRU case, the video application has been a great influence on the best effort tasks, which lead to the low performance. Not only the worst average frame rate is 5.3fps, but also a great jitter amplitude. Isolation algorithm has better performance under the LRU algorithm, but the average frame rate is only 15fps, which still maintained a low level.

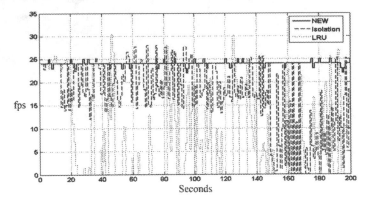

Fig. 6. The worst frame rate of four video applications and the best effort task running in parallel

The main reason for this phenomenon is that when the task of these two algorithms exhausted their own memory block, memory pages will be replaced leading to block tasks running. If replacement of pages is frequent, the task blocking phenomenon will increase, which results in task delay, and reduces the frame rate. Finally, it will affect the overall system performance.

When resources are low, the proposed memory allocation algorithm still maintain average worst frame rate 24fps, and the jitter amplitude is small. As a result, the video application is running very stable. Mainly due to the algorithm in the task's private memory block resources are exhausted, it can also set aside a block of memory from the shared use of memory resources, and there are a series of measures to avoid page-replacement operation. Such blocking time is greatly reduced, and the average frame rate is improved. Finally, the stability is enhanced. If we give the memory isolation algorithm as much as possible to allocate a large block memory, the CPS node performance will be improved. However, this allocation will result in excessive waste of memory resources, and it will reduce the CPS node system performance.

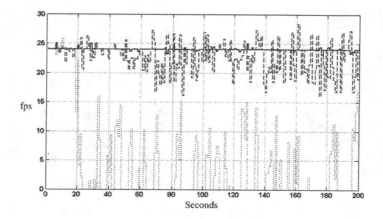

Fig. 7. The worst frame rate of twelve video applications and the best effort task running in parallel

This article put twelve parallel H.264 video applications running on quad-core processing platform. Figure 7 shows that the comparison with worst-case frame rate in three allocation methods. In this test, we give each test task memory pages allocated 2,500 private memory blocks. If system used this algorithm, we should allocate the same amount of shared pages reserved memory blocks. The average worst frame rate of LRU replacement algorithm is 6.1fps with great jitter amplitude. Memory isolation algorithm performance is higher than LRU, and the worst average worst frame rate achieves 20fps. However, the larger jitter amplitude will destroy the stability of the system, resulting in system performance degradation. Compared with these two algorithms, the proposed algorithm has the highest average frame rate 25fps, and the frame rate jitter amplitude is small. Therefore, the low-memory situations caused by the best effort tasks or parallel tasks, we propose the memory allocation algorithms to protect real-time and stability characteristics which is more effective than others.

5 Conclusion

As real time characteristic is the key attribute for CPS, most algorithms uses preemptive scheduling mode. Combining with preemptive and non-preemptive scheduling, this article proposed a reserved threshold-based real-time scheduling and memory allocation algorithm for CPS. Under the schedulable condition, the algorithm maximizes the execution times of the preempted tasks and reduces the task switching frequency by creating slack time and reserved threshold of the task sets. At the same time, the algorithm effectively allocates memory for parallel real time system. Experimental results show that, in condition of limited memory resources, the new algorithm achieved a higher schedulable rate of and memory resource utilization. As a result, the new algorithm gives effective guarantee of the CPS in real time and stability.

References

1. Lee, E.A.: Cyber physical systems: Design challenges. In: 2008 11th IEEE International Symposium on Object Oriented Real-Time Distributed Computing (ISORC), pp. 363–369. IEEE (2008)
2. Lee, E.A., Seshia, S.A.: Introduction to embedded systems: A cyber-physical systems approach. Lee & Seshia (2011)
3. Li, J., Gao, H., Yu, B.: The concept, characteristics, challenges and research progress of CPS. In: 2009 Computer Science and Technology Development Report, Beijing, CCF, pp. 1–17 (2010)
4. Li, R., Xie, Y., Li, R., Li, L.: Survey of Cyber-Physical Systems 49(6), 1149–1161 (2012)
5. Mao, X., Miao, X., He, Y., et al.: Citysee: Urban CO2 monitoring with sensors. In: IEEE INFOCOM, Orlando, FL, USA (2012)
6. Liu, Y., He, Y., Li, M., et al.: Does wireless sensor network scale? A measurement study on GreenOrbs. In: 2011 Proceedings IEEE INFOCOM, pp. 873–881. IEEE (2011)
7. Du, X.Z., Qiao, J.Z., Lin, S.K., et al.: The Design of Node Operating System for Cyber Physical Systems. Procedia Engineering 29, 3717–3721 (2012)
8. MinSeong, K., Andy, W.: Applying fixed-priority preemptive scheduling with pre-emption threshold to asynchronous event handling in the RTSJ. Concurrency and Computation: Practice and Experience 23(14), 1609–1622 (2011)
9. Ding, W., Guo, R.: Preemption Threshold Scheduling Algorithm with Higher Fault-Tolerant Priority. Journal of Software 22(12), 2894–2904 (2011)
10. Keskin, U.: Exact response-time analysis for fixed-priority preemption-threshold scheduling. In: Proceedings of Emerging Technologies and Factory Automation (ETFA), Bilbao, pp. 1–4. IEEE Press (2010)
11. Chen, Y., Wang, X., Zhao, H., et al.: Ready queue optimization research in task scheduling. Journal of System Simulation 18(4), 877–882 (2006)
12. Eswaran, A., Rajkumar, R.: Energy-aware memory firewalling for QoS-sensitive applications. In: Proceedings of the Euromicro Conference on Real-Time Systems, pp. 11–20. IEEE Press, Palma de Mallorca (2005)
13. del Mar Gallardo, M., Merino, P., Sanán, D.: Model Checking Dynamic Memory Allocation in Operating Systems. Journal of Automated Reasoning 42(2), 229–264 (2009)

A Localization Algorithm
Based on Virtual Beacon Nodes
for Wireless Sensor Network

Li Ma*, Jianpei He, and Dongchao Ma

North China University of Technology
mali@ncut.edu.cn

Abstract. The position service is becoming more and more important for WSN applications. In order to resolve the problem of low positioning accuracy in WSN, a new positioning algorithm based on virtual beacon nodes is proposed. In this algorithm, the space is divided into several equal areas by anchor nodes; PIT theory is used to estimate the preliminary regional; the best virtual beacon nodes is calculated through the approach degree; finally, an unknown nodes position can be calculated by computing the centroid of the selected anchor nodes. This algorithm adopts the RF signal to locate unknown node.It can not only avoid the overlapped error in a range-based localization algorithm, but also avoid high complexity.

Keywords: virtual beacon node, localization algorithm, computing complex, location accuracy, approach degree.

1 Introduction

Wireless sensor networks (WSN) with low power consumption, ad-hoc network, cheap node cost, small size, strong adaptability and excellent features, it has been widely used in military, industrial, medical, environmental monitoring and other fields. Accurate positioning of sensor nodes is an important condition for WSN applications, for example, the monitoring of the zone human cannot enter or hostile area. The sensing data without the position of sensors is meaningful in these places. In addition, the location information of Sensor node can be used to improve the efficiency of WSN routing and the quality of network coverage, balance network load and automatically configure the topology, etc. Therefore, the positioning of WSN node not only has become an important support technology, but also an extremely important research direction in recent years.

In large-scale WSN, sensor nodes, according to their own location information, may be divided into two kinds of nodes: beacon nodes and unknown nodes. Beacon nodes obtain their location information through artificial deployment or GPS. They have a smaller proportion. Unknown nodes get their location information through localization algorithm. The existing localization algorithm

---

* Corresponding author.

L. Sun, H. Ma, and F. Hong (Eds.): CWSN 2013, CCIS 418, pp. 271–280, 2014.

can be divided into two categories: Range-based versus Range-free [1]. Range-based approaches measure the Euclidean distances or angle information between the unknown node and beacon nodes through RSSI [2], TDOA [?]jour3,AOA [4].Range-based approaches calculate the location of the unknown node by Tri-lateral France, trigonometry or maximum likelihood estimation method. These approaches improve positioning accuracy by adding additional hardware and communication overhead. By contrast, Range-free approaches perform localization relying only on network connectivity measurements. Range-free approaches have lower communication overhead with lower positioning accuracy and demanding network deployment. Typical algorithms are Centroid [5], DV-HOP [6], APIT [7],etc.

No matter which positioning method is used, in theory, the number of beacon nodes has a direct impact on the positioning accuracy. In addition, the simulation of the existing location algorithms also show the higher the ratio of beacon nodes, the higher the positioning accuracy, but more beacon nodes will increase the computational overhead of WSN, network overhead and network costs. To this end, the literature [8] proposed a localization idea based on virtual node, literature [9] proposed iteration idea - convert unknown nodes to beacon nodes, to some extent, can improve the positioning accuracy, but each has drawbacks. Literature [8] combines the idea of BP neural network, but uses a centralized location algorithm, the algorithm selects secondary beacon nodes by comparing minimum number of hops between the virtual nodes and unknown nodes to beacon nodes, but requires a higher degree of connectivity of network, and does not consider the distribution of virtual beacon nodes impact on the algorithm;The iteration idea of literature [9]mainly make the positioned nodes as new beacon nodes, but this will cause superposition error and large communication load.

According to the above problem, this paper presents a positioning algorithm based on Virtual Beacon nodes (Virtual Beacon Localization, VBL), aimed at minimizing the accumulative errors caused by iteration and the power consumption caused by large amount of computation and communication. VBL algorithm evenly grids the localization region, and then combines with RSSI, closeness and Centroid to achieve positioning. This method does not need additional hardware, in the case of slightly increased computational complexity, it have greatly improved positioning accuracy and can be used in practical applications, especially in some special occasions.

2   Theoretical Foundation

2.1   Radio Signal Propagation Model

Many factors will cause positioning error in sensor nodes localization, the radio signal model is one of them, a good model can guarantee the accuracy of positioning, so it is important to choose the model. The existed models are obtained by modifying the ideal physical model; and Shadowing model, RIM model and Free - space model are commonly used models. Taking into account the presence of signal intensity in different directions of the irregularity cannot be ignored, so this paper choose the combination of the RIM model and Shadowing model [10]. RIM model:

$$K_i = \begin{cases} 1 & \text{if } i = 0 \\ K_{i-1} + Rand \times DIO & \text{if } (0 < i < 360 \, and \, \|K_0 - K_{359}\| \leq DOI) \, . \end{cases} \quad (1)$$

Shadowing model:

$$P_r = P_r(d_0) - 10 \times \beta log \frac{d}{d_0} + X_{db} \, . \quad (2)$$

then,

$$P_r = P_r(d_0) - 10 \times \beta log \frac{dK_i}{d_0} + X_{db} \, . \quad (3)$$

Pr(d) is signal strength at a distance d; Pr(d0) is signal strength at the reference distance d0; b is the path loss coefficient; Xdb is a Gaussian random distribution, Ki represents the loss coefficient from different directions path, DOI indicates the ratio of maximum path loss. The coordinates of virtual beacon nodes and beacon nodes are known, we can calculate d through formula 4, and calculate RSSI through formula 3.

$$d = \sqrt{(X_i - X_j)^2 + (Y_i - Y_j)^2} \, . \quad (4)$$

2.2   Grid Array

Through analyzing the literature, location accuracy can be increased through using the grid array. So the VBL algorithm will use the grid array. The communication distance of the sensor nodes is limited and the collected data need send to Sink node through the routing. So this paper will establish coordinate system and Sink node as the origin, then share the whole coordinate system, the grid side length is L. All the intersections are virtual beacon nodes, the coordinates of virtual nodes can be expressed as (n * L, m * L), where $n, m \in \mathbf{Z}$.

2.3   The Approach Degree

Degree is concepts of the fuzzy theory, describes the proximity of two fuzzy sets. This paper takes RSSI collection that the unknown nodes and virtual beacon nodes receive the signal strength from the beacon nodes as two fuzzy sets, A and B, then, uses degree to measure the similar degree. Taking into account the characteristics of wireless sensor networks, we use the biggest-smallest approach degree which has lower computational complexity.

Assuming that there are n beacon nodes and m virtual beacon nodes in the communication range of an unknown node, the unknown node will receive a group RSSI relative to beacon nodes, $R_S = (R_{S1}, R_{S2}, \cdots, R_{Sn})$; Similarly, there is a group RSSI: $R_g = (R_{g1}, R_{g2}, \cdots, R_{gn})$, for a virtual node.So equation 5 can be expressed:

$$Degree(R_s, R_g) = \frac{\sum_{i=1}^{n} min(R_{si}, R_{gi})}{\sum_{i=1}^{n} max(R_{si}, R_{gi})} . \tag{5}$$

Then calculate the degree between virtual beacon nodes and unknown nodes, and choose some virtual beacons which have highest degree as secondary beacon nodes.

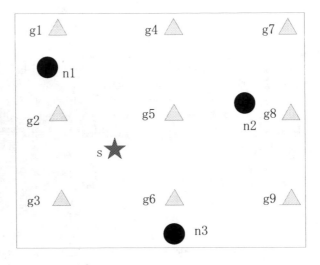

Fig. 1.

As shown in Figure 1, the black dot represents the beacon node, the triangle represents the virtual node, red five-pointed star represents unknown node. Calculate RSSI that virtual nodes (e.g. g_1) and unknown node s relative to beacon nodes n_1, n_2 and n_3; calculate $Degree(R_s, R_{g1})$ through formula 6, in the same way, the RSSI of g2, g3, g4, g5, g6, g7, g8 and g9 can be calculated, assuming threshold is 4, so select g2,g3,g5,g6 as secondary beacon nodes.

2.4   Preliminary Area

When there are more than three beacon nodes in the communication range of unknown node, the unknown node will record the order of beacon nodes, and group these beacon nodes. Assuming an unknown node successfully receives four beacon nodes, the order of these 4 nodes: A, B, C and D; the first group is ABC, and the corresponding signal strength are RSSI1, RSSI2 and RSSI3.

There are two cases position that unknown nodes relative to $\triangle ABC$: (1) Inside the triangle (2) outside the triangle:

Based on the PIT method to judge whether the unknown node inside the triangle: Assuming that s is unknown node, the points: s1, s2, s3, are the midpoint of the lines: AB, AC and BC. Coordinates of points A, B, C are known, so the coordinates of s1, s2, s3 can be simply calculation through midpoint formula, and then plug in formula 4 and 2 to calculate RSSI, and then respectively compare RSSI that s receives the signal of A, B, C. According to the theory of PIT: if one of points RSSI (s1, s2, s3) is bigger or smaller than unknown node RSSI, we argue that s outside the $\triangle ABC$, or inside. If node is outside $\triangle ABC$, the next triangle group will be judged until inside a triangle.

For the case that unknown node inside the triangle, as shown in figure 2, comparing the size of RSSI, if $RSSI1 \leq RSSI2, RSSI1 \leq RSSI3, RSSI2 \leq RSSI3$, the unknown node is in the shaded area in Figure 3, where E is the triangular circumventer.

Proof: using reduction to absurdity argument:

If the unknown node in I region, so $RSSI1 \leq RSSI2, RSSI1 \leq RSSI3, RSSI2 \geq RSSI3$, but with the known condition $RSSI2 \leq RSSI3$ contradictory,so unknown node is not in area I. Similarly, we can prove unknown node is not in area II, III, IV, V. Therefore unknown node is in the shaded area in Figure 2.

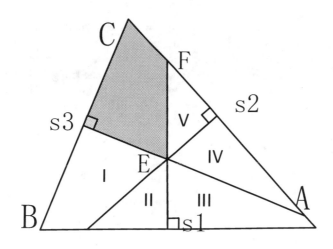

Fig. 2.

3 VBL Localization Scheme

3.1 Localization Scheme

For the problem of low positioning accuracy in WSN, a new positioning algorithm based on virtual beacon nodes is proposed. The basic idea is as follows:

when positioning an unknown node, it need send information to beacon nodes, then it will receive some packets which include RSSI from beacon nodes, and calculate the preliminary area of unknown node. The coordinates of virtual beacon nodes are known, so we can calculate RSSI that virtual nodes relative to beacon nodes, then select secondary beacon nodes, finally the centroid coordinate of these secondary beacon nodes is the location of unknown node.

3.2   Localization Algorithm Steps

a) Establish a coordinate system, and share the whole coordinate system;
b) Obtain preliminary area;
c) Calculate RSSI that virtual beacon nodes which are preliminary area in relative to beacon nodes;
d) Select secondary beacon nodes;
e) Calculate coordinate of unknown nodes through Centroid formula:

$$(x, y) = (\frac{x_1 + x_2 + \cdots + x_J}{J}, \frac{y_1 + y_2 + \cdots + y_J}{J}) . \tag{6}$$

3.3   Algorithm Analysis

The time complexity of this stage depends on triangle area which is composed of three beacon nodes, the bigger the triangle area, the more the virtual beacon nodes, and the higher the computation complexity.So we can use number of grids in shaded area to evaluate algorithm complexity, because the grid is composed of virtual beacon nodes. Assuming that node communication radius is R, the worst case is that unknown node is the external triangle. Assuming that unknown node in the shaded area, as shown in Figure 3, line CE parallel to the Y-axis coordinate, line DE parallel to the X-axis coordinate, the grid width is L, s1, s2, s3 are respective midpoint of line AB, AC, BC; The coordinates of A, B, C are $(X_a, Y_a), (X_b, Y_b), (X_c, Y_c) \rightarrow (X_{s2}, Y_{s2}) = (\frac{1}{2}(X_a + X_c), \frac{1}{2}(Y_a + Y_c)), (X_{s3}, Y_{s3}) = (\frac{1}{2}(Xc + Xb), \frac{1}{2}(Yc + Yb))$, the length of line DE is d1: $d1 = \|X_{s3} - X_c\| \rightarrow$ The area of the delta CES is S0: $S0 = \frac{1}{2}(R * d1) = \frac{1}{4}R * \|X_b - X_c\|$; because $R2 < ((X_b - X_c)^2 + (Y_b - Y_c)^2) < 4 * R2 \rightarrow S0 < \frac{1}{2}R2$, shaded area is S: $S < R2$, the grid area is L^2, $\rightarrow$the number of grid in shaded is $N : N < (\frac{R}{2L})^2$.

4   Performance Analysis and Simulation Results

4.1   Simulation Environment

To verify the performance of VBL algorithm, we use MATLAB7.13 for simulation. Using random deployment model, all the wireless sensor nodes are randomly distributed in region. there are 200 nodes which are randomly distributed in the $200m \times 200m$ square area. And DOI equals 0.1, J equals 10, b equals 5, dot represents the unknown node, star represents the SINK node, asterisk represents beacon node.

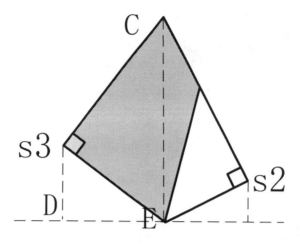

Fig. 3.

4.2 Experimental Results and Analysis

Under the condition of the signal transmission model, we compare VBL algorithm with Centroid[6] and RN-BP[12]. In actual situation of outdoor, the communication radius is between 50m and 100m. In average location error simulation, the radius is set to70m. The mean location error uses the formula (7), the actual coordinates of node is x_i, the estimated coordinate is x_i^*, and mean location error is A_{error}

$$A_{error} = \frac{1}{N} \sum_{i=1}^{N} \|x_i - x_i^*\| . \tag{7}$$

1) Centroid algorithm: unknown nodes receive three or more packets from beacon nodes, then, calculate the centroid of polygon that is composed of beacon nodes. The coordinates of the centroid of the polygon are the coordinates of unknown nodes. The algorithm is simple, but strict to the network, especially the proportion of beacon nodes.

2) RN-BP algorithm: it uses the characteristics of neural network, firstly estimates location of the unknown nodes, and then uses the virtual node which was trained in network with small error, if there is an unknown node that has the same hop with virtual node to beacon node, to upgrade the unknown node to beacon node. Re-train the network until all nodes are located.

4.2.1 Influence of Mesh Width on Mean Location Error

VBL algorithm uses a grid array coordinate system, so we observe the effect on mean location error by changing the mesh width in this section. Beacon nodes density is 20%. After running many times of VBL algorithm, the result as the figure 4 showsthat mean location error changes little when mesh width in 4m to 7m, but if continue to increase the width, the location start to appear serious deviation which is mainly due to the virtual nodes becoming sparse.

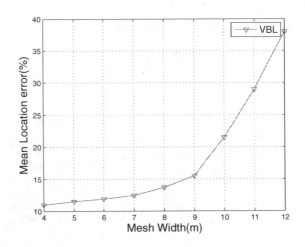

Fig. 4.

4.2.2   Influence of Beacon Nodes Ratio on Mean Location Error

In this section, we observe the effect on algorithm of RN-BPCentroidVBL by changing the ratio of beacon nodes. The beacon node varies in the range of 6% to 30%, the mesh width is 6m, the result as the figure 5 shows; with the increase of ratio of beacon nodes, mean location error of the three algorithms is reduced, the dependence of Centroid algorithm for beacon node is larger, so range error decreases quickly, but this make network costs increase greatly. While the other two algorithms dependent on the beacon nodes is not great, especially, the author proposed VBL algorithm, when the ratio is in range of 5% to 17%, VBL algorithm is better than RN-BP algorithm, and the decreasing of mean location error is not significant after the ratio is close to 16%.

4.2.3   Influence of Communication Radius on Mean Location Error

In this section, we observe the effect on mean location error in algorithms of RN-BPCentroid and VBL by changing radius. Communication radius varies in the range of 50m to 100m and the mesh width is 6m and beacon nodes ratio is 20%. After several simulations of the three algorithms, the result as the figure 6 shows that with the increase of radius, the location errors of the three algorithms are reduced, but after $R > 70m$, the location error of Centroid algorithm increases. Because the increase of radio cause more beacon nodes participate in operation, and all beacon nodes share the same weight when calculating the centroid coordinates, but beacon nodes are not uniform distribution. And because the increase of radio will make the maximum distance of a hop increase, and

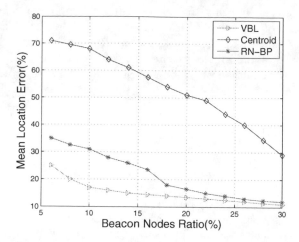

Fig. 5.

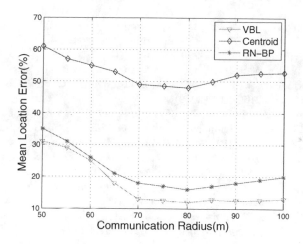

Fig. 6.

there will be error when algorithm selects virtual nodes in RN-BP algorithm. After $R > 70m$, mean location error of VBL algorithm has little change, because VBL selects secondary beacon nodes by comparing the RSSI.

5 Conclusion

Localization has been extensively studied by practices and theoreticians over the past decade. In this paper, VBL algorithm based on virtual beacon nodes is proposed, aimed at positioning accuracy problems. It combines RSSI and range-free positioning mechanism by using the biggest-smallest approach degree to calculate the coordinate of unknown nodes. Experiments show that VBL algorithm has better performance and is suitable for application in WSN. However the introduction of virtual nodes increase the network communication overhead, the maximum degree of reduction of traffic will be the next major work.

Acknowledgments. This research work was Supported by Beijing Natural Science Foundation (4132026,4122023).

References

1. Zeng, F.-Z., Sun, Z.-Z., Luo, J.: Improved node localization algorithm for wireless sensor network. Journal on Communications 29(11), 62–66 (2008)
2. Zaruba, G.V., Kamangar, F.A., Chlamtac, I.: Indoor location tracking using RSSI readings from a single Wi-Fi access point. Wireless Networks 13(2), 221–235 (2007)
3. Fujiwara, R., Mizugaki, K., Nakagawa, T., et al.: ToA/TDoA hybrid relative positional system using UWB-IR. IEEE Radio and Wireless Week 65, 679–682 (2009)
4. Malajner, M., Peter, P., Gleich, D.: Angle of Arrival Estimation Using RSSI and Omnidirectional Rotatable Antenas. IEEE Sensors Journal 12(6), 1950–1957 (2012)
5. Niculescu, D., Nath, B.: DV based positioning ad hoc networks. Journal of Telecommunication Systems 22(1), 267–280 (2003)
6. Zhang, D., Liu, F., Wang, L., Xiu, Y.: DV-HOP localization algorithms based on centroid in wireless sensor networks. In: Consumer Electronics, Communications and Networks, pp. 3216–3219 (2012)
7. Chiti, F., Pierucci, L.: APIT2: a bit of improvement for applications in critical scenarios. In: The 6th International Wireless Communications and Mobile Computing Conference, New York (2010)
8. Sun, K., Liu, R.-J.: BP localization algorithm based on virtual nodes in wireless sensor networks. Transducer and Technologies 29(9), 122–124 (2010)
9. Zhao, J., Pei, Q., Xu, Z.: APIT Localization Algorithms for Wireless Sensor Networks. Computer Engineering 33(5), 109–111 (2007)
10. Zhou, Q., Zhu, H.-S., Xu, Y.-J.: Smallest enclosing circle based localization approach for wireless sensor networks. Journal on Communications 29(11), 84–90 (2008)

Light-Weight Multi-channel Scheduling Algorithm for Industrial Wireless Networks with Mesh-Star Hybrid Topology

Pengxiang Ji[1], Wei Liang[2,*], Xiaoling Zhang[2], and Meng Zheng[2]

[1] Shenyang Ligong University, Shenyang 110159, China
Lab of Industrial Control Network and System[**], Shenyang Institute
of Automation, Chinese Academy of Sciences, Shenyang 110016, China
[2] Lab of Industrial Control Network and System, Shenyang Institute
of Automation, Chinese Academy of Sciences, Shenyang 110016, China
weiliang@sia.cn

Abstract. Industrial monitoring and control applications set strict real-time performance to industrial wireless networks. Transmission scheduling is one of the key technologies to guarantee the real-time performance of industrial wireless network. For the mesh-star topology, this paper first analyzes the lower limit of the required time slots and channels for completing transmission, and then designs a light-weight multi-channel real-time transmission scheduling algorithm. The simulation results show that the proposed algorithm yields better network performance in comparison to other scheduling algorithms, in terms of time overhead and throughput.

Keywords: Industrial wireless networks, WIA-PA, Transmission scheduling, Multi-channel.

1 Introduction

As wireless sensor network (WSNs) technologies are becoming more mature, research on WSNs has shifted from theoretical research to applications, where industrial wireless network is a representative example. At the same time, industrial applications require reliable and real-time data transmission for the deployed industrial wireless networks[1]. Due to the fact that multi-channel transmission scheduling can greatly improve network throughput and in the meanwhile effectively avoid communication conflicts, it currently becomes a hot spot topic in industrial wireless networks.

WIA-PA(Wireless Networks for Industrial Automation-Process Automation)[2] is developed for process automation of industrial wireless network specification in China, and becomes the second international wireless

---

* Corresponding author.
** Lab. of Networked Control Systems, Chinese Academy of Sciences, Shenyang 110016, China.

L. Sun, H. Ma, and F. Hong (Eds.): CWSN 2013, CCIS 418, pp. 281–292, 2014.

standard after WirelessHART, achieving 96% of the membership vote certification of the International Electrotechnical Commission (IEC). Different from WirelessHART, WIA-PA adopts the mesh-star (two-layer) hybrid network topology.

So far, there have been lots of works on multi-channel scheduling problem for mesh networks. In order to maximize the number of parallel transmission links subject to interference, the number of channels and interfaces constraints, Das A.K. et al.[3] put forward two mixed integer linear programming models for the static multi-channel scheduling problem. However, a feasible polynomial time algorithm is not given in Alicherry M. et al.[4] proposed a centralized routing joint channel assignment algorithm, whose disadvantage is the lack of consideration for sharing channels among conflicting links. Tang J. et al.[5] and Wang X. et al.[6] proposed a distributed joint routing and channel assignment algorithm, respectively. These methods may lead high routing maintenance rate and thus exhaustive overhead. Raniwala A. et al.[7] proposed a heuristic channel allocation strategy for multi-interface wireless mesh networks. According to a certain order, we color the edges in the graph based on the rule that selects the least used color within the conflict domain. Edge coloring algorithm is basically with a high algorithmic complexity since conditions , e.g., vacant interface and common channels, have to be considered. On the other hand, other scholars investigates the scheduling algorithm for networks with specific topologies. Zhang H. et al.[8] proposed an optimal link scheduling algorithm for convergence transmission in WirelessHART networks, which only works for line-cluster networks. Zhang X. et al.[9] proposed a two-stage transmission real-time scheduling algorithm, in which the lower limit of the needed time slot and channel numbers is analyzed, and the optimization scheduling of linear network and tree network is also realized.

In summary, highly dynamic industrial wireless channels as well as the rigorous real-time performance requirement imposed by industrial applications commonly leads highly complex solution method. In addition, current researches concentrates on structures such as mesh structure, line-clusters and tree clusters, and do not apply to the mesh-star hybrid network topology (i.e., WIA-PA). For this, this paper proposes a novel light-weight multi-channel scheduling algorithm for industrial wireless networks with mesh-star hybrid topology. The proposed algorithm could effectively avoid transmission conflictions, and reduce the complexity of the algorithm at the same time, which implies the easy implementation in practical applications. Finally, the verification of the algorithm and comparative analysis are done via simulations.

2   Analysis and Design of the Algorithm

2.1   Network Model

WIA-PA proposed by Chinese Wireless Industrial Networking Alliance is the sub-standard of WIA standard series. Based on the IEEE 802.15.4, WIA-PA defines the system structure and communication specification of WIA for process automation.

Five types of physical devices are defined in WIA-PA network standard[2]:

- Host computer: Computers used by users, maintenance personnel and management staff interacts with the WIA network;
- Gateway device: Devices that connect WIA network with other factory network equipment;
- Routing device: Devices which is responsible for field device management, packet forwarding, and other functions;
- Field device: Devices equipped with sensors or actuators, installed in the industrial field and connected directly to the production process;
- Handheld devices: Handheld portable devices to finish primary control.

WIA-PA network also defines the following two types of main logical devices[2]:

- Network Manager that is responsible for configuring the network, scheduling the communications of routing devices, managing the routing table, monitoring network performance;
- Security Manager that is responsible for the entire network security policy configuration, key management and device authentication.

The hybrid structure of a classic WIA-PA network is shown in Figure 1. The first layer is the mesh structure consisting of the gateway and routing devices. Network manager and security manager for system administration can be configured at the gateway or host computer; the second layer is the star structure, also known as cluster, which consists of routing devices, field devices and handheld devices. Routing devices in WIA-PA network undertake the function of cluster heads and field devices undertake the function of cluster member. The field devices are responsible for collecting and transmitting data through routing devices to the gateway, while routing devices and the gateway do not generate data.

2.2   Scheduling Model

Assuming all the nodes in the network have the same communication capability, any of the two nodes are classified as neighbor nodes if these nodes are within each other's communication range. Gateway, where the location information of each node and its neighbor nodes is stored, is charge of the transmission scheduling of the whole network. The mesh type network can be constructed as a undirected graph $G = (V, E)$ according to the graph theory, among which $V = \{GW, R, F\}$ means all the devices in the network; GW means Gateway; R means a set of all the routing devices; F means a collection of all the field devices; E is the collection of all the links in the network. Before the transmission starts, each field device is capable of producing up to a set of data, at the same time waits for the routing device forwards the data to the gateway. Routing topology $T = (V', E')$ according to the transmission path is proposed in this paper,

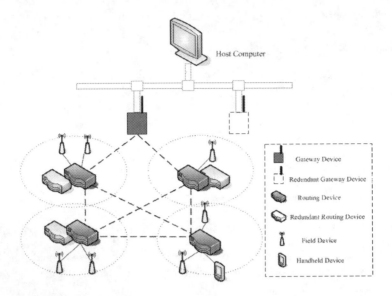

Fig. 1. An example of WIA-PA network with mesh-star hybrid topology

$V' \subseteq V$ means routing devices on the path and each routing device carries a set of field devices within the cluster, $E' \subseteq E$ means the path of transmission links.

According to the characteristics of network topological structure we analyse the requirement of time slot number and channel number for mesh-star network in this paper, and design network transmission scheduling algorithm based on the time slot number and channel number.

We set x_{ijt} indicates the activities at slot t. If the device i sends data to the device j in the time slot t, then $x_{ijt} = 1$, otherwise $x_{ijt} = 0$. $I(i)$ and $O(i)$ represent the set of link that enter and leave the device i respectively. $p_t(i)$ represents the cache space of the device i after the end of the time slot t, and sets $p_0 = 1$. g_{ij} represents in a period, the number of the message in the cluster which the routing device R_{ij} as the cluster head. T means the frame length as units of time slots. Most of the work for industrial wireless sensor network using multi-channel communication now. For efficiently using on resources of frequency rationally, the optimizing of time slots and channels (i.e., to obtain as few as possible the number of time slots and channels to complete the entire network transmission) must be satisfied by transmission scheduling algorithm simultaneously. Based on the above symbol definitions, we achieve the following optimized transmission scheduling model for time slots and channels.

The objective function:

$$minimize \ T \tag{1}$$

$$minimize \ C = \max_{t \in [0,T]} \sum_{(i,j) \in E'} x_{ijt} \tag{2}$$

The constraints:

$$\sum_{(j,i)\in I(i)} x_{jit} + \sum_{(i,j)\in O(i)} x_{ijt} \leq 1, \forall i \in V, \forall t \in [0, L] \tag{3}$$

$$p_L(GW) = \sum_{i,j} g_{ij} \tag{4}$$

$$p_t(i) = p_{t-1}(i) + \sum_{(j,i)\in I(i)} x_{jit} - \sum_{(i,j)\in O(i)} x_{ijt}, \forall i \in V, \forall t \in [0, L] \tag{5}$$

$$x_{ijt} \in \{0, 1\}, \forall (i, j) \in E' \tag{6}$$

Among them, the formula (1) is super-frame length to minimize. C in the formula (2) represents the number of channels used, which equals to the number of devices for parallel transmission in network. The formula (3) is half-duplex limitation that forbids devices sending and receiving data simultaneously. The formula (4) represents that the field devices have produced all packets forwarded to the gateway after a superframe period. The formula (5) represents the message storage state and the update cache space. The formula (6) identifies the link status at each time slot.

2.3 Analysis of Time Slot Number and Channel Number in Mesh-Star Hybrid Topology

Analysis of Time Slot Number. Each routing node in the mesh network has a depth in the routing graph. The depth is defined as the minimum number of hops from a device to the gateway device. Supposing the entire network time is synchronized, one-time data transmission is permitted in a time slot. Each device in the network is equiped with half-duplex SISO radio transceiver. Therefore, we need to meet the constraints that devices can not simultaneously send and receive data when designing transmission scheduling policy. At the same time, it is required that devices should use different channels to complete transmission simultaneously to avoid conflicts in a same time slot. According to the above conditions, the transmission formula of time slot number as follows:

$$Ts = F_{r1} + 2\sum_{i=2}^{N} F_{ri} \tag{7}$$

Which i is an integer, F_{ri} means that the number of field devices within the cluster of the routing device nearest to gateway, F_{ri} represents the number of field devices within the cluster of the depth of i routing device.

In the network, R_1 responsible for completing the two tasks: 1) Forwarding (receive and transmit) data from other routing devices; 2) Send data generated within the cluster itself to the gateway. R_1 forwarding the data transmitted by R_2 requires $2\sum_{i=2}^{N} F_{ri}$ time slots at least; R_1 sending data in the cluster itself to

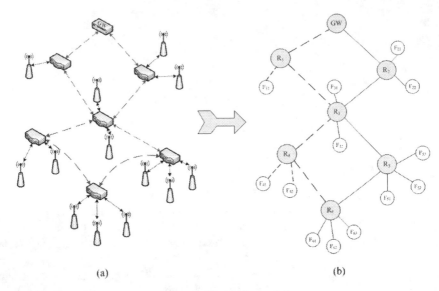

(a)   (b)

Fig. 2. Network model

the gateway requires F_{r1} time slots at least. Therefore, in a superframe period, the minimum number of time slots to complete a single path transmission is the two cumulative numbers of time slots.

Figure (2) shows the network configuration diagram of a mesh network topology with WIA-PA as the prototype, which defines the solid line is a routing path that is a depth of 4 routing device R_4 as the starting point in Figure 2(b). Analysis the routing nodes R_2 closest to gateway in path ρ, all the data on the entire path through R_2 are required to forward to the gateway, so the number of time slots to complete the transfer consumed by R_2 equal to the number of time slots for the full path to complete transmission. In addition to R_2 forwarding the data carried in the cluster itself to the gateway device, forwards the data transmitted from R_3, R_5, R_6 the summation of two parts is the number of time slots required to complete the transfer in path ρ.

$$Ts = F_{r2} + 2 \times (F_{r3} + F_{r5} + F_{r6}) \tag{8}$$

$F_{r2}, F_{r3}, F_{r5}, F_{r6}$ represent respectively the the number of field devices within the cluster carried by R_2, R_3, R_5, R_6.

Analysis of Channel Number. Due to the constraints of SISO RF chip, the maximum number of channels which is required for two devices communicate with each other under the same path:

$$Ch = \max \left(\left\{ \begin{array}{ll} \frac{R_N+1}{2} & N = 2k-1(k=1,2,3...,n) \\ \frac{R_N}{2} & N = 2k(k=1,2,3...,n) \end{array} \right. , C \right) \tag{9}$$

R_N means the number of routing devices in this path.

Thus we come to the conclusion that the routing topology and resource allocation strategies of path ρ in Figure 3.

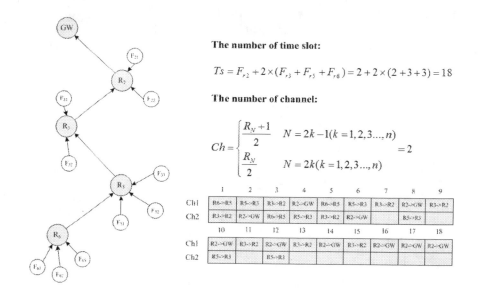

The number of time slot:

$$Ts = F_{r2} + 2 \times (F_{r3} + F_{r5} + F_{r6}) = 2 + 2 \times (2 + 3 + 3) = 18$$

The number of channel:

$$Ch = \begin{cases} \dfrac{R_N + 1}{2} & N = 2k - 1 (k = 1, 2, 3 \dots, n) \\ \dfrac{R_N}{2} & N = 2k (k = 1, 2, 3 \dots, n) \end{cases} = 2$$

	1	2	3	4	5	6	7	8	9
Ch1	R6->R5	R5->R3	R3->R2	R2->GW	R6->R5	R5->R3	R3->R2	R2->GW	R3->R2
Ch2	R3->R2	R2->GW	R6->R5	R5->R3	R3->R2	R2->GW		R5->R3	

	10	11	12	13	14	15	16	17	18
Ch1	R2->GW	R3->R2	R2->GW	R3->R2	R2->GW	R3->R2	R2->GW	R2->GW	R2->GW
Ch2	R5->R3		R5->R3						

Fig. 3. An example on resource allocation for mesh topology

It is not difficult to find that the dotted line (i.e. path σ) in Figure 2(b) include the routing device R_3 existing in path ρ. During the transmission of path σ, R_3 plays a forwarding role uniquely, because the data within the cluster of R_3 has been transmitted already. Path σ , according to the above method, is similar to the path ρ s that generates resource allocation strategies and these two strategies are merged together to generate the entire network scheduling scheme that is distributed by the gateway eventually.

As is vividly depicted in the scheduling policy, once a path is chosen, the data on the path will be transmitted completely. Therefore, the principle to build a routing path is to select the deepest depth of the routing device, which acts as the starting device to reduce the number of paths in the overall network. This strategy enables saving the limited channel resources, inproving the transmission efficiency of the entire network.

2.4   Algorithm Implementation

According to the above analysis about the number of time slots and channels, we design a novel algorithm for path searching. The core of the algorithm includes:

- Determine the routing device which has the maximum number of hops away from the gateway and transmission path 1.

– According to the preceding analysis of the structure, calculation of the required time slot and channel number.
– The search algorithm based on path deposit the full path scheduling into the resource allocation table; if there is multiple paths in the network, following the same method to generate path $2 \sim N$ scheduling, and dispatching all scheduling merged into the network resource allocation table eventually. Gateway releases the scheduling result.

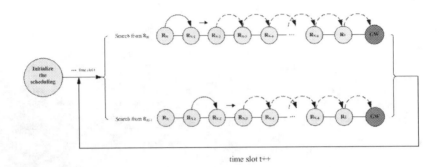

Fig. 4. Searching process

The general steps of algorithm are as follows:

1. Initialize $G = \emptyset$;
2. According to the neighbor table to determine the maximum number of hops routing device R_N ;
3. R_N is the starting device to determine the transmission path;
4. Initialize the number of time slots Ts and the number of channel Ch ;
5. Judge whether the time slot number t is greater than Ts, if true distribute the transmission scheduling results, or start to search the device which begin transmitting;
6. As shown in figure 4, at a certain time slot t, if the transmission device is R_N, $R_N \Rightarrow R_{N-1}$ occupies one channel, and then we check successively whether or not R_{N-2}, R_{N-3} ... R_1 send or forward to gateway directions, if $R_i(i \in [1, N]$) sending or forwarding, then $R_i \Rightarrow R_{i-1}$ ocuppies the next channel. We continue to search from R_{i-2} to gateway directions and so on until the completion of the parallel transmission at this time slot or the number of channels greater than or equal Ch, and then the next time slot allocates in the same manner. Otherwise we check successively whether or not R_{N-3}, R_{N-4} ... R_1 send or forward from R_{N-1};
7. At last, if t is larger than Ts, then the proof is complete this scheduling and the result will be distributed by the gateway.

The flow chart of the above algorithm is shown in figure 5.

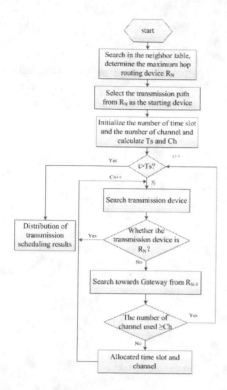

Fig. 5. Flow chart

3   Simulation

The performance of multi-channel scheduling algorithm analysed by Matlab simulation software, and we makes a comparison with WirelessHART centralized transmission scheduling[8] and a classic centralized channel edge coloring algorithm proposed by paper[7] on time overhead and network throughput. The Parameters in simulation is shown in Table 1.

Table 1. Parameters in simulation

Simulation Parameters	value
Packet length	128byte
Scope of network topology	$100 \times 100 m^2$
Number of channel	16
Length of time slots	31.25ms
Maximum number of network hops	Variable
Transmission power	15.16mw
Received power	35.28mw

The transmission scheduling algorithm reduces 6 to 8 times to complete transmission scheduling time overhead compared with WirelessHART centralized approach; although edge coloring algorithm has a good rapidity, it spends a certain amount of computation time on routing identification and judgment on coloring, the time cost of the algorithm is also higher nearly 1 times than the algorithm in this paper. Therefore, this algorithm significantly saves network resources, and is proved the feature of light and rapid.

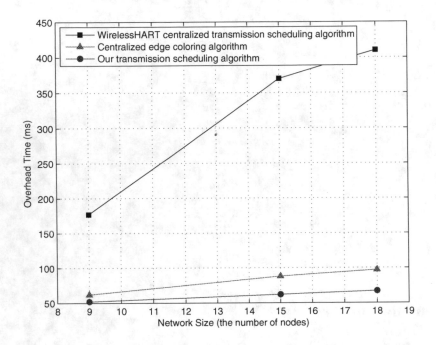

Fig. 6. Comparison of time overhead

In comparison of network throughput shown in Figure 7, it can be seen as the network size increases, the network throughput of proposed algorithm and centralized edge coloring algorithm stabilize at an average of around 20Mbps. However average throughout of our algorithm is obviously higher than that of centralized edge coloring algorithm, due to the maximum utilization of the available transmission channel. Compared to the WirelessHART centralized transmission scheduling algorithm, our algorithm is higher than 4 to 5 times. It is noticeable that the algorithm presented in this paper lowers time overhead , and obains the ideal network throughput as well.

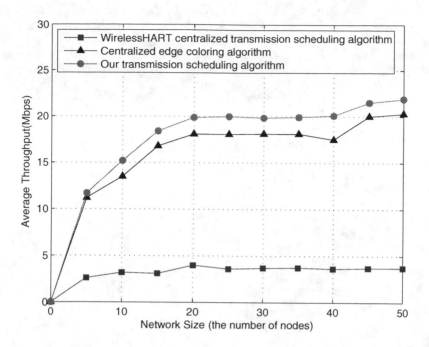

Fig. 7. Comparison of average throughput

4   Conclusion

For mesh-star industrial wireless networks, this paper for the first time analyzes the lower limit of the number of required time slots and channels for completing periodical transmission. In addition, a light-weight multi-channel scheduling algorithm that guarantees real-time transmissions is also proposed. Simulation shows that the time overhead of the algorithm is reduced and the efficiency of data transmission is improved, in comparison to other scheduling algorithms.

Acknowledgements. This work was supported by the Natural Science Foundation of China under contact (61174026, 61304263), the National High Technology Research and Development Program of China (863 Program: 2011AA040101), and Strategic Priority Research Program of the Chinese Academy of Sciences (XDA06020402).

References

1. Sun, D., Cao, J., Zheng, J.: A Cluster Routing Algorithm of WSN for Industrial Measurement and Control. Information and Control 41(6), 779–785 (2012)
2. Liang, W., Zhang, X., et al.: Survey and Experiments of WIA-PA Specification of Industrial Wireless Network. Wiley Wireless Communications and Mobile Computing 11(8), 1197–1212 (2011)

3. Das, A.K., Alazemi, H.M.K., Vijayakumar, R., et al.: Optimization Models for Fixed Channel Assignment in Wireless Mesh Networks with Multiple Radios. In: Proc. of IEEE SECON. IEEE Computer Society, Santa Clara (2005)
4. Alicherry, M., Bhatia, R., Li, E.: Joint Channel Assignment and Routing for Thoughput Optimization in Multi-radio Wireless Network. IEEE Journal on Selected Areas in Communications 24(11), 1960–1971 (2006)
5. Tang, J., Xue, G., Zhang, W.: Interference Aware Topology Control and QoS Routing in Multi-channel Wireless Networks. In: MobiHoc 2005, USA (2005)
6. Wang, X., Garcia-Luna-Aceves, J.J.: Distributed Joint Channel Assignment, Routing and Scheduling for Wireless Mesh Networks. Computer Communications 31(7), 1436–1446 (2008)
7. Raniwala, A., Gopalan, K., Chiueh, T.: Centralized Channel Assignment and Routing Algorithms for Multi-Channel Wireless Mesh Networks. Mobile Computing and Communications Review 8(2), 50–65 (2004)
8. Zhang, H., Soldati, P., Johansson, M.: Optimal Link Scheduling and Channel Assignment for Convergecast in Linear WirelessHART Networks. In: The 7th International Symposium on Modeling and Optimization in Mobile, Ad Hoc, and Wireless Networks (WiOPT 2009), Seoul, Korea, pp. 1–8 (2009)
9. Zhang, X., Liang, W., Yu, H.: Two-stage and real-time scheduling algorithm for converge cast in wireless sensor networks. Control and Decision 27(5), 761–767 (2012)

Digital Greenhouse System via WSN*

Zhikui Chen and Jian Zou

School of Software Technology,
Dalian University of Technology
116621 Dalian, China
zkchen@dlut.edu.cn, jan.tsou@gmail.com

Abstract. The paper designs an agricultural digital greenhouse system via Zigbee+GPRS. Environmental sensors and CC2530 RF chip as the core designs a series of nodes collecting information in greenhouses. These nodes generate networks based on ZigBee protocol, Environmental parameters and real-time images upload to a centralized monitoring host for analysis, storage and display via GPRS. In order to improve the network stability and extend the life of the network, this paper uses SDT algorithm to avoid redundant data transmission, and optimizes image acquisition through the frame difference method. The objective of the study, can change the straightforward way of greenhouse crops, achieve accurate, intensive, intelligent cultivation, increase production, reduce cost, and promote the WSN application in the field of agriculture.

Keywords: Digital Greenhouse, ZigBee, CC2530, SDT, WSN.

1   Introduction

Wireless Sensor Network (WSN), a combination of sensor technology, embedded computing technology, modern networking, wireless communication technology and distributed information processing technology, is widely used in the agricultural greenhouse, through various integrated micro-sensors to monitor real-time collaboration, perceive and collect a variety of environments or monitor objects [1].

Agricultural greenhouses can grow a variety of vegetables and fruits, while not subject to seasonal constraints. inside carbon dioxide concentration, temperature, humidity and light intensity directly affect the growth of plants, besides greenhouses are generally not set up in urban areas, which leads to the high cost of human duty and weakness of real-time, requiring remote monitoring greenhouse environment parameters and real-time images. Zhang Qibo etc. designed the remote AD590-based digital display temperature measurement and control instrument [2]. Li et al. designed ZigBee and embedded system based greenhouse temperature monitoring system [3]. Li Mingjun who used GPRS communication technology designed the greenhouses intelligent monitoring system [4].

* The Natural Science Foundation of Liaoning Province of China under Grant No.2013020014.

L. Sun, H. Ma, and F. Hong (Eds.): CWSN 2013, CCIS 418, pp. 293–302, 2014.
© Springer-Verlag Berlin Heidelberg 2014

those systems, achieved remote monitoring, had their own strengths with different technical methods, but did not explain the actual problems encountered while deploying and solutions, For example, in large-scale deployment of nodes, how to solve data congestion problem, how to upload pictures to use less traffic and not occupy the bandwidth heavily. GPRS is relatively narrow bandwidths, the system should ensure that the most useful data prior to upload.

This paper first introduces carbon dioxide concentration acquisition node and temperature-humidity acquisition node and light intensity acquisition node design, and then summarizes the approaches to reduce power consumption and to optimize the network, and finally discuss how to implement remote monitoring.

2   System Design and Implementation

The system, using a ZigBee protocol [5] widely used in WSN and drawing on experiences in domestic and international agricultural digital greenhouse system, designs system architecture shown in Figure 1, where E1, E2 represent information collection node, including carbon dioxide concentration and temperature and humidity, etc. some routing nodes can be properly deployed if necessary.

According to ZigBee protocol stack architecture [6], this system can be divided into three layers, the sensing layer can be thought of IEEE 802.15.4 MAC layer protocol and physical layer is responsible for collecting information and send to coordinator node (the routing node may be routed through), which forwards the data to the gateway, the gateway extract useful data added greenhouses unique information to sent to the monitoring host, which puts the data into the appropriate location for remote viewing based on the greenhouses information.

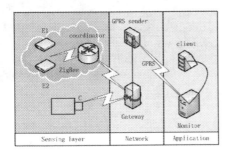
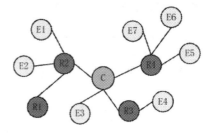

Fig. 1. System framework   Fig. 2. Topology structure

ZigBee network in this system includes a coordinator node, some routing nodes and data collection nodes. Routing nodes simply responsible for the data transfer can be removed if the greenhouse area is not large, furthermore, the controlling nodes, such as ventilation control, humidification control, etc, only need to connect a digital switch, will not be described here. The paper talks about the hardware and software design and implementation only for the coordinator node and data collection nodes.

2.1   Coordinate Node

ZigBee as an ad hoc network has a clear distinction with WiFi, which has huge energy consumption and weakly supports for multi-hop, WiFi networks usually setup for star structures, while ZigBee has a wide range of simple routing algorithms and fast data transmission features [7], and more for the structure shown in Figure 2, where C is representative of the coordinator node, Ri represents the routing nodes, Ei represents the data collection nodes.

In a ZigBee network, each node has two addresses, a 64-bit IEEE extended address and a 16-bit network address [8] which is allocated by the parent node in the network when the node joins. The short address effective internal is used to maintain the network structure, while the 64-bit long address is the modifiable hardware address, an external unique identifier for the node.

Each parent node can connect upto C_m child nodes, in which R_m sub-routing nodes exist at most; the maximum depth of the network is L_m. When a data acquisition node without routing functionality comes to the network, the depth of its parent is d, and the node is nth child, then the node's short address A_n can be calculated according to formula (1) [9], where A_k is the parent node's address, $Cskip(d)$ indicates address offset that the parent node with depth of d assigns to its child.

When a routing node joins the network, its network address An is calculated according to formula (2) [9]. In the formula (1), (2) the $Cskip(d)$ is calculated by the equation (3) [9].

$$A_n = A_k + Cskip(d) \times R_m + n \tag{1}$$

$$A_n = A_k + 1 + Cskip(d) \times (n - 1) \tag{2}$$

$$Cskip(d) = \begin{cases} 1 + C_m \times (L_m - d - 1) & , if R_m = 1 \\ \frac{1 + C_m - R_m - C_m \times R_m^{L_m - d - 1}}{1 - R_m} & , otherwise \end{cases} \tag{3}$$

According to the formula (1), (2), (3) the system calculates the communication address of each node. The coordinator node records all of the addresses in the network to maintain the dynamic changes of the network to ensure that the data collected is sent correctly to the application layer.

2.2   Carbon Dioxide Concentration Acquisition Node

(1) Hardware Structure

Part circuit of the carbon dioxide concentration node shown in diagram 3 includes CC2530 RF chip, MG811 carbon dioxide concentration sensor (amplified output signal), the power supply circuit and a reset circuit. MG811 output analog signal to the ports P0, CC2530 obtains the digital correlation values of the carbon dioxide concentration through a build-in analog-digital converter. MG811 solid electrolyte sensor is working properly when core temperature grows up to 500 degrees, while the kernel and the surrounding air is in direct contact, so the ambient temperature changes can affect the sensitivity of the sensor, and tCOM port is used to solve the problem of the temperature compensated output.

The data sheet of MG811 writes that this type of CO_2 sensor has good sensitivity and selectivity; is weakly affected by temperature and humidity changes; has good stability and reproducibility. MG811 is a solid electrolyte sensor, whose signal output impedance is very high, which means it is not a good idea to measure the output signal directly with the common voltmeter or multimeter. Add a termination impedance conversion circuit in the sensor output signal level when designing, which can reduce the output impedance to normal measurable level, the impedance conversion op amp must use high input impedance type, say CA3140.

(2) Software Design

Figure 4 shows the relationship between EMF and the concentration of carbon dioxide with a temperature of 28, relative humidity of 65%, and an oxygen concentration of 21%, wherein EMP represents the potential difference between the sensitive electrode and the reference electrode, the variable is in accordance with the Nernst equation:

$$EMP = E_c - (R \times T)/(2F) \ln^{P(CO_2)} \tag{4}$$

$P(CO_2)$ shows the carbon dioxide partial pressure, E_c is a constant, R is the gas constant, T is the absolute temperature, F is the Faraday constant.

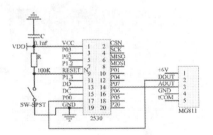
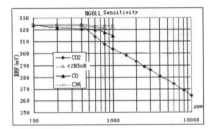

Fig. 3. Circuit diagram of the carbon dioxide concentration acquisition node

Fig. 4. MG811 Sensitivity

MG811 output is an analog signal (amplified) 0V~2V, from Figure 4 (the original signal) can be seen the lower the concentration the higher the output voltage. Generally normal clean air contains CO_2 350ppm. In order to get a more accurate value, the system need MG811 temperature compensation output, when the ambient temperature changes, the output voltage signal changes therewith, which means the temperature change amount is converted to the corresponding output voltage variation, and thus through the program to compensate for the temperature change.

2.3   Temperature and Humidity Acquisition Node

(1) Hardware Structure

Part circuit of temperature and humidity acquisition node shown in Figure 5 comprises CC2530 RF chip, SHT11 temperature and humidity sensors, power supply circuit and a reset circuit. SHT11 using I2C interface, where VDD is the power input with the scope of 2.4V~5.5V, GND is ground, SCK is the serial clock input, connected with the CC2530 SCK, DATA is the serial data line, two-way transmission. As long as add I2C interface program to the CC2530, the system can collect temperature and humidity.

(2) Software Design

SHT11 requires a timing sequence Start Transfer shown in Figure 6 before sending a command: When SCK is high DATA toggles low, followed by SCK goes low, then DATA flip to high with high SCK. After that the address code and instructions are required, the address currently only can be 000, temperature directive 00011, humidity directive 00101, followed by the 8th SHT11 SCK clock after whose falling edge the DATA drops down (ACK bit) until the 9th SCK clock falling edge (recovery high), indicating that the command has been completely sent, the rest is waiting for data to return. If necessary, reset the connection according to the timing sequence shown in Figure 7.

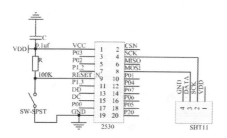

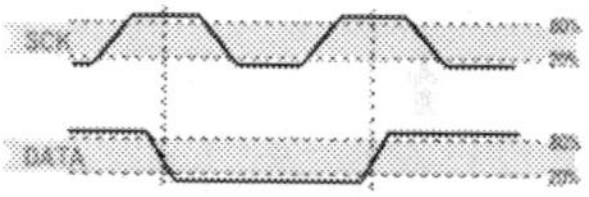

Fig. 6. Start Transfer

Fig. 5. Circuit diagram of the temperature and humidity acquisition node

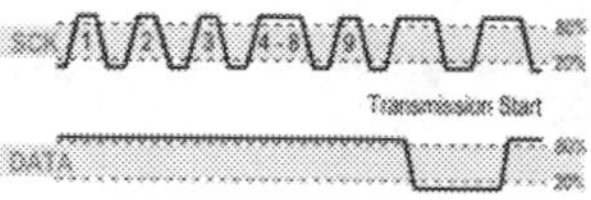

Fig. 7. Reset sequence

2.4 Light Intensity Acquisition Node

(1) Hardware Structure

Part circuit of light intensity acquisition node shown in diagram 8 comprises CC2530 RF chip, TSL2550 light intensity sensor, the power supply circuit and a reset circuit. TSL2550 uses SMBus interface, where VDD is the power input with the scope of 2.7V~5.5V, GND is ground, SMBCLK is the serial clock input connected to the CC2530 P0.0 pin, SMBData is a two-way transmission data line. the system can capture the light intensity, adding SMBus interface code the CC2530.

(2) Software Design

TSL2550 is a kind of light sensor with two wired digital output, a built-in 8-bit command register is used to configure the sensor with the command format shown in Figure 9, where S and P represent the start and end, WR is 0, A represents ACK . In addition, TSL2550 has two read-only data registers, which memorize channel 0 and channel 1 collected light intensity separately, users read channel 0 (1) need to set the command register 0x43 (0x83), read data command format is shown in Figure 10, where RD is 1.

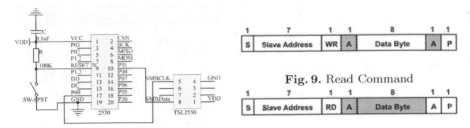

Fig. 8. Circuit diagram of the light intensity acquisition node

Fig. 9. Read Command

Fig. 10. Write Command

3   Reducing Power Consumption and Network Optimization

So far, the system has been able to work correctly, but once mass nodes deployed, the system will encounter problems of network congestion and power consumption, the following will describe how to overcome these problems and ensure the normal operation of agricultural greenhouses.

3.1   Utilizing SDT Algorithm to Avoid the Redundant Data Transmission

It is obvious that environmental parameters in the shed are actually process data, that contains a lot of redundant information, which information loss will not affect the overall distribution of data and trends, and then there is no need to spread in the network, a way affect network bandwidth, the other increase the pressure of the coordinator node. For example, a one-hour time change of the temperature in the greenhouse is actually not very large, but does not rule out a sudden change, which means it should ensure those significant changes in the data uploaded successfully but imperceptible changes discarded.

In this paper, the idea of SDT algorithm [10] is used to avoid redundant data transmission. SDT algorithm is a compression algorithm with linear trend, for a given data, first specify the maximum permissible errors, such as temperature error is 0.3, and then locate the trend line as long as possible, so when the temperature and humidity collection node returns the temperature, compare with the last upload, if the error is less than 0.3, discard the data after collection or else upload temperature, meanwhile refresh the temperature profile with the collection about the last upload, reserved for the next reference.

Figure 11 shows the effect of using SDT to avoid the transfer of redundant data in one hour, where a red dot indicates the temperature taken every minute, and blue represents the actual temperature uploaded, each covers a red point, so there are 60 red dots and 32 blue dots, then the actual amount of data transferred only 53% of the original, greatly reducing the pressure on the network. Of course, the actual efficiency of the method and pace of environmental change has a direct relationship, if the environment changes dramatically (greenhouse rarely encountered), this method is not very obvious; but if the environment changes slowly (in most cases this is) the method effect is quite significant.

3.2 Utilizing Frame Difference Method to Reduce the Image Transmission

The system uses GPRS to upload real-time images, but in the actual process, uploading an image in regular intervals will be bandwidth-intensive, which will affect other environmental parameters upload for inherently narrow bandwidth of GPRS, taking advantage of inter-frame difference method which get rid of the image frame not changed obviously can reduce the amount of data uploading.

Frame difference method [11] first determines a grayscale threshold T, then the formula (5) is calculated to get binary image $D(x, y, t_i)$, where (x, y) represents pixel, $F(x, y, t_i)$ represents the pixel in the gray value at time t_i.

Then, using equation (6), the equation (7) calculate the accumulated value sum and the cumulative num of the motion area, to obtain the mean gray level difference $avg = sum/num$, then upload the image when avg is greater than the error threshold T_{avg} and update $F(x, y, t_{i-1})$, or else do not have to upload the image.

$$D(x, y, t_i) = \begin{cases} 0 & , |F(x, y, t_i) - F(x, y, t_{i-1})| < T \\ 255 & , |F(x, y, t_i) - F(x, y, t_{i-1})| \geq T \end{cases} \tag{5}$$

$$sum = \begin{cases} sum + |F(x, y, t_i) - F(x, y, t_{i-1})| & , D(x, y, t_i) = 255 \\ sum & , D(x, y, t_i) = 0 \end{cases} \tag{6}$$

$$num = \begin{cases} num + 1 & , D(x, y, t_i) = 255 \\ num & , D(x, y, t_i) = 0 \end{cases} \tag{7}$$

3.3 Using Active Transport to Reduce the Query

In the process of data collection program query response mechanism is commonly used, namely, data collection node always listens air signal for the requests from the coordinator node, then performs data acquisition and replies to the coordinator node, after that gets into the listening state again, reason for doing this is by reducing computation amount of data collection nodes to reduce power consumption, however, in the system with real-time requirements that increases the coordinator query data packets, which gives the coordinator node too much pressure.

Aimed at the situation above, the flowchart shown in Figure 12 is designed for the data acquisition nodes, compared with the query response mechanism the program increases the collection times, but thanks to the approach in section 3.1 , the system not only does not increase the number of packets in the network, but also leaves the network more fluently because of removing the regular query program in the coordinator node; in addition, the method of using the hardware timer interrupt to trigger data acquisition saves excessive loss of energy.

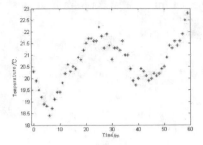

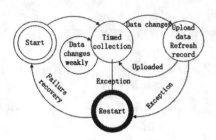

Fig. 11. Effect of utilizing SDT algorithm to avoid the redundant data transmission

Fig. 12. Data acquisition node work flowchart

4   Teleprocessing Monitor

First, open a remote host port (non-80 port) for GPRS upload data, each shed has a GPRS transmitter node for uploading real-time environmental parameters and images, these uploaded data package contains the unique identifier of the greenhouse character, when the remote host receives the packet, the identifier will be extracted and bind to the TCP connection which received the packet. If there is a previously bind, but different from the new connection (GPRS reconnection), the system releases the bound TCP connection and creates a new bind between the identifier and the accepted TCP connection. With this binding relationship, the remote host can send arbitrary commands to arbitrary greenhouses, such as ventilation, humidification. Figure 13 and Figure 14 is physical pictures of data acquisition nodes.

Users authenticated to access the remote host can see the information of their own greenhouses (the user has been registered by greenhouse identifier), for example, a user registered three greenhouses where planted strawberries, vegetables and pineapple separately, then he will see the screen shown in Figure 13, which includes selection buttons left of the greenhouses (vegetable is selected), and the live image and environmental parameters in the middle, as well as the control buttons right side (currently vegetable greenhouse is heating up and adding carbon dioxide).

5   Comparison and Analysis

Agricultural digital greenhouses can provide people vegetables and fruits regardless of seasons, it is a life-changing paradigm, and what makes it different from traditional greenhouses is that it can save human resources, people at work can feel the joy of farming at the same time, and this system compared with other similar systems has the following characteristics:

(1)Low cost, low power consumption All nodes used are of modular design, the deployment amount can be specified according to the size of the greenhouses,

Fig. 13. Temperature and humidity node

Fig. 14. Carbon dioxide concentration node

Fig. 15. Overall effect screenshots

data acquisition using the interrupt mode, reducing the number of queries, cutting the ZigBee protocol stack by removing some of the complexity not commonly used, can reduce power consumption as much as possible, making the network run more smoothly and long lasting.

(2)Multi-function integration The system can not only collect temperature, humidity, light intensity and carbon dioxide concentration, but also real-time images, allowing users to keep abreast of greenhouses state. In addition users can connect to the server through the greenhouses binding way, which allows users to control greenhouse environment remotely, eliminating the tedious manual operation. So many features can be integrated together is one of the characteristics of the system.

(3)Deploy a larger scale Using the idea of SDT algorithm creates more intelligent data acquisition node so that it can independently determine whether the data is uploaded, thereby reducing data transmission frequency, which greatly optimizes network performance, so that the network can accommodate naturally the number of nodes increase, by contrast, the system can be deployed in greater greenhouses in agriculture.

(4)Real-time feature Considering the cost of the long-distance wireless communication, GPRS is a reasonable choice only, but low bandwidth leads the transmission of video basically unrealistic, transferring images which in turn produces the real-time constraints, from this viewpoint, in this paper, inter-frame difference method is capability of both low cost and real-time.

6   Conclusion and Prospect

In this paper, ZigBee technology, GPRS network and B/S mode are used to build a digital greenhouse system to achieve environmental acquisition, image acquisition and remote monitoring capabilities, meeting the requirements on low-cost and automated agriculture, but the system also have sustainable space of development, such as applying 3G/4G technology to provide more comprehensive data services, converting the image acquisition into a video capture; introduction of agricultural research parameters, so that the greenhouse can automatically adjust to fit the greenhouse crop growth, reducing labor participation; increasing the data collection nodes to gain more refined figures and so on.

References

1. Li, C., Hailing, J., Yong, M., et al.: Overview of Wireless Sensor Networks. Journal of Computer Research and Development 42(1), 163–174 (2005)
2. Qibo, Z., Zhongwu, L., Fengzhi, P., et al.: Digital Display Equipment for Long-Distance Monitoring and Controlling Temperature of Greenhouse. Journal of Jilin Agricul Tural University 21(1), 80–82 (1999)
3. Lili, L., Wei, S.: Design of Embedded Wireless Temperature Control System for Agricultural Greenhouse. Chinese Agricultural Science Bulletin 27(33), 278–282 (2011)
4. Mingjun, L., Wenming, Y.: Intelligent Monitoring System via GPRS. Application of Electronic Technique 32(8), 83–85 (2006)
5. Wang, N., Zhang, N.Q., Wang, M.H.: Wireless sensors in agriculture and food industry–recent development and future perspective. Computers and Electronics in Agriculture 50(1), 1–14 (2006)
6. Bakey, N.: ZigBee and Bluetooth strengths and weaknesses for industrial applications. Computing & Control Engineering Journal 16(2), 20–25 (2005)
7. Ming, G.: zigBee Routing Protocol. Zhengzhou Henan. Information Engineering University (June 2006)
8. Marsden, I.: NetworkLayerOverviewEB/OL (October 5, 2009), http://www.zigbee.org/en/events/documellts
9. Ran, P., Sun, M.-H., Zou, Y.-M.: ZigBee Routing Selection Strategy Based on Data Services and Energy-balanced ZigBee Routing. In: IEEE Asia-Pacific Conference on Services Computing, APSCC 2006. IEEE (2006)
10. Mah, R.S.H.: Process Trending with Piecewise Linear Smoothing. Computers and Chemical Engineering 19(2), 129–137 (1995)
11. Meier, T., Ngun, K.N.: Video Segmentation f or Content -Based Coding. IEEE Trans. on Circuits and Systems f or Video Technology 9(8), 1190–1203 (1999)

Application and Realization of Indoor Localization Based on Hidden Markov Model

Xinlang Ding, Yubin Chen*, Qiao Gui, and Chong Xiong

Institute of Software, Nan Chang Hang Kong University, Nanchang 100084, China

Abstract. Considering the low localization accuracy caused by uncertainty of indoor environment changes and many unexpected factors like man-made interference, this paper presents an indoor space localization method based on Hidden Markov Model. By adding indoor localization component program to the system of off-the-shelf WSN deployment, this method can collect mobile-node's RF characteristic parameters relation to the indoor positioning , without changing the network topology and system function. Then these parameters are processed by Hidden Markov Model to eliminate the effect of indoor environment changes and man-made interference, consequently getting mobile-node's precise localization in the room.

Keywords: Indoor Localization, Hidden Markov Models, Eigenvectors.

1 Introduction

With the development of information society, services of localization information perception in an indoor environment has a growing strong demand for the reason that indoor environment places the role of mainly daily activities, research for indoor location technology will deeply promote the development and popularization of IT industry in our country. In open outdoor environment, indeed global positioning system GPS can provide accurate positioning information, and the technology is relatively mature, but it is very difficult to play a effective role in indoor environment which surrounded by concrete. In recent years, the rapid development of short-range radio technology made indoor localization technology advanced rapidly. In general, indoor localization can use the technology of sensor, which finish the task by sensing the object into a specific area with the aid of pre-deployed sensor and its transmission network. Now, there are many typical systems such as infrared sensor localization systems, vibration-sound sensor localization system, ultra-wideband localization system, etc. However, sensor technology requires specialized hardware facilities, equipment requires considerable investment, and the effect is not ideal. Limited by sensing range of the sensor and sensor network deployment, localization can not provide a wide range

---

* This work was supported by Foundation of Jiangxi Educational Committee Grant No.GJJ11168),Natural Science Foundation of Jiangxi Province, China (No.20122BAB211028).

L. Sun, H. Ma, and F. Hong (Eds.): CWSN 2013, CCIS 418, pp. 303–312, 2014.

of coverage, The localization accuracy is also limited according to different sensor types. Currently, WLAN (Wireless Local Area Network) has been widely deployed worldwide. For this reason, scholars have proposed the use of WLAN to achieve indoor localization. Thus, user can not only enjoy the convenience of WLAN transmission of information, but also can obtain location information immediately, thereby enhancing the function of WLAN, which is called to kill two birds with one stone. The problems of indoor localization mainly includes: the link quality is not reliable, the wireless channel environment is complex, ambient noise, fading phenomenon seriously, and the final result of the received positioning is not steady. By contrast, WSN indoor localization method based on Hidden Markov Model involves pattern matching field, it is able to observe the sequence acquisition by determine the HMM model, training is a good solution to these problems. Indoor localization system includes two important aspects: first, to establish a complete WLAN localization scene fingerprint database; According to the signal strength and location of the fingerprint database, The localization based on HMM can obtain the best corresponding state sequence.

2   Related Work

Wireless sensor network is a completely new information-obtained stage, it can be used in a wide range of applications for detecting large scale complex tracking tasks, but most applications are based on localization technology for wireless sensor networks. Now, it has developed a lot of algorithms to resolve node localization problem in itself [2]. Indeed there exist many WSN localization methods, but each method is only suitable for certain application, there isn't an algorithm in common use. The difficulty of localization technology for wireless sensor network is the lack of node's energy and resources. The current localization algorithm can be divided into two categories by the localization method: Range based (and Range free. By measuring the distance or angle between nodes, Range-based can calculate the nodes location using trilateration and triangulation or maximum likelihood estimation method:RSSI,TOA,TDOA and AOA are the most common ranging technology. However, the TOA and VOA requires special equipment support, and they can be seriously affected by the stadium and path, RSSI is seriously dependent on the channel transmission model Pathloss but the indoor wireless channel is very unpredictable, because the reflected signal with the walls, floor and ceiling can cause serious interference to channel receiving antenna. In the indoor environment, there exist serious multipath interferences, because the distance between known points and points to be measured is usually not too far and the propagation of radio waves drives too fast, The difference between positioning method of Range based and Range free is that the former method does not measure distance directly, but use network connectivity to estimate node from distance or coordinates of anchor nodes, the methods of Range-based is numerous, but most of them stay theoretical research, in addition, the accuracy of localization is generally low and closely related to the intensity of network connectivity and node. Therefore, the localization method of Range based and Range free both has limits in the scope of application. We propose a new indoor localization method based on Hidden Markov Model, the method's characteristic is that we can learn the movement model of the mobile node from the actual data and analyze spatial hierarchical significance of mobile node movement by probability analysis. In this way we can not only improve the localization accuracy but also the speed of localization.

3   The Implementation

Indoor localization realized localization by matching the information to be localized with the node information in the fingerprint database [6], therefore, the first step is to establish node status fingerprint database. Process of node training and localization are quite similar to the classical algorithm based on HMM, the way to get knowledge observable sequence is the main difference. We introduce HMM algorithm to node localization, describes an indoor localization method based on HMM.

3.1   Determination of the Status of Node HMM

For one certain node in the indoor localization, we should first confirm the relationship of HMM with it, and then get the according of mathematical model for the node. According to the characteristic of behavioral characteristics of indoor nodes possess difference at different time, assuming that the node's characteristic condition have horizontal characteristics, then the major characteristic of the node(node ID, coordinate, RSSI value, LQI value) will appear in order in horizontal direction, this means that we can build the node as a model of the horizontal direction. According to the definition of HMM and characteristic condition of node [7], we can divide the node into four status, respectively relate to the node ID, coordinate, RSSI value, LQI value, where the number of status $N = 4$, to establish a data fingerprint database based on the four status value collecting from every signal receiver in the reference point. Status structure and the non-zero transition probabilities a_{ij} are shown in Fig. 1.

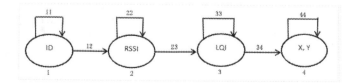

Fig. 1. The horizontal HMM model

3.2   Observation Sequence

According to the definition of hidden Markov model and the feature of ASN status values related to distance, the mobile node at each reference point measures the characteristics of collected data to establish fingerprint database, the mobile node feature continuous vector-valued data multiple acquisitions and generate sequence of observations to those observed sequence as input, the training process obtains an optimized set of HMM parameters and establishes the final HMM models. For the mobile node, the first characteristic value need to be collection and pretreatment, and then, using the trained HMM model does calculations, the final model output node position information in indoor positioning.

The Precision of Indoor Space Division by Grids. The nodes need precision location, divide and number the WSN nodes in indoor space, every cell's sizes determine the precision of located nodes. The precision of located nodes is the deviation between node lab position and theory position. This precision is depending on actual requirements; normal indoor node's precision can be 2 meters. The size of the grid is refers to the maximum of its center of mass to the edge of the distance. It is better to divide cell equality, and number every cell.

Samples of Node Information. There are many ways to generate the observed sequence by sampling node information. The easiest way is draw directly from every four features of corresponding state data as observation values. However, this method has two defects. First one is too many factors disturb the locating of nodes, which affects the node status value. Second one is huge observation vectors can cost plenty time and works to locate. So, the best way is using Kaman filtering algorithm to manage samples and using ASN mentioned above.

Training Nodes of Hidden Markov Model. In order to achieve the positioning of interior nodesa group of nodes of hidden Markov model has to be trained . When positioning , each set of data information in the fingerprint database is a node of HMM. Sampling was carried out on the node, it generates sequence of observations, using observation sequence for each space area of a HMM parameters trains a set of optimized model of the node. The training of steps are as follows.

Step 1: according to each associated ASN extraction sequence of observations, the node area of training for uniform segmentation must be derived.

Step 2: a general HMM ($\lambda = (A, B, \pi)$) which is used to determine the state of the model number must be established. A general HMM model which is used to determine the state of the model number must be established. According to the definition of HMM and the characteristics of the ASN, we can divide the node into four status, respectively relate to the node ID, coordinate, RSSI value, LQI value, where the number of status $N = 4$. As shown in Fig. 1 is a HMM of WSN indoor positioning.

ID each node has a unique serial number to distinguish the node type.
RSSI Received Signal Strength Indicator (Received Signal Strength Indicator).
LQI the strength of the received packets / Quality (the Link Quality Indicator).
X, Y A node in the region of the positioning coordinates, denoted as the serial
   number of blocks.

$$
A_{mitial} = \begin{bmatrix}
a_{1,1} & a_{1,2} & 0 & \cdots & 0 & 0 \\
0 & a_{2,2} & a_{2,3} & \cdots & 0 & 0 \\
\vdots & \vdots & \vdots & \ddots & \vdots & \vdots \\
0 & 0 & 0 & \cdots & a_{N-1,N-1} & a_{N-1,N} \\
0 & 0 & 0 & \cdots & 0 & a_{N,N}
\end{bmatrix} \tag{1}
$$

Step 3: The training data obtained with N states for the corresponding calculation of HMM initial parameters, the state transition probability of matrix A
must be initialized at this point, we assume that a state can only be transferred
to the state itself or the next state, in this way it can reduce the system complexity. Setting status i can only be returned to the state itself or be transferred
to $j = i + 1, a_{ij} = 0, j < i$ or $j > i + 1$. For the initial state probability distribution, setting $\pi_i = 1(\pi_i = 0, \pi \neq 1)$, that is to say, we suppose that from the
first state HMM beginning. The observation probabilities for initialization, we
assume $b_{ik} = 1/M, 1 \leq i \leq N, 1 \leq k \leq M$. Finally, initialize a hidden Markov
model $\lambda = (A, B, \pi)$.

Step 4: The forward-backward algorithm to calculate the vector O of $P(O|\lambda)$
in this model. There is the need to be focused that although $O = [o_1, o_2, \cdots, o_M]$
has been given, the resulting state of O is not unique. Because the value of each q_t
is not unique. Because the value of each q_t can produce o_t in a certain probability.

In (2) :π_{q_1} is initially probability in state of q_1, $b_{q_1}(o_1)$ is the state of q_1's
probability of generating observation o_1; $a_{q_1 q_2}$ is the state q_1 transition probability to the state q_2. Since each group can produce a sequence of states that
probability, each state q_i as a different N possible values. Therefore, a total of a
similar path are N^M .The sum of the probabilities of these paths to get up on
our requirements $P(O|\lambda)$, namely

$$
P(O|\lambda) = \sum_{q_1=s_1}^{s_N} \sum_{q_2=s_1}^{s_N} \cdots \sum_{q_M=s_1}^{s_N}
$$
$$
\pi_{q_1} b_{q_1}(o_1) a_{q_1 q_2} b_{q_2}(o_2) a_{q_2 q_3} b_{q_3}(o_3) \cdots a_{q_{N-1} q_N} b_{q_N}(o_M) \tag{2}
$$

The concept is not complicated, but computationally intensive, (2) contains
$(2T - 1)$ Multiplication, (3) contains $(2T - 1)N^M$ Multiplication. In order to
realize the calculation of $P(O|\lambda)$, the need to find a more efficient algorithm.

Taking into account that the above calculation process actually made a lot of
reduplicate counting, thus the basic idea to improve algorithm is: consolidate recursive algorithm. The specific strategies can be divided into three categories[8]:

1. Forward recursion method: assign $a_t(i)$ as the partly probability under given
   model parameter process from beginning to the time t generating partly

observation sequence $o_1 \sim o_t$ and status at the time t is s_i, denoted as $a_t(i) = P[o_1, o_2, \cdots, o_t; q_t = s_i/\lambda]$. To get relationship between $a_t(j) = P[o_1, o_2, \cdots, o_{t+1}; q_{t+1} = s_j/\lambda]$ and $a_t(i)$, the algorithm is as follows:

$$a(i) = \pi_i b_i(o_i) \tag{3}$$

$$a_{t+1}(j) = [\sum_{i=1}^{N} a_t(i) a_{ij}] b_j(o_{t+1}) \tag{4}$$

$$P(O|\lambda) = \sum_{j=1}^{N} a_M(j) \tag{5}$$

Formula (3) is the process of initialization, formula (4) is the recursive process, formula (5) end by $t = M$. Thus we know that forward recursive algorithm required number of multiplications is about $N^2 M$, so that volume calculation of formula (2) reduced much.

2. Backward recursive method: $\beta_t(i)$ the partly probability under given model parameter λ, and $q_t = s_t$ Namely: $\beta_t(i) = P[o_t, o_{t+1}, \cdots, o_T/q_t = s_i, \lambda]$. To get relationship between $\beta_{t+1}(j) = P[o_{t+1}, o_{t+2}, \cdots, o_T/q_{t+1} = s_j, \lambda]$ and $\beta_t(i)$, the algorithm is as follows.

$$\beta_T(i) = 1, \; i = 1, 2, \cdots, N \tag{6}$$

$$\beta_t(j) = [\sum_{i=1}^{N} a_{ij} b_j(o_{t+1})] \beta_{t+1}(j) \tag{7}$$

$$P(O|\lambda) = \sum_{j=1}^{N} \beta_t(j) \tag{8}$$

Formula (6) is the process of initialization, formula (7) is the recursive process, formula (8) end by $t = 1$.

3. Forward and backward recursive method: namely to combine the forward recursive method with the backward recursive method, apply the forward one during time $o \sim t$, apply the backward one during time $T \sim t$ (value t can select randomly between $1 \sim T$). At this point:

$$P(O|\lambda) = \sum_{i=1}^{N} a_t(i) \beta_t(i) \tag{9}$$

Compared with common method to solve $P(O|\lambda)$, forward backward algorithm has obvious advantages, it can significantly reduce the computational complexity.

Step 5: After the initial model to determine, using Baum-Welch revaluation algorithm to recalculate initial Hidden Markov Model, get a new $\lambda = (A', B', \pi')$. Then calculate the $P(O|\lambda')$ observation sequence O under the model by forward and backward recursive algorithm or Viterbi algorithm. To estimate the model which is closest to observation sequence O, assign threshold value C, when $|P(O|\lambda') - P(O|\lambda)| < C$ ($P(O|\lambda')$ is of convergence at this time), this is to get the trained Hidden Markov Model, otherwise assign $\lambda = \lambda'$ and repeat this step to $P(O|\lambda')$ is of convergence, the closest observation sequences HMM is shown in Fig. 2:

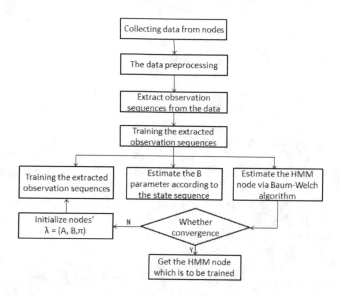

Fig. 2. Node training process

3.3   Node Localization

For indoor mobile node to be located, we should collect data localization information packet from deployed WSN several anchor sensor node, first to reduce noise for RF characteristic parameter from the sample data by Kalman filtering method, then put into input of Hidden Markov Model. It requires the several trained nodes Hidden Markov Model before localization, namely to establish the node database well, only on this basis can do the localization. Assuming that fingerprint database already exist K Hidden Markov Model nodes, its localization algorithm is as follows:

Step one: Extract observation vector sequence from nodes to be located.

Step two: Calculate similar probability $P(O|\lambda_n)$ between observation vector sequence and every node in the node fingerprint database via forward and backward recursive method.

Step three: Similar probability reflects the similarity of observation vector sequence of the nodes to be located and the node Hidden Markov Model from data fingerprint database, that is if $P(O|\lambda_i), i \in (1, 2, \cdots, K)$ is the biggest in the $P(O|\lambda_k), k \in (1, 2, \cdots, K)$, then λ_i is the closest Hidden Markov Model to nodes to be located. At this point, localization finished.

4   Analysis of the Experimental Result

4.1   Influence of Difference Parameters to Localization Performance

In the HMM model, the status transition probability matrix A, the output probability matrix function B and the initial status probability distribution π is the best parameter to represent model, however, we should also pay enough attention to select another parameter, in our indoor localization experiment, ignorance of the following two model parameter will reduce accuracy, while the appropriate selection of them will be more favorable to model, the two effect of HMM parameters are: Total status HMM model N, the number of training samples M, they are determines whether the model success for the localization of the nodes to a certain extend. This section will explore on influence of the above several combinations to model localization performance.

If we do the experiment for every possible combinations of the parameters, amount of experiment will be very huge, therefor this experiment made the assumptions: Parameter can be independent changed to a certain extent, we can adjust parameters by subjectively, and can only do experiment to one combination once, for every parameter combination, we should define the merits and demerits of the RMSE measuring localization performance, the less the value, the localization performance of the model better.

Table 1. The HMM model accuracy under different parameters

Number of states N	Number of training nodes samples M					
	15	13	10	7	4	2
1	73.4	71.0	67.2	76.1	80.8	77.3
2	66.5	62.4	69.0	67.3	82.1	89.3
3	56.9	58.3	63.8	78.6	80.4	72.2
4	58.3	61.4	66.5	87.2	78.1	82.9

Selection of the Number of Training Samples. Number of training node affects strongly to the accuracy of localization during state of model training, less training sessions, the training is not sufficient, and the training model may not enough to describe node characteristics changes. We can infer that use of such a model exits great localization error, so we can further determine the effect of M to localization performance by adding number of training node. Fig. 3 shows that generally error when $M > 10$ apparently less than $M < 10$, this is consistent with the expected conclusion. Therefore, the training model should be fully trained to improve localization accuracy.

Selection of the Number of Status. Status of N in HMM model determines the number of feature descriptions of an object. If observation sequence is long, we should choose a large value of N to capture more features.

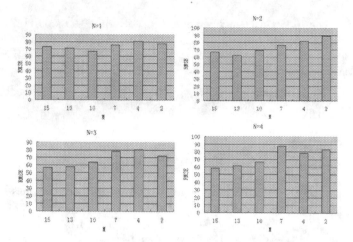

Fig. 3. Experiment results with various numbers of samples M

We run extensive experiments to test the impact of the number of states on the localization performance. The experimental results are shown in Fig. 4. Under the condition that the training data is relatively sufficient, the localization error is smaller when N takes an appropriate value. When $M < 10$, due to the fact that the change of localization model cannot fully characterize the change of the feature of localization object, there is no obvious regularity. Because the observation length of training data is very small, the localization error is small when N takes higher value. The localization algorithm complexity of calculation is proportional to N. The smaller N is, the more quickly the localization is. Therefore, we have to compromise to select the appropriate N value, considering both location speed and localization accuracy.

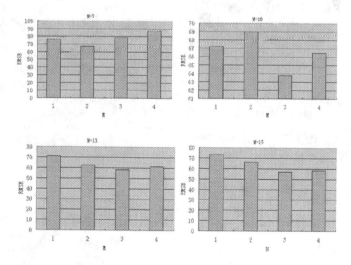

Fig. 4. Experiment results with various number of states N

To sum up, the following conclusions can be obtained: 1) we should provide sufficient training data to fully train the model; 2) we should select the proper number of states according to the observation sequence length to improve both speed and accuracy.

5   Conclusion

By using the idea of Hidden Markov Model, the node is regarded as a model. According to three algorithms of HMM, we can set up it with nodes to design indoor node's training and localization algorithm. Then use Kalman Filtering technology to resolve the node data before the processing of training and positioning so as to extract some effective node status observation, This method improves the localization accuracy, and reduces the operation time.

References

1. Torres-Solis, J., Falk, T.H., et al.: A review of indoor localization technologies: towards navigational assistance for topographical disorientation. Ambient Intelligence, 51–84 (2010)
2. Rohrig, C., Muller, M.: Indoor location tracking in non-line-of-sight environments using a IEEE 802.15. 4a wireless network. In: IEEE/RSJ International Conference on Intelligent Robots and Systems, IROS 2009. IEEE (2009)
3. Bahl, P., Padmanabhan, V.N.: RADAR: An in-building RF-based user location and tracking system. In: Proceedings of the IEEE Infocom, Israel (2000)
4. Zhou, G., He, T., Krishnamurthy, S., Stankovic, J.A.: Impact of Radio Irregularity on Wireless Sensor Networks. In: Proceedings of MobiSys 2004, Boston, MA (2004)
5. Elnahraway, E., Li, X., Martin, R.P.: The limits of localization using RSS. In: Proceedings of the 2nd International Conference on Embedded Networked Sensor Systems, Baltimore, MD, USA (2004)
6. Nagpal, R., Shrobe, H., Bachrach, J.: Organizing a global coordinate system from local information on an ad hoc sensor network. In: Zhao, F., Guibas, L.J. (eds.) IPSN 2003. LNCS, vol. 2634, pp. 333–348. Springer, Heidelberg (2003)
7. Kjærgaard, M.B.: A taxonomy for radio location fingerprinting. In: Hightower, J., Schiele, B., Strang, T. (eds.) LoCA 2007. LNCS, vol. 4718, pp. 139–156. Springer, Heidelberg (2007)
8. Mitilineos, S.A., Kyriazanos, D.M., Segou, O.E.: Indoor Localization with Wireless Sensor Networks. Progress in Electromagnetics Research 109, 441–474 (2010)
9. Indoor Localization System using Wireless Sensor Networks for Stationary and Moving Target (2009)
10. Welch, G., Bishop, G.: An introduction to the Kalman filter (1995)
11. Paul, A.S., Wan, E.A.: RSSI-based indoor localization and tracking using sigma-point kalman smoothers. IEEE Journal of Selected Topics in Signal Processing 3(5), 860–873 (2009)

DV-hop-MSO Based Localization Algorithm in Wireless Sensor Networks

Xiaoyu Lv[1], Xuemei Sun[1,*], Xuefeng Zhou[2], and Guowei Xu[1]

[1] School of Computer Science and Software Engineering,
Tianjin Polytechnic University
Xiqing, 300387, Tianjin, China
`seesea_sun@163.com`
[2] School of Electronics and Information Engineering,
Tianjin Polytechnic University
Xiqing, 300387, Tianjin, China

Abstract. Wireless Sensor Networks (WSNs) play an important role in making the dream of ubiquitous computing a reality. It has the potential to influence and improve everyone's life with a variety of applications in the future. However, there are a number of issues in deployment and exploitation of these networks that must be dealt with for sensor network applications to realize such potential. Localization is one of the supporting technologies in wireless sensor networks, which can not provide the physical locations of events, but also help to improve the routing efficiency, optimize the network coverage and control the topology etc. Therefore, localization is one of the important issues of the WSN. This paper proposes an improved DV-hop localization algorithm for WSNs. The new localization algorithm, which not only maintains the advantages of DV-hop localization algorithm, but also overcomes the shortcomings of Mass-Spring Model (MSO) algorithm that it is easy to fall in to local optimum, make use of the advantages of error inhibition of MSO to solve the problem of calculation error in traditional DV-hop which use weighted least square estimates to calculate the coordinate of unknown nodes. Experimental results show that our proposed method is effective and robust, especially the node localization more accurately than DV-hop localization algorithm at the same network environment.

Keywords: Wireless sensor networks, Mass spring model, Localization algorithm, DV-hop.

1 Introduction

Wireless sensor network (WSN) is thought as one of hot researches in recent years, which contains communication parts and data processing units. The study of wireless sensor network techniques includes many technologies such as wireless communication, distributed information processing and embedded computing.

---

* Corresponding author.

L. Sun, H. Ma, and F. Hong (Eds.): CWSN 2013, CCIS 418, pp. 313–323, 2014.

In fact, WSNs have made the concept of pervasive computing more realistic. We could use WSNs as applications to monitor the glacier, ocean water and so on. As soon as the technologies of WSN improved, a variety of applications for WSNs are widely used in human life. However, there are a number of issues in deployment and exploitation which must be dealt for applications of WSNs. Nodes localization, which is the subject of this paper, is one of the basic problems that must be solved for using WSNs more effectively.

As we all know, there is a vital need of nodes localization for using WSNs more sufficiently. In WSNs, we could use localization algorithm to determine relative or absolute positions of nodes. While designing location algorithm for WSNs, there are many factors that we should to be considered. First of all, the accuracy of localization algorithm is needed to be considered, that is, we prefer that localization algorithm has higher localization accuracy as well as less computation. On the other hand, we should choose the appropriate localization algorithm for different WSNs. The last but not the least, we also should considered the other factors, for example, anchor nodes ratio, self-applicability, fault tolerance system, power consumption and so on.

There are two kinds of nodes in WSNs, one is called anchor nodes or beacon nodes which could know its position by using GPS equipment, and the other one is called unknown nodes which dont know but could utilize the message of beacon nodes to determine its position. Considerable efforts have been made in the field of localization in WSNs. Due to using devices to measure the distances between nodes or not, proposed localization algorithms can be categorized mainly into two categories: range-based and range-free. Range-based algorithms are those which use range measurement equipment, The methods used for measuring distance in these devices is usually a received signal strength indicator, time difference of arrival, time of arrival and direction of arrival or angle of arrival. After receiving the messages from the neighbor nodes, each node uses a method like triangulation to compute its position. Despite centralized localization algorithms are excellent approximations, they are impractical for large-scale sensor networks due to high computation and communication costs. The problem with distance measurement is that the ranging process (or hardware) is subject to noise, and complexity/cost of algorithms increases with the accuracy requirement. In contrast, range-free algorithms do not hold any assumption of existence of any range measurement devices on sensor nodes. Therefore, considering the consumption and power dissipation, range-free algorithms are better choices if they achieve an acceptable accuracy.

As a traditional range-free algorithm for WSNs, DV-hop localization algorithm not only demands the ability to measure distances between nodes for sensors, but also is uncomplicated to realize and moderate computation and communication costs. For kinds of sensor networks, the DV-hop localization algorithm could compute the average distance of each hop and achieve a satisfactory accuracy. This paper first shows a brief review of the DV-hop localization algorithm, and aims at solving the problem of calculation error in traditional

DV-hop localization algorithm by using Weighted Least Square Estimates which further increases positioning accuracy.

2   Tranditional DV-hop Localization Algorithm

2.1   Tranditional DV-hop Localization Algorithm

The DV-hop algorithm is a kind of range-free techniques based on the multi-hop ranging as well as the distance vector routing mechanism which was proposed by Dragons Niculescu of Lutegesi University of United States. The basic idea of DV-hop algorithm is: the unknown node itself only exchanges information with its adjacent/neighbor nodes, the distance between the unknown node and the anchor node is represented by average hop distance and the shortest path between two nodes, and then it uses trilateral measurement to obtain the node location information. To acquire higher positioning accuracy, each beacon node would always revise the hop distance as well as gain the optimum average hop distance. So DV-hop algorithm is one of the most widely applied algorithm for WSNs. The DV-hop algorithm could be divided into the following 3 steps:

First step: The unknown nodes first calculate the minimal hops between the beacon nodes. Then the beacon nodes broadcast their location information packets to the neighbors, including jumping section of the field, and the value is initialized to 0. Receiving node records the minimum hop count of each node, while ignoring the larger hop group from the same anchor node, then the jump number is added 1 and transmitted to neighbor nodes. Through this method, all nodes in the network could be able to record each beacon node under the minimum number of hops.

Second step: calculate the actual distances between unknown nodes and the anchor nodes. Each anchor node estimates the actual average hop distance using formula (1), according to the location information and the hop count of the other anchor nodes from the above step.

$$HopSize_i = \frac{\sum_{j \neq i} \sqrt{(x_i - x_j)^2 + (y_i - y_j)^2}}{\sum_{j \neq i} h_j} \tag{1}$$

Among them: (x_i, y_i) , (x_j, y_j) are the coordinates of the anchor node i, j ;h_j is the hop account between anchor node i and the anchor node j (ij).

Anchor nodes broadcast its localization information packet and the average hop distance. Unknown nodes, which not only record the message of first received from the adjacent beacon nodes but also renew the messages at any times and transmit the information to neighbor nodes. Then unknown nodes fix the nearest anchor nodes average hop distance and calculate the distance to every anchor node, according to the records of hop account.

Third step: The unknown nodes use trilateration or maximum likelihood estimation method to calculate the coordinates of the unknown nodes, according to the records of hop distance to each anchor node. When the distances P which are from all the anchor nodes to the unknown nodes, we can use formula (2) to calculate:

$$\begin{cases} (x_1 - x)^2 + (y_i - y)^2 = d_1^2 \\ \cdots \\ \cdots \\ (x_n - x)^2 + (y_n - y)^2 = d_n^2 \end{cases} \tag{2}$$

To make this system of equations linear, subtract last equation from first $(n-1)$ equations. We get a system of $(n-1)$ equations as shown in (3).

$$\left.\begin{array}{l} x_1^2 + y_1^2 - x_n^2 - y_n^2 - 2(x_1 - x_n) - 2(y_1 - y_n)y = d_1^2 - d_n^2 \\ x_2^2 + y_2^2 - x_n^2 - y_n^2 - 2(x_2 - x_n) - 2(y_2 - y_n)y = d_2^2 - d_n^2 \\ \cdots \\ x_{n-1}^2 + y_{n-1}^2 - x_n^2 - y_n^2 - 2(x_{n-1} - x_{n-1}) - 2(y_{n-1} - y_n)y = d_{n-1}^2 - d_n^2 \end{array}\right\} \tag{3}$$

Rewriting in the form of AX = B ,where A , B ,and X are given by equations (4), (5), and (6), respectively:

$$\mathbf{A} = \begin{bmatrix} 2(x_1 - x_n) & 2(y_1 - y_n) \\ 2(x_2 - x_n) & 2(y_2 - y_n) \\ \cdots \\ \cdots \\ 2(x_{n-1} - x_n) & 2(y_{n-1} - y_n) \end{bmatrix} \tag{4}$$

$$\mathbf{B} = \begin{bmatrix} x_1^2 + y_1^2 - x_n^2 - y_n^2 + d_n^2 - d_1^2 \\ x_2^2 + y_2^2 - x_n^2 - y_n^2 + d_n^2 - d_2^2 \\ \cdots \\ \cdots \\ x_{n-1}^2 + y_{n-1}^2 - x_n^2 - y_n^2 + d_n^2 - d_{n-1}^2 \end{bmatrix} \tag{5}$$

$$\mathbf{C} = \begin{bmatrix} x \\ y \end{bmatrix} \tag{6}$$

We can get the coordinates of the unknown node through using the standard minimum mean variance estimation method to formula (7):

$$X = (A^T A)^{-1} A^T b \tag{7}$$

2.2   Error Analysis of DV-hop Algorithm

DV-hop algorithm assumes that the minimum hop path between nodes is like a straight line, which is not always possible in practical applications. This assumption emerges an error in the distance estimated by hop count and average hop distance. The other main drawback of DV-hop algorithm is the communication range. The communication range of each node in the networks is not a standard circle and quite anomalistic polygon. Because of the influence of network topology, the each hop distance is different from others. As if we use the average distance of each hop to estimate the distance between nodes, the error will increase with the number of hops because of accumulated error. In this paper, we tried to reduce the ranging error of DV-hop algorithm.

3   Localization Algorithm Based on Mass-Spring Optimization

A mass spring model (MSO) [5] uses WSNs as the system model which composed of many particles as well as springs connected with the composition of the particle. We could use the particle representation of sensor nodes and take the spring which connected sensor nodes and its neighbor nodes as the connectivity between each pair of neighbor nodes in the network. So each of the measured range between neighbor nodes would be regard as the spring free length connecting two nodes. The main procedure of the localization as follows: 1) Convert the network structure into a mass spring model (MSO), and randomly generate some sensor nodes in the network coordinates; 2) Because the coordinate of anchor nodes in WSNs could be acquired through GPS positioning, we could take the anchor node as fixed particle and the sensor nodes as the activity particles. The initialization process above is equivalent to impose a force on each node. The positions of the unknown nodes would be moved under the action of the force until the system energy $E = \sum_{i=1}^{N} E(S_i)$ reaches the minimum value while the $E(S_i)$ is on behalf of the energy of each node. Expression is as follows:

$$E(S_i) = \sum_{neighbor\, S_i} (dist_{est}(S_i, S_j) - dist_{true}(S_i, S_j))^2 \tag{8}$$

Among them: $dist_{est}(S_i, S_j)$ and $dist_{true}(S_i, S_j)$ are the estimated distance and the actual distance between the nodes S_i and S_j.

3) To minimize the total energy E in a distributed manner, each sensor nodes concurrently minimizes its local energy $E(S_i)$. For this purpose, each node S_i translates its position by a vector $\alpha_i F(S_i)$, where $\alpha \in (0, 1)$ is chosen such that the new energy $E(S_i)$ is smaller than the old energy. This position-translation process is repeated until the energy cannot be improved significantly further, or the number of repetitions exceeds some threshold. An example choice for α_i, as recommended and evaluated in [5], is $1/2m_i$, where m_i is the number of neighbor nodes of S_i.

4   Localization Algorithm Based on DV-hop-MSO

The traditional DV-hop algorithm and its improvement algorithms in WSNs have the problem of calculation error while using Weighted Least Square Estimates to calculate the average hop distance to fix the coordinate of unknown nodes. The calculation error would make some mistakes for the positioning accuracy.

For the mass spring model algorithm (MSO), because the coordinate of node in WSN is initialized to be a random value, so it is very easy to cause the coordinate in local optimal. While we take the communication distance between nodes as the spring free length in the construction of mass spring model which has some stretching and compression, the MSO would adjust the action force that emerged by the error in process of calculating the average hop range and also acquired lower localization error. That is to say, the error between the measured distance and the prediction distance of the nodes could be optimized by the MSO algorithm. If the nodes coordinates in WSN has been initialized as a relative accurate value, then the MSO algorithm would obtain better positioning effect so as to optimizing the performance of algorithm.

Because the advantages and disadvantages of these two algorithms can be complementary, this paper combines the DV-hop algorithm and the mass spring model (MSO) to propose a positioning algorithm based on DHM. Since DV-hop has not ability to measure the true distance between nodes, we make some change for MSO algorithm. We use the communication range r of each sensor in lieu of the true distance.

The energy of a sensor Si is now defined as:

$$E(S_i) = \sum_{neighbor S_i} (dist_{est}(S_i, S_j) - r)^2 \tag{9}$$

The force on Si pulled by Sj is redefined as:

$$F(S_i) = \sum_{neighbor S_i} (dist_{est}(S_i, S_j) - r) \times u(S_i, S_j) \tag{10}$$

After making some changes for mass spring model, we could combine DV-hop localization algorithm and the mass spring model to construct a new algorithm the DV-hop-MSO positioning algorithm.

The positioning algorithm based on DV-hop-MSO is mainly divided into the following two steps:

1) The DV-hop positioning algorithm acquires the preliminary locations of nodes in WSN in order to estimate the coordinates of the nodes;

2) Use mass spring model to refine coordinates of nodes, and improve positioning accuracy;

Through the above analysis, the main steps of DV-hop-MSO in this paper are as follows:

1) By using DV-hop method to calculate the average hop distance, in further to estimate the positions of the unknown nodes;

2) Change WSN into the structure of mass spring model and let the initial coordinates of the particle be the location of Si. Use the DV-hop localization algorithm presented in the previous sections. We also take the spring length of the adjacent particles as the communication distance r of nodes and assume the anchor node as fixed particle as well as the unknown node would be the node that can move.

3) According to mass spring model, the unknown node would be keep moving under the function force of the vector until meeting the minimum energy E;

4) Let f_x and f_y be the x-dimension and y-dimension magnitudes of this force, respectively. Then compute possible new location:

$$x_{new}(S_i) = x_{current}(S_i) + \frac{f_x}{2m_i} \tag{11}$$

$$y_{new}(S_i) = y_{current}(S_i) + \frac{f_y}{2m_i} \qquad (12)$$

5) Compute possible new energy $E_{new}(S_i)$ according to (19) using the new location.If $(E(S_i) > E_{new}(S_i))$, update the current position:

$$x_{current}(S_i) = x_{new}(S_i) \qquad (13)$$

$$y_{current}(S_i) = y_{new}(S_i) \qquad (14)$$

Until the energy of the system to meet the minimum value.

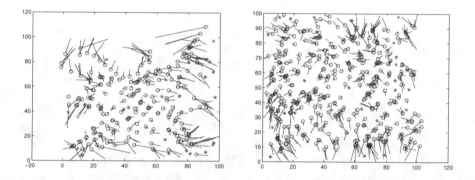

Fig. 1. The positioning error map based on DV-hop

Fig. 2. The positioning error map based on DV-hop-MSO

5 Experimental Results and Simulation Study

5.1 Parameter Model of Wireless Sensor Network

In this paper, we take the Matlab as simulation platform to conduct a simulation study on a network of 300 sensors located in a 100m*100m 2D area. In our simulation network environment, we assume uniform random distribution for the sensor locations and the selection of the beacon sensors. We consider that the levels of network density is 10m(in other words, it means communication range) and the beacon population is 10%. Then we take simulation experiments by using the DV-hop and DV-hop-MSO positioning algorithm in the same network environment. In order to reduce the error caused by ambient noise, we take gauss error to simulate the noise error in process of measurement. Assume the actual distance between nodes is d, then the measured range is $d = d * (l + N(0, er))$, Among them : $N(0, e,)$ is the Gauss error function which the average value is 0 and the standard error is e.

5.2   Analysis of Simulation Results

Fig. 1 and Fig. 2 show the positioning results of DV-hop and DV-hop-MSO respectively. In Fig.1 and 2, the circles indicate node location coordinates, while the short-term on circle means the range and direction that deviating from the actual positioning coordinates of the unknown nodes. As shown in Fig. 2, the average localization error for DV-hop is 59% while the average localization error for DV-hop-MSO is 53%. As can be seen from the simulation results, DV-hop-MSO proposed in this paper could partly improved the positioning accuracy by using the DV-hop location result as the initialization value for the node coordinates in mass spring model.

5.3   Analysis of Algorithm Performance

Influence of Anchor Nodes Density on the Positioning Error. The anchor node density refers to the percentage of the number of anchor nodes and the number of sensor nodes in total in WSNs. Assuming that the proportion of anchor nodes are 5%, 10%, 15% , ..., 35%, namely the number of the anchor nodes in the wireless network are 15, 30, 45,...and 105. Comparing the influence of average location error for traditional DV-hop algorithm and the localization algorithm based on DV-hop-MSO in different proportion of anchor nodes. As shown in Fig. 3, with the percentage of anchor nodes increases, the average positioning error of two algorithms is a decreasing trend. Under the same conditions, the average location error of the DV-hop-MSO algorithm is smaller than traditional DV-hop algorithm. It can be seen from the figure, when the anchor nodes in 10% - 25% ratio, the positioning error of the DV-hop-MSO algorithm decreased greatly; when the anchor node ratio is greater than 25%, the positioning error of the DV-hop-MSO algorithm tends to a bit inflection. The main reason is that although the number of the anchor nodes increase, the whole information of

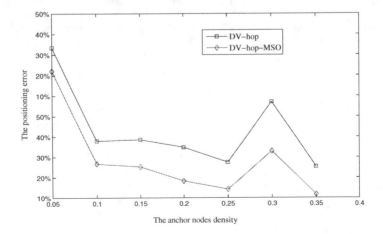

Fig. 3. Localization error when the anchor nodes density changes

all anchor nodes can used totally. The positioning error will be also increased in some times. On the whole, the out performance of DV-hop-MSO is better than DV-hop localization algorithm.

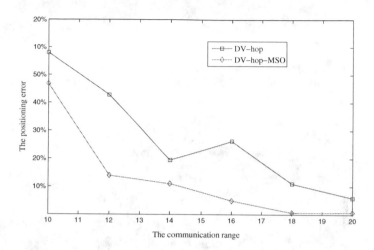

Fig. 4. Localization error when communication range changes

The Effect of Network Connectivity on the Positioning Error. In WSN, the average number of neighbor nodes of a node that can communicate directly is called the node connectivity which determines by the following two factors: the density of nodes and the communication radius [4]. The network connectivity will be changed while changing the density of nodes and the communication radius. In this paper, the number of nodes in the network is 300, the number of the anchor nodes is 15, and we change the network connectivity by changing the communication radius of nodes and verify the relationship between the positioning error and the network connectivity. The communication radius are equal to 10m, 12m, 14m, 16m, 18m, 20m repetitively. It can be seen from the following figures, comparing with the traditional DV-hop algorithm, the DV-hop-MSO algorithm reduces the positioning error and has better performance.

The Impact of Total Number of Nodes on Positioning Error. This experiment is to study the effect of total number of sensor nodes in WSN on the average positioning error of the algorithm. Let the total number of nodes in the network are 300, 400 and increased by step length 100 until 1000. The anchor nodes density is 10% and the communication range is 10m. In the case of the other conditions remain unchanged, we compares the average location error of DV-hop and the DV-hop-MSO algorithm, and then analyzes the influence of the total number of nodes on the node location error in the network. As shown in Fig. 5, with the total number of nodes in the network increasing, the location errors of the traditional DV-Hop algorithm and DV-hop-MSO algorithm are

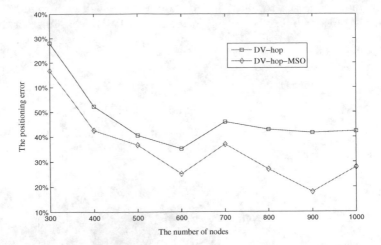

Fig. 5. Localization error when the number of node changes

decreased. Furthermore, under the same conditions, the positioning error of the DV-hop-MSO algorithm is smaller than the traditional DV-hop algorithm, so we can know that the DV-hop-MSO algorithm is more preponderant than the traditional DV-hop algorithm.

6   Conclusion

This paper summarizes the characteristics of the DV-Hop algorithm based on the analysis of DV-Hop algorithm, and proposed a new localization algorithm DV-hop-MSO. Through the original analysis and experimental results, it can be seen that the improved algorithm significantly increases the accuracy of the nodes localization compared with conventional DV-HOP algorithm, under the premise of maintaining simple, low cost. It is an effective scheme for the node localization in wireless sensor networks. In the future work, we will study how to make the localization algorithm in this paper gain higher positioning accuracy as well as to reduce the nodes communication and computation at the same time, so as to minimize the energy consumption of nodes and improve the algorithms utility value, and it will be a very meaningful and valuable research topic.

References

1. Niculescu, D., Nath, B.: Ad Hoc Positioning System (APS). In: Proceedings of the IEEE GlobeCom, San Antonio, AZ (November 2001)
2. Mingyu, S., Yin, Z.: DV-HOP localization algorithm based on improved average hop distance and estimate of distance. Application Research of Computers 28(2), 648–650 (2011)

3. Xinsheng, W., Yanjing, Z., Haitao, L.: Improved study based on DV-HOP localization algorithm. Computer Science 38(2), 76–78 (2011)
4. Jiangang, W., Fubao, W., Weijun, D.: Application of weighted least square estimate on wireless sesor network node localization. Application Research of Computers 22(9), 41 (2006)
5. Priyantha, N.B., Balakrishnan, H., Demaine, E., Teller, S.: Anchor-Free Distributed Localization in Sensor Network. In: Proc. of the First ACM Intl Conf. Embedded Networked Sensor Systems (SenSys) (2003)
6. Tran, D.A., Nguyen, T.: Localization in Wireless Sensor Networks Based on Support Vector Machines. IEEE Trans. Parallel Distributed Syst. 19(7), 981–994 (2008)

A Novel Routing Algorithm
Base on Non-uniform Distribution
Double Fusion Nodes for WSN

Zongang Liu[1], Tong Wang[2,*], Xiaoxue Du[3], and Jianjun Yu[1]

[1] Unit91550, Dalian, Liaoning116023, China
{LiuZongang,YuJianjun}@126.com
[2] College of Information and Communication Engineering,
Harbin Engineering University, 150001 Harbin, China
WangTong@hreu.edu.cn
[3] Equipment Department of Naval North Sea Fleet, Qingdao, 266071, China
DuXiaoxue@126.com

Abstract. Considering the unbalance of network energy consumption caused by one-hop communication in hierarchical fusion algorithm of wireless sensor networks, this paper presents a novel improved hybrid fusion algorithm DNDC based on LEACH using the idea of non-uniform. In this novel algorithm, fusion node is firstly selected which is mainly used for data receiving and processing in the cluster. Then, based on the difference of distance from fusion node to base station, vice fusion nodes of non-uniform are chose, which is mainly responsible for data forwarding from fusion nodes. DNDC can balance the network energy consumption. Furthermore, routing data path for the new type of algorithm is improved by using ant colony optimization algorithm. The enhanced algorithm ADNDC can prolonged the survival time of the network .Simulation shows that the two proposed algorithms DNDC and ADNDC have integrated the advantages of planar fusion algorithm and hierarchical fusion algorithm. ADNDC can not only balance the network energy consumption but also extend the network lifespan. Besides, the ADNDC algorithm can be applied to large scale networks or the network which has large proportion of (vice) fusion nodes.

Keywords: wireless sensor networks, non-uniform distribution, double fusion nodes, ant colony optimization.

1 Introduction

Data fusion technology is nowadays a hot spot of the research of Wireless Sensor Network (WSN) because many nodes disperse densely in WSN, the collected

* This paper is supported by the National Natural Science Foundation(61102105) ; the National Postdoctoral Science Foundation under Grant No. 20080440840; the National Research Foundation for the Doctoral Program of Higher Education of China under No. 20102304120014; the Natural Science Foundation of Heilongjiang Province of china under Grant No. F201029.

L. Sun, H. Ma, and F. Hong (Eds.): CWSN 2013, CCIS 418, pp. 324–336, 2014.

date exist a great deal of redundance, and these redundant data will bring a huge energy Consumption. Thus, the expenditure of network energy can be decreased effectively by reducing the amount of network data communication via the data fusion. Further more, the energy expenditure caused by selecting a node to data fusion is also different. So fusion algorithm based on routing is a major research in fusion technology.

Fusion algorithm is divided into two categories in WSN: Plane fusion algorithm and hierarchical fusion algorithm. In the Flat-type network, data rout in the multi-hop manner, the fusion is executed by all the routing nodes which are contacted. We usually use the two-hop communication in hierarchical network; one hop is from cluster members to the fusion, while the other is from the fusion to the base station. In the hierarchical algorithm, the fusion is executed by the fusion nodes which send the fusion data to the base station. As the plane type algorithm is not conducive to the expansion of the network, the majority of the current study is based on hierarchical network, and LEACH [3] is the most typical hierarchical fusion algorithm in WSN.

2   LEACH and Its Improved Algorithm

2.1   LEACH Algorithm

LEACH algorithm is divided into two stages: Clustering stage and stabilize stage. In the stage of establishing clusters, each node randomly select a positive number less than one, if it is less than the threshold value T(n), then the node becomes as a fusion node to broadcast message to the network system . The node which is not elected will join to a cluster according to the strength of the received information signal; fusion node will allocate time-slice to transmit data for all the nodes in the cluster. The threshold selected by the fusion node is calculated by the formula (1):

$$T(n) = \frac{p}{1 - p \times (\gamma mod \frac{1}{p})}, n \epsilon G \tag{1}$$

p is the probability of selecting fusion node, and r is the number of rounds has been carried out,G represents a set of unselected nodes within a cycle, T (n) will be 0 if the node has been elected fusion node before. But LEACH algorithm cannot equalize the energy between the clusters, for fusion node communicates with the base station directly. It takes more energy to communicate with the base station for areas which are far away, and then comes to the "*hot zone*"problem. Especially in the larger network, this problem will become increasingly obvious, so LEACH is not suitable for large-scale network environment.

2.2   Improved Algorithm Based on LEACH

Consider the deficiencies of LEACH, some of the early studies[4][5] has mainly improved communication mode between the fusion nodes and the base station , so fusion node could communicate with the base station through multi-hop mode, therefore the algorithm is also known as a hybrid network algorithm .Early the improved algorithm could solve the "hot zone" problem effectively , however , it comes to the new "hot zone " problem to fusion node that near the base station , due to the large amount of energy consumption used for forwarding data sent by the remote base station end.

In order to solve these two problems above at the same time, Soro and others for the first time propose the Uneven Cluster-Based thought [6], On this basis , Li Cheng et al proposed a WSN routing protocols [7] based on unequal clustering, the algorithm can well balance the energy of the network, but it makes the protocol overly complex for the nodes in the network in the same round cycle cannot all serve as the same number of fusion node.

Song Mao et al proposed the unequal clustering algorithm[8] based on ant colony optimization , Qin Zhichao et al proposed the unequal clustering algorithm[9] based on particle swarm optimization , These type of unequal clustering algorithms based on intelligent optimization algorithm , not only have good energy balance ,but also could enhance the robustness of the network , but due to the same reason of unequal clustering characteristics , the protocol process is too complicated , and they do not apply to small-scale networks because of the high cost for optimization process.

Zhou Qin et al proposed a fusion algorithm [10] based on double cluster head, the clustering algorithm is simple and easy to achieve, but the energy balance of the algorithm is not good enough for it has less consider the problem of the distance between the fusion node to the base station, and equally to the LEACH algorithm, it does not apply to large-scale network. Liu Zhijun et al proposed a fusion algorithm [11] based on the unequal clustering of double cluster heads, same with the other non-uniform clustering algorithms; the algorithm has the better energy balance, but with a high complexity which is not fit for the WSN.

3   DNDC Algorithm

On the basis of LEACH algorithm, we design a data fusion algorithm based on non-uniform distribution double fusion nodes, which uses non-uniform thought for reference.

3.1   Fusion Node Selection

D select an ACH(Assistant Cluster Head) within clusters. ACH is mainly responsible for forwarding data among clusters. The probability which produces ACH increases with the decrease of the distance between FN (Fusion Node) to BS (Base Station) .Such a design can solve "hot spots" problem near BS area in multiple hops routing. The threshold T (d) generated by the formula (2): NDC and LEACH produce FN of equal probability P. According to the distance to the BS, FN calculates a threshold T (n), and compares it with the random number which is produced by the campaign of FN. If it is greater than a, FN can

$$\mathrm{d} = (1 - \frac{d}{d_{max}})^k \tag{2}$$

d represents the distance of FN to BS,d_{max} represents the maximum distance of the network nodes to the BS , k is the adjustment coefficient.

FN which can produce ACH will calculate the residual energy of all the nodes in the cluster and the ratio of the distance Ere /d to the BS, and choose one of the biggest ratio of nodes in cluster as ACH. In addition, DNDC uses multiple hops to communicate between clusters, after FN fusing all the data in the cluster, it pass the data to BS by ACH. Thus we can balance the energy consumption between clusters and solve "hot spots"in the far BS area.

3.2   The Process of DNDC Algorithm

Fusion Nodes Generation Phase. BS start network and broadcast information, including their location information, all received information of N (the Node) and report their location information to the base station .Then BS calculates the d_{max}, broadcast to all the N in the network, and starts the network clustering.

After receiving information of the BS, N will begin to campaign fusion node in accordance with the P values provided by BS. The information provided by BS besides d_{max}, and P includes the cycle time to clustering,after such clusters being formed, we will know after how many times of transmission data stability then to clustering. Once a N campaign succeed,it will broadcast to the network the elected information CHMsg (addr, ID, CH), the information contains FN address,node ID and elected sign CH.

After UN (Unselected Node) receiving the broadcast FN, it choose clusters according to the strength of the information signal, and send cluster information JoinMsg (addr, ID, Ere, CID)to FN, the information contained in the Node's own address, ID, residual energy and the ID of FN.

FN after receiving a N cluster request, puts it in its own cluster members list, and store the the location information of N and residual energy. FN then distribute a sequence used to transmit data for each N in the cluster and send the confirmation AKMsg (ID, CID, DATA), which contains ID of N in the cluster and FNID as well as the temporal information distribute to N in the cluster.

Node Generation Phase of the Vice Fusion Node. After the formation of clusters, FN began to select ACH. FN will store the elected N in the routing list after selected Successfully and broadcast information of AHMsg (ID, addr) to network, which contains the ID and address of the elected N .Once the elected N received information it will know that it is elected for the ACH, it will throw the timing information away which is assigned by FN, and establish a routing table, used to store the forwarding path of the data of FN .After other clusters (vice) fusion node receive the information, they will calculate the distance between FN to the BS , FN or ACH will throw the information packet if it is far than the distance of itself to the BS , or put the N stored in the routing list.

The Stable Transmission Stage of Network. When the ACH have finished, the network entered a stable stage .N within each cluster is will sent data to the

FN, FN After data fusion according to their own timing , and sends the result to ACH in the cluster .The cluster of ACH, FN will select the nearest ACH as the next hop N from the routing list if there is no ACH in the cluster .The FN near the base station may have a empty routing list for no ACH in the cluster, then it will sent the data to the BS directly. ACH will select the nearest as the next hop N from the routing list after receiving the information , until there is an empty routing list of ACH , it will also direct sent the data to the BS.

When the clusters conduct several rounds of data transmission stably, the network will enter a new round of clusters and stable process. Same with the LEACH algorithm, in1/p round, the N which is elected as FN before can no longer participate in the election of FN.

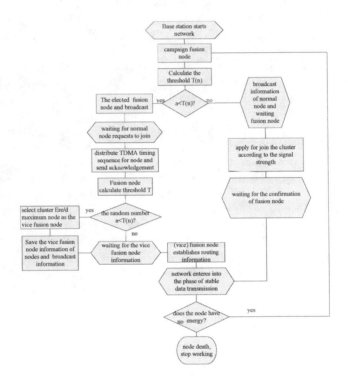

Fig. 1. The flow chart of DNDC algorithm

4   THE ADNDC Algorithm

DNDC algorithm has just been greatly improved in the energy balanced compared to LEACH algorithm, but has not significantly improved the survivability life of the network. This is mainly because the data transmission path of FN, which is simply selected based on the shortest distance from its own, so the chosen path is not optimal, it will consume a lot of network energy.

In order to make the routing path optimized, we should make the energy consumption at least for the data transmission in the routing list with the selected process. Based on this basic, we could optimize the data transfer path of the DNDC algorithm by using ant colony algorithm. ADNDC algorithm is based on ant colony algorithm to optimize the path of the DNDC algorithm(a novel DNDC algorithm based on ACO).

The difference between ADNDC algorithm and DNDC algorithm is that exist a path optimization step of ant colony after the selection of ACH in the second stage, and a different selecting form of a next hop node of data transmission in the third stage of stable stage. The main work process of ADNDC algorithm is as follows:

First, all the FN in the network will broadcast ant to all the ACH in the routing list after the selection of ACH, so only the ACH within the FN list could receive ant sent by FN, the ant contains a routing list R_list which involved the ID information of ant that has through all the nodes. And also contains the total energy E_{total} that ant need in transmission, node j could calculate the energy E_{ij} required by the transmission of data between node i, j , and add it to the ant E_{total}. The routing list which contains the ant node currently could detect ant node just based on the information in the list to determine whether to accept forwarding ants. There is only direct communication path between the FN and the BS if the FN routing list is empty, so it will not broadcast ant.

Once received the ant ACH will add their own ID number to R_list and update the E_{total} values of ant,then check the routing list, if it is empty, the ACH will direct sent the ant to BS, or replace with its own routing list to the original N_list information of ant, then broadcast the ant out.

BS will add up the number of path from each FN to BS and the consumption of energy information required by each path after all ant of the network has arrived BS, then the pheromone value for updating each ACH could be calculated according to the statistics, and at last broadcast out the information of the pheromone value each (vice) fusion node need for updating. (Vice) fusion node will update the pheromone according to the received information. Calculated by equation (3):

$$\tau_{ij} = \tau_{init} + \Delta\tau_{ij} \tag{3}$$

τ_{ij} means the initial pheromone content between every two (sub) fusion nodes, generally valued as 1. $\Delta\tau_{ij}$ indicates the updated value, which is calculated using the formula (4):

$$\Delta\tau_{ij} = \sum_{k=1}^{m} \Delta\tau_{ij}^{k} \tag{4}$$

M means the number that all the fusion nodes have passed through between the (vice) fusion node i to j in the path leading to BS, different from the traditional ant algorithm which m represents the number of ants. $\Delta\tau_{ij}^{k}$ could be calculated by equation (5):

$$\Delta\tau_{ij}^{k} = Q/E_{toatal}^{k} \tag{5}$$

Q is a constant, E^k_{total} represents the total energy consumption of passing the k-path between (vice) fusion node i and j, which difference from the traditional ant colony optimization algorithm. We use the energy consumption value on the path.

As soon as the pheromone of the whole (vice) fusion node has updated, the network enters the stabilization phase of data transmission. Same as the DNDC algorithm, node within each cluster will be sent to the fusion node to fuse data, and send the data to BS directly or through a multi-hop communication of the ACH by FN. But different with the DNDC algorithm, (vice) fusion node of the ADNDC algorithm select the next hop not based on the shortest distance in the routing list, but based on probability. The calculating formula is as follows:

$$p_{ij} = \frac{\tau^\alpha_{ij}\eta^\beta_{ij}}{\sum_{s\epsilon R}\tau^\alpha_{is}\eta^\beta_{is}}, j\epsilon R \qquad (6)$$

Similar to the traditional ant colony algorithm, η_{ij} represents the visibility between (vice) fusion node i and j, its value equals to $1/d_{ij}$, α express the pheromone adjustment coefficients while β express the visibility adjustment coefficients, and R represents the routing list of the (vice) fusion node i.

(Vice) fusion node choose node from the routing list with the largest probability of calculation as next hop, once the node in the routing list come to a failure, it will be removed from the list and instead choose another node with the largest probability of calculation as next hop.

4.1   Experimental Analysis

Experimental Parameters Set. Set the network as a X*X rectangular area, the base station location is(0.5*X75+X) on the axis . In order to compare the influence of the network size on two different algorithms, the test will take two different values of X, and choose two different groups of p values and adjustment coefficient k values of ACH selected by network. In two different size network, ant colony optimization part expresses the adjustment coefficient ? and ? of pheromone and visibility take values 5 and 1 respectively. The initial pheromone concentration between (vice) fusion nodes is1, $Q = 100 \times 10^{-8}$.

Simulation Results and Analysis. In several different sizes of networks, we compare the network survival nodes number and the total network consumption with time in ADNDC algorithm, DNDC algorithm and LEACH algorithm.

The Network I Simulation. Figure 3 is in the network of P = 0.1, k = 4 and the area size of 100 x100nodes number 100, the initial energy of nodes is 2J to simulate. Generally think when WSN nodesdeaths is more than eighty percent, the whole network is dead. So we carried out ten times simulation in the network one, calculate the first nodes death time and the entire network average death time respectively in the DNDC algorithm and LEACH algorithm .In ADNDC

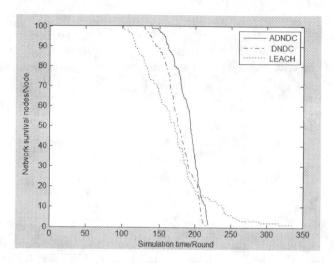

Fig. 2. The comparison chart between survival nodes number of network one and time

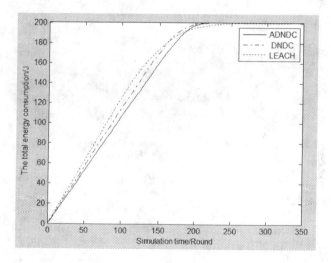

Fig. 3. The comparison chart between survival nodes number of network one and time

algorithm, the average death time of the first node is 131, and the entire network is 203; In the DNDC algorithm, the average death time of the first node of is 138, the entire network is 209; in the LEACH algorithm, the first node of the average death time is 105, the entire network is 201.

The Network II Simulation. Figure 4 is in the network of P=0.2k=2 and the area size of 100 x100nodes number 100, the initial energy of nodes is 2J to simulate. After ten times simulation ,the statistical results shows that in ADNDC algorithm, the average death time of the first node is 155,and the average death

time of the entire network is197.In the DNDC algorithm , the average death time
of the first node is 156, the average death time of the entire network is 189; in
the LEACH algorithm he average death time of the first node is 70, the average
death time of the entire network is 193.

The Network III Simulation. Figure 5 is in the network of P=0.1k=4and
the area size of 200x200nodes number 200, the initial energy of nodes is 4J to
simulate. After ten times simulation, the statistical results shows that in ADNDC

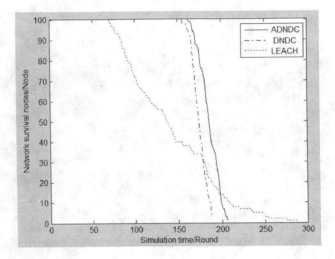

Fig. 4. The comparison chart between survival nodes number of network two and time

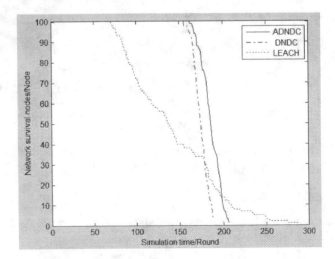

Fig. 5. The comparison chart between total energy consumption of network two and
time

algorithm, the average death time of the first node is 136, and the average death time of the entire network is 349.In DNDC algorithm, the average death time of the first node is 109, and the average death time of the entire network is 342. In LEACH algorithm, the average death time of the first node is 50, and the average death time of the entire network is 321.

The Network IV Simulation. Figure 6 is in the network of P=0.2k=2and the area size of 200x200nodes number 200, the initial energy of nodes is 4J to

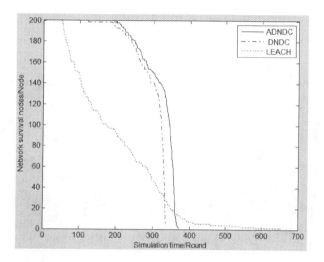

Fig. 6. The comparison chart between survival nodes number of network three and time

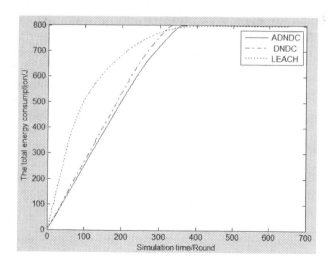

Fig. 7. The comparison chart between total energy consumption of network three and time

simulate. After ten times simulation, the statistical results shows that in ADNDC algorithm, the average death time of the first node is 169, and the average death time of the entire network is308.In DNDC algorithm, the average death time of the first node is 147, and the average death time of the entire network is260. In LEACH algorithm, the average death time of the first node is 26, and the average death time of the entire network is264.

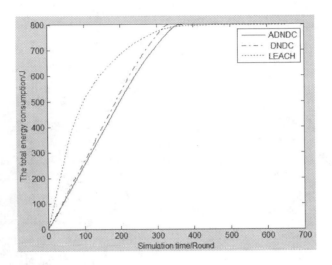

Fig. 8. The comparison chart between survival nodes number of network four and time

Analysis of Results. Compare to the LEACH algorithm in the first network, algorithm ADNDC and DNDC algorithm not only has a better energy balance but also a longer lifetime of the network analyzing from the experimental data. But algorithm ADNDC is somewhat less certain to DNDC algorithm, for it has a smaller scale which leads to the decrease of number of the (vice) fusion node which forwards data in the network. In addition, the selected fusion node P value is a little small of the first network while the selected vice fusion node K value is a little large, which leads to the decrease of the proportion of the (vice) fusion node which forwards data in the network.

Therefore, in such a network, compared to the energy consumed in the ants way-finding, the energy that the network has saved by using the ant colony algorithm to optimize the path is not a small number, so in this case, it is not appropriate to use the ant colony optimization algorithm to optimize the path of the DNDC algorithm for it not only increase the complexity of the algorithm but decrease the performance of the network.

On the basis of the network I, the network II has just changed the value of the probability P of the selected fusion node and the value of K of the selected sub-fusion node. In such networks, the energy balance of the algorithm ADNDC and DNDC algorithm is better than LEACH algorithm, the performance of the lifetime of the network with algorithm ADNDC is better than that with LEACH

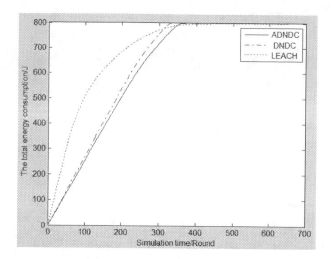

Fig. 9. The comparison chart between total energy consumption of network four and time

algorithm, while the survival performance of network with DNDC algorithm is less than the LEACH algorithm. This is because the larger the value of k, the smaller probability of selecting ACH there will be, its performance is more close to LEACH. And due to the shortcomings of the DNDC algorithm itself, it consumed much more energy in routing data, so the performance of the network lifetime is less than that with LEACH algorithm. While the ADNDC algorithm has solved the shortcomings of the DNDC algorithm, its performance is better than the LEACH algorithm. In addition, as the proportion of the number of the (vice) fusion node which forwards data in the network has increased, the performance of ADNDC algorithm is better than DNDC algorithm.

The size of the network becomes large in network III, IV respectively compared to the network I, II. Similar to network I, II, while the proportion of the number of the (vice) fusion node which forwards data in the network is a little larger. But regardless of the probability of the selected fusion node or the adjustment coefficient value of the selected sub-fusion node, performance of ADNDC algorithm is better than both the LEACH algorithm and the DNDC algorithm. In a large-scale network, the (vice) fusion node participated in data routing will be more, while the energy saved by ant colony optimization path compared to the energy consumed in the path-finding process becomes much. The bigger the size of the network, the larger the gap will be. In this case, the use of ant colony optimization to optimize the path of DNDC algorithm is very suitable.

5   Conclusion

The proposed fusion algorithms of DNDC and ANDC have a good energy balance according to the uneven network energy consumption caused by one-hop routing of the hierarchical LEACH in WSN. The DNDC algorithm is simple and easy to achieve, suitable to small scale network which has a smaller proportion of the (vice) fusion node. ADNDC algorithm solves the optimization problem of the routing data path of DNDC, but adds more complexity of the algorithm at the same time. It is suitable for large-scale or large network which has a larger proportion of the (vice) fusion node.

References

1. Kumari, P.: Wireless Sensor Network. LAP Lambert Academic Publishing AG and Co KG (2012)
2. Bleiholder, J., Naumann, F.: Data Fusion. ACM Computing Surveys 41(3), 102–109 (2008)
3. Heinzelman, W., Chandrakasan, A., Balakrishnan, H.: Energy-efficient communication protocol for wireless micro sensor networks. In: Proceedings of the 33rd Hawaii International Conference on System Sciences (HICSS 2000), pp. 8020–8029. IEEE Press, Maui (2000)
4. Lindsey, S., Raghavendra, C.S.: PEGASIS: Power-Efficient Gathering in Sensor Information Systems. In: Proceedings of the IEEE Aerospace Conference, pp. 1125–1130 (2002)
5. Younis, O., Fahmy, S.: HEED: A Hybrid, Energy-Efficient, Distributed Clustering Approach for Ah Hoc Sensor Networks. IEEE Transactions on Mobile Computing 3(4), 660–669 (2004)
6. Soro, S., Heinzelman, W.: Prolonging the Lifetime of Wireless Sensor Networks Via Unequal Clustering. In: Proceedings of the 5th International Workshop on Algorithms for Wireless, Mobile, Ad Hoc and Sensor Networks, Denver (2005)
7. Li, C.-F., Chen, G.-H., Ye, M.: An Uneven Cluster-Based Routing Protocol for Wireless Sensor Networks. Chinese Journal of Computers 30(1), 27–36 (2007)
8. Song, M., Chenglin, Z., Zheng, Z.: An Improved Fuzzy Unequal Clustering Algorithm for Wireless Sensor Network. In: International ICST Conference on Communication and Networking in China, pp. 245–250 (2001)
9. Qin, Z.-C., Zhou, Z., Zhao, X.-C.: A Ring-Based Clustering Routing Protocol for WSN Using Particle Swarm Optimization. Journal of Beijing University of Posts and Telecommunications 35(5), 26–30 (2012)
10. Zhou, Q., Li, L.: A Multi-hop Routing Protocol Based on Double Cluster-heads for Wireless Sensor Networks. Journal of Wuhan University of Technology(Information and Management Engineering 32(2), 202–205 (2010)
11. Liu, Z.-J., Li, L.-Y., Yang, S.-H.: Improvement of LEACH Protocol Based on Dual Cluster Head Non-uniform Clustering. Microelectronics and Computer 28(11), 81–84 (2011)

Based on the Law of Bill Traversal of Underwater Optical Image Restoration Algorithm for Color Pixel Matrix

Hao Xu, Bing Zheng*, and Tingting Lin

Department of Electric Engineering, Ocean University of China,
266100 Qingdao, China
bingzh@ouc.edu.cn

Abstract. Because of the physical properties of the water, the light diffuse propagation attenuation occurs when the light go through water and light of different wavelength ranges in which the diffuse attenuation will be different, so the color of water image will become bluish. This paper proposed an algorithm to traverse the pixel matrix calculating diffuse attenuation factor, which can reduce diffuse attenuation factor calculating accumulated error in the process of poor, widening wave calculation, so that the image is not to be restored to recover pixel blind spot rate low, the error is small. In this paper, the color noise ratio was used to evaluate the quality of the image. Through experiments that the method used color restoration to get better results, the experimental noise ratio is 3.614%.

Keywords: underwater image, color restoration, Beer's law, diffuse attenuation coefficient.

1 Introduction

Scientific research in the field of underwater research is a very important area, and in the underwater operations will often through photography technology to capture an image of an object underwater research object of study to study. However, due to the reasons for the aqueous medium, the captured image will be distorted color, which is mainly due to the aqueous medium with severe diffuse light attenuation.

Water-borne diffuse light attenuation include both absorption and scattering [1].

Absorption effect is caused by the water molecules in the aqueous medium, dissolved substances, plankton and suspended particles produced by direct absorption of light. Since the solubility of substances in different waters, phytoplankton and zooplankton and suspended particles are different types and concentrations, different waters have a great degree of absorption of light different; physical characteristics of the light, light of different wavelengths in the same water absorption of

---

* Corresponding author.

L. Sun, H. Ma, and F. Hong (Eds.): CWSN 2013, CCIS 418, pp. 337–344, 2014.

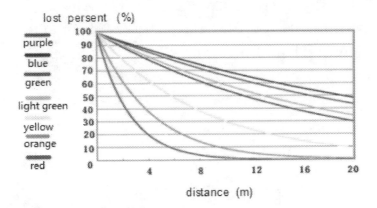

Fig. 1. Relationship between light intensity and the propagation distance

the spread can be different [2]. Figure 1, the light intensity at different wavelengths in water losses as a percentage relationship between the propagation distance.

Scattering effect is mainly due to water molecules, plankton and suspended particles scattering of light, so that the light deviated from the original path and cause energy losses. Diffuse light attenuation coefficient in the water reflects the total effect of the two, so that different light attenuation coefficient of water there is a great difference, the same waters of different wavelengths of light attenuation coefficient is also very different.

From the above analysis, such as shorter wavelength blue light underwater propagation loss is small, while the red light at longer wavelengths such as underwater propagation loss is large, so the image will appear bluish underwater dim phenomenon [3]. And the light and the light propagation loss of the total distance, the loss rate increases as the distance increases gradually linear.

2   Beer's Law

2.1   Suppose

This will be based on the following three assumptions, the different wavelengths of light attenuation coefficient is estimated [4].

1) May be represented by each color image RGB color representation;
2) There is no visible water floats, so the acquired image color noise is 0;
3) In the best light and angle compensation obtain images, so the image is the best underwater images.

The aim is to keep the wavelength, respectively, discrete, easy quantitative analysis; excluded due to underwater obstacles cause image noise, easy ignoring small factor correlation; requirements for image quality, easy to exclude non-main factors.

2.2   Overview of Beer's Law

Beer's law, the photon's performance in a medium, is the monochromatic beam irradiating the surface of an absorbent medium, by a certain thickness of media, since the medium absorbs a portion of light, transmitted light intensity will decay. The greater the concentration of the absorbing medium, the thicker the thickness of the medium, the more remarkable attenuation of the light intensity is. See equation below:

$$I = I_0 e^{-k_\lambda z}$$

I: The observed intensity
I_0: The original light intensity
k_λ: Wavelength of the light attenuation factor
z: Optical transmission distance in the medium
The diffuse attenuation factor is calculated from this:

$$k_\lambda = \frac{\ln I_0 - \ln I}{z}$$

3   Diffuse Attenuation Factor Analysis of Algorithms

Every pixel can expressed as vector $\overline{color} = (R, G, B)$. The image is expressed as a two-dimensional matrix of pixels. Let pixel matrix $T_{(x,y)}$, then each image pixel color values are available from the three-dimensional matrix $T_{\overline{color}} = (R_{(x,y)}, G_{(x,y)}, B_{(x,y)})$ [5].

The three-dimensional matrix of pixel color values of the three dimensions of the projection transformation were done, the pixel can be obtained three-dimensional color value matrix, which matrix for each pixel in the light reflected monochromatic beam, wavelength is a certain value $\lambda_{(x,y)}$.

$$R_{(x,y)} = \pi_R(T) \tag{1}$$

$$G_{(x,y)} = \pi_G(T) \tag{2}$$

$$B_{(x,y)} = \pi_B(T) \tag{3}$$

Values of these three matrix pixel monochrome grayscale image conversion, get three monochrome pixel values of light intensity matrix:

$$I_{R(x,y)} = Gray(R_{(x,y)}) \tag{4}$$

$$I_{G(x,y)} = Gray(G_{(x,y)}) \tag{5}$$

$$I_{B(x,y)} = Gray(B_{(x,y)}) \tag{6}$$

Under ordinary conditions so we can get the three pixel monochrome image intensity value matrix, then obtain three monochromatic beam diffuse attenuation factor matrix:

$$k_R = \frac{\ln I^0_{R(x,y)} - \ln I_{R(x,y)}}{z} \tag{7}$$

$$k_G = \frac{\ln I^0_{G(x,y)} - \ln I_{G(x,y)}}{z} \tag{8}$$

$$k_B = \frac{\ln I^0_{B(x,y)} - \ln I_{B(x,y)}}{z} \tag{9}$$

Diffuse light attenuation is nonlinear, the propagation distance of the light intensity is the same as the attenuation factor can diffuse the same. The attenuation factor of the array to the same intensity of light transmitted from the same premise of diffuse attenuation factor of the same, by the three-dimensional matrix of pixel color values can be estimated diffuse attenuation inverse of the original three-dimensional image matrix of pixel color values, even if the color is restored.

4   Color Underwater Image Restoration Algorithm Steps

In mind the need to restore the color images of (z to obtain a picture of the object distance from the camera), under the same conditions as the reference image, the reference pictures under normal conditions, the reference picture, respectively Figure 2 and Figure 3.

Fig. 2. underwater standards swatches, z is 30cm

The basic idea: to estimate diffuse through the reference picture attenuation factor, attenuation factor used to estimate the diffuse color to restore the picture [6].

Step 1: Obtain a three-dimensional reference picture pixel color value matrix $T'_{z\_color} = (R^z_{(x,y)}, G^z_{(x,y)}, B^z_{(x,y)})$;

Step 2: Apply the formula (1) (2) (3) for the three-dimensional matrix of pixel color values T'_{z_color}. Projection to three dimensions, to obtain three-dimensional matrix of pixel monochrome $R^z_{(x,y)}, G^z_{(x,y)}, B^z_{(x,y)}$;

Step 3: Apply the formula (4) (5) (6) for three values of the pixel matrix monochrome grayscale image conversion, gets its pixel values of the light intensity matrix monochrome $I^z_{R(x,y)}, I^z_{G(x,y)}, I^z_{B(x,y)}$;

Step 4: Repeat the picture T'_0 No.1,2,3 step of obtaining the value of the image pixel intensity monochromatic matrix $I^0_{R(x,y)}, I^0_{G(x,y)}, I^0_{B(x,y)}$;

Step 5: Apply the formula (7) (8) (9) calculate the diffuse attenuation factor k_R', k_G', k_B';

Step 6: Get image repeat No.2 steps to get the picture of the three-dimensional pixel monochrome matrix $R_{(x,y)}, G_{(x,y)}, B_{(x,y)}$

Step 7: Find T_z traversal of T_z' with equal intensity pixels, this pixel point inverse diffuse attenuation:

$$R^0_{(x,y)} = R_{(x,y)} e^{k_R' z} \tag{10}$$

$$G^0_{(x,y)} = G_{(x,y)} e^{k_G' z} \tag{11}$$

$$B^0_{(x,y)} = B_{(x,y)} e^{k_B' z} \tag{12}$$

Step 8: Color restored picture as $T = (R^0_{(x,y)}, G^0_{(x,y)}, B^0_{(x,y)})$

5 Algorithm Advantages and Disadvantages to Be Desired

5.1 Advantages and Disadvantages

Advantages:

Based on the Beer's law for color restoration, the most important task is to estimate the diffuse attenuation coefficient. The diffuse attenuation coefficient by a number of factors, in the same waters of a homogeneous most important factor is the light wavelength and the distance attenuation, in particular wavelength, which is continuous in the range, leads us to capture all light wavelengths unrealistic.

Fig. 3. Air standard color, z is 30cm

(1) This algorithm is to be treated through the standard palette color image restoration restored, bypassing the diffuse attenuation factor acquisition, through the existing standard color image and the general conditions of underwater image color contrast, used directly to calculate the standard Beer's law swatch diffuse all wavelengths of light attenuation factor, and then use the diffuse attenuation factor to be set to the color returned to the same wavelength on the image of the diffuse light attenuation factor assigned.

(2) According to the standard color gamut to get different color gamut recovery, with 24 color palette, then restored it to 24 color images; with 48 swatches, then restored it to 48 color images.

Disadvantage:

(1) Subject to the color quality of recovery to restore the picture by two reference picture quality decisions;

(2) Since the reference picture of the discrete light intensity of three primary colors RGB is to be recovered may not all include all of the light intensity of the color image, it will cause some of the pictures to be restored pixel diffuse attenuation factor can not be obtained, it can not be restored, to make the color noise ratio:

$$Noise = \frac{R_{T \neq T'} + G_{T \neq T'} + B_{T \neq T'}}{3 \times N_{T(x,y)}} \times 100\% \qquad (13)$$

$R_{T \neq T'}$ is a two-dimensional pixel monochrome R-value can not match the number of pixels of T_z.

$G_{T \neq T'}$ is a two-dimensional pixel monochrome G-value can not match the number of pixels of T_z.

$B_{T \neq T'}$ is a two-dimensional pixel monochrome B-value can not match the number of pixels of T_z.

$N_{T(x,y)}$ is the total number of pixels T_z.

5.2   Improved

As the picture on the color value of each pixel is relevant, the use of correlation, with the noise surrounding pixel diffuse attenuation factor to estimate the noise out of the diffuse attenuation factor, resulting in color restored.

6   Experimental Result

The original image T_z, the restored image T, the noise number is 4424,the rate of the noise number is 3.6136%.

     (a) The Original Image   (b) The Restored Image

Fig. 4. Experimental Result

7   Conclusions

As we can see, this method can kind of increase the contrast of the image. The image is till bluish, the red color is very little, the true image is vivid and full of red color. Back-scattering effect is strongly influenced in this picture.

In further work, a better method should be proposed to recover the color of the underwater image. At least, the red color part should be recovered to get a better result.

References

1. Alpine, A.E., Cloern, J.E.: Trophic interactions and direct physical effects control phytoplankton biomass and production in an estuary. Limnology and Oceanography 37(5), 946–955 (1992)

2. Mudg, M., et al.: Principles and practices of robust, photography-based digital imaging techniques for museums (2010)
3. Raimondo, S., Silvia, C.: Underwater image processing: state of the art of restoration and image enhancement methods. EURASIP Journal on Advances in Signal Processing (2010)
4. Jensen, J.R.: Introductory digital image processing: a remote sensing perspective. Univ. of South Carolina, Columbus (1986)
5. Comaniciu, D., Meer, P.: Mean shift: A robust approach toward feature space analysis. IEEE Transactions on Pattern Analysis and Machine Intelligence 24(5), 603–619 (2002)
6. Iqbal, K., et al.: Underwater Image Enhancement Using An Integrated Color Model. IAENG International Journal of Computer Science 32(2), 239–244 (2007)

Privacy Protection Based on Key-changed Mutual Authentication Protocol in Internet of Things

Li Peng[1,2], Wang Ru-chuan[1,2], Su Xiao-yu[1], and Chen Long[1]

[1] College of Computer, Nanjing University of Posts and Telecommunications,
Nanjing, Jiangsu 210003, China
[2] Jiangsu High Technology Research Key Laboratory for Wireless Sensor Networks,
Nanjing, Jiangsu 210003, China
lipeng@njupt.edu.cn

Abstract. This paper concentrates in the privacy protection in Internet of things. It firstly focuses on the security issues and attack risks of Internet of things from four aspects, which are perception layer, transport layer, application layer and the integrated networking system. And it puts forward some proposals on wireless sensor network and RFID (Radio Frequency Identification) security system structure. The researches are theoretical basis in security defense of Internet of things. Furthermore, in order to reduce the security risks in Internet of things communication process, this paper puts forward key-changed mutual authentication protocol. The protocol integrates random number generator in the tag and reader, and adopts the one-way Hash function, key refresh in real time, key backup and other mechanisms. The analysis shows that this protocol is able to be well applied to low cost Internet of things system and effectively prevent the network from replay, replication, denial of service, spoofing and tag tracking attacks.

Keywords: Privacy Protection, Security Risk, Key-changed Mutual Authentication, Internet of things.

1   Introduction

The Internet of things is regarded as the application extension of Internet. The innovation based on the user experience is the key point of the development of Internet of things. The concept of the Internet of things breaks the tradition mode of thinking pattern and plays an important role in smart home, logistics system, medical care, industrial monitoring, and military battlefield. Along with the wide range applications of wireless sensor networks node and RFID to Internet of things, security risks of Internet of things are becoming more and more significant [1].

The paper mainly focuses on the security issues and attack risks of Internet of things from the three levels, which are perception layer, transport layer, and application layer. It puts forward some proposals on wireless sensor network

L. Sun, H. Ma, and F. Hong (Eds.): CWSN 2013, CCIS 418, pp. 345–355, 2014.

and RFID security system structure. In addition, it proposes the key-changed mutual authentication protocol to enhance the privacy protection in the Internet of things, and together it analyzes the detailed description of the protocol and its security feasibility.

2   Security Risks Analysis in Internet of Things

2.1   Security Risks in the Perception Layer

The perception layer is essential in Internet of things, for it needs to realize the communication between objects. The perception layer is mainly responsible for information collection and recognition. The perception layer includes sensor nodes, RFID cards, short distance radio communication, low power routing and other important technologies. The technologies themselves have security risks, so that they bring safe problems to Internet of things. The security risks in the perception layer are summarized as follows:

(1) Radio interference in sensor signal. In the wireless sensor network, the malicious nodes perceptual interference attacks usually occur in two situations, which are hidden terminal and exposed terminal. The attacker disguises itself as a normal communication node, sending invalid packet constantly so as to occupy the channel resources in either case. As a result, the surrounding neighbor nodes can not start the send process when sending nodes detected around. So it interrupts normal operation of network eventually and reduces network efficiency.

(2) Card copy attack. Card number reading operation in ID card is of no restriction. Compared to the ID card, IC card security seems better. The corresponding password authentication is needed in data reading or writing operation. While the ID card is simple, the card number is easier to read or copy. The replication RFID card can be used for routine attendance and access control, so that the application of RFID loses the original meaning.

(3) Wireless sensor attack. As a significant part of the Internet of things, wireless sensor network determines the perception layer, even the operation and execution efficiency of Internet of things. Therefore, the risk problem of wireless sensor network attack appears particularly important.

(4) Device power consumption attack. This attack causes node energy resource depletion through continuous communication by the use of protocol vulnerabilities. For instance, it repeats sending the packets by using the fault in link layer retransmission mechanism, which draining node resource ultimately. In 802.11 MAC protocol, it utilizes RTS(Request To Send), CTS(Clear To Send) and ACK(data ACKnowledge) mechanism. If a malicious node sends RTS packets to a node continually, the node should respond CTS packet, which leads to node resource depletion eventually.

(5) Network node heterogeneity risk. From bottom to top, it involves a variety of heterogenous networks, such as wireless sensor, RFID network and mobile communication network, etc. The networks have higher requirements to security mechanisms when communication or fusion.

(6) The node betrayed problem. The Internet of things seems to be large networks composed of many small heterogeneous networks. While each node among heterogeneous networks needs to cooperate, it may generate risks.

2.2   Security Risks in the Transport Layer

Internet is the core and foundation of Internet of things, and Internet of things is the extension and expansion of Internet-based network. The transport layer is mainly responsible for transmission information. The key technologies include network access technology, routing technology, the convergence of heterogeneous networks, gateway equipments and so on. These important facilities may have safety problems in hardware and software protocols [2,3].

(1) Node forgery and identity spoof attack. A malicious user with forged identity entrances into Internet of things, accesses to resources or data, uses network illogically. Some key points are introduced as following: The attacker gets into the Internet of things through forged RFID and accesses to network resources illogically. By man-in-the-middle attack or identity fraud ways, it filches user authentication key, encryption key and session key, and steals user privacy data. In wireless sensor network, forgery node accesses to internet, initiating a DoS (Denial of Service) attack or disrupting network routing network.

(2) Network routing protocol attack [4]. Seen from the attack source, one is malicious attacker external, and the other is the security node internal. An attacker outside increases the network load by inserting through the wrong routing information, or modifying the routing protocol to disrupt the operation. It generates a large number of retransmissions or invalid route information. As to the internal security node, it refers to the illogical identity of user node, which is broken into by malicious node in the network. The malicious node then broadcasts incorrect routing information, so that it affects other users working normally [5].

(3) Malicious code injection attacks in wireless. As the wireless sensor network channel resource is limited, the way to illogically use channel resources is the most effective attacking way. This type of attack is characterized by an attacker sending useless signals ongoing, so as to occupy the channel resource and hinder the normal transmission and communication node. The basic types can be divided into continuous attack and intermittent attack.

2.3   Security Risks in the Application Layer

The top of Internet of things is the application layer, and it is responsible for information processing and utilization. The application layer is the ultimate user oriented hierarchy. Application layer mainly includes the massive information processing, middleware, information forecast and other key technologies. There are some security vulnerabilities summarized as follows [6,7].

(1) Data and context privacy attack. It includes five aspects. Firstly, positioning threat: user with electronic label may be monitored and exposed position. Secondly, layout threat: the tag around forms specific RFID pattern, the tag

relations can be used to track. Thirdly, breadcrumb threat: it establishes identity item associated database by collecting specific figure. Fourthly, transaction threat: a certain RFID reader can guess the relationship between users and affairs when the tagged articles varying from one pattern to another. Finally, RFID card information leak: the same specification of RFID card recording different information through the RFID reader may leak large amounts of irrelevant information.

(2) Denial of service attack. DoS attack may occur in various levels of interconnection. In the perception layer, attackers prevent communication between RFID waves and tag. In the network layer, attackers use the loopholes existing in network, such as broadcast routing request, to attack network. In the application layer, it exists DoS flow attack risks.

(3) Privacy stealing technology. Attackers interest in all privacy information in the Internet of things network. For example, RFID tag information on the goods and reader with wiretap function can read all RFID label information of consumers. The traditional network may protect some important confidential information, however, in the Internet of things, because of too much information source, attacker may infer public information derived from some other private information by locking information sources of a target.

(4) Illogical tracking. One benefit of RFID is increasing transparency of supply chain, however new risks brought to data security. Attacker can illogically track by revealing key supply chain. RFID technology belongs to the non-contact automatic identification technology, the privacy of security threats are: illogical reading, position tracking, tapping, DoS , and reproduction attacks [8].

2.4   Security Risks in the Integrated Internet of Things System

Internet of things, as computer communication, faces threats from malicious code. Similarly, Internet of things tends to use network security protection technology, but the technology is not absolutely safe itself. The paper summarizes the possible malicious code attacks as well as protection system against risks of Internet of things [9-11].

(1) Malicious code attack. The malicious code needs to detect the sensor node, consider the current scanning strategies of various worms, and propose scanning strategy in the wireless sensor networks. During the diffusion process, it applies the topology discovery technology to malicious code. The effect of comprehensive attack has high degree, and it has integrated function with viruses, worms and back door, etc.

(2) The protection technical attack. Network firewall, as a protective measure, sets successfully once, it is difficult to detect the hosts behind it under normal circumstances. In Internet of things network, data are transmitted through the packets, and each packet has a certain format, which is called the protocol. The camouflage technology of data packet refers to the data packet constructed of attack protocol actually.

3   Privacy Protection Protocol Based on Mutual Authentication

Due to the tag information leakage and the use of unique identifier tag to malicious track, the tradition RFID tag potentially exists security risks. This chapter aims at the security flaws on the relevant authentication protocol based on Hash function, and puts forward a kind of Key-changed Mutual Authentication Protocol (KMAP). This protocol has forward security property, it resists illogical RFID intrusion methods, such as tag trace, replay attack and tag copy attack[12,13], etc.

3.1   The Design Requirement of the Protocol

A mature and efficient RFID authentication protocol requires the following characteristics [14]:

(1) Low cost. The tag in low cost often has low computational power and limited memory unit. Symmetric encryption algorithm and asymmetric encryption algorithm have a higher safety performance, but they are not suitable for low cost RFID systems due to the large consume on the tag computing and the storage resources. The characteristics require higher demand for safety design on RFID protocol, and corresponding with specific password mechanism.

(2) Anonymity. RFID electronics tags typically store user privacies, such as identity information and current position. Therefore, in the process of the wireless communication protocol, it is of important to prevent leak of key information.

(3) Reliability. The RFID authentication protocol not only needs the ability to prevent tag replication attack, spoofing attack, eavesdropping attack and other common attacks, but also needs the ability to prevent attacks on the RFID device itself , such as the false synchronization attack, which the attacker makes the logical tag authentication failed by causing inconsistency data between tags and database.

(4) Mutual authentication. The RFID authentication protocol needs the reader to tag logicality identity authentication, and needs the tag to ensure the logical of the reader as well. The tag authentication is valid after confirming the logical identity status.

3.2   The Protocol Assumption

(1) Tag has low resistance. It can handle simple operations such as Hash calculation, random number generation, XOR and shift function.

(2) The backend server is appropriate to handle calculation of high-strength and complex data retrieval requirement.

(3) The attacker cannot find out the original data by the one-way Hash function.

(4) The attacker cannot obtain the internal data in tag by force bruting the inside circuit.

(5) On account of the unsafety channel between the reader and the tag, the attacker may eavesdrops, intercepts and modifies the information transferred on the channel. On the contrary, the attacker has no opportunity to get message from the channel between the reader and the backend server [15-16].

3.3　The Symbol Definition

The symbol definitions of KMAP protocol are showed in Table 1.

Table 1. The tag used in KMAP protocol

Symbol	Description
T	tag
R	$reader$
D	$backend server$
$PRNG$	$random number generator$
l	$bits number of data unit$
$H()$	$one-way Hash function$
$\oplus$	$XOR operator$
Rr	$random number reader generated (length l)$
Rt	$random number tag generated (length l)$
ID	$unique identification tag (length l)$
Key	$tag storage secret key (length l)$
Ko	$original secret key value (length l)$
Kn	$updated key value (length l)$

4　Key-changed Mutual Authentication Protocol

4.1　The Description of the Protocol

The backend server database mainly includes 4 columns, that are Index, ID, Key, and Pointer. The Index column is the self growth data sheet. ID column is the only sign number of tag. Key column is the random key that the reader distributes to each tag. And Pointer column is the data record associated pointer used to ensure data consistency. As a result, it prevents false synchronization attack.

The protocol initialization process. For ID tags,the reader generates a random key length l, then it inserts the initial recorded in the tags data table (ID,Key,0). It also sends the key value to the specified tag. The tag stores the Key value received, it gets into the locked state. At this moment, the initial recording in the tag is (ID, Key).

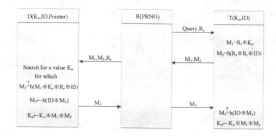

Fig. 1. KMAP Protocol authentication flowchart

4.2 Mutual Authentication Flowchart

The procedure of RFID authentication is shown in figure 1.

(1) The reader R generates a random number Rr, and send a query to the tag using random number Rr. The response includes three cases, that are no tag response, one tag response, and multiple tags response. The communication fails when no tag response; and frame-slot aloha algorithm conflict arbitration is performed when multiple tags response, which is shown in figure 2. Specific reader is selected by the conflict arbitration algorithm.

(2) The selected tag T generates a random number Rt when receiving a query request and related random number Rr from the reader. Then, the tag computes M1=Rt $\oplus$ Ko, M2=h(Rt$\oplus$Rr$\oplus$ID). Finally, it responses M1 and M2 to the reader.

(3) The reader receives M1 and M2, and sends M1, M2 and random number Rr to the server.

(4) The backend server receives M1, M2 and random number Rr, and retrieves the database to find out whether the data (Ko,ID) exists in the tag lists, which makes M2=h(M1$\oplus$Ko$\oplus$Rr$\oplus$ID). The reader authentication is successful when (Ko,ID) is identified, so that the tag is logical, and failed when no (Ko,ID) is identified. At this stage, the backend server requires only a simple operation Hash function, which tries to find out the (Ko,ID) to meet the equation M2=h(M1$\oplus$Ko$\oplus$Rr$\oplus$ID) and corresponding Pointeri. If the authentication is successful, the backend server then computes M3=h(ID$\oplus$M1), and generates new Kn=Ko$\oplus$M1$\oplus$M2. If Pointeri = 0, a new data table record j= (j,Kn,ID,i) index is inserted. If Pointeri 0, Pointeri is updated (Pointeri,Ko,ID,i). Finally, it sends M3 to the reader.

(5) When the tag receives the M3 from the reader, it compares h(ID$\oplus$M1) with the received M3. If equality holds, then the label reader authentication success, which means two-way authentication between the reader and tag is achieved. The tag unlocks and opens all functions to the reader, and updates key to Kn=Ko$\oplus$M1$\oplus$M2. Otherwise, it regards the reader as illogical, and the authentication process is failed.

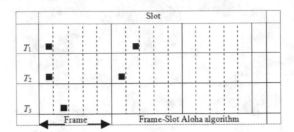

Fig. 2. Aloha conflict arbitration

5 The Security and Feasibility Analysis

5.1 Safety Analysis

(1) Confidentiality. The communication messages between the tag and reader are encrypted by Hash or XOR operation. The attacker fails to parses true content of the tag by intercepting packets between wireless communication channels.

(2) Integrity. The transmission data and the authentication process in protocol both ensure the data integrity with Hash. If an attacker makes unauthorized tampering with the data, it may make the tag and the reader authorization failed during the execution of protocol.

(3) Anonymity. The KMAP protocol uses the random number generator and the real-time refresh mechanism to ensure the anonymity of the tag. In the authentication phase, the information in transmission is a pseudo-random sequence computed by Hash or XOR with random numbers and secret key value without real tag information. At the same time, when each protocol is completed, the tag and the backend server update the old value of key Ko by the formula $Kn=Ko \oplus M1 \oplus M2$. That is why the tag has anonymity.

(4) Mutual authentication. First, in order to ensure the identification of the tag, the backend server queries if there is a matching record in the database according to the data returned from the tag. And then, it encrypts the ID information of the tag with the security key that the tag and the reader shared. The tag encrypts the information to confirm the logical status of the reader.

(5) Forward security. KMAP protocol takes the real-time refresh mechanism. The tag and the background server update the old value of key K by the equation $Kn=Ko \oplus M1 \oplus M2$. Even the attacker intercepts the current session key, it is unable to obtain the next session.

5.2 Analysis of Protocol Anti-attack

(1) Replay attack. The tag and the reader both integrate a random number generator, which produces random numbers length of l bit for each session. The probability of the same number is 2l each time. The length of low cost RFID protocol is 60 bits, so the chance to obtain authentication by making replay attack to the interactive information is very small.

(2) Replication attack. If an attacker gets a tag secret key value in some way, and clones a new tag successfully. Due to the KMAP protocol uses the real-time refresh mechanism, both of the database and the tag secret key change after the logical tag completing an authentication. It leads the replication tag failure to the authentication successfully.

(3) Denial of service attack. In the protocol of KMAP, the database stores the old key before authentication and the new key produced in each authentication at the same time. When an attacker makes the DoS attack to the RFID system, it may cause the value of the tag secret key different from the value of the newest secret key in the database. The database recovers the synchronization with tag secret key.

(4) Spoof attack. Due to the tag and the reader use random numbers in the interactive process and encrypt the message with XOR computing or Hash function, the attacker may not acquire the value session information in the tag response by imitating the reader.

(5) Tag tracking. The tag and reader generates random numbers Rt and Rr respectively. When initialing the protocol, the reader sends a query request. After the tag receiving the request, it computes M1=Rt⊕Ko, M2=h(Rt⊕Rr⊕ID) and sends M1, M2 to the reader. M1 performs Hash operation uses random number R1 XOR operation, the same to the M2 with random number R2, which makes uncertainty of the tag responses.

(6) Intermediate attack. The interactive information M2, M3 between the tag and the reader is the message abstracts encrypted by Hash functions. Any change to the transmission data in the communication process by the intermediate node will interrupt the protocol.

5.3   Related Security Protocols Comparison

The paper also compares the proposed KMAP protocol with Hash-lock protocol, Random Hash-lock protocol, Hash chain protocol, Hash-based ID variation protocol. As a result, it shows that KMAP protocol has better security

Table 2. Protocol security performance comparison

Security performance	Hash-lock protocol	Random Hash-lock protocol	Hash chain protocol	Hash-based ID variation protocol	KMAP
Information privacy	Yes	Yes	Yes	Yes	Yes
Forward security	No	No	Yes	No	Yes
Non-traceability	No	No	Yes	Yes	Yes
Indistinguishability	No	No	Yes	Yes	Yes
Anti-replay attack resistance	No	No	No	No	Yes

performance in information privacy, forward security, non-traceability, indistinguishability, and anti-replay attack resistance. The results are listed in Table 2.

6 Conclusions

As to the lack of unified understanding and standard of the secure system structure frame, analysis of the security architecture of Internet of things is needed. The main research carries out from the four aspects, which are perception layer, transport layer, application layer, and the Internet of things system, so as to strengthen the security of Internet of things. The application layer is mainly based on the security of data information, while the transmission layer is based on network security, and the perception layer is mainly concentrated in the security of sensor node itself.

According to the lack of security in traditional protocols, the key-changed mutual authentication protocol is proposed to protect the privacy in Internet of things. The protocol integrates random number generator in the tag and reader, and adopts the one-way Hash function, key refresh in real time, key backup and other mechanisms, so as to ensure the confidentiality, integrity, anonymity, mutual authentication and forward security during the communication process. And analysis of protocol anti-attack shows that the proposed protocol can effectively resist replay attack, replication attack, denial of service attack, spoofing attack and tag tracking attack. As a result, it reduces the security risks in Internet of things.

Acknowledgment. The subject is sponsored by the National Natural Science Foundation of P. R. China (No 61170065, 61373017, 61103195, 61203217), the Natural Science Foundation of Jiangsu Province (No BK2012436, BK20130882), Scientific and Technological Support Project of Jiangsu Province (No BE2012183, BE2012755Scie), Scientific Research and Industry Promotion Project for Higher Education Institutions (No JHB2012-7), Science and Technology Innovation Fund for higher education institutions of Jiangsu Province(No CXZZ12-0479).

References

1. Sharma, S., Sahu, A., Verma, A., et al.: Wireless Sensor Network Security. In: Second International Conference Computer Science and Information Technology (CCSIT 2012), pp. 317–326 (2012)
2. Li, P., Wang, R., Zhou, Y., Dai, Q.: Research on Network Malicious Code Dendritic Cell Immune Algorithm Based on Fuzzy Weighted Support Vector Machine. In: Wang, R., Xiao, F. (eds.) CWSN 2012. CCIS, vol. 334, pp. 181–190. Springer, Heidelberg (2013)
3. Sakthidharan, G.R., Chitra, S.: A survey on wireless sensor network: An application perspective. In: 2012 International Conference on Computer Communication and Informatics, pp. 1–5 (2012)
4. Oh, S.Y., Cornell, B., Smith, D., et al.: Rapid detection of influenza A virus in clinical samples using an ion channel switch biosensor. Biosensors and Bioelectronics 23(7), 1161–1165 (2008)

5. Peng, S.C.: A Survey on Malware Containment Models in Smartphones. Applied Mechanics and Materials 263, 3005–3011 (2013)
6. Menahem, E., Shabtai, A., Rokach, L., et al.: Improving malware detection by applying multi-inducer ensemble. Computational Statistics and Data Analysis 53(4), 1483–1494 (2009)
7. Gao, F., Hu, Z.H.: The Security Mechanism for Wireless Sensor Networks. Applied Mechanics and Materials 256, 2392–2395 (2013)
8. Holm, H., Sommestad, T., Almroth, J., et al.: A quantitative evaluation of vulnerability scanning. Information Management and Computer Security 19(4), 231–247 (2011)
9. Shaila, K., et al.: Mobile node authentication using key distribution scheme in wireless sensor networks. International Journal of Ad Hoc and Ubiquitous Computing 12(1), 34–45 (2013)
10. Jain, P., Goyal, S.: An Adaptive Intrusion Prevention System Based on Immunity. In: International Conference on Advances in Computing, Control, and Telecommunication Technologies, Trivandrum, Kerala, India, pp. 759–763. IEEE, Piscataway (2009)
11. Sun, F.X.: A Danger Theory Inspired Security Evaluation Paradigm for Computer Network. Advanced Materials Research 179(1), 1333–1337 (2011)
12. Folcik, V.A., Broderick, G., Mohan, S., et al.: Using an agent-based model to analyze the dynamic communication network of the immune response. Theoretical Biology and Medical Modelling 8(1), 1–25 (2011)
13. Nohl, K., Evans, D., Starbug, Plotz, H.: Reverse-Engineering a Cryptographic RFID Tag. In: USENIC Security Symposium, pp. 185–194. USENIC Association (2008)
14. Chang, Z.-H.: Research of RFID Privacy Protection Authentication Protocol and Application. The PLA Information Engineering University, Henan (2008)
15. Ohkubo, M., Suzuki, K., Kinoshita, S.: Hash-chain based Forward-Secure Privacy Protection Scheme for Low-cost RFID. In: Proceedings of the 2004 Symposium on Cryptography and Information Security (SCIS 2004) (2004)
16. Henrici, D., Muller, P.: Hash-based enhancement of location privacy for radio-frequency identification devices using varying identifiers. In: Proceedings of the 2nd IEEE Annual Conference on Pervasive Computing and Communications Workshops (PERCOMW 2004), Washington, DC, USA, pp. 149–153 (2004)

Development of Management Training System Based on RFID and Cloud Computing

Hongyan Ma

Qingdao Ocean Shipping Mariners College,
Qingdao, Shandong, China
mahyan@163.com

Abstract. Enhancing the human resource management in different levels is a critical success factor to advance the performance of management for universities.However,the traditional training system is lack of insufficient capital investment, deficient training resources, single model, few platforms, etc. In order to deal with those problems mentioned above, a novel of mangement training system based on RFID and cloud computing is proposed in the network platform. By the RFID read-write device control center collecting data, it transmits the data to the cloud, then implements centralized and distributed management of human resources.The human resource management can be sustainable development through this system.

Keywords: teacher training, RFID, cloud computing.

1 Introduction

In the era of economic globalization, the development of human resources will become a global strategic focus. In colleges and universities, the quality of teachers determines school-running quality, efficiency of schools, academic level and comprehensive strength. In recent years, a lot of efforts have been made in the development and training of talents [1].

With the emerging of popularization of higher education and the expansion of college enrollment, the problems existing in the teaching staff are highlighted increasingly. In the construction of teaching staff in universities, it is worthy of thinking about how to improve teacher management and teachers' quality. And the solving of all these problems depends on teacher training and optimization. Teacher training, as an important part in the construction of teaching staff, is the basis of high-level teaching staff construction, which concerns the survival and development of universities. Therefore, it is a basic task with strategic significance to strengthen teacher training, improve their quality and ability, and thus guarantee high-quality teachers for sustainable development of universities. With the development of information society and the transformation of the education, internet has become popular and information of education develops fast, which means the needs to improve training modes and means in teacher training

L. Sun, H. Ma, and F. Hong (Eds.): CWSN 2013, CCIS 418, pp. 356–362, 2014.

of universities. Therefore, the exploration and study of teacher development platform under the network environment is of theoretical and practical significance in promoting teachers' professional development and professional level. Through mass data resources from the Internet, this paper aims at constructing teacher training system of universities based on RFID and cloud computing, with the help of powerful data processing ability of cloud computing [2-3]. More ever, drawbacks of management, inappropriate training method, unadvanced training content, and low professionalism of instructors add the gaps of real result and expected outcome, thus fall to realize their demands. So the problems in teachers?development of universities can be concluded into as followings [4-7].

2 Overview

In this section, we review RFID,cloud computing and SaaS. RFID(Radio Frequency Identification) is a non-contact automatic identification technology [8]. Cloud computing is an internet-based application mode, through which the shared resources and information from software and hardware can be provided to computers and other devices as required. SaaS (Software as a service) is a completely innovative software application mode of 21st century, owning to the development of Internet and the mature of software.

2.1 RFID

RFID enables identification from a distance, and unlike earlier bar-code technology, it does so without requiring a line of sight. RFID systems consist of the RFID tag, the RFID reader, and the data processing subsystem. Typically the RFID tags consist of a microchip that stores data and a coupling element, used to communicate via radio frequency communication. The RFID tags may be either active or passive. Active RFID tags have an on-tag power supply and actively send an RF signal for communication, passive RFID tags obtain all of their power from the interrogation signal of the RFID reader and either reflect or load modulate the RFID reader signal for communication. The RFID readers consist of a radio frequency module, a control unit, and a coupling element to interrogate electronic tags via radio frequency communication. The data processing subsystem which utilizes the data obtained from the RFID reader in some useful manner.

2.2 Cloud Computing

Cloud computing is the blending outcome of parallel computing, distributed computing, grid computing and other computer technology and network technology. Cloud Computing aims at integrating some low-cost computing entities into a system with powerful computing ability through the Internet, which indicates the hybrid evolution and jump of virtualization, utility computing, IaaS, PaaS, SaaS, etc. Cloud computing, with nearly unlimited storage space, has a strong computing power and can support a variety of software services. It is essentially a combination of server virtualization technology and IaaS, whose core is to provide users with services in the form of renting computing resources, after the virtualization of computing resources of a certain or a few data centers. In the narrow sense, computing refers to the delivery and usage pattern of IT infrastructure, obtaining needed resources through network in on-demand and easily extensible form. The operation of enterprise data center will be more similar with Internet by distributing calculation in plentiful distributed computers instead of local computers or remote servers, which enables enterprises to switch resources into application, and to access computer and storage system as required. This can be compared to a mode with centralized power supply turned from an old simplex dynamo model, which means that the computing capacity can turn to commodity into circulation, like gas, water and electricity, with convenient use and low cost. The largest differences lie in that it is transmitted through the internet [7,9].

2.3 SaaS

SaaS has a similar meaning with "on - demand software? the application service provider (ASP) and hosted software. It is a model providing software through Internet, which means that manufacturers arrange application software on their own servers in a unified manner, and customers can order required application software services from manufacturers through Internet, according to actual demand, who should pay manufacturers the cost based on the number and time of ordered service. Obtaining the services from manufacturers through Internet, customers tend to rent web-based software to manage enterprise business activities, with no deed to maintain software. The service providers will manage and maintain software with full authority. Software manufacturers offer customers Internet application, but also software offline operation and local data storage, enabling customers to use the ordered software and services anytime and anywhere. For many small enterprises, SaaS is the best choice to adopt advanced technology, which can avoid the purchase, construction and maintenance of infrastructure and application.

3   Management Training System Based on RFID and Cloud Computing

3.1   Initialization

The efficient allocation and use of training resources directly affect the quality of university teachers. There is an unbalanced development in universities of different regions and different levels both in hardware and software. Even in a university, there also exists incompatibility between different departments and majors in resource utilization and allocation. Based on cloud computing platform, the users can make good use of real-time information on Internet, without installing any application software, which not only saves users terminal resources, but also avoids the maintenance. The users can use software directly by connecting to the corresponding server through network, which will reduce use cost of terminal software effectively, and avoid troubles of installation and updating as well [10].

3.2   Architecture Model of Teacher Training Platform

The architecture model of teacher training platform of universities based on RFID and cloud computing is shown in figure 1. Control center collects data by the RFID read-write device.The model is management system of cloud computing based on SaaS. Cloud computing mode usually relies on SOA architecture and Web Service technology. SOA is a service-oriented system, by which Web services related to teacher training management can be expanded. All these application modules, together with their based database processing, network transmission, platform interface, and other hardware and software form the teacher training cloud of universities as is shown in figure 1.

Physical resource layer is composed of data storage, network transmission and so on, all of which distribute in many different places, and are through private or public network communication. They should share the same communication mechanism, to ensure data updating. Virtual resource layer is made up of the software used for basic data management and information processing, such as database management system, web site service system, data reception processing system, UDDI, etc.

These systems are used for the processing of underlying information, and their stability determines the effectiveness of all application service in application service layer. Application service layer, with various kinds of application services available for teacher training management platform, is the software contacted and used directly by users. This layer includes user management, schedule management system, learning management system, resource management system, resource aggregation system, interactive system, questionnaire survey and assessment system.

3.3   The Functions of Each System

The functions of each system are as follows:

(1) User management system: the management on user registration, user information, user group, role permission and permission assignment etc. The user management system perform its funciton with the use of a campus card which is based on RFID. By reading, discriminating and disposing the data of campus card, the system can be used for the cardholder's identification, financial application, E-wallet and security assurance. Firstly, we will initialize the personal basic information and create the background database when transact campus

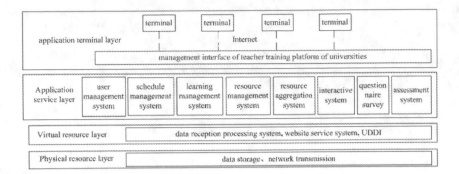

Fig. 1. Architecture model of teacher training platform of universities based on RFID and cloud computing

card. Secondly, the card helps the cardholders connect to the financial institutions, operations like the information transfer, electronic wallet payment can be conducted successfully .

(2) Schedule management system: according to the specific demand, different schedules can be formulated, such as school calendar, meeting schedule, course arrangement, teaching calendar, etc.;

(3) Learning management system: it can be realized to make online learning plan, to organize online learning courses, and to manage learning content and students grades, etc, which is applicable to teachers' pre-service training and other special training;

(4) Resource management system: to issue and manage all kinds of teaching resources, including video, pictures, animation, software, documentation and other kinds of files, and to count and analyze resource usage.

(5) Resource aggregation system: to aggregate all kinds of tools used commonly, such as search engines (Baidu, Google, etc.), academic journals library (CNKI, Wan fang, etc.), video, online library, public class (public class of Netease, MIT etc.);

(6) Interactive system: different BBS program can be set according to different majors. Users can communicate and discuss topics of common interest in corresponding column, as the functions and permissions of general BBS.

(7) Questionnaire survey system: questionnaire type and content can be lay out according to customer's specific use, which supports various types of survey questions, makes counting and analysis of the results, and produces data reports in a variety of forms (figure, table data);

(8) Assessment system: support multi-user online reviews of various projects evaluation, according to the specific purpose is different, make different evaluation criteria, can be used as a subject, online reviews, microteaching, etc. Terminal is integrated with all kinds of application services extensible platform, the platform has the function of dynamic integration of various kinds of access interface can provide various application service one-stop interface.

3.4   Request Oriented Scheduling Mechanism

We develop the teacher training platform based on B/S structure, using SaaS application provided by the Web browser. The SaaS application structure can be divided into four layers: user interface layer, balance the layer, application logic layer and database layer. In order to achieve the appearance of the system, function of configurability, efficient, flexible scheduling and resource, this paper designed the request oriented scheduling mechanism is shown in figure 2. The workflow engine can assemble a new process and implement it correctly. Business application request has been received from the tenant by analyzing the rules. The rules engine decide how to deal with the next step and send the reply to the workflow engine. The workflow engine will activate associated business service module under the guidance of the rules engine. For the user resource request, business service module will submit request to the business management module, and business management module will schedule the teacher staff training resources to the browser, then complete resource scheduling.

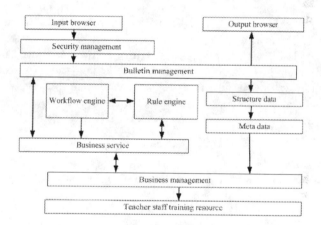

Fig. 2. Request oriented scheduling mechanism

4   Analysis System Characteristics

With adoption of SOA architecture and SaaS of web service, teacher training system of universities based on RFID and cloud computing demonstrates obvious advantages, compared with the existing system.

(1) Traditional teacher training system is fragmented. It is very common that each school sets up their independent rooms, and configures corresponding administrator, leading to redundant construction of IT resources. But the core of cloud computing is unified management. Owning to platform of cloud computing, all these resources can be unified and managed in a unified way, which not only can reduce maintenance cost, but also avoid unnecessary waste of resources.

(2) With Web Service model, teacher training system of universities based on cloud computing enables users to access all kinds of resources in training system just by browser. All information and resources of users are stored in service platform of cloud computing, which can realize the safety, unity, privacy and sharing of users resources.

(3) Teacher training system of universities based on RFID realizes identity recognition, financial application, etc. It combines network and information system, greatly improves the efficiency of management of universities and makes the management of training teachers more convenient.

5   Conclusion

The most important element in human resources of universities is the quality of teachers. Since teaching staff construction of university is a systemic project, university should create a teaching staff with reasonable structure and sustainable innovation, so as to maintain sustainable development of universities. In order to deal with those problems mentioned above, a novel of management training system based on RFID and cloud computing is proposed in the network platform. By the RFID read-write device control center collects data, it transmits the data to the cloud, then implement centralized and distributed management of human resources. Meanwhile it designs modules and functions of university teacher training system based on RFID and cloud computing, which will be definitely beneficial to university teacher training and improvement of training effectiveness, thus pushing forward the work of university teacher training.

References

1. Fu, Y.: Raising Main problems in training teachers and putting forward some countermeasures. Ournal of Social Science of Jiamusi University 22(1), 91–92 (2004)
2. Yali, T.: Conception of teacher training model in higher institutes. Journal of Qiongzhou University 15(6), 35–36 (2008)
3. Zheng, S., Wu, L., Lu, D.: Strengthening teaching management and innovation to improve clinical teaching quality. China Higher Medical Education (5), 56–59 (2006)
4. Qingyan, Z.: On training of college teachers in china. Journal of Beijing Institute of Technology (Social Sciences Edition) 4(4), 6–8 (2002)
5. Mingxue, C.: Problems and countermeasures of human resource management informatization. Market Modernization 23, 282 (2008)
6. Guangcong, W.: On the informatization of university human resources management. Journal of Ningbo University (Educational Science Edition) 1, 79–82 (2010)
7. Wu, Z.: Human resource management system model based on cloud computing research. China Computer Communication, 142–144 (2012)
8. Finkelzeller, K.: The RFID Handbook, 2nd edn. John Wiley & Sons (2003)
9. Armbrust, M., Fox, A., Griffith, R., Joseph, A.D., et al.: Above the clouds: a berkeley view of cloud computing. Technical Report (11), 120–131 (2009)
10. Zeng, W., Zhao, Y., Qu, K., Song, W.: Research on cloud storage architecture and key technologies. School of Computer Science and Engineering, South China University of Technology, 212–217 (2010)

Author Index